palgrave advances in world histories

Palgrave Advances

Titles include:

Marnie Hughes-Warrington (*editor*)
WORLD HISTORIES

Phillip Mallett (*editor*)
THOMAS HARDY STUDIES

Lois Oppenheim (*editor*)
SAMUEL BECKETT STUDIES

Jean-Michel Rabaté (*editor*)
JAMES JOYCE STUDIES

Frederick S. Roden (*editor*)
OSCAR WILDE STUDIES

Forthcoming:

Patrick Finney (*editor*)
INTERNATIONAL HISTORY

Robert Patten and John Bowen (*editors*)
CHARLES DICKENS STUDIES

Anna Snaith (*editor*)
VIRGINIA WOOLF STUDIES

Nicholas Williams (*editor*)
WILLIAM BLAKE STUDIES

Jonathan Woolfson (*editor*)
RENAISSANCE HISTORIOGRAPHY

Palgrave Advances
Series Standing Order ISBN 1–4039–3512–2 (Hardback) 1–4039–3513–0 (Paperback)
(*outside North America only*)

You can receive future titles in this series as they are published by placing a standing order.
Please contact your bookseller or, in the case of difficulty, write to us at the address below
with your name and address, the title of the series and the ISBN quoted above.

Customer Services Department, Macmillan Distribution Ltd, Houndmills, Basingstoke,
Hampshire RG21 6XS, England

palgrave advances in world histories

edited by

marnie hughes-warrington

First published 2005 by
PALGRAVE MACMILLAN
Houndmills, Basingstoke, Hampshire RG21 6XS and
175 Fifth Avenue, New York, N.Y. 10010
Companies and representatives throughout the world

PALGRAVE MACMILLAN is the global academic imprint of the
Palgrave Macmillan division of St Martin's Press LLC and of
Palgrave Macmillan Ltd.
Macmillan® is a registered trademark in the United States,
United Kingdom and other countries. Palgrave is a registered
trademark in the European Union and other countries.

ISBN 1–4039–1277–7 hardback
ISBN 978-1-4039-1278-7   ISBN 1-4039-1278-5 paperback

This book is printed on paper suitable for recycling and
made from fully managed and sustained forest sources.

A catalogue record for this book is available
from the British Library.

Library of Congress Cataloging-in-Publication Data
Palgrave advances in world histories / edited by Marnie Hughes-Warrington.
    p. cm.
  Includes bibliographical references and index.
  ISBN 1–4039–1277–7 — ISBN 1-4039-1278-5 (pbk.)
  1. Historiography. 2. World history. I. Hughes-Warrington, Marnie.
D13.P323 2004
907'.2—dc22

2004050043

10 9 8 7 6 5 4 3 2 1
14 13 12 11 10 09 08 07 06 05

Transferred to digital printing in 2007.

contents

notes on the contributors

Craig Benjamin is Assistant Professor in the Department of History at Grand Valley University State University, Michigan. He is the co-editor (with David Christian) of *Worlds of the Silk Roads* (1998) and *Realms of the Silk Roads: Ancient and Modern* (2002).

David Christian is Professor of History at San Diego State University. He is the author of *Living Water: Vodka and Russian Society on the Eve of Emancipation* (1990); *Imperial and Soviet Russia: Power, Privilege and the Challenge of Modernity* (1997); *A History of Russia, Central Asia and Mongolia: Volume 1: Inner Eurasia from Prehistory to the Mongol Empire* (1998); and *Maps of Time: An Introduction to Big History* (2004).

Ricardo Duchesne is Associate Professor of Sociology at the University of New Brunswick, Canada. He completed his PhD in the interdisciplinary programme in Social and Political Thought at York University, Toronto. He is currently working on some of the significant intellectual landmarks in the rise of the West, and the related phenomena of modernity.

J. Donald Hughes is John Evans Professor of History at the University of Denver, Colorado. He is the author of *An Environmental History of the World: Humankind's Changing Role in the Community of Life* (2001) and *Pan's Travail: Environmental Problems of the Ancient Greeks and Romans* (1984). He is a founding member of the American Society for Environmental History and the European Society for Environmental History, and past editor of *Environmental Review* (now *Environmental History*).

Marnie Hughes-Warrington is Senior Lecturer in the Department of Modern History at Macquarie University, Sydney, Australia. She is the author of *Fifty Key Thinkers on History* (2000) and *'How Good an Historian Shall I Be?': R. G. Collingwood, the Historical Imagination and Education* (2003).

Michael Lang is Assistant Professor in the Department of History at the University of Maine. He has published on German intellectual history and on the history of globalization.

Patrick Manning is Professor of History and African-American Studies at Northeastern University in Boston, where he directed the World History Center from 1994 to 2004. He is the author of *Navigating World History* (2003) and lead author of *Migration in Modern World History, 1500–2000* (2000), a CD-ROM. He also writes on the history of slavery and the African diaspora.

Bruce Mazlish is Professor of History at the Massachusetts Institute of Technology. His chief publications include *The Riddle of History* (1965), *James and John Stuart Mill* (1975), *A New Science* (1989), *Conceptualizing Global History* (with Ralph Buultjens, 1993), *The Fourth Discontinuity* (1993) and *Civilization and its Contents* (2004).

Deborah Smith Johnston is a secondary school educator in Lexington, Massachusetts and an adjunct in the History Department, Northeastern University. Deborah has presented workshops on world history education both in the US and internationally.

Judith P. Zinsser is Professor of History at Miami University, Ohio. Her chief publications include *Feminism and History* (1994), *Indigenous Peoples and the United Nations System* (1994), and *A History of their Own: Women in Europe from Prehistory to the Present* (with Bonnie Anderson, 1988, rev. edn 2000). She is currently completing a biography of the Marquise du Châtelet.

1
world histories

marnie hughes-warrington

Compare any two maps of the world and a host of differences will become apparent. Placenames vary across time and culture, but so too do the geophysical and biological features represented and the determination of a 'centre' and a 'top'. In one map, for instance, a landmass labelled 'North America' may be centre and top, in another it may be 'Europa'; one may chart the flow of rivers, another human migration. Smaller differences are also apparent, from the colours used – for example, blue means water, pink means British Empire – to the fonts used in labels. World histories too come in a wide array of forms, varying in rhetorical structure, organizing principles and labels, foci and spatial and temporal breadth. Differences are most apparent when multiple works are produced on the same problem, period or event. To take just one example, in recent years the works of – among others – Andre Gunder Frank, Ken Pomeranz, R. Bin Wong and Angus Maddison have stimulated a lively debate on areas of growth in the eighteenth-century world economy and, more generally, 'Eurocentrism' in the writing of world history.[1] The volume of works produced on this topic is now so large that there are surveys devoted to it.[2]

Such differences of opinion among historians can help to illuminate the presuppositions that give form to their activities, and awareness of these may in turn stimulate changes in practice. The value of historiography – the study of the nature and purpose of histories – is often acknowledged at times of debate. Many historians, however, are reluctant to acknowledge the value of historiographical examinations of uncontested activities. To their view, attention to historiography is akin to expecting a driver to understand exactly how their car engine works before starting it, with the result that they take an extraordinarily long

1

time to get anywhere or do not start at all. This view of historiography is mistaken because it presumes that it is an adjunct to historical practices and can be disentangled from them. Every time an historian engages in writing, research and teaching, they make or affirm assumptions that define, refine, contract or extend their activities. Some assumptions are subject to great historical and cultural variation, while others are affirmed so often and for so long that they appear to be unalterable or as subject only to minor indiscernible alterations. Some are openly debated, while others are so deeply held that they cannot be clearly enunciated. Regardless, all historiographical assumptions are subject to change and open to question.[3]

The explicit, critical consideration of historiographical assumptions is no easy matter, and historians may struggle to bring into focus what they so often take for granted. R. G. Collingwood captures this difficulty well when he argues that we tend to be 'ticklish' in our presuppositions.[4] But the discomfort is worth bearing for at least two reasons. First, historical practices are *ethical* practices, infused by decisions or affirmations of what world history *ought to be*. Selections, methods, representations, definitions and labels support or establish patterns of relations among various peoples – past and present – animals and our geophysical environment. Put simply, historians privilege and they exclude. Historiographical reflection is valuable because it can bring patterns of privilege and exclusion to light, and may encourage historians to augment or even radically readjust their practices. Second, historiographical reflection might help to address the questions of those who are unsure as to just what world history is and what world historians do.

defining a field

This last point is no small matter, for as Bruce Mazlish notes in Chapter 2, issues of terminology complicate any study of world histories. Claims for 'universal history', 'ecumenical history', 'regional history', 'area studies', 'comparative history', 'world-system history', 'macrohistory', 'transnational history', 'big history' and the 'new world' and 'new global histories' have waxed and waned and sometimes even jostled for attention. Each of these terms has been used with the conviction that it offers the best treatment of historical phenomena. But problematically, few world historians have given much thought to their relationship or kinship with one another. Nor have they given much thought to the relations of world history with other forms of history or even the concept of 'history' itself. At best, they have articulated a distinction between their own practices and those of 'national historians'. World historians may view this division as a useful way of highlighting their contribution of a viable, alternative view of the past. But left unexamined, it may also affirm a hierarchical relation of national history as 'default' and world history as 'other'.

Historians generally arrive at their criticisms of world histories by comparison to national histories. To national histories are attributed the positive qualities of methodological rigour and access to historical meaning. World histories, in contrast, are considered derivative: they are viewed as an amalgam of smaller national histories and thus as dependent on the historiographical presuppositions and methodologies of them. This relation may be represented thus:

historical meaning←national history←world history

Here, historical meaning is achieved only via the intermediary of national history. This arrangement is problematic because it rests upon the unquestioned positioning of national history as a solid, desirable and unchanging foundation for history. Furthermore, it leaves unexamined the assumption that world history and national history are discrete.

So what is world history and how, if at all, do world histories differ from other forms of history? To begin, world history is not a thing, but an activity, and various physical forms of expression such as lectures, books, journal papers and classroom lessons are *criteria* for it. An historian, for instance, may point to a book and say 'that's a world history', even if they cannot elucidate why. 'World history' should thus be defined through an examination of the various forms of expression taken as its criteria, not apart from or prior to them. As Collingwood has written of the concept of 'science':

> To criticise the conceptions of science is the work of science itself as it proceeds; to demand that such criticisms should be anticipated by the theory of knowledge is to demand that such a theory should anticipate the history of thought.[5]

So too, historiography does not precede the activity of world history. The best way of understanding the concept of world history is therefore to examine it at work in world histories.

Where should we start our examination of world history at work? It would be wonderful if the history of world histories began with one of those great anecdotes that light up the history of science, like the dramatic tale of Charles Doolittle Walcott, who fell off his horse and chanced upon the Burgess Shale, a mother lode of Precambrian fossils.[6] Unfortunately we have no tale like this available to us, for there is, as far as we know, no revolutionary moment at which world histories came into being and no individual for us to claim as progenitor. Nor can we assume that the result of our search will be a seamless, cumulative narrative in which generations of writers pass on their methodological gains and offer us a consistent collection of conceptual criteria. Rather, as with much history, sometimes we have so little evidence that it is like watching tiny snippets of different television channels broken up by interminable periods of static.

Additionally, as suggested above, few world historians have explored the interrelations of different approaches within the field, with the result that few see their efforts as associated with those of ancient historians. The prime outcome of this neglect of connections has been the limitation of historiographical analyses of the field to the period following global exploration in the sixteenth century or even to the twentieth century. In his entry on 'World History' for the *Encyclopedia of Historians and Historical Writing*, for instance, Craig Lockard assumes that the field is of 'relatively recent origin' because:

> comprehensive history with a universal perspective became feasible only with the great increase of knowledge and the evolution of a more international orientation during the past century.[7]

Lockard's conclusion is not unusual, for none of the recent works on the historiography of world history, such as Paul Costello's *World Historians and their Goals* (1994), Jerry Bentley's *Shapes of World History in Twentieth-Century Scholarship* (1996), Philip Pomper, Richard Elphick and Richard Vann's *World History* (1998), Ross Dunn's *The New World History* (2000), Benedikt Stuchtey and Eckhardt Fuch's *Writing World History 1800–2000* (2003) and Patrick Manning's *Navigating World History* (2003), looks back before the sixteenth century in any depth.[8] World historians may argue for a 'big picture' of the past, but when it comes to their own history, they have opted for a limited and limiting view.

This prevailing view is limited because it rests upon two problematic presuppositions. First, it treats 'world' as synonymous only with earth or globe. 'World', as world-system historians have long argued, also refers to any complex whole, sphere, realm or domain *taken for* an entire meaningful system of existence or activity by historians or historical agents. The ancient universal historian Pompeius Trogus (fl. 5 CE), for instance, knew only a fraction of the globe as we know it, but Justinus judged that his *Philippic History* encompassed 'the annals of every period, king, nation and people'.[9] The 'world' in world history, I therefore contend, refers not to the earth in its entirety – both including and apart from human experience – but to the *known* or *meaningful* world of an individual or group.

Second, the prevailing view is limited by parochialism of the present, or the claim that the more recent a phenomenon, the more complex and worthy of study it is. To my view, world histories emerged much earlier than global exploration, at least as early as the ancient tradition of universal history writing. The few studies we have of universal history begin with Ephorus (405–330 BCE) and the climate of cosmopolitanism that arose after the conquests of Alexander of Macedon. In his 30-volume history, Ephorus surveyed the entire military and political history of the Greeks, a project that necessarily involved having something to say about all the groups with whom the Greeks came into contact. He was sure, though, that his wide survey was designed to make clear the significance of the Greeks. Raoul Mortley similarly acknowledges the historiographical impact of Alexander, but he has also tried to demonstrate the influence of Aristotelian peripatetic philosophy on the emergence of the genre, defining 'peripatetic universal history' as:

(i) an interest in universal figures, and in the truths which belong to the whole world; (ii) an interest in moral aspects of biographical facts since moral ideas were of the generalisable kind sought by post-Aristotelian historians; (iii) an interest in acts (*praxeis*) as that which provides the best guide to the inner moral man, the 'signs of the soul'; (iv) the interest in tradition whether mythical or factual, since true tradition is held to contain truth.[10]

But the formulation of definitions and origin theories is complicated by the fact that less than 5 per cent of Hellenistic literature has survived. José Miguel Alonso-Núñez has therefore opted for the more inclusive description of universal historians as 'those who deal with the history of mankind from the earliest times, and in all parts of the world known to them'.[11] Yet even his definition does not readily accommodate the efforts of those who composed works like biographical catalogues, which were exhaustive not in temporal and geographical scope, but in the use of biographies to illuminate universal social, moral or political principles. Further, his use of the word 'mankind' begs the question whether his worldview is itself universal. To this we must add the observation that we are not always sure whether extant histories might originally have been parts of universal histories: for example, commentators have argued that the Roman historian Arrian's (c. 92–c. 180 CE) *Anabasis Alexandri* and *Indica* ought to be considered as one work, and that the Indo-Persian Mulla 'Abd al-Husayn Tuni's (d. 1489) *Ma'athir-i-Mahmud Shahi* is a fragment of a universal history.[12]

Even the treatment of universal history writing in the periods favoured by current writers appears too selective, being restricted almost exclusively to European writers. Names like Jean Bodin (1530–1596), Voltaire (1694–1778), Giambattista Vico (1688–1744), Johann Gottfried Herder (1742–1803), Immanuel Kant (1724–1804), Friedrich Schiller (1759–1805), the Marquis de Condorcet (1743–1794), G. W. F. Hegel (1770–1831), Leopold von Ranke (1795–1886) and Karl Marx (1818–1893) feature again and again. They are used to lend weight to the argument that universal history writing hit either its zenith or nadir with philosophies of history in the nineteenth century, and then was superseded by more professional and methodologically sound world and national history writing in the twentieth century. Writers and historiographical traditions from outside Western Europe are not entirely absent from this view of the past, but are generally cited to demonstrate the intellectual reach of European colonization.[13]

The disconnection of and gap between surveys of ancient and modern universal histories is problematic. But problematic too is the privileging of documents common to commentators on ancient and modern works. Furthermore, scholars of both periods frame their histories as stories of diffusion, beginning in Europe and spreading to the rest of the world. Are universal histories, and world histories, simply a Western elite, masculine, cultural product that spread to or was forced upon the rest of the world?

whose worlds?

Even if we restrict ourselves to an examination of documentary evidence alone, it is clear that there were and are parallel or intersecting traditions of world history writing outside Western Europe. The rise of Islam in the sixth century, for example, fostered the development of universal chronography organized either by annual entries (*ta'rikh 'ala al-sinin*) or by caliphal reigns (*ta'rikh 'ala al-khulafa*). There is a good deal of evidence to suggest that Judaeo-Christian, Persian and Syrian historiography influenced Islamic chronography, but Muslims also exported historiographic forms. One striking feature of Islamic universal chronography from the sixth to the twelfth centuries, for instance, was the widespread and strict use of *isnads* or 'name tags' tied to the beginning of an account of the past. If the account was a report of the words or deeds of a religious figure (*hadith*), the *isnad* ideally comprised an unbroken series of transmitters from the book's compiler to a witness; if the report was of other words or deeds (*khabar*) then it did not need to be so complete.[14] Abu Ja'far al-Tabari's universal history *Tarikh al-rusul wa-l-Muluk* (*The History of the Prophets and Kings*, 911–23 CE) marks the culmination of this tradition, before later writers eschewed *isnads* as a narrative or methodological intrusion and as a waste of space.[15]

China boasts an even longer historiographical tradition, with private histories and official histories – records compiled by or for the ruling class – dating from at least 279 BCE. It is estimated that the 25 officially approved histories contain 20 million characters, which is roughly equivalent to 45 million English words.[16] These official histories, as Hok-lam Chan has argued, are notable for the presence of fictive claims, used to align sources with Confucian and political historiographical norms such as commemorative adornment, political legitimation and moral edification.[17] However it is the synchronic, encyclopaedic structure of Chinese official histories, developed first by Sima Tan (d. c. 110 BCE) and Sima Qian (145–80 BCE), that most sets them apart from other historiographical traditions. The first four official histories, the *Shiji* (*Records of the Grand Historian*) begun by Sima Tan and completed by Sima Qian, the *Hanshu* (*History of the Former Han Dynasty*) by Ban Gu (32–92 CE), the *Sanguozhi* (*History of the Three Kingdoms*) by Chen Shou (d. 297 CE) and the *Hou Hanshu* (*History of the Later Han*) by Fan Ye (398–445 CE) established a quadripartite division of histories into imperial annals (*benji*), tables (*biao*), treatises (*shu*) and biographies or memoirs (*juan* or *liezhaun*). The first part documented major events in imperial families; the second, month-to-month events for government offices; the third, knowledge of an enormous range of activities, from official rites to music, food to law and punishment; and the fourth, accounts of virtuous and infamous individuals and collective biographies for groups such as scholars, assassins and eunuchs. Though modified, this structure was employed in official histories right up to *Qingshi gao* (*Draft History of the Qing Dynasty*, 1928).[18] Accompanying that tradition were chronologically arranged universal histories, the form of which was established by Sima Guang (1019–1086) in the *Zi Zhi Tong Jian* (*Comprehensive Mirror to Aid in Government*). The internal history of China thus promises much for those interested in historiographical exchange and hybridity.

Western tradition, too, is more varied than is generally acknowledged. Anyone who looks to existing surveys of world histories might be led to the conclusion that they are high cultural masculinist products. As Judith Zinsser argues in Chapter 9, however, women were not absent from the activity of writing world history, but prevailing historiographical assumptions 'mask, appropriate or minimise women's presence, contributions, and achievements'. Arguably, too, prevailing assumptions have led to the neglect of more 'mundane', 'popular', 'ordinary' or even 'lesser quality' world histories by men and women alike. Finally, just as world historians have recognized that peoples do not stay tidily within the boundaries of states, we must expect that world histories too are – to a lesser or greater degree – the products of interaction and exchange. My use of the word 'Western', for instance, begs the question of whether I have bestowed too much unity on a group of people and drawn too clear a division with other parts of the world.

These examples are just the surface of a history of world history, the depths of which we are yet to chart because of limitations in our historiographical assumptions. If we open up our examination to include non-documentary materials, then the gaps in current accounts become even more numerous. It is worth considering, for instance, whether the idea of world history has a relationship with the oral and pictorial creation myths or stories told by peoples around the world.[19] This might seem an odd connection, but there is good reason to it. The language, structure, modes of transmission and means of verification are different, but they share a common purpose.

world histories and purpose

The purpose of world histories and creation myths is to construct a world of meaning and order that is not so much right or wrong as useful.[20] A good illustration of what is meant here can be found if we return to the map analogy that opened this chapter. Maps represent features thought helpful for a particular person or group. The map displayed around the campus where I work, for instance, does not include the many trees, only the buildings. That makes sense, as few people come to a university to find a tree, but many need help to navigate their way to a building for a class. So too, mythmakers and world historians select certain phenomena and ways of representing phenomena to make the past intelligible to a particular audience: for example, while the word 'Renaissance' was unknown to twelfth-century Europeans, the term will be clearly understood by many readers today as meaning a period of revival.[21] Moreover, the selections and explanations of the mythmaker or historian serve to orient their audiences to their own present and future. In Australian Aboriginal 'Dreamings', for instance, past events are organized spatially and morally rather than temporally in order to bind people to one another and 'in country'.[22] In another 'world', John Knox presented a universal history of female monarchs – *The First Blast of the Trumpet Against the Monstrous Regiment of Women* (1558) – to show that the rule of any woman is 'repugnant to nature, contumelious to God, a thing most contrary to his revealed will and approved ordinance, and... the subversion of good order, or all equity and justice'.[23] And over 400 years later, Andre Gunder Frank argued in *ReOrient* (1997) that lifting Europe and the United States out of the world economy has serious political as well as historiographical consequences, consequences that do indeed seem to have been played out since September 11, 2001.[24] The differences between these 'worlds' clearly show us the potential difficulties for those outside looking in on them, but it is similarly clear that they are united in their purpose of orientation. Many world historians do not write overtly about the present or future, but in their selections and presentations they express their views of what knowledge is worthwhile, and what the world that they live in ought to be like. World histories are thus *world order* histories.

The selections and presentations of world historians generally 'go without saying', to borrow Roland Barthes' phrase, but simply because they cannot be given a justification it does not follow that they are defective or undependable or that the people who act according to them are foolish. They often do not decide to reject or accept presuppositions at all, any more than they decide to be human beings rather than chimpanzees. Presuppositions do not have to be simply arbitrary and volatile *or* immutable and invariant: they can also be social and conventional, changing over time. Nor do they have to be obvious *or* hidden: they can be both. And as we noted above, their usefulness, acceptance and degree of explicitness does not mean that they are immune to analysis or change.

Constellations of presuppositions not only shape world histories and creation myths; they also form the (always shifting) foundation upon which all our intellectual activity, and indeed the very possibility of intellectual activity, rests. As presuppositions are the means by which people construct a meaningful and organized world, I contend that seen through the lens of purpose, *all* histories are world histories. Where histories differ is in the degree to which the purpose of world construction is explicit. The definition of 'world history' therefore does not turn simply on methodology. Philosophical universal histories, for example, do not offer the archetypal form for world history, for although writers like Hegel and Kant sought to expose the presuppositions at work in human history they remained oblivious to some of their own, such as the connection of rationality with masculinity.[25] Nor does the definition turn on spatio-temporal scale. Biographies and microhistories might be built out of the same presuppositions that shape big histories of humanity and the universe. Furthermore, as noted above, 'world' should not to be taken as synonymous with Earth or globe alone. The world of the ancient Greek universal historian Polybius (c. 200–c. 118 BCE) nestled on the edges of the Mediterranean, whereas that of the big historian David Christian stretches out to the farthest reaches of the universe. World histories, I believe, share the feature of being a construction of and thus a guide to a meaningful world. This is not to say that differences in methodology and scale are unimportant, rather that neither is the defining criterion of world history.

Given the paucity of historical and historiographical analyses of world histories, the definition of world history that I have suggested can only be provisional. Closer attention to a wider range of sources might lead us to question or even abandon it and to bring matters of scale and methodology back into focus. An immediate priority is thus the historical – incorporating historiographical – analysis of world history at work. Though a long and hard task, the study of world histories is nevertheless important because it can help us to work through a basic question that applies to all histories: 'What and who is history *for*?'[26] The explicit world constructions of many world histories are also a good starting point for those new to historiography, as decisions of omission and inclusion are often more apparent to non-specialists. Little historical training is needed, to take just one example, to see that a world historian has omitted mention of Africa. If, in studying world histories, we begin to appreciate the shaping role of presuppositions, then we may seek them in all histories. World histories, therefore, provide an important and accessible route to the consideration of 'history'.

the purpose and structure of this book

As we have seen, there are countless ideas and issues that a volume on world histories could address. I, and the nine other world historians that have joined me in this project, have thus selected topics, sources and lines of argument that we believe will best realise the twofold aim of historiography described above, to illuminate the ethical nature of historical practices and to clarify the nature of world history. First, this book is intended to be of assistance to readers new to the field who seek an introduction to what world history is and what world historians – past and present – do. The effect of this work, we hope, will be like seeing differences and similarities across world maps, and then wondering why they are so. Second, we hope that those more familiar with the field will find this work a stimulant for discussion, debate and reflection on world historical practices, many of which currently go without saying, and some of which ought to be augmented or even challenged.

The ten contributors to this book (myself included) agree on a number of issues. But as you read on, fracture points and lines of disagreement will become apparent. For those differences and disagreements we make no apology, for they reflect a healthy variety of viewpoints that cannot be easily collapsed or reconciled because they point to deep seated differences of opinion about what world history is and what it ought to be. It is our hope that readers will scrutinize the disagreements and agreements alike and use them to gain a clearer view of their own presuppositions about the field.

As noted above, any study of world histories is complicated by the range of terms used to describe the field. In Chapter 2, Bruce Mazlish traces the historical emergence of the terms 'regional history', 'universal history', 'ecumenical history', 'eschatological history', 'comparative history', 'world-system history', 'macrohistory', 'big history', 'new world history' and 'new global history'. This historical analysis informs his philosophical analysis of the relationship among these various terms, and with the concepts of 'world history' and 'history'. Mazlish notes the presence of 'local' differences, but concludes that world histories share empirically grounded practices that seek to give 'a transcendental meaning, theological or historical, to the human experiences of the past'.

In Chapter 3, Patrick Manning develops Mazlish's conclusion, identifying the methods, materials and analytical frameworks that both connect world histories to and distinguish them from other genres of historical writing and the notion of 'history' itself. World histories cannot be differentiated from other histories, Manning argues, if we look only for a single method, type of sources or analytical concept. They are instead best characterized by multiplicity: first, in the use of a varied range of data from many spatio-temporal locations; second, in the combination of many methods from a broad range of disciplines; third, in the diverse backgrounds and purposes of authors; and finally, in the mixture of small and large scale spatio-temporal perspectives.

The interrelation of various spatio-temporal scales in world history writing is of particular interest to David Christian. In Chapter 4, he calls for critical scrutiny of the prevailing association of 'history' with the study of a relatively narrow range of phenomena, from the experiences of individuals to nation states or groups of nation states. To his view, this association is not 'natural' or logical, but the product of nineteenth-century professionalization which favoured the intensive study of nation states through primary documents. In so limiting themselves, Christian maintains, historians have excluded or marginalized the illiterate, including all people from prehistory, those who do not fit tidily within the parameters of nation states because of nomadism or cultural interaction and human relations with the organic and inorganic environment. As a remedy, he calls for the study of the past on multiple scales, ranging from a human lifetime to the age of the universe.

Issues of scale are closely related to decisions about where the study of world history should begin and end. World histories may start, for instance, with the rise of states, writing, the hominids, the formation of the earth or even the beginnings of the universe. Why? Further, why have so many world historians shown an interest in the future? In Chapter 5, Craig Benjamin investigates some of the practical and philosophical dimensions of decisions made by both ancient and modern world historians about the parameters of their work. While noting that variations in world histories are often shaped by personal decisions and prevailing cultural milieux, Benjamin identifies a clear pattern of spatio-temporal expansion in the history of world history writing – an expansion that has come into increasing conflict with the wider historiographical tendency towards contraction since the emergence of 'professional' history in the nineteenth century.

Writing world history involves decisions not only about methods, materials, scale and parameters, but also about the selection, arrangement and emphasis of historical events. World historians are, whether or not they like or even recognize it, stylists: they shape their works according to literary conventions. In Chapter 6, I note that there is, however, little in recent historiographical scholarship that can help us to better understand the narrative shapes of world histories. Questioning both prevailing 'rise of the professional West' historiographical narratives and the 'narratological' theory of Hayden White, I argue for the recognition of greater narrative variation in world histories, particularly prior to the twentieth century, and for more reflection on the presuppositions that shape histories of the field.

'The West' is also the focus of Chapter 7, with Ricardo Duchesne documenting the shift in treatments of this concept and analytical frame in world histories since the end of the nineteenth century. Many world histories written up to the 1960s conjoined the liberal idea that civilization was moving in a desirable direction with triumphalist attitudes towards peoples and cultures considered 'outside' it. We are mistaken, though, Duchesne argues, if we believe that all world histories were the product of racial arrogance and ethnocentric malice or that historians were untroubled by ethnocentrism. Tracking the emergence of sustained criticism against 'the West' and 'progress' in history, through the two examples of the 'negative philosophy of history' of Max Horkheimer and Theodor Adorno and the cultural relativism of anthropologists like Franz Boas, Duchesne's challenging conclusion is that a 'narrow-minded, anti-Western theology' and 'anti-progressivism' has taken hold of contemporary world history writing. Western affirmation, he reminds us, is not synonymous with either isolationism or unethical triumphalism.

The centre and margins of world history writing come under further scrutiny in Michael Lang's exploration in Chapter 8 of the 'modern' and 'postmodern'. Lang explains the interest of postmodernists in language and representation and their claims that the knowledge, truth and methodological claims of world history scholars are 'naturalized' Euro- and Americano-centric presuppositions. To postmodernists, world histories are constructions, not descriptions, of the world by and for hegemonic groups. They are 'grand', 'master' or 'meta' narratives that legitimate selected ideals and gloss over conflicting views and discontinuities. Yet, Lang notes, postmodernism promotes its own world history, a unified narrative of the rise and end of 'modernity'. Herein lies a paradox between world historical construction and deconstruction, one that is paralleled in the studies of 'subaltern' scholars, who work both within and against naturalized Eurocentric world history.

Exclusion and marginalization are not determined solely on the basis of culture. As Judith Zinsser argues in Chapter 9, gender scholars also struggle within and against the naturalized presuppositions of world historians. It is not the case, as Zinsser shows in wide range of examples, that women did not write world history, or that women were not significant historical agents; rather, past and present historiographical presuppositions mask or minimize their activities. But the recovery and inclusion of the activities of women is not sufficient, because no group functions in isolation. Zinsser thus calls for the critical examination of gender relations, the ways in which sexual difference and definitions have been created and given significance both in history and in the activity of writing history.

World history writing is a masculinist activity, she concludes, and until world historians transform it, they will fail in their aim to write the history of humanity.

In Chapter 10, I analyse the deconstruction of world history scholarship from another angle, that of the 'death of the author' and the rise of the 'auditor' or 'reader'. Drawing on a range of examples, I show that while the writers of world histories have long recognized the role of readers in the making of meaning, they have tried to maintain authority by recommending manners or orders of reading. Their efforts, though, must be seen alongside those of readers and publishers in shaping texts. Focusing in on 'future histories' of science fiction writers, Julian Barnes' novel *History of the World in 10½ Chapters* and Mel Brooks' film *History of the World Part I*, I demonstrate how readers appropriate and refashion the concepts, styles and assumptions of world histories. In doing so, they cross back and forward across 'elite' and 'popular' culture, leading us to wonder whether these are useful categories of analysis. These findings challenge conventional author-oriented treatments of world histories, and form the basis for a call for more research into their reception.

Much of Chapters 1–10 are focused on human–human relations. In Chapter 11, J. Donald Hughes widens our view to take in human relations with the physical environment. While the idea that human history is shaped in part by the physical environment may be found in the writings of ancient historians, it came to the forefront of world history scholarship in the latter half of the twentieth century. World histories from that time onwards, Hughes claims, show an increasing interest in questioning the assumption that humans are special, apart, supreme; in research from the historical sciences; and in topical environmental issues such as global warming, land and water degradation and threats to biodiversity. Hughes charts the rise of environmental world histories and critically examines claims that they are determinist and declensionist.

Finally, in Chapter 12, Deborah Smith Johnston takes us beyond world history texts to assess the potential and problems of world history education. Drawing on interviews and policies, she reveals varying views of purpose and procedure that go some way to explaining both the ascendancy of high-school programmes in the United States and their public contestation. She then highlights the necessity of historiographical engagement by students and teachers, dialogue between school and university educators, the connection of pedagogy with research and international collaboration. Her chapter is an important reminder that historiography is not mere semantics; that ethical decisions and affirmations shape what and how we teach and whom we reach.

notes

1. A. G. Frank, *ReOrient: Global Economy in the Asian Age* (Berkeley, CA: University of California Press, 1998); K. Pomeranz, *The Great Divergence: China, Europe, and the Making of the Modern World Economy* (Princeton, NJ: Princeton University Press, 2000); R. Bin Wong, *China Transformed: Historical Change and the Limits of European Experience* (Ithaca, NY: Cornell University Press, 1997); and A. Maddison, *The World Economy: A Millennial Perspective* (Paris: OECD, 2001).

2. P. Vries, *Via Peking Back to Manchester: Britain, the Industrial Revolution and China* (Leiden: CNWS, 2003).

3. I am grateful to both Ludwig Wittgenstein and to R. G. Collingwood for this insight. For a fuller discussion, see M. Hughes-Warrington, *'How Good an Historian Shall I Be?'*: R. G. Collingwood, the Historical Imagination and Education (Exeter: Imprint Academic, 2003), chapter 3.

4. R. G. Collingwood, *An Essay on Metaphysics*, ed. R. Martin, rev. edn (Oxford: Oxford University Press, 1998), p. 44.

5. R. G. Collingwood, *The Idea of History*, ed. W. J. Van der Dussen, rev. edn (Oxford: Oxford University Press, 1993), p. 230.

6. For a critical discussion of the form and function of this anecdote, see S. Gould, *Wonderful Life: The Burgess Shale and the Nature of History* (London: Vintage, 2000).

7. C. Lockard, 'World History', in K. Boyd (ed.), *Encyclopedia of Historians and Historical Writing* (Chicago, IL: Fitzroy Dearborn, 1999), vol. 2, pp. 1330–1.

8. P. Costello, *World Historians and their Goals: Twentieth Century Answers to Modernism* (De Kalb, IL: Northern Illinois University Press, 1994); J. Bentley, *Shapes of World History in Twentieth-Century Scholarship* (Washington, DC: American Historical Association, 1996); P. Pomper, R. Elphick and R. Vann (eds), *World History: Ideologies, Structures, Identities* (Malden, MA: Blackwell, 1998); R. Dunn (ed.), *The New World History: A Teacher's Companion* (New York: Bedford/St. Martin's, 2000); B. Stuchtey and E. Fuchs (eds), *Writing World History 1800–2000* (Oxford: Oxford University Press, 2003); and P. Manning, *Navigating World History: Historians Create a Global Past* (New York: Palgrave Macmillan/St. Martin's Press, 2003).

9. J. C. Yardley and R. Develin (eds and trans.), *Justin. Epitome of the Philippic History of Pompeius Trogus* (Atlanta, GA: American Philological Association Classical Resources Series 3, 1994), preface, p. 2.

10. R. Mortley, *The Idea of Universal History from Hellenistic Philosophy to Early Christian Historiography* (Lewiston: Edwin Mellon, 1996), p. 197.

11. J. M. Alonso-Núñez, 'The Emergence of Universal Historiography from the 4th to the 2nd Centuries BC', in H. Verdin, G. Schepens and E. de Keyser (eds), *Purposes of History in Greek Historiography from the Fourth to the Second Centuries BC* (Leuven: Orientaliste, 1990), p. 197. See also J. M. Alonso-Núñez, *The Idea of Universal History in Greece: From Herodotus to the Age of Augustus* (Amsterdam: J. C. Gieben, 2001).

12. W. Schmitthenner, 'Rome and India: Aspects of Universal History During the Principate', *Journal of Roman Studies*, 69 (1979) 90–106; Z.- D. A. Desai, 'The Fifteenth Century Ma'athir-i-Mahmud Shahi Written in Gujarat: Dynastic History, Monographic History or Universal History?', *Journal of the Pakistan Historical Society*, 46(3) (1998) 63–8. On the treatment of geographical,

ethnographic and historical works as aspects of unified universal histories, see K. Clarke, *Between Geography and History: Hellenistic Constructions of the Roman World* (Oxford: Oxford University Press, 1999).

13. See A. Ekert, 'Fitting Africa into World History: A Historiographical Exploration', V. Lal, 'Provincialising the West: World History from the Perspective of Indian History', R. K. S. Mak, 'The "Middle Kingdom" Struggles to Survive: The Chinese Worldview in the Nineteenth Century' and J. A. Thomas, 'High Anxiety: World History as Japanese Self-Discovery', all in Stuchtey and Fuchs, *Writing World History 1800–2000*.

14. A notable exception to this norm was al-Mas'udi's *Kitab al-Tanbih wa'l-ishraf*. See A. Shboul, *Al-Mas'udi and his World* (London: Ithaca, 1979).

15. C. F. Robinson, *Islamic Historiography* (Oxford: Oxford University Press, 2003), pp. 15–16, 35–6.

16. H. H. Dubs, 'The Reliability of Chinese Histories', *The Far Eastern Quarterly*, 6(1) (1946), 23, 26.

17. H.- I. Chan, 'The Rise of Ming T'ai-tsu (1368–98): Facts and Fictions in Early Ming Official Historiography', *Journal of the American Oriental Society*, 95(4) (1975) 679–715.

18. On Sima Qian's approach, see G. Hardy, *Worlds of Bronze and Bamboo: Sima Qian's Conquest of History* (New York: Columbia University Press, 1999).

19. I am grateful to David and Chardi Christian for this insight. See D. Christian, *Maps of Time: An Introduction to Big History* (Berkeley, CA: University of California Press, 2004).

20. M. Gleiser, *The Dancing Universe: From Creation Myths to the Big Bang* (New York: Plume, 1997), chapter 1.

21. On the regular use of anachronism in histories, see W. H. Walsh, 'Colligatory Concepts in History', in P. Gardiner, *The Philosophy of History* (Oxford: Oxford University Press, 1979), pp. 139–40.

22. See for example D. B. Rose, 'Ned Kelly Died for our Sins', *Oceania*, 65(2) (1994) 175–86.

23. J. Knox, *The First Blast of the Trumpet Against the Monstrous Regiment of Women* [1558] (Amsterdam: Da Capo, 1972), p. 9. See I. Maclean, *The Renaissance Notion of Woman* (Cambridge: Cambridge University Press, 1980).

24. Frank, *ReOrient*, pp. 357–9.

25. G. Lloyd, *The Man of Reason: 'Male' and 'Female' in Western Philosophy* (Minneapolis: University of Minnesota, 1984); and B. R. Barber, 'Spirit's Phoenix and History's Owl or the Incoherence of Dialectics in Hegel's Account of Women', *Political Theory*, 16(1) (1988) 5–28.

26. K. Jenkins, *Re-Thinking History* (London: Routledge, 1991), p. 18.

recommended resources

Alonso-Núñez, J. M., *The Idea of Universal History in Greece: From Herodotus to the Age of Augustus* (Amsterdam: JC Gieben, 2001).

Barrow, J., *Theories of Everything* (Harmondsworth: Penguin, 1991).

Bentley, J., *Shapes of World History in Twentieth-Century Scholarship* (Washington, DC: American Historical Association, 1996).

Clarke, K., *Between Geography and History: Hellenistic Constructions of the Roman World* (Oxford: Oxford University Press, 1999).

Costello, P., *World Historians and their Goals: Twentieth Century Answers to Modernism* (De Kalb, IL: Northern Illinois University Press, 1994).

Dunn, R. (ed.), *The New World History: A Teacher's Companion* (New York: Bedford/ St. Martin's, 2000).

Gaddis, J. L., *The Landscape of History: How Historians Map the Past* (Oxford: Oxford University Press, 2002).

Gleiser, M., *The Dancing Universe: From Creation Myths to the Big Bang* (New York: Plume, 1997).

Green, A., and Troup, K., *The Houses of History* (Melbourne: Manchester University Press, 1999).

Hardy, G., *Worlds of Bronze and Bamboo: Sima Qian's Conquest of History* (New York: Columbia University Press, 1999).

H-World [electronic discussion forum], online at <www.h-net.org/~world/>.

Hughes-Warrington, M., *Fifty Key Thinkers on History* (London: Routledge, 2000).

Journal of World History (1990–)

Manning, P., *Navigating World History: Historians Create a Global Past* (New York: Palgrave Macmillan/St. Martin's Press, 2003).

Mortley, R., *The Idea of Universal History from Hellenistic Philosophy to Early Christian Historiography* (Lewiston: Edwin Mellon, 1996).

Pomper, P., Elphick, R., and Vann, R. (eds), *World History: Ideologies, Structures, Identities* (Malden, MA: Blackwell, 1998).

Robinson. C. F., *Islamic Historiography* (Oxford: Oxford University Press, 2003).

Schneide, A., and Schwierdrzik, S. W. (eds), *Chinese Historiography in Comparative Perspective*, special issue of *History and Theory*, 35(4) (1996).

Stuchtey, B. and Fuchs, E. (eds), *Writing World History 1800–2000* (Oxford: Oxford University Press, 2003).

World History Association, online at <www.thewha.org>.

World History Connected: The e-journal of Teaching and Learning, available at <www. worldhistoryconnected.press.uiuc.edu>.

Zeitschrift für Weltgeschichte, vol. 1, 2000–.

2
terms

bruce mazlish

In a volume devoted to 'world histories', it figures naturally that 'world history' will be the central term. Yet to truly situate it in historical discourse, we must place it among other, related terms. Such comparison is essential, above all, because world history implicitly subsumes all other histories under its domain-name. Partial recognition of this fact is embodied in the plural, 'histories', in the title of this book.

Among the related terms that figure under the rubric of world histories are regional history, universal history, ecumenical history, eschatological history, comparative history, world-system history, macrohistory, big history, world history, and global history; and, indeed, now new global history. We must ask, therefore, how do these overlap with one another, and in what ways might they share common characteristics? Alternatively, the question is what are the significant differences among these approaches? Or do they largely represent a conceptual muddle, indicative of the historian's difficulties in discerning meanings and patterns in the story of the past?

Rather than seeking mechanically and abstractly to address these questions, let us deal with them 'historically', that is, looking at their emergence over time. There are two observations we must make before entering on this task. The first is to be aware that 'world' history may not be engaged in equally by all parts of the world (though, of course, they participate as objects of study in it). While there are numerous attempts at wide-ranging explanations of the human past made in non-Western civilizations, world history appears to be a specially Western preoccupation. Or is it? Here we have a question to be researched further by students of the subject. Certainly the discipline of 'world histories' is a late development, one which calls for its own historical explanation.

My second observation is even more important. It is to note that all of our terms are in conjunction with the word 'history.' We need history before we can have any of the variants on world histories given above. As is well known, history, meaning inquiry in the Greek, mainly enters 'history' with Herodotus and Thucydides. It is a fifth-century BCE creation, developing at the same time as the inquiry into nature and its presumed laws, undertaken by the Ionian and Greek thinkers of the period. The concept of history represents a great breakthrough in human understanding of the world, culturally rather than physically. Previously, humans tried to understand their past by constructing myths, inventing sagas and legends, and offering accounts of a religious nature. In this realm, gods reign, in a timeless space. Now, after Herodotus and his contemporaries, systematic inquiry into the past is to be undertaken in terms of human happenings, explicable in secular terms, ideally using documents, aiming at causal explanation as well as narrative accounts, and open to challenge, that is, renewed inquiry. The past is no longer unbroken, but given precise dates. As M. I. Finley, the great scholar of antiquity, puts it, 'Dates and a coherent dating scheme are as essential to history as exact measurement is to physics.'[1]

Even this brief observation about the nature of history poses for us major questions about world histories in regard, for example, to their use of evidence – documents are often not available – coherent dating, narrative strategies, employment of causal schemes, and so forth. In short, world histories are forms of history and must be understood and evaluated in terms of the emergence, nature, and meaning of history and its accompanying methodological and historiographical challenges. This should be the framing context as we now turn to the variants of world history.

*

Herodotus not only was the originator in regard to history per se, but can also be regarded as being perhaps the first in extending it beyond the local. As one commentator puts it, 'It was Herodotus who passed beyond chronicle to both reasoned historical narrative and to a "universal" history, extending outside Hellas to the known world.'[2] In this sense, then, history is world history from its very beginning. Although the father of history had as his declared aim mainly to preserve the memory of the great war between the Greeks and Persians, his canvas also included other peoples around him, such as the Egyptians. At the very least, then, he aimed at what we might call a regional history. Was it, in fact, also universal? What is crucial, of course, is what is meant by universal, that is, what is the idea of the cosmos and of the political universe, known to the Greeks of the time? Even a cursory observation tells us that history such as Herodotus' was of very limited universality even in his time.

Yet the genre was launched. Efforts at universal history, as reflected often in the titles given to such works, proliferated. A detailed historiography is not our intent here. We note only a few early landmarks. Thus, as the *Encyclopaedia Britannica* tells us, Ephorus with his 29 books presents us with 'the first universal history'. Another source cites writers like Diodorus of Sicily (c. 90–21 BCE), whose assertion that peoples of different times and places 'could be connected by universal history' resulted from his belief that 'historians, in recording the common affairs of the inhabited world as though they were those of a single state, have made of their treatises a single reckoning of past events'.[3]

Such efforts attempted to give a mainly secular account of the then-known inhabited world and its happenings. With the coming of Christianity a major shift in focus and conception took place. Christ's birth, seen as a unique and one-time event, introduced the notion of linearity into universal history and thus a new attitude toward dating. Now there was a pivotal before and after point. The older, more general conception of circularity was displaced. This was a metamorphosis whose effects transformed historical perspective from that time to the present.[4]

The other part of this shift was to introduce the notion of teleology into universal history. The past was given meaning as a prelude to an inevitable future. The aim of earthly happenings was to prepare the way for salvation. History, like the Bible, was to be read as an introduction to the end of days and the second coming of the Messiah. Where the Greeks in their histories had sought to relegate the gods to the background, if not to eliminate them in their accounts, it might be said that Christians practising universal history had reintroduced them, but now in the figure of one God.

Almost all such universal histories drew upon St Augustine, the fourth-century Bishop who uniquely resurrected the genre, and his dichotomy of the City of Man and the City of God. It was the latter that gave meaning to the chaos of earthly life – this veil of tears – which otherwise was of no importance by itself. Two works, among many, can epitomize for us the genre of Christian universal history. The first is from the twelfth century, Bishop Otto of Freysing's *The Two Cities* (his preferred title for his *Chronicle of Universal History to the Year 1146 AD*). Declaring that only the 'faculty of reason' can release one from the obscurity of past events, his reasoning is not that of historians such as Herodotus – the Bishop admits that he is 'without proper training' – but of theologians such as Augustine and Orosius. As he tells us,

> Following in their steps I have undertaken to speak of the Two Cities in such a way that we do not lose the thread of history, that the devout reader may observe what is to be avoided in mundane affairs by reason of the countless miseries wrought by their unstable character, and that the studious and painstaking investigator may find a record of past happenings free from all obscurity.[5]

More theology than history, Bishop Otto's *Two Cities* bears little resemblance to what would now figure in a history of the early middle ages (a periodization unknown to him, and in which he would have had little interest; he had a different dividing line). Yet it is representative of much that had been written under the heading of universal history. Its final and most glorious representative, however, is worth greater scrutiny. It involves another Bishop, Jacques Benigne Bossuet (1627–1704), whose *Discourse on Universal History* was published in 1681, at the height of the early Enlightenment.

Though half a millennium had passed between Bishop Otto and Bossuet, the essential reading of history was the same, with the centrality of Christ at its core. What was different was the context of Bossuet's universal history. In the seventeenth century the scientific revolution was in full swing, taking cultural and social form in an early Enlightenment that challenged the belief in miracles, oracles, and other 'violations' of nature's laws preached by the churches. A century or so earlier, a Reformation had split the Church, making a major new breach in theological unity. Taking advantage of this more open setting, numerous dissenting voices arose. Cartesians were in the forefront of new thinking, with the Spinozists challenging traditional readings of the Bible and Church authority to the point of atheism.[6]

Into this maelstrom of opinion, Bossuet sought to restore the legitimacy of the older Christian view of history. Although privately himself favourable to Cartesianism, he rejected a philosophical interpretation in place of a theological one, and portrayed the events of human history as caused by Providence and occurring as part of a divine plan. The past is divided into twelve epochs and seven ages, on religious grounds, and key events are the Creation, the Deluge, the birth of Christ, and the conversion of the Roman Emperor Constantine. Secular events are noted, such as the fall of Troy, but are of relatively little importance. Evidence is in terms of the Bible and myths, and theology takes the place of history in interpreting them. The rise and fall of empires is treated as part of the divine plan.

Bossuet's real enemy is Spinoza, the leader of the philosophical doubters. The *Universal History* is intended to be a defence of God and King, not an inquiry in the sense history had acquired with Herodotus and his Greek and Roman heirs. The fact that Pierre Bayle and others had begun to explore the past in even more sceptical and empirical terms than the ancients figured not at all in Bossuet's account. Though the Bishop made occasional gestures toward the modern, and wrote in beautiful prose, his *History* in essence was 'eternal', in the sense of still being about the Two Cities. Myth and theology, with accompanying miracles, are centre stage, and causality is explained in terms of God's intentions rather than that of humans. Though many faithful continued to hold to a version such as Bossuet's, intellectually, his *Discourse* can be seen as the last gasp of significant Christian universal history, still viewed as eternally valid.

*

As a category of world histories, the universal appeared to be at an end. Such a conclusion is too simple. What happened is that universal history *à la* Bossuet turned into a secular version, under the heading of philosophy of history. Here the emphasis is on philosophy, whereas before it had been on theology. Such history did not so much search for a meaning *in* history as impose one on it. In the process, however, it paid attention to more of the facts of secular history than its predecessor. As a result, we need to treat philosophy of history briefly as a variant of world histories.

The term 'philosophy of history' was coined by Voltaire in 1765, and then incorporated in his Introduction to his *Essai sur les Moeurs et l'Esprit des Nations* four years later. The title speaks volumes about the shift underway. The focus is no longer, in principle, on the religious or political meaning of history but on its larger cultural aspects. It is in this context that religion figures, as part of the culture, for our Enlightened philosophe seeks what is useful in history and finds it, for example, in the book of Zend, of the Parsis! In his *Essai*, Voltaire had started with geology, entered into anthropology, and then proceeded to recorded history in order to show human development from its beginnings. Fragmentary and speculative, his account was nevertheless an attempt to trace a genesis for mankind other than the traditional Biblical one.[7]

Numerous variants of philosophy of history followed. Familiar names in the list would be Turgot; Condorcet; Scottish Enlightened thinkers such as Adam Ferguson, with his stadial notion of human progress; Herder, with an increased stress on the cultural; Vico, with a partial return to cyclical history; and even more portentous names such as Kant, Hegel, Comte and Marx. Each in his own way foreshadowed elements of what would emerge later, in greatly changed forms, as divergent shapes of world histories.

A few further words will suffice. As is well known, Kant entitled one of his works *Idea for a Universal History from a Cosmopolitan Point of View* (1784), thus echoing the older tradition. In the *Idea*, Kant treated human actions as, like all other natural phenomena, subject to general laws. In what otherwise appeared a senseless mass of human events, the German philosopher perceived a teleology: the unintended consequence of man's actions was increased federation of nations and an approximation of eternal peace. More philosophy than history, Kant's notions passed almost by osmosis into more empirical accounts by historians in the future.

The same can be said of Hegel's *Philosophy of History*, though it was much more embedded in the details of the past, even though with an emphasis on religious systems. Hegel was, in fact, dealing with worldviews. For him, history was the story of the march of the Idea and of Freedom through time, coming into being dialectically. Initially universal in his outlook, Hegel was in fact enormously Eurocentric and parochial in his own view, embracing the notion of ancient, medieval, and modern periodization, the latter reflecting Western superiority. His influence on Marx, who purportedly stood him right-side up, is obvious; less so is his influence on many ordinary historians who followed him perhaps unknowingly.

Marx's economic, or materialist, interpretation of history is so powerful an influence on 'working' historians that it is easy to overlook its fitting into the genre of philosophy of history. Yet, like Hegel, Marx also sees a dialectic to history, culminating teleologically, in his case, in communism. Marx, however, also borders on writing a version of what today we would call world history. In his analysis of history as the passage to capitalism (as a way station to communism), he comes close to writing *a history* of capitalism. He also sees its world-historical aspirations, grounding his explanation in the bourgeoisie's drive to a world market. In addition, he intuited the way in which the world was being interconnected and its people drawn together in tight-knit relations of production and distribution. The *Manifesto*, in its first section, is a limited account of world history. Its impact on future world historians has been almost incalculable.

In touching upon philosophy of history as a precursor of world histories, I have neglected innumerable figures. Comte should have been accorded a paragraph along with Kant, Hegel and Marx. All sorts of lesser figures could have been noted. So, too, I have neglected mention of more mundane historians in the nineteenth century, who wrote general, or universal, or world histories (and would have to be mentioned in a more historiographical account). These practising historians, in fact, have had less influence on the present-day practice of world histories than the philosophers of history. It is the likes of Voltaire and those after him who serve as the bridge from eschatological, universal histories to ecumenical, secular histories, with Marx rooted with one foot in the last-named, the philosophies of history, and with the other foot in what we now are prepared to call world histories.

*

I have been paying attention up to now to the large-scale efforts, theological and or philosophical, to understand the past on a grand scale. In fact, Western historians from the nineteenth century until the middle of the twentieth, and even beyond, were mainly occupied with the nation state as the subject of their research and narratives. Their focus, of course, coincided if it did not originate with the French Revolution, with its emphasis on nationalism. A little earlier, the American Revolution had taken place, and the history of the USA is really symmetrical with the nation born from that struggle; what came before is part of European or colonial history. With the success of these Western revolutions, their merging with the forces of the Industrial Revolution, and their embodiment in capitalist and imperialist expansion, the supremacy of the nation state as the form in which social relations took place and could be understood reigned supreme. Henceforth the history of all other societies was placed, sooner or later, on this procrustean bed. Their earlier history was seen as a prelude to their entrance upon the stage of nations, along with a role in international affairs.

It is essential that we be aware of this dominant mode of writing history if we are to understand the advent of world history in the twentieth century. It is the reaction to this 'tradition' after World War II, coupled with the earlier work in universal and philosophy of history, that serves as the major explanation for the rise of the new mode of trying to understand the past. The world history that emerges is first and foremost an effort to go beyond not only a national perspective but to transcend a Eurocentric orientation. This is the work mainly of practising historians, rather than philosophers or sociologists. We must examine it carefully as both an intellectual aspiration and an institutional accomplishment.

One piece of unfinished business remains before we enter upon the details of professionalized world history. It is to call attention to two further figures in what is basically still philosophy of history. The first is Oswald Spengler, whose *Decline of the West* first appeared in 1918. There are three aspects of his work that bear special mention. The first is his rejection of historical linearity in favour of a return to a theory of cycles. The second is his 'Copernican discovery', whereby the West is displaced from its central position in history, and we are presented with a number of major cultures, each going through their fated cycles of birth and death. The third is his insistence that the last stage of every culture is 'civilization', when a petrifying world city replaces the organic existence based on mother earth. With all his mysticism and sweeping platitudes, not to mention his ideological predilections, Spengler nevertheless inspired others to transcend Western parochialism and to rise above nation states so as to view cultures – what we, departing from his usage, would call civilizations – as the main subjects of history.

The second figure to be noted here is Arnold Toynbee. When presented with Spengler's *Decline* in 1920, Toynbee asked himself whether his whole projected inquiry had been anticipated by the German writer. Consoling himself with the conviction that his own work was focused more on the origins of civilizations and on dealing with them by the method of English empiricism, Toynbee pressed on to write *A Study of History*, in ten volumes. His central insight, as he declared later, was that 'The smallest intelligible fields of historical study were whole societies and not arbitrarily isolated fragments of them like the nation-states of the modern West or the city-states of the Graeco-Roman world.'[8]

Focusing on 19 (or 21) civilizations, he looked at their origins in terms of such notions as challenge and response, withdrawal and return, mimesis, creative minorities, the effects of environment, and what he calls new ground, blows, and penalizations. As becomes clear, his is an ecumenical history, with 'etherialization' as a desired outcome of a civilization's trajectory on its way to breakdown. Covering a vast panorama of the past, Toynbee's history is on a grand scale, treating of civilizations rather than nation states, and embracing the comparative perspective. Written during the period surrounding the two world wars, Toynbee's vision seemed to offer emancipation from the narrow confines of nationalist antagonisms. For this reason, and more ideological ones as well, he was placed by Henry Luce on the cover of an issue of *Time Magazine*.

Historians, however, as they came to look more closely at Toynbee's English empirical method found unacceptable flaws in the data. Other more theoretically minded historians found his concepts ill-defined and flaccid. Thus, his reception amidst professional historians was quite distinct from that among the general public. Yet even for some of the former, his work was an inspiration. More than anyone else, it seemed, Toynbee held forth the vision of history transcending its Eurocentric bias, and rising to the level of true comparative history, with civilizations as the central actors.

One who admittedly fell under his spell was William McNeill, arguably the most important figure in the structuration of contemporary world history. An esteemed professional historian, holder of a chair at Chicago, a President of the American Historical Association, McNeill was an insider who chose to be an outsider, promoting an approach that was initially anathema to many in the mainstream. His pioneering work was *The Rise of the West: A History of the Human Community* (1963). Following Toynbee's lead, McNeill focused on civilizations. In his case, however, these were not so much hermetic entities as interacting systems. Inspired by various anthropologists, McNeill emphasized cultural borrowing as well as the separate civilizations. Blessed by a blurb from Toynbee, the book became an instant success.

Looking back at it some years later, McNeill was aware of its limitations. As he remarked, he still operated in terms of civilizations as largely separate fixtures, though interacting, and while escaping from Eurocentrism to a large degree, had neglected the role of Chinese civilization, for example, as well as giving undue attention to Latin Christendom. Admitting that he had been 'too much preoccupied by the notion of civilization', he recognized the need for more attention to a 'trans-civilizational process', in which 'encounters with strangers were the main drive wheel of social change'.[9] Turning his attention subsequently to plagues and population movements, long-distance trade, the spread of religions, McNeill showed in concrete form how one might do world history. In his hands, it became a masterly art of constructing syntheses and narrative accounts of transnational and post-Eurocentrically viewed movements of the past.

McNeill, though first among equals, was joined by a number of other pioneers in seeking to break past the boundaries of nation-state history. Another outstanding figure was Leften Stavrianos, who also wished to de-Europeanize history and called for 'a view from the moon'.[10] Recognizing that the standard 'History of Western Civilization' survey offered by many universities was no longer tenable after a second world war, Stavrianos and his supporters argued for its replacement by 'World

History'. Waging an uphill battle, the idea caught on and gradually came to prominence in the curriculum. Aided by the establishment in 1982 of a World Historical Association and the publication of a *Journal of World History* in 1990, it now had institutional support to go along with the work of such established figures as Philip Curtin and younger scholars such as Christopher Chase-Dunn, Ross Dunn and Jerry Bentley (the editor of the *Journal*), to mention only a few.

At this point, rather than going into further particulars about the movement, it is more fruitful to step back and see, so to speak, world history in the large. The first question to be asked concerns its definition. Other than being a transcendence of Eurocentrism and of Western civilization courses, what is its content? Recognizing that definitional questions can be a quagmire sinking any inquiry, it is still a necessary exercise. On what do world historians focus and what, if anything, do they leave out? One answer seems to be given in the original 'Invitation to Membership' of the World Historical Association: 'the whole history of the whole world'.[11] While adherents of the WHA often deny it, this does *seem* to imply that there is no obvious principle of selection. This sombre conclusion is supported by the titles publishers list in their catalogues under 'World History' as well as by the books reviewed in the *American Historical Journal* under the heading 'Comparative/World.'

Other answers are more cautious. As Jerry Bentley judiciously puts it, 'interactions between peoples participating in large-scale historical processes' are 'one of the central concerns of world history'.[12] This is certainly more in line with McNeill's intentions, and has the virtue of ruling out various other concerns in history, for example microhistory. There is still, of course, a certain vagueness to this definition: would every historian of the Industrial Revolution, say, as it develops in one country, necessarily be a world historian, and if not, why not? What stands out in the end is that world history is open-ended, tends to the comparative, is concerned with long-term and large-scale happenings, and has a penchant for thinking in terms of civilizations.

Under the tent of world history so defined numerous historians of non-European areas can come in from the periphery of the discipline and assume central roles. It is noteworthy how many of its figures began outside the modern Euro-American scene: in ancient history (McNeill and Stavrianos, for example), or African (Philip Curtin and Patrick Manning), or Middle Eastern (Marshall Hodgson); Asian historians are increasingly identifying themselves as world historians. A most useful fallout of this fact is that the old survey course has been greatly enriched by the addition of sections on Asia, Africa, the Middle East and other areas previously missing from the Table of Contents.

And as we shall see more extensively in Chapter 12, world history's appeal can be seen in the numerous courses now taught, for example, in North American high schools, thus cutting across the divide between secondary and university education. A few graduate degree programmes can be found, for example, at Hawaii and one or two other universities. However, at least one such programme – that at Northeastern – is folding for lack of financial support. Yet the increasing demand for the teachers of world history at university level is manifested in the growth of job listings. Almost always, however, such a course is an add-on to the quest for a specialist in Asian, African or Latin American history. Nor is it clear what training is requisite for the teaching of world history; there is almost an assumption that any historian who glances outside Europe and the US can undertake this most extensive and far-reaching effort at understanding the past.

Thus the triumph of the world history cause is tinged with troubling matters. Questions are raised not only as to the absence of a principle of selectivity but also as to exactly how far it has actually escaped the Eurocentric perspective. One astute observer, Gilbert Allardyce, has called attention to the field's lack of conceptualizing power, say, in the form of an elegant idea of how to order all human experience.[13] Perhaps an even more telling criticism is that there is no clear idea of how to conduct research in the field; it seems mostly to lend itself to synthesis of other's work, say, that of area specialists, and to an emphasis on teaching.

While the lacunae of world history are serious, especially that regarding the research necessary to advance the field, they should not obscure the field's solid advances. Synthesis and teaching are hardly to be looked upon askance. While world history's tendency to base itself upon civilizations is and should be increasingly subject to examination, its commitment to rising above the nation, its desire to avoid Eurocentrism, its embrace of the comparative method, and its general ecumenical intentions impress most observers as praiseworthy. These trump its possible weaknesses and ensure its compatibility with the present *Zeitgeist*, making world history a 'growth' industry of a worthwhile sort.

*

Among contemporary world histories there is another version that carries the word 'world' in its heading, but couples it with systems analysis. It has two branches. One involves the *Annales* School, and is associated with the great French historian, Fernand Braudel. The other draws inspiration from Karl Marx, and has been forwarded mainly by a sociologist at Binghamton University (SUNY), Immanuel Wallerstein, where a Fernand Braudel Center has been established, symbolizing the connection between the two branches.

Let us look at Braudel first. He can well lay claim to being the foremost historian of the twentieth century, starting with his book *The Mediterranean and the Mediterranean World in the Age of Phillip II* (1949). It is a magisterial work, based on an incredible range of research, and beautifully written. It is truly a masterpiece of scholarship. In it, the author deploys the *Annales* ideas about the *longue durée*, about structure, *conjuncture* and everyday events in exquisite detail and to great effect. By structure, Braudel has in mind economic systems, states, societies, and civilizations, all at work in the field of warfare. By *conjuncture*, he has in mind the history of events, 'surface' disturbances, 'the actions of individual men', what his colleagues called '*l'histoire événementielle*'. The interplay of structure and *conjunture* occurs against an even more fundamental background, man's relations to the environment, an 'almost timeless history'. As he informs us, he was inspired by the geographers who taught him at the Sorbonne.

We, of course, are primarily concerned with the relation of Braudel's work to world history, and thus must bypass any larger treatment of him. And even in regard to world history our remarks must be brief. In fact, in his great book on the age of Phillip II, Braudel is really writing regional history. As he tells us, there is a unity and coherence to the Mediterranean region, lived and breathed alike by Turks and Christians, who thus shared a common destiny. This is a sea that stood at the threshold of modern times, for from the 1580s on Spain turned toward the Atlantic and a transatlantic destiny. Only then can we really talk about a chapter in world history.

The essential question, Braudel informs us, is that of boundaries; from it all others flow. To draw a boundary around anything is to 'adopt a philosophy of history', which is also equated with historical narrative.[14] It should come as no surprise that Part One of the book is called 'The Role of the Environment', whose first chapter is on 'The Peninsulas: Mountains, Plateaux, and Plains'. These are the boundaries behind which people live, and across which they move and interact. It bears repeating, however, that we are still in a regional, not a world setting. Yet the book is perceived by many to be a contribution to world history because it does transcend the national boundaries observed by other historians.

There is one other small point to be made before moving on to Braudel's own efforts to transcend the regional and truly enter upon world history.

It is his belief that a work of synthesis inspires a new crop of specialized research. Here we may have a partial answer to the charge levelled against world history that it has no research component. In Braudel's case, of course, he means research into the history of the Mediterranean, a delimited subject, and even here he holds out the prospect that the task is beyond a single historian and in the future should be undertaken by large research teams.

The Mediterranean could well be the life work of any other historian. There is a second Braudel, however, who wrote a three-volume work on *Civilization and Capitalism, 15th–18th Century*. Here he quite specifically says, 'I wanted my study to cover the whole world if such a thing could be done.'[15] The vehicle making this possible was capitalism, for it too, in actuality, sought to cover the whole world. Starting with what he calls the market economy, not that of Smith and Marx but of the world of self-sufficiency and barter of goods and services within a very small radius, Braudel posits as its opposite capitalism, which is multi- and transnational. Again, his capitalism is not that of free-trade economists but the monopolies of the Fuggers and Welsers. Never mind, this capitalism was intensely transnational, radiating out into the broader world beyond Europe. Linking his version of the market economy and capitalism, Braudel portrays the material civilization in which they had their being in the fifteenth to the eighteenth centuries.

But Braudel has something larger in mind: a world economy. The handmaidens of its construction are capitalism and the Industrial Revolution. Between them they will create a worldwide trading network. At its centre will be world cities – Venice, Amsterdam – dominating the capitalist economy, early or late. This centre, which Braudel also calls core (not an original usage), is matched by peripheries in every quarter of the world; and thus we are introduced to the famous core–periphery. In an amazing display of erudition and imagination, Braudel illustrates his system in vivid detail. Again, it is a *tour de force*.

Braudel himself tells us that he used extensively Werner Sombart's monumental *Der Moderne Kapitalismus* (in which, I should add, the term 'capitalism' is first introduced), 'a fantastic combination of erudition and analysis'. Noting specifically that this book and almost all other general works are confined to the European context, Braudel declares that 'I am convinced that history would benefit immeasurably from comparisons made on the only valid scale – that of the world.' Practising what he preaches, he has become a world historian, moving beyond his own region.

Not all members of the *Annales* School moved with him. Theirs is another story. And Braudel is largely unique – a genius. The major development of his work in regard to world histories took another turn, at the hands of what has come to be called world-system analysts. We need to turn to that school now.

*

The leading figure in world-system analysis is unquestionably Immanuel Wallerstein. Unlike the historian Braudel, he trained as a sociologist, was heavily indebted to Marx (and later of Fanon and Prigogine, as well as Braudel), and did his early work as an Africanist. In the course of two decades, seeing himself as one of the few scholars who, knowing French, could study the continent across European linguistic barriers, he moved beyond Africa to the world; or rather a 'world-system' perspective. Going beyond Braudel's early work, the American sociologist insisted that both a systemic and an historical viewpoint were required; that is, that the most plausible unit of analysis was an 'historical social system'.[16] (It should be noted that Wallerstein's first book was published in 1974, anticipating Braudel's work on capitalism by five years.)

In three volumes, from 1974 to 1988, Wallerstein analysed *The Modern World-System*, the title of his extended work. As with Braudel, we will not go into much detail but only touch on the major themes. It is Wallerstein's argument that following upon a crisis of feudalism, an historical social system, a new social system revolving around capitalism emerged around the sixteenth century. It was characterized by the emergence of national states, a major geographical expansion, and the rise of an international division of labour, organized around the notions of core, periphery, semi-periphery and the external arena. Capital is central to this system, now worldwide.

It is a system marked by constant change, though the essentials stay the same. What is so impressive is the way Wallerstein marshals the historical data and places it in his schema. Thus, for example, in Volume II, devoted to *Mercantilism and the Consolidation of the European World-Economy, 1600–1750*, drawing on existing scholarship, he employs it to examine the question of the alleged seventeenth-century crisis (which he accepts as occurring), and deals eloquently with the early hegemony of the Dutch and then its challenge by the English in two separate phases covering the seventeenth and eighteenth centuries. It is a conflict, we should note, in the core. I should also add that the chapter on the Dutch, when I first read it long ago, seemed to me worth the price of admission alone.

Wallerstein saw his work as rooted in epistemology, where the choice of the unit of analysis was crucial. After the sixteenth century, that unit had become the world. Moreover, the 'theory of capitalist development [was] only a part of a larger theory of sociohistorical change'.[17] It was not necessarily the last word, and was itself marked by continuing crises. And it is at that point that possible contradictions in Wallerstein's scheme intrude forcefully upon our consciousness.

In a later statement, he declared that 'World-system analysis... is not a theory but a protest against neglected issues and deceptive epistemologies... a call for intellectual change.'[18] This seems to fly in the face of the obvious, and to make a claim for some form of objectivity – analysis – free of theory. Surely the idea of a world-system is itself a theory, and as with most theory, laden with value? The question, then, is what effect his theories and values have on his work.

Admirers will claim that it informs it; detractors that it pushes too much material into a predetermined 'system'. In any case, as he deals with later periods of capitalism, Wallerstein takes more openly political positions. He believes, for example, that under capitalism people have been and are both objectively and subjectively less well off than in pre-capitalist times – a version of Marx's theory of increasing immiserization? – that there is less liberty, equality and fraternity than in earlier times, and that the embrace of universals – science – has been used largely as a weapon in the subjection of local peoples and their traditions. In this mode, it is clear that part of the appeal of Wallerstein's world-system approach is its political aspect.

Its other, and earlier, appeal was that it offered a new version of world history, lucidly written and forcefully argued, both systemic and historically grounded in detail. This way of going beyond the Eurocentric, shorn of its political overtones, could be built upon by others who, as we shall see, both contracted and expanded his work. More immediate challenges appear in two forms. The first is the accusation that the world-system approach is too *econocentric*, to coin a phrase, for its singular emphasis on the economic. The work and insights of intellectual and cultural history, for example, are simply missing. They would undoubtedly add complexity and meaning to Wallerstein's generally negative treatment of modernity and, implicitly, the Enlightenment. It is 'enlightening', to pun a bit, that the latter movement is totally missing in Wallerstein's account of capitalism.

The second is to ask in what way Wallerstein's analysis differs from that of a host of other scholars who seek to address the question of why capitalism and modernity arose in the West. McNeill, as we have seen, tried to deal with this question in his first book. More recently, other scholars have engaged in the debate begun so prominently by Max Weber. David Landes, who has been accused of Eurocentrism, has tried his hand. So have scholars such as R. Bin Wong and Kenneth Pomeranz, who can less likely be dismissed in these terms.[19] What Wallerstein has done is to add or impose a 'system' on the historical debate: depending on one's viewpoint, is this a gain or a loss – perhaps an imposition of a procrustean bed? An even more subversive question has been raised by some of his critics: is Wallerstein's world-system itself also fundamentally Eurocentric (and not just econocentric)?

Whatever the answers to these questions, there can be no denying the importance of Wallerstein's work for world history. Its impact has been facilitated by his skill as an organizer. The Braudel Center is a continuing base for his operations, and its *Review* a vehicle for the promotion of his views (though it also encourages challenges and counter-arguments). If we recall the similar institutional achievements of world history – its journal and association – it would appear that one measure of any version of world history's success lies, not surprisingly, not only in its intellectual claims but in the means of promoting them.

In any event, while Wallerstein is the leading figure in world-system analysis, other major contributors also should be mentioned. One is Janet Abu-Lughod, who 'contracts' (my term) Wallerstein, while building on his theories. This paradox emerges because she argues that a world-system had existed prior to the sixteenth century in a part of the world other than the West. In her book *Before European Hegemony: The World System A.D. 1250–1350* (1989), and in various articles, she argues that a system of world trade and even cultural exchange prevailed in the Middle East heartland, linking East and West. The balance could have tipped either way, with the rise of the East rather than the West; moreover, when the latter occurred it was because of borrowings from the earlier world-system. For Abu-Lughod the period from the thirteenth to the sixteenth century constituted a 'crucial turning point in world history'.[20]

Abu-Lughod is 'contracting' Wallerstein because, while recognizing his major contribution, she is treating it as a parochial and limited version of world history. In her eyes, he is still writing from the perspective of Western Europe. In this view, Abu-Lughod seems to be saying, Wallerstein is betraying the broader aspirations of world, or what she prefers to call global, history. A true world-system history would be one that is decentralized and truly global, going beyond the simple additive process that studies the rise and fall of different civilizations 'as if they were relatively independent of one another'.

Originally a follower of Wallerstein, Andre Gunder Frank became a critic by expanding his analysis far beyond its originator's theses. In the largest sense, Frank argued that the modern capitalist world system was not only the continuation of Abu-Lughod's version of it in the 1250–1550 period but of all previous periods of history when viewed in a world-system perspective. More specifically, Frank pointed out that China, not Northwest Europe, was the dynamic core of the system and Europe its periphery until the late eighteenth century. In short, Frank vastly expanded the world-system perspective and stood Wallerstein on his head in the process.

Frank's numerous works, but especially his *ReOrient: Global Economy in the Asian Age* (1998) joined the growing debate on the nature, causes, and timing of the West's surge to supremacy. Why was it the West and not the superior China of the eighteenth century that entered upon an Industrial Revolution? If that revolution had not occurred in the West would it have emerged elsewhere, at a different time? What would be the shape of world history if it had been Asia and not Europe that rose to global dominance in the modern period? To answer such questions we must look from the Asian perspective as much or more than from the European: hence ReOrient. In doing so, argues Frank, we will be doing real world-system analysis.

Without going into further details here – for example, about the actual data Frank uses, the shrillness of his tone as noted by his critics, his polemical Marxist bent, his single-minded attention to the economic – one can note that he has made a major contribution to the world-system literature. Along with Wallerstein and Abu-Lughod, and others not named, he has helped promote a variation of their work, which, while having many affinities with world history as previously described, has tried to give a principle of selectivity and an agenda for research that, to some observers, seemed missing in the more ecumenical version derived from Toynbee and even McNeill.

*

Yet another variant of world histories is what has come to be called 'big history'. It emerged in the context of world history and its teaching, but then took its own turn. David Christian, of Macquarie University, Australia, giving 'An Introduction to World History' course, asked himself when it all began. His answer was with the Big Bang; and a few years later his article 'The Case for "Big History"' appeared in the *Journal of World History*. Recognizing that the term was rather grandiose, he could think of none better for his take on world history, and thus this subgenre continued under his 'big history' label, even after others joined his effort.

Among these others – and, indeed, they are relatively few in number though not in influence – was the prominent Dutch historian, Johan Goudsblom (the author of a major book on fire, and a follower of Norbert Elias) who, in turn, introduced the idea to his colleague, Fred Spier. Together the two mounted a big history offering at the University of Amsterdam, 1995–96, as part of a 'Big History Project', out of which emerged Spier's *The Structure of Big History* (1991, revised 1996).

In back of these three men, and their successors, was work in the natural sciences, circling about cosmology, evolutionary biology and evolutionary psychology, all viewed as historical sciences. Going back to the Big Bang and the origins of life, these sciences provided the necessary prologue to history conceived on a 'big' scale, that is, the story from the beginning of the universe. For Christian, it all amounts to 'a single, and remarkably coherent story, a story whose general shape turns out to be that of a Creation Myth, even if its contents draw on modern scientific research'.[21] For Spier, there is 'one single, uncomplicated, conceptual scheme' covering all of cosmic, planetary, world, and human history'.[22] Going back to the beginning 13 billion years ago, the Dutchman deals with it all in the course of just over 100 pages.

There is much talk of regimes, patterns, equilibrium systems and the like, and a central concern with issues of order and disorder. Such usage is especially congenial for Spier, who started as a biochemist and then shifted to anthropology and historical sociology. In taking all of the past, inhuman and human, as their subject, Christian, Spier and others openly acknowledge that they are doing big history, or macrohistory; for one scholar, Marnie Hughes-Warrington, they can be most fruitfully 'located in the tradition of universal history'.[23] What has changed, of course, from the time of the ancients on to our present is our conception of the universe.

Such large-scale history seems more like prehistory than history as generally practiced as a discipline. It draws upon evolutionary sciences and archaeology, the hinge to the coming of humans and their records (incidentally, 'archaeology' is a term first coined in the mid-nineteenth century), rather than on the written documents that mark the emergence of civilizations. Indeed, humans seem absent from the account, or when they appear, do so either as abstractions or microscopic figures in the larger landscape (and not to be viewed in terms of microhistory). Hence a potential gap seems to yawn between conventional world history, centrally concerned as it is with civilizations, and big history.

One work that, perhaps unintentionally, bridges the gap and in any case stands as an exemplary attempt at a sort of big history is Jared Diamond's *Guns, Germs, and Steel*. He, too, starts as a non-historian, with his own training in physiology, from whence he expanded into evolutionary biology and biogeography. His declared aim is to 'develop human history as a science, on a par with acknowledged sciences such as astronomy, geology, and evolutionary biology'.[24] Where Spier had devoted about 100 pages to 15–20 billion years, Diamond treats of 2.5 million years in about 450 pages. If Spier stands within the tradition of universal history, Diamond is best seen as standing within the tradition of philosophy of history, solidly grounded in empiricism.

In Diamond's view, there are a set of identifiable ultimate causes and proximate causes of what happened in history. Though the ultimate cause appears to be food production, Diamond really operates with a constellation of causes that include geography, climate, ecology, and the orientation of the axes of the continents. Against this epistemological background, he raises specific big questions, the main one being what he calls 'Yali's Question':[25] why were New Guineans (Diamond had done much of his fieldwork in New Guinea) so far behind Westerners in 'development'? Seeking to answer this and related questions, he ranges widely and brilliantly over the long stretch of time, geologically and historically, up to the sixteenth century; but not much beyond.

It is a truly impressive book. Equally clear, it goes well beyond the Eurocentric perspective (and if anything, takes a New Guinean perspective). Rather than asking why the West arose, it asks why New Guinea didn't. Situated on the margin of both world history and big history, it is a model for doing work that transcends both geographical and disciplinary boundaries. Yet challenges surround Diamond's work. What has happened to non-material forces, such as religion and culture? What room is there for human agency? What sort of history is it that ignores hermeneutics and the social construction of meaning?

These are the same challenges that surround all of big history. Christian, Spier, Diamond and similar figures all draw on the same developments in the evolutionary natural sciences, and seek to apply them to the species, *Homo sapiens*. Their work, and that of big history, is a testament to the human desire to know the whole of the past, envisioned in one swooping vision, overleaping the limited and limiting boundaries humans have sought to place on the earth.

*

In turning to our last version of world histories, global history, we are confronted not only with additional problems of time, methodology and epistemology, but with a conceptual muddle. Many practitioners of world history use the word 'global' as a synonym. For example, a series is being published under the aegis of the American Historical Association, whose editor speaks of 'new global or world history' as if they were one and the same. The elision is found in numerous other authors. Yet both etymology and analysis bring the synonymity into doubt.

A quick glance at the dictionary shows that 'World' comes from the Middle English for human existence as it refers to the earth with its inhabitants and all things upon it. The word 'Globe' comes from the Latin, with its first definition as something spherical or rounded, for example, a heavenly body. The valence of the two terms is very different.[26] 'Global' points us in the direction of space, where humans can stand outside our planet and see it whole, as 'Spaceship Earth'. Interestingly, this perspective can usefully be traced back to the Copernican Revolution, which views the globe imaginatively, as if from outer space. It coincides with the widespread construction of actual 'globes' – a history unto itself, made manifest in numerous paintings subsequently – that is, of spherical maps.

Critics of this view may wish to dismiss it as semantic quibbling. It points, however, to the fact that global history embodies a principle of selectivity that is missing from world history as generally practised. Global history, when not confused with world history, seeks to inquire into the one strand of the latter that can be addressed under the heading of globalization. Where world history may take all of the past for its subject, global history restricts its attention to the theme of globalism. While this theme can be traced back to the beginnings of human existence – hunter-gatherers wandering the globe – it becomes a matter of sustained consciousness only sometime in the second half of the twentieth century. And thus a matter of disciplined historical inquiry.

A world-system thinker such as Wallerstein dismisses it testily, as in his comment that, in contrast to his long-lasting structures, global history represents one of 'those momentary expressions of reality that we so regularly reify into fashionable theories. The enormous recent furore concerning so-called "globalization" is an example of the latter.'[27] World history practitioners, as we have seen, tend to take the global under their wings imperialistically, and to pooh-pooh its claims to an autonomous existence. Others, such as Anthony Hopkins and his colleagues, in the book *Globalization in World History* (2001), attempt to show how, while the former is a part of the latter, it needs to be studied as a separate theme, in its own terms.

The tension concerning what I have labelled a conceptual muddle is effectively *echoed* in the important article by Martin Geyer and Charles Bright, 'World History in a Global Age'. As they remark, there is a crisis of 'Western imaginings... the world we live in has come into its own as an integrated globe, yet it lacks narration and has no history'.[28] A number of scholars faced with this challenge have tried to respond in various ways. Interestingly, in the beginning they came mostly from sociology and anthropology rather than history. Thus Roland Robertson drew upon comparative religion and international affairs to write his book *Globalization* (1992). Manuel Castells' three volumes on the Information Revolution (1996–98) has become a classic. The anthropologist Arjun Appadurai has approached globalization culturally in his *Modernity at Large* (1996).

Historians have been latecomers to the effort to discern the shape of globalization as a scholarly enterprise. Many if not most world historians have little knowledge of the work of the sociologists and anthropologists, an observation that points to the interdisciplinarity required of work in global history. The competitive advantage of historians, however, is exactly that they bring a sustained historical perspective to the subject. Like the world historians, global historians also seek to rise above Eurocentrism and see the world whole. Only their world is in fact a globe, with all that that portends as suggested above.

In addition to those who wish to write the history of globalization as a part of world history, there are an increasing number who wish to pay special attention to the new globalization, that is, the manifestations of globalism since the end of World War II. To distinguish their work, they have added the term 'new' to global history. Nevertheless, while starting in the near present, they go as far back into the past as is necessary or helpful in regard to any single part of their inquiry.

A brief description of some of their tenets will suffice for this emerging subfield of history. It begins with a provisional definition of globalization as the increasing interrelation and interdependency of increasing numbers of people, accompanied in present times by a transcendence of existing boundaries and the erosion of sovereignty in its national form, and by a heightened compression of space and time. Aware of new actors and forces brought into being by globalization, its practitioners envision a history that revolves about certain new factors at work in our contemporary 'world'.

One early attempt to deal with the subject emphasized the following basic facts of our time: the step into space, with its accompanying sense of being in one world as seen from outside the earth's atmosphere; satellites in outer space, linking the peoples of the world in real time in unprecedented fashion; nuclear threats that reveal the inadequacy of the territorial state any longer to protect its citizens from either military or ecologically related invasions; environmental problems that overleap lines drawn on a map; and the enormous expansion of multinational corporations of a global nature. Others, for example, human rights and global consumerism, could be added. All are marked by a synergy and synchronicity among them. It is also noteworthy that the subject must be addressed constantly in terms of the global and the local, and the interactions among them.[29]

New global history is certainly a nascent version of world histories. In the eyes of various critics, it is too 'contemporary' and impossible to carry out; too limited in its view of when globalization starts; and too broad in its coverage and interests. Time will shed light on the validity of such charges.

As the newest entry, it beckons for further work and workers. It, too, like world history and world-system analysis, will need to create institutional supports in order to flourish. A few existing university courses herald more to come. Conferences and the volumes resulting from them are visible evidences of this new subfield's existence. As a work in progress it envisions a journal and an association devoted to its purposes, as well as network links. Only the future will tell if new global history will flourish, to take its place next to the other variants on world histories discussed at length in this chapter.

*

In the end, we must remember that all world histories are a form of history, and thus subject to the strictures of that form of inquiry. Those strictures include an insistence on an empirical basis – facts – subject to continued challenge and renewal; on the verification of documents; on the placing of them in context; on induction subject to constant review; on the use of theories; and then the return of the theories to the data. In short, world histories like any other history must aim at a form of scientific method suitable to the materials with which they deal, thereby offering an alternative to myth.

World histories themselves cannot become new forms of myth, but must remain part of the practice of history. No different in this respect from microhistories, the different versions of world histories, however, go to the other end of the spectrum in terms of the scale of their object of study. World histories focus on the widest range of human relations possible, ranging over all known time and space. In practice, of course, pieces of the whole are chosen for investigation, and the local treated as an opening to the world or globe.

All of the versions of world histories that we have scanned – universal, philosophy of history, world history, world-system analysis, big history, global and new global history – have in common the desire to transcend the local lines of their time. Their 'locality', however, is in constant change, with the question of what is the universe, what the world, and what the global undergoing important and continuing mutations. A universal history predicated on a 6000-year span and a world whose geography is half unknown is different from a Big History going back 13 billion years and spinning out into infinite space.

Overall our world histories share some common characteristics, but also exhibit 'local' differences. The most essential common feature is a desire to transcend their existing geographic limitations. Of equal importance, they have sought to give a transcendental meaning, theological or historical, to the human experiences of the past. In the process, they all go beyond parochial earthly time/space coordinates. Today, however, world histories may be seen as moving not only to a new sense of that earth and its boundaries but to a sense of a globe that is itself part of a new space. Historical consciousness now needs to take this novel 'global positioning system' into account as it goes about the task of reviewing past efforts and constructing future world histories.

notes

1. M. I. Finley, *The Use and Abuse of History* (Harmondsworth: Penguin, 1985), p. 15. See especially the first chapter, 'Myth, Memory and History', for a splendid account of the emergence and differentiation of history from mythical approaches. In fact, of course, the emergence was gradual, for Herodotus does include mythical stories in his inquiry. Additionally, he draws extensively on interviews – oral history – in place of documents, which frequently were non-existent.
2. K. H. Waters, *Herodotus the Historian* (Norman, OK: University of Oklahoma Press, 1985), p. 175. This may well be the best single book on Herodotus, though generally neglected.
3. For Ephorus, see the *Encyclopaedia Britannica*, 11th edn, vol. 9, p. 678. For Diodorus, see M. Hughes-Warrington, 'Big History,' *Historically Speaking*, 4(2) (2002) 17.

4. An excellent account of this transformation is given by C. N. Cochrane, *Christianity and Classical Culture* (New York: Oxford University Press, 1957); see especially p. 483. Though an 'old' book, its discussion is hardly outdated.

5 Excerpts from *The Two Cities* may conveniently be found in *Main Currents of Western Thought*, ed. F. Le Van Baumer, 2nd, rev. edn (New York: Alfred A. Knopf, 1964), pp. 92 and 94.

6. For a wonderful account of the context sketched here, see J. I. Israel, *Radical Enlightenment* (Oxford: Oxford University Press, 2001). Israel is exhaustive and, certainly for the average reader, vastly over-detailed in his account, and should only be dipped into.

7. The treatment here of Voltaire and those that follow is, needless to say, without depth, intended only to mark their existence for our present purposes. My own attempt to deal with them at more length can be found in *The Riddle of History: The Great Speculators from Vico to Freud* (New York: Harper & Row, 1966). A bibliography accompanies each chapter, but an immense amount of literature on these subjects has appeared subsequently, as any internet search will show. The chapter on Marx in the *Riddle* should be supplemented by my *The Meaning of Karl Marx* (New York: Oxford University Press, 1984), whose bibliography points to other works on him and, especially, his contribution to history.

8. A. Toynbee, *Civilisation on Trial and other Essays* (New York: Oxford University Press, 1946), pp. 9–10.

9. See W. H. McNeill, '*The Rise of the West* After Twenty-Five Years', *Journal of World History*, 1(1) (1990) 13, and 'The Changing Shape of World History', *History and Theory*, 34(2) (1995) 14–26.

10. Quoted in G. Allardyce, 'Toward World History: American Historians and the Coming of the World History Course', *Journal of World History*, 1(1) (1990) 40. This is a detailed account of its subject, and fundamental on the subject.

11. A printed mailing from R. Rosen, Executive Director, World Historical Association, n.d.

12. J. Bentley, review of *Conceptualizing Global History*, ed. Bruce Mazlish and Ralph Buultjens on H-Net Book Review, available at <www.h-net.msu.edu> (August 1995).

13. Allardyce, 'Toward World History', p. 67.

14. F. Braudel, *The Mediterranean and the Mediterranean World in the Age of Phillip II*, trans. S. Reynolds, 2 vols (New York: Harper & Row, 1972–73 [1949]), vol. 1, pp. 18, 21. In regard to the next paragraphs, see pp. 15 and 18.

15. F. Braudel, *Civilisation and Capitalism 15th-18th Century*, trans. S. Reynolds, 3 vols (New York: Harper & Row, 1981–84), vol. I, p. 25. In regard to core and periphery see vol. III, pp. 39–40, and to Sombart, vol. III, p. 18.

16. I. Wallerstein, *The Essential Wallerstein* (New York: New Press, 2000), p. xvii. In the introduction to his *The Modern World-System. Capitalist Agriculture and the Origins of the European World-Economy in the Sixteenth Century* (New York: Academic Press, 1974), Wallerstein gives a short but interesting account of how he worked his way toward the notion of world-system analysis.

17. I. Wallerstein, *The Modern World-System II* (New York: Academic Press, 1980), p. 8.

18. Wallerstein, *The Essential Wallerstein*, p. xxii. In chapter 8 of this book, 'World-Systems Analysis', the author offers what he feels is the clearest exposition

of his position, denying it to be a theory. Wallerstein's views, incidentally, were hardly static, developing and changing over time; the same could be said for most of our practitioners of other versions of world histories. Space, however, precludes tracking these changes.

19. For an excellent treatment of some of these figures and the general subject, see G. Stokes, 'The Fates of Human Societies: A Review of Recent Macrohistories', *American Historical Review*, 106(2) (2001) 508–25.

20. J. L. Abu-Lughod, *The World System in the Thirteenth Century: Dead-End or Precursor?* (Washington, DC: American Historical Association, 1994), p. 2. The larger book is *Before European Hegemony: The World System AD 1250–1350* (New York: Oxford University Press, 1989).

21. Quoted in Hughes-Warrington, 'Big History', p. 16. In general, this short article is a very useful treatment of its subject.

22. F. Spier, *The Structure of Big History* (Amsterdam: University of Amsterdam Press, 1996), p. 2.

23. Hughes-Warrington, 'Big History', p. 17.

24. J. Diamond, *Guns, Germs, and Steel: The Fates of Human Societies* (New York: W. W. Norton, 1997), p. 408. For a long review-essay on Diamond and Spier, see B. Mazlish, 'Big Questions? Big History?', *History and Theory*, 38(2) (1999) 232–48.

25. Diamond, *Guns, Germs, and Steel*, p. 239.

26. For a full exposition of this idea see B. Mazlish, 'Comparing Global History to World History', *Journal of Interdisciplinary History*, 23(3) (1998) 385–95.

27. Wallerstein, *The Essential Wallerstein*, pp. xviii–xix. Wallerstein's position may reflect the fact that the new globalization embodies a decentralized, networked society and calls into question, either explicitly or implicitly, the further usefulness, unless seriously modified, of the concepts of core and periphery. So, too, does new global history's attention to creolization, or hybridity, potentially undermine the dogma of homogenization-cum-imperialism as the inevitable result of global processes.

28. M. Geyer and C. Bright, 'World History in a Global Age', *American Historical Review*, 100 (1995) 1037, 1041.

29. Cf. the introduction to *Conceptualizing Global History*, eds B. Mazlish and R. Buultjens (Boulder, CO: Westview Press, 1993), pp. 1–24. For more on new global history, see the website <http://www.newglobalhistory.org/>.

recommended resources

Abu-Lughod, J. L., *Before European Hegemony: The World System AD 1250–1350* (New York: Oxford University Press, 1989).

Abu-Lughod, J. L., *The World System in the Thirteenth Century: Dead-End or Precursor?* (Washington, DC: American Historical Association, 1994).

Allardyce, G., 'Toward World History: American Historians and the Coming of the World History Course,' *Journal of World History* 1(1) (1990) 23–76; reprinted in R. Dunn (ed.) *The New World History* (New York: Bedford/St. Martin's, 2000), pp. 29–58.

Braudel, F., *The Mediterranean and the Mediterranean World in the Age of Phillip II*, trans. S. Reynolds, 2 vols (New York: Harper & Row, 1972–73 [1949]).

Braudel, F., *Civilisation and Capitalism 15th-18th Century*, trans. S. Reynolds, 3 vols (New York: Harper & Row, 1981–84).

Cochrane, C. N., *Christianity and Classical Culture* (New York: Oxford University Press, 1957).

Diamond, J., *Guns, Germs, and Steel: The Fates of Human Societies* (New York: W. W. Norton, 1997).

Finley, M. I., *The Use and Abuse of History* (Harmondsworth: Penguin, 1985).

Geyer, M., and Bright, C.,'World History in a Global Age', *American Historical Review*, 100 (1995) 1037–41.

Hughes-Warrington, M., 'Big History', *Historically Speaking*, 4(2) (2002) 16–17, 20.

Israel, J. I., *Radical Enlightenment* (Oxford: Oxford University Press, 2001).

Le Van Baumer, F. (ed.), *Main Currents of Western Thought*, 2nd edn (New York: Alfred A. Knopf, 1964).

Mazlish, B., *The Riddle of History: The Great Speculators from Vico to Freud* (New York: Harper & Row, 1966).

Mazlish, B., *The Meaning of Karl Marx* (New York: Oxford University Press, 1984).

Mazlish, B., and Buultjens, R. (eds), *Conceptualizing Global History* (Boulder, CO: Westview Press, 1993).

Mazlish, B., 'Comparing Global History to World History,' *Journal of Interdisciplinary History*, 23(3) (1998) 385–95.

Mazlish, B., 'Big Questions? Big History?, *History and Theory*, 38(2) (1999) 232–48.

McNeill, W. H., 'The Rise of the West After Twenty-Five Years', *Journal of World History* 1(1) (1990), reprinted in *The Rise of the West*, rev. edn (Chicago, IL: University of Chicago Press, 1993).

McNeill, W. H., 'The Changing Shape of World History', *History and Theory*, 34(4) (1995) 14–26.

Spier, F., *The Structure of Big History* (Amsterdam: University of Amsterdam Press, 1996).

Stokes, G., 'The Fates of Human Societies: A Review of Recent Macrohistories', *American Historical Review*, 106(2) (2001) 508–25.

Toynbee, A., *Civilisation on Trial and other Essays* (New York: Oxford University Press, 1946).

Wallerstein, I., *The Modern World-System II.* (New York: Academic Press, 1980).

Wallerstein, I., *The Essential Wallerstein* (New York: New Press, 2000).

Waters, K. H., *Herodotus the Historian* (Norman, OK: University of Oklahoma Press, 1985).

3
methods and materials
patrick manning

Studies of world history overlap substantially in their content and analysis with studies set at national, local and other levels. World history is more, however, than the accumulation of local and national knowledge, for it addresses patterns at a larger scale that may not be observable or explicable at more localized levels, and it addresses the linkages among localized and broader scales. As a result, certain of the methods and materials of world historians are common to historical studies in general, while others are distinctive and characteristic of global studies. This chapter presents an effort at identifying the distinctive methodological characteristics of world history: the range of its scope and scale, the balance of its various materials and methods, and the attention to how best to combine these elements of historical analysis.

models for historical research

World historical writing has coexisted with several other styles and forms of historical research and writing. National history is the most fully developed genre in historical studies, having been dominant in academic historical studies for over a century. But other genres of historical writing, each with its characteristic rhetoric, materials and audience, have long traditions and continue to reproduce themselves and in some cases to thrive. Thus dynastic history is distinct from national history in its biographic focus, though the two fields overlap in political and diplomatic analysis. Military history, while generally written within national or imperial traditions, gives particular emphasis to the tension between the contingency of events on battlefield and the influence of underlying social and economic structures. Ecclesiastical history focuses on religious doctrine and institutions. Philosophic histories, attempting to make sense of the world and its transformations, have been largely speculative, but their authors have maintained a continuity of discourse by linking their interpretations to those of earlier writers. Historical geography has been an eclectic field, sometimes empirical and sometimes speculative, organizing evidence more by place than by time. Area-studies history expanded dramatically in the late twentieth century: it consisted partly of multidisciplinary social science, but was also partly an extension of national history beyond the limits of Europe and North America. Other significant fields of historical study include family history, local history, institutional history, and the long-established tradition of assembling chronologies.

Each of these genres of historical writing entails a characteristic model of research and writing. For each genre, the model recommends its subject matter, its documents, the logic of its analysis, the boundaries of its purview, the style of its writing and its audience. These varying models for historical research and writing overlap significantly with each other. Medieval history, for instance, is a broad category of historical study, encompassing work in economic, social, political and intellectual history. Yet medievalists working on Europe share a common exposure to Latin texts and a tradition of encompassing a wide region within their purview.[1] Similarly, medievalists working on the Islamic world, on China and on Japan share skills in a major literary language and a tradition of working across the wide region in which that language was dominant among the elite.

World history, now formalizing itself as a field, is visibly proceeding through a review of the various other models for historical research, drawing on their various approaches, and developing new approaches where necessary. Already we can see that, in this initial organization of the field, there will be several directions and not just one. As was made clear in the previous chapter, the differences have already shown up in the terminology: world history, global history, universal history, contemporary history and big history.[2]

Certain distinctive patterns in world-historical interpretation appeared in the earliest stages of historical writing, and have continued to the present. World history in early times, as now, reflected an effort to link knowledge over the widest range in time and space. Such broad exploration of the past, pressing on the frontiers of knowledge, tended to be dominated by historical philosophy. Commonly the writers were in the service of a state or religious institutions. Herodotus collected historical information through his travels and interviews, and wrote for a Greek public. Sima Qian similarly relied on travels and interviews but also on the written record of the Han state, and wrote for an audience of state officials in the first century BCE. In the early centuries of Christianity, Eusebius sought to show the unity of the world and its Christian destiny through a chronological history that included an estimate of the date of creation. By the tenth century, the Arab historians al-Tabari and al-Mas'udi had created more extensive universal histories, relying on the growing volume of available records and written speculations. Otto of Freysing, the twelfth-century German bishop and chronicler, wrote *The Two Cities*, a multivolume history of the world from creation to 1146 that attempted a comprehensive history fitting with Christian revelation.[3] In the seventeenth century a French bishop, Bossuet, wrote a more concise universal history that conveyed many of the same messages as Otto but reached a far wider public. The difference was that Bossuet, along with Ottoman universal historians of the same era such as Mustafa Ali and Evliya Celebi, had to account in their interpretations for the discovery of the Americas and new religious and social conflicts at home.

Works of such eighteenth-century writers as Vico and Voltaire relied more on their reading of other published works than on original research.[4] Yet for each of them, the expansion of scientific and geographical knowledge provided additional issues to address. Some of the great historical works of the eighteenth century were works of primary scholarship, including Gibbon's history of Rome. Others, such as Raynal's *History of the Two Indies*, were collective works of synthesis. When the philosophers Kant, Herder and Hegel wrote of the past, they drew on a new framework that emphasized categorization of all elements of the world, and a sense of change that began to be called 'progress'.[5]

One distinction among world-historical writers, of earlier and later times, separates those primarily presenting a narrative conveying a broad social vision (often with an underlying moral or social message) and those primarily presenting an argument centring on selected conclusions (with narrative for illustration). In the eighteenth century, Voltaire and Gibbon wrote narratives, while Vico's writings in world history were intended to sustain an argument about the place of language in human development. Authors of both these categories of world histories, as indeed the authors of most studies, drew heavily on the writings of earlier authors, and refocused their interpretations to address the concerns and questions of their own era. In some cases they used direct evidence or interviews as sources. In the nineteenth century Hegel and Marx each invoked world history to expound their analytical visions, and Lewis Henry Morgan drew upon world history to convey his vision of the succession of savage, barbarian and civilized stages. Leopold von Ranke's final project was a multivolume history of the Western world, based on secondary sources, of which the eighth and final volume led into the fifteenth century. Perhaps the case of H. G. Wells makes clearest the strengths and weaknesses of this long tradition of amateur work in world history. Wells, a journalist and novelist, took on the task of outlining world history. He read widely and consulted systematically with leaders of English scholarly life, and reproduced their prejudices as well as their breadth of vision. His volume was original in its assembly of materials from many sources, and the maps and figures illustrating it were equally original.

The professionalization of national history set new standards for evaluating world history, and influenced the boundaries of world history.[6] The professional practice of national history in European languages developed in what can be thought of as two waves. First, beginning in the mid-nineteenth century, a few individuals wrote synthetic statements for a popular audience, linking reviews of national history with implications of national destiny. These authors – Bancroft in the US, Michelet in France, and equivalents elsewhere – developed historical writing to a level sufficient to inform and inspire the national consciousness.[7] Their work addressed a range of diplomatic, political and social issues. Second, toward the end of the century a university-based guild of professional historians developed, to explore the specifics of the national past. Leopold von Ranke has become the culture hero for this sort of historical analysis. Such analysis focused on assembly of primary textual sources, particularly from the archives of foreign ministries in the conduct of diplomacy, but also from parliamentary debates and personal correspondence.[8] As a result, the preferred publication became the historical monograph, providing an apparently exhaustive analysis of a given topic, usually in national political history. The broad, synthetic work aimed at a general audience came to be thought of as amateur history, while the detailed monograph aimed at an audience of historians came to be seen as professional history. The way to gain admission to the guild of professional historians was through completion of a doctoral dissertation: a first monograph, in which the new scholar demonstrated her (or generally his) skill in documenting the past within a selected set of evidence.

The materials of professional, national historians were manuscript and print documents, generally from coherent archives. Guides to archives grew to assist in their analysis. The authority of the written text became such that other sorts of documents were seen as inferior: oral evidence, material and expressive culture. The scholarship of national historians followed an artisanal approach, emphasizing keeping track of numerous factors, balancing continuity and change over time, and constructing an edifying narrative. The materials were organized and analysed with attention to chronology, and relying on the historian's intuitive and empirical sense of the links within them. Theories played little role in the work of national historians. The framework was that of the national community. Studies might be written of a given city or community or region, but the objective was generally to throw light on the nature and evolution of the nation.

After being organized on the above principles, the practice of national history experienced a century of growth and transformation.[9] For instance, studies of social history began to grow in importance among national historians as the twentieth century proceeded. Such studies responded to a need for public discussion of how contending groups within the nation accommodate and make their place. But the expansion of social history changed the practice of historical study: the range of sources became wider, the limits on archival holdings were less precise, and principles of social theory began to creep in.[10] And then area-studies history arose as an effort to extend the model of national history to regions beyond Europe and North America.[11]

Yet even in the century during which the model of national history held unmistakable primacy in historical studies, historians pursued studies based on other models, and maintained a vision of historical studies that was more general than national history. One clear indication of this more general vision of historical studies appeared in the occasional introductory manuals for history written by prominent historians. The best-known of these manuals, written by such scholars as Karl Lamprecht, R. G. Collingwood, Marc Bloch and J. H. Hexter, were the work of innovative rather than conventional historians, so they escape a mechanical concentration on studies of national destiny.[12] Nevertheless, their terms of reference reflect the primacy of the national framework in historical studies of their time.

professionalization of world history

In recent years the study of world history has been undergoing a professionalization that is parallel (if on a more modest scale) to the earlier professionalization of national history. (The present volume, indeed, plays a part in the process of professionalizing world history through its critical review of major aspects of the field.) Some obvious indications of this process are such institutional changes as the formation of professional associations, the publication of scholarly periodicals, the holding of annual conferences and, with the advances in technology, the formation of electronic discussion groups. It is possible that world history may develop a set of subfields, organized by temporal, spatial, topical or methodological divisions.

More substantial than institutional changes are the accompanying expansion and deepening in the materials, methods, and frameworks of analysis with which world historians analyse the past. Analysis of these issues is made complex by their breadth and inclusiveness, a result of the fact that world history has not yet broken itself down into subfields. This discussion addresses the emerging patterns, materials, methods and frameworks in professional study of world history, and then goes on to address the institutions of world history and the intersection of professional and amateur (or general-audience) presentations of world history.

The materials for world history include, first, the materials shared with local and national studies of history. Much of world history for recent times is comparative in its organization, and relies on the national archives and data collections used within the units under comparison. These include governmental text documents, oral documents, social statistics and economic data. In addition, world historians draw on materials from a growing range of disciplines that are creating and analysing historical data. These include medicine, environmental and climatological studies, and cultural studies. For instance, the field of ethnomusicology has expanded dramatically, combining data on musical performance with analysis of its social context in comparative studies of many regions of the world. While the materials used by world historians are much the same as those used by national historians, the world historian faces the additional complexity of using multiple archives, data collected under different conditions in multiple regions, and linking them into a coherent empirical picture.[13]

While historical studies generally concentrate on the nineteenth and twentieth centuries, and world historians follow this trend in large measure, their interest in large-scale and long-term analysis leads them inexorably to consideration of earlier times. Thus, data on birth and death rates over time, on climatic change, on volcanism and the implications of volcanism for climate, and the results of archaeological studies commonly gain attention from world historians.

It remains the case that world historians largely rely on secondary sources rather than on their own primary research. This lack of direct engagement with source materials may be seen partly as a deficiency. But the review and interpretation of published historical works also provides a service: the historical literature is now enormous, and the review and assessment of this literature is for professional historians, not just for textbooks. (Indeed, national and local historians put a great deal of their energy into reviewing and interpreting published works, in addition to their work on primary documents.) The massive work of John Richards on the environmental history of the early modern world relies largely on print materials, especially secondary works. Similarly, the even larger volume by Dirk Hoerder on global migration in the past millennium draws overwhelmingly on published works.[14] Both studies combine published sources and traditional historical methods, but open substantially new interpretations at a global level.

Beyond that, however, world historians cannot rely simply on secondary materials, because world history is more than an exercise in global overview: it is also the linkage of global and local. Philip Curtin published an early world-historical monograph focusing on trade diasporas, relying largely on secondary works but also on his original research. Years later Claude Markovits completed a parallel study for merchants from Sind, based on primary sources, and entered into discourse with Curtin.[15]

The methods of world historians have expanded in range at least as much as the materials. By methods I mean at least three categories of method, which may be called the technology of historical research, artisanal methods and analytical methods. The category of technology encompasses everything from pencil and paper to computers. Computers have changed significantly the work of the historian. They enable preservation and display of documents, rapid copying and entry of data, storage and searching of data, quantitative and qualitative analysis, easy retrieval of secondary works, and improved communication among historians. Work at a world-historical scale is much easier to envision with the assistance of computers.[16] The artisanal methods of historians include the eclectic techniques of data recovery and interpretive analysis long associated with the historical profession. At the level of research these include the techniques of archival and library study, involving recovering, storing and analysing data. At the level of interpretation they involve the reflective work of assembling all the methods and materials into a coherent interpretation.

The analytical methods of history include those associated with disciplinary fields of study ranging from economics to law to music history. The topical strength of world history has been in political, military and commercial history, and in the conflict of religious communities. Social history – including analysis of class, race, gender, ethnicity and family – has been slow to develop in studies of world history, in large part because these structures are generally understood to operate at local and national rather than transnational levels. Environmental history and medical history, in contrast, have been readily understood to involve phenomena that cross national and other borders, and world historians have contributed major works in these fields. While cultural phenomena are commonly thought to operate within social communities, the importance of cross-cultural interaction in recent times has been widely noted, and historical studies have responded in particular with analysis of cultural encounters of distinct social groups.[17] Other new topics and frameworks gaining attention from world historians include game theory, evolutionary psychology, migration theory, and evolutionary studies of human nature including gender relations and violence.

This panoply of methods entering the discourse of world history suggests another sort of artisanal task for world historians: the devising of techniques for assembling and linking multiple methods. Historians in other fields have chosen either to specialize in a single method or, more commonly, to learn to adopt the language and some simplified versions of the methods in various fields without learning them in detail. For world history, it seems that many practitioners will have to learn how to balance and connect several methodologies within a single study.

The frameworks for professional study of world history range widely. There is far more to the choice of frameworks than the difference between nations and localities. In spatial frameworks, one may also consider empires, oceanic basins, links of local to global, and comparisons of these. In analytical frameworks, various world historians work with civilizations, world systems, the ecumene, big history, notions of social evolution and historical materialism. This range of possible frameworks demonstrates that there are many sorts of subfields in world history, even though it remains a small field.

Given the range of possible frameworks, and the impact of the chosen framework on the resulting interpretation, it is advisable for authors and readers to be explicit about their choice of framework. In addition, it is not sufficient for an analyst to adopt a given framework and stick with it, since it rapidly becomes clear that any process appears differently when seen from a range of standpoints. No framework is so obvious as to be unproblematic.

In past years world historians have primarily been self-trained deviants from national history or visitors from fields of study outside history. Thus it is that even those who are considered leading researchers and teachers in world history are often reluctant to identify themselves as world historians.[18] On the other hand, even in this amateur era, the institutions of associations, conferences and journals developed, and some manuals for world history have begun to appear.[19]

The materials, methods and frameworks of professional world history are created and propagated by a developing set of institutions. The demand for publications and teaching in world history has now grown to the point where it is clear that the future will bring expansion of programmes of graduate study. In these programmes it is becoming necessary to determine the appropriate courses of study for world historians, and the appropriate first major research project for new world historians. That is, the doctoral dissertation in world history and the monograph in world history must be recognized in some sort of professional consensus. The delineation of the institutions of graduate study is made difficult in part because of the difference, among graduate students, of those making the study of global processes their top priority, those wishing to study world history as a secondary field (perhaps for teaching rather than research), and those wishing only an introductory acquaintance with world history.

The professional study of world history cannot, however, safely be considered in isolation either from other fields of professional history or from the study of world history by those who are not professionals in the field.[20] World historians, who specialize in phenomena that cross boundaries, need to give particular attention to the boundaries of professionalism in their field. To begin with, it is necessary to distinguish at least two types of non-specialists who participate in world-historical studies. First are those who are specialists in other fields of study, and whose studies have led them into exploration of their specialty over a long time period and a wide region. These amateurs are generally strong in the methodology of their chosen field, but inexperienced in the practice of history. Examples of distinguished amateur world historians of this sort include the physiologist Jared Diamond and the sociologist Immanuel Wallerstein; less well-known but intriguing examples include authors of a global history of physical education and a history of domestic animals.[21] A second sort of amateur includes those who are non-specialist writers focusing on narrating world-historical issues for a general audience. H. G. Wells was such an amateur world historian (in contrast to his professional contemporary, Oswald Spengler). More recently, the journalist Mark Kurlansky has produced works of global historical interest on the cod, salt, the Basques and the year 1968.[22] A third category of amateur world historian is that described above: non-specialists who are appropriating world historical material in the service of advancing an argument that goes beyond the interpretation of history. Included in this category is the game-theoretical approach of Robert Wright in *Nonzero*. He has used a review of human history and biological evolution to convey the point that a non-zero-sum side of life is always present, pointing toward growth and complexity.[23] Fourth, however, given that the overlap of fields of study is unavoidable in world history, it is important to avoid setting arbitrary limits to distinguish professional from non-specialist involvement in world history. The point is to recognize that these different tendencies exist, and to use them so as to best advance the understanding and appreciation of world history.

Another important issue at the boundaries of professional world history – one that will be examined in more depth in Chapter 12 – is the practice of teaching world history. While some teachers of world history at both secondary and post-secondary levels are best seen as professionals in the field, most teachers are and will remain non-specialists, though hopefully well-prepared non-specialists. Teaching is partly professional and partly so much for a general audience that it cannot become professional. Many of the people teaching world history have no training in the field, and this will remain the case for a long time. The demand for the teaching of national history is different from that for national history: world history is less likely to be sustained by (and deformed by) patriotic impulses than world history. There exists no clear constituency relying on world history as there is for various sorts of national history or community history. On the other hand, it can also be shown that levels of global consciousness fluctuate with time and events, so that the teaching of world history does depend on public perceptions.[24]

The question of audience for the work of world history poses problems analogous to those for national history. That is, the professional world historian will doubtless begin with an audience of other world history professionals and, if ambitious, seek to extend that audience to include professional historians outside of world history and beyond that to an audience of the general public, which is subdivided by national and other outlooks. This complexity provides a reminder that there is no reason for world history to become fully professionalized, as an important element of its contribution lies in opening discussion for general audiences.[25]

world history and theory

The expansion of studies in world history provides an opportunity for historians to become more deeply involved in theory. This opportunity comes partly because historians are widening their interests and exploring new issues in the past. It is also because scholars in other fields, as they encounter temporal dimensions of work in their discipline, are writing up the results as history. As these scholars enter historical discourse, they bring their theories with them. World historians, because their work addresses so many topics, thereby encounter theory in the natural sciences, social sciences and humanities.[26]

Historians have tended to draw minimally on theory. History is most basically an empirical field, concentrating on locating and assembling data into narrative form. Some historians write of the exceptions rather than the rules, while others write decisive analyses: both groups tend to present interpretations through interplay of a large number of factors. Theorists, in contrast, categorize distinctive factors and focus on formalizing systematic relationships among them, using the minimum number of variables for efficiency of explanation. Yet the two types of explanation rely heavily on each other.

'Knowledge' is both empirical evidence and relationship among analytical categories into which we place the evidence. Patterns in the past help project future trends. Current issues undergoing a mix of historical and theoretical investigation include global warming, economic growth, technological change, political centralization, patterns of disease, language change, kinship systems, and the changes and exchanges in cultural production. The theories in each of these areas developed in response to empirically identified problems.[27] The theories, in turn, led to identification of new evidence.

Historians often think of information about the past as being held in a literal or figurative archive. The notion of the fixed archive is, however, misleading in certain senses. All of the evidence we have from the past exists in the present: we are unable to go directly to the past to experience it, and are limited to exploring remnants of the past that have survived to the present. But depending on the skill of our analysis, we may be able to identify evidence that was not previously recognized or valued. Thus, while the physical remnants from the past may be fixed and declining, our work of analysis creates new evidence of the past. The quantity and variety of historical evidence has expanded in interaction with the technology and theory of analysis.[28]

The work of world historians, from the most descriptive level to the most fully theorized level, thus interacts with theory. Here are brief characterizations of the relationship between theory and history at several levels. The most common and best established link of history and theory is the historical background to a theoretical discussion. Such background, which sets the theoretical analysis in context, also shows the significance of the issue under analysis.

A more theoretically engaged type of work by historians is that of applying a theory to the past. In this case, the historian assumes the validity of the theory, and explores its implications in a historical situation. For instance, the application of price theory to Indian Ocean trade or the application of world-system theory to the economy of the South Atlantic will yield theoretically informed interpretations. A more simplified version of this approach is for the historian simply to appropriate the results of an economist or world-system analyst, without any further analysis of evidence.

Historians may also analyse the theories, rather than simply adopt them. One aspect of analysing theory is the logical critique and perhaps refutation of a theory. One famous such example is E. P. Thompson's critique of the theory of class conflict proposed by Louis Althusser, in which Thompson argued that 'the logic of history' refuted Althusser's analysis.[29] Another aspect of analysing theory is empirically testing a theory, often against an alternative theory, to see whether the theory is affirmed or refuted.

Two further theoretical activities of historians, even more proactive than those above, are the creation of new theories and the linking of existing theories. Of these, the world historian is most likely to be involved in linking existing theories. For instance, analysts of cultural encounter may draw upon theories in anthropology, sociology and literature, and may link aspects of them to provide a theory relevant to world historical problems.[30] Similarly, studies of migration will lead the historian to economic, sociological and demographic theories of migration. There is an opportunity to link these theories to each other, to provide a more comprehensive analysis of migration.

The development and application of modernization theory was an effort at worldwide political and social analysis that was influential from the 1950s into the 1980s. As theory, it was ultimately revealed to be mainly an ideological restatement of the hierarchy of the colonial world. In practice, however, modernization studies facilitated the expansion of area studies generally, and thereby contributed to growth in world historical studies.[31] Notions of co-evolution, as these developed in biology and anthropology, were soon applied to early stages of human history.[32] Genetics and linguistics came to have great importance in the study of human evolution and early human migration. Oceanography and geology combined to develop explanations of the El Niño phenomenon and its climatic implications.[33] Studies in medical history, facilitated partly by the increasing availability of computers and spreadsheets for analysis but also by epidemic disease, expanded sharply in the late twentieth century. And, over the long term, debates over the philosophy and theories of historical materialism – in economics, politics, popular culture and sociology – have informed a great deal of historical work.[34]

Theory, despite the benefits brought by its increasing prominence in world historical studies, also has its disadvantages. Theories develop most fully for situations in which there are large quantities of data, so that theories and theorists tend to neglect situations where data are scarce. A clear example of this phenomenon is in the areas of economics and economic history, where the wealthy regions of the world are analysed in most detail, and the economic patterns of other regions are treated implicitly as insignificant. Such imbalances, however, may be adjusted with time. Thus the field of demography, which focused for a long time on the data-rich regions of Europe and North America, then found the problems lacking in interest, and turned to study of the rest of the world, where problems were more interesting and the challenges of developing good data were also interesting.[35]

Expansion of theory makes it harder to pin down the distinction between primary and secondary sources, in that much of the data historians use will have been processed by other analysts. But the distinction will not go away: it will be reformulated into those areas where the historian knows the data well as opposed to those where the historian adopts the conclusions of previous analysis, rather than working significantly with the data.

general methods in world history

The specific methods of a world historian embarking on a study of the past depend on the subject matter, the question under study, the available data, the discipline and the investigator's analytical strategy. No single formula can prepare the analyst for the specifics of a world-historical investigation. There may be advanced, however, some general principles for conceptualization and execution of a study in world history. These principles are distinct from historical practices generally in that world historians work on extensive and highly interactive topics. The following is a brief statement of such principles as I envision them, in seven steps.[36]

The first step is the articulation of a research agenda. This task involves selecting a topic and an objective for analysis. A research agenda is a response to two sorts of questions: questions by historians about gaps or contradictions in the historical record, and questions of contemporary society, seeking background and explication for the unfolding of contemporary global processes. The historical questions may address, with varying priority, the origins, timing, dynamics and legacy of past processes. The formal statement of the research question should set the limits of the study in space, time, and in topical coverage.

Next is a step I call exploratory comparison. Once a topic and its context are selected, but before settling on the details of the research, the analyst should identify comparisons of the selected topic and other historical situations. The point here is to break out of stereotypical and unimaginative analysis by seeking out possible patterns and relationships that might not first have been envisioned. For instance, in a study of the interaction of empires in the eighth century CE, the analyst should explore comparisons with systems of large political units in earlier times and up to the present day, and should also consider interactions among small political units, to gain a broader sense of which patterns in imperial interaction are quite general, and which were specific to the eighth century. After this stage of brainstorming, the design of the actual research should be strengthened considerably.

The step of formulating and implementing the research design focuses especially on developing an appropriate model for the dynamics of the historical situation under study. To create a model, one must select a discipline or disciplines on which to draw. For instance, the fields of economics, politics, anthropology, genetics and art history all have well-established analytical models. The model articulates statements of the historical dynamics under study: the types of interactions and changes that are to be investigated or hypothesized. The historical dynamics, thus modelled, are analysed within a framework with several dimensions. It restates the limits of analysis in space, time, and topics. It identifies the units of study (the cases and networks to be explored) and the procedures for study (the comparisons and linkages among the units). The model and its framework are used to implement the strategy for solving the historical problem. With these structures, the historian locates and organizes historical data, and links the data to the model. In an orderly analysis, the data and the model appear to be consistent.

But following this detailed linkage of data and model, the world historian should seek to connect the subsystems of the historical situation under study. That is, in addition to confirming the details, the historian should look for larger relationships in the material.

The step of verifying the conclusions of an analysis is too often explored only at an implicit and informal level. The reader of a world-historical analysis should have a clear statement from the author on whether the analysis has simply been proposed as a plausible argument, or whether it has been verified at some level. While it will be difficult indeed to have 'proof' of the validity of interpretations of world history, it is possible for historians to identify and implement several sorts of procedure that give varying types of indication on whether and how the analysis has been verified.[37]

Even after all the above work is completed, the analytical work of the world historian is not complete. Because situations in world history entail so many different perspectives (perspectives of analysis, perspectives of historical figures), it is best for the historian to adopt another set of perspectives, different from those used in the analysis to this point, and replicate the analysis from these alternative perspectives.[38] Presumably the results of the analysis will vary measurably in this replication. The degree of interpretive difference brought by shifting perspective itself becomes a part of the interpretation. A further replication from still different perspectives may be advisable.

The last stage, of course, is presenting the results. The main point here is that the presentation of the results should convey the complexity of the analysis, but also convey the simplest and strongest interpretation that is consistent with the evidence and the framework. It may be noted that the succeeding steps in my summary of world-historical method alternate in breadth: one making the analysis more specific, and the next making the analysis broader. This set of points in world-historical method is quite general, and it can be helpful in clarifying a strategy of research and its implementation. Similarly, reviewing the same list of points will assist readers and reviewers in assessing the studies they evaluate.

conclusion:
priorities for professional study of world history

Just as professionalized national history requires extensive formal training and practice, so will professionalized world history require extensive formal preparation. Necessarily, the training in world history will be more varied for world history today, as the extent of our knowledge and the range of techniques has broadened so greatly in the last century. But some set of common techniques and practices is central to keeping world historians in touch with each other, to build a general discourse on world history. Thus, world historians should specialize in order to get to the depths of specific types of evidence and theory, but should maintain systems of exchange and connection to avoid extremes in specialization.

notes

1. R. J. Barendse, 'The Feudal Mutation: Military and Economic Transformations of the Ethnosphere in the Tenth to Thirteenth Centuries', *Journal of World History*, 14 (2003) 503–29; S. Morillo, 'A "Feudal Mutation"? Conceptual Tools and Historical Patterns in World History', *Journal of World History*, 14 (2003) 531–50.
2. W. H. McNeill, *The Rise of the West: A History of the Human Community* (Chicago, IL: University of Chicago Press, 1963); B. Mazlish, 'An Introduction to Global History', in B. Mazlish and R. Buultjens (eds),*Conceptualizing Global History* (Boulder, CO: Westview, 1993); G. Barraclough, *An Introduction to Contemporary History* (Harmondsworth: Penguin, 1967); D. Christian, *Maps of Time: An Introduction to Big History* (Berkeley, CA: University of California Press, 2004).
3. Otto, Bishop of Freysing, *The Two Cities: A Chronicle of Universal History to the Year 1146 AD*, trans. C. Christopher Mierow (New York: Columbia University Press, 2002). This work draws on precedents of Augustine and Orosius. The last of eight books projects the Second Coming, the Last Judgement, and the beginning of the Divine state.
4. For reviews of early work in world history, see P. Manning, *Navigating World History: Historians Create a Global Past* (New York: Palgrave Macmillan/St. Martin's Press, 2003); E. Breisach, *Historiography: Ancient, Medieval, and Modern* (Chicago, IL: University of Chicago Press, 1983); and J. B. Bury, *The Idea of Progress: An Inquiry into its Growth and Origin* (New York: Dover, 1932).
5. G. Vico, *The New Science of Giambattista Vico*, trans. T. G. Bergin and M. H. Fisch (Ithaca, NY: Cornell University Press, 1984); Voltaire, *The Philosophy of History* (London: Vision, 1965); E. Gibbon, *The Decline and Fall of the Roman Empire*, 6 vols (London: Everyman, 1993 [1776–78]); G.-T.-F. Raynal, *Histoire philosophique et politique des etablissemens et du commerce des Europeens dans les deux Indes*, 3rd edn (Amsterdam, 1781); J. G. Herder, *On World History*, trans. E. A. Menze and M. Palma (Armonk, NY: Augsburg Fortress, 1997); G. W. F. Hegel, *Lectures on the Philosophy of World History*, trans. H. B. Nisbet (Cambridge: Cambridge University Press, 1975).
6. For general reviews of historiography, see Breisach, *Historiography*; and G. G. Iggers, *Historiography in the Twentieth Century: From Scientific Objectivity to the Postmodern Challenge* (Hanover, NH: Wesleyan University Press, 1997).
7. G. Bancroft, *History of the United States of America from the Discovery of the Continent*, 10 vols (Boston, MA: Little, Brown, and Co., 1873–74); J. Michelet, *History of the French Revolution*, trans. C. Cocks (Chicago, IL: University of Chicago Press, 1967). See the review of nineteenth-century historical writers by H. White, with emphasis on rhetoric and philosophy rather than historical reconstruction, in his *Metahistory: The Historical Imagination in Nineteenth-Century Europe* (Baltimore, MD: Johns Hopkins University Press, 1973).
8. L. von Ranke, *The Secret of World History: Selected Writings on the Art and Science of History*, trans. and ed. R. Wines (New York: Fordham University Press, 1981); P. Novick, *That Noble Dream: The 'Objectivity Question' and the American Historical Profession* (Cambridge: Cambridge University Press, 1988).
9. For examples of the review of national history in the United States, see Novick, *That Noble Dream*, and D. W. Noble, *Death of a Nation: American Culture and*

the *End of Exceptionalism* (Minneapolis, MN: University of Minnesota Press, 2002).

10. P. Burke, *History and Social Theory* (Ithaca, NY: Cornell University Press, 1992).

11. As an example of the strength of reference materials developed for area-studies fields, the *Handbook of Latin American Studies,* long a print publication, is now published online by the US Library of Congress at <http://lcweb2.loc. gov/hlas/>.

12. K. Lamprecht, *What is History? Five Lectures on the Modern Science of History* trans. E. A. Andrews, (New York, 1905); R. G. Collingwood, *The Idea of History,* ed. W. J. Van der Dussen, rev. edn (Oxford: Oxford University Press, 1993); M. Bloch, *The Historian's Craft,* trans. Peter Putnam (Manchester: Manchester University Press, 1992); and J. H. Hexter, *The History Primer* (New York: Basic, 1971).

13. For a work relying on archives in Portugal, the Netherlands, Britain, India and Indonesia, see R. J. Barendse, *The Arabian Seas: The Indian Ocean World of the Seventeenth Century* (Armonk, NY: M. E. Sharpe, 2002).

14. J. F. Richards, *The Unending Frontier: An Environmental History of the Early Modern World* (Berkeley, CA: University of California Press, 2003); D. Hoerder, *Cultures in Contact: World Migrations in the Second Millennium* (Durham, NC: Duke University Press, 2003).

15. P. D. Curtin, *Cross-Cultural Trade in World History* (Cambridge: Cambridge University Press, 1984); C. Markovits, *The Global World of Indian Merchants, 1750–1947: Traders of Sind from Bukhara to Panama* (Cambridge: Cambridge University Press, 2000).

16. Two examples of studies of world-historical research that involve substantial reliance on computers in analysis are A. Maddison, *The World Economy: A Millennial Perspective* (Paris: OECD, 2001); and P. Manning, *Slavery and African Life: Occidental, Oriental, and African Slave Trades* (Cambridge: Cambridge University Press, 1990).

17. I. C. Campbell, 'The Culture of Culture Contact: Refractions from Polynesia', *Journal of World History* 14 (2003) 63–86.

18. Deborah Smith Johnston conducted interviews of 70 scholars and teachers associated with world history, of whom a majority, including several well-known scholars, declined to label themselves as world historians. Johnston, *Rethinking World History: Conceptual Frameworks for the World History Survey* (PhD dissertation, Northeastern University, 2003).

19. World history manuals include F. Spier, *The Structure of Big History: From the Big Bang until Today* (Amsterdam: University of Amsterdam Press, 1996); Manning, *Navigating World History;* and Christian, *Maps of Time.*

20. As an heuristic exercise, one can imagine creating a bibliography of works relevant to world history with subcategories distinguishing the contributions of professional world historians from those of scholars in area-studies history, national history, topical analysis in history (e.g. a focus on gender), and other disciplines (e.g. medicine or anthropology). Review of such a list might yield suggestions on how better to organize professional study of world history.

21. J. Diamond, *Guns, Germs, and Steel: The Fates of Human Societies* (New York: Vintage, 1997); I. Wallerstein, *The Modern World-System: Capitalist Agriculture and the Origins of the European World-Economy in the Sixteenth Century* (New

York: Academic Press, 1974); R. A. Caras, *A Perfect Harmony: The Intertwining Lives of Animals and Humans throughout History* (New York: Basic, 1996).

22. H. G. Wells, *The Outline of History, Being a Plain History of Life and Mankind* (London: George Newnes, 1920); O. Spengler, *The Decline of the West*, trans. C. F. Atkinson, 2 vols (New York: Alfred A. Knopf); M. Kurlansky, *The Cod: A Biography of the Fish that Changed the World* (Harmondsworth: Penguin, 1997); M. Kurlansky, *Salt: A World History* (New York: Walker and Co., 2002).

23. R. Wright, *Nonzero: The Logic of Human Destiny* (New York: Vintage, 2001). In an earlier study, the same author made the case for evolutionary psychology: *The Moral Animal. Why We Are the Way We Are: The New Science of Evolutionary Psychology* (New York: Vintage, 1994).

24. Johnston, *Rethinking World History*; S. Wineburg, *Historical Thinking and Other Unnatural Acts: Charting the Future of Teaching the Past* (Philadelphia, PA: Temple University Press, 2001).

25. C. Ponting, *A Green History of the World: The Environment and the Collapse of Great Civilizations* (Harmondsworth: Penguin, 1989); Felipe Fernandez-Armesto, *Civilizations: Culture, Ambition, and the Transformation of Nature* (New York: Free Press, 2001).

26. Diamond, *Guns, Germs, and Steel*; K. Pomeranz, *The Great Divergence: China, Europe, and the Making of the Modern World Economy* (Princeton, NJ: Princeton University Press, 2000); L. Benton, *Law and Colonial Cultures: Legal Regimes in World History, 1400–1900* (Cambridge: Cambridge University Press, 2002).

27. In addition to the existing theories being brought into historical analysis (economic theory, literary theory, evolutionary biological theory, plate tectonic theory), new theories are being developed, especially in fields of cultural study. Film theory, new developments in anthropological theory, linguistic theory, notions of creolization in visual art and language, and other sorts of formalized conceptions are also being applied to issues in world history.

28. William S. Atwell, 'Volcanism and Short-Term Climatic Change in East Asian and World History, c. 1200–1699', *Journal of World History*, 12 (2001) 29–98.

29. E. P. Thompson, *The Poverty of Theory and Other Essays* (London: Merlin, 1978). The main essay in this collection was a critique of Louis Althusser, *Pour Marx* (Paris: Maspero, 1965); see also Louis Althusser and Etienne Balibar (eds), *Lire 'Le Capital'*, 2 vols (Paris: Maspero, 1965).

30. I. C. Campbell, 'The Culture of Culture Contact'.

31. Works based on modernization theory that encouraged the expansion of area-studies history included David E. Apter, *The Political Kingdom in Uganda: A Survey of Bureaucratic Nationalism* (Princeton, NJ: Princeton University Press, 1961); and Manfred Halpern, *The Politics of Social Change in the Middle East and North Africa* (Princeton, NJ: Princeton University Press, 1963).

32. W. Durham, *Coevolution: Genes, Culture, and Human Diversity* (Stanford, CA: Stanford University Press, 1991).

33. B. M. Fagan, *Floods, Famines, and Emperors: El Niño and the Fate of Civilizations* (New York, 2000); Mike Davis, *Late Victorian Holocausts: El Niño Famines and the Making of the Third World* (London: Verso, 2001).

34. C. Chase-Dunn and T. D. Hall, *Rise and Demise: Comparing World Systems* (Boulder, CO: Westview Press, 1997); E. O. Wright, *Classes* (London: Verso, 1985).

35. J. Z. Lee and W. Feng, *One Quarter of Humanity: Malthusian Mythology and Chinese Realities, 1700–2000* (Cambridge, MA: Harvard University Press, 1999).
36. Manning, *Navigating World History*, pp. 313–21.
37. The terms I have used for these procedures of verification are plausibility, inspection, debate, hypothesis-testing and feedback-testing. Manning, *Navigating World History*, pp. 301–6.
38. For instance, Kenneth Pomeranz, in his analysis of early modern economies, adopts a series of regional perspectives to yield a more nuanced overall conclusion: the perspectives of the industrial centres of Britain and China, the perspectives of Europe generally and China generally, and the perspective of the world economy as a whole. Pomeranz, *Great Divergence*.

recommended resources

Barendse, R. J., *The Arabian Seas: The Indian Ocean World of the Seventeenth Century* (Armonk, NY: M. E. Sharpe, 2002).

Benton, L., *Law and Colonial Cultures: Legal Regimes in World History, 1400–1900* (Cambridge: Cambridge University Press, 2002).

Breisach, E., *Historiography: Ancient, Medieval, and Modern* (Chicago, IL: University of Chicago Press, 1983).

Burke, P., *History and Social Theory* (Ithaca, NY: Cornell University Press, 1992).

Chase-Dunn, C. and Hall, T. D., *Rise and Demise: Comparing World Systems* (Boulder, CO: Westview Press, 1997).

Christian, D., *Maps of Time: An Introduction to Big History* (Berkeley, CA: University of California Press, 2004).

Curtin, P. D., *Cross-Cultural Trade in World History* (Cambridge: Cambridge University Press, 1984).

Davis, M., *Late Victorian Holocausts: El Niño Famines and the Making of the Third World* (London: Verso, 2001).

Diamond, J., *Guns, Germs, and Steel: The Fates of Human Societies* (New York: Vintage, 1997).

Fernandez-Armesto, F., *Civilizations: Culture, Ambition, and the Transformation of Nature* (New York: Free Press, 2001).

Hegel, G. W. F., *Lectures on the Philosophy of World History*, trans. H. B. Nisbet (Cambridge: Cambridge University Press, 1975).

Herder, J. G., *On World History* , trans. E. A. Menze and M. Palma (Armonk, NY: Augsburg Fortress, 1997).

Hoerder, D., *Cultures in Contact: World Migrations in the Second Millennium* (Durham, NC: Duke University Press, 2003).

Iggers, G. G., *Historiography in the Twentieth Century: From Scientific Objectivity to the Postmodern Challenge* (Hanover, NH: Wesleyan University Press, 1997).

Kurlansky, M., *Salt: A World History* (New York: Walker and Co., 2002).

Kurlansky, M., *The Cod: A Biography of the Fish that Changed the World* (Harmondsworth: Penguin, 1997).

Lee, J. Z., and Feng, W., *One Quarter of Humanity: Malthusian Mythology and Chinese Realities, 1700–2000* (Cambridge, MA: Harvard University Press, 1999).

Maddison, A., *The World Economy: A Millennial Perspective* (Paris: OECD, 2001).

Manning, P., *Slavery and African Life: Occidental, Oriental, and African Slave Trades* (Cambridge: Cambridge University Press, 1990).

Manning, P., *Navigating World History: Historians Create a Global Past* (New York: Palgrave Macmillan/St. Martin's Press, 2003).

Markovits, C., *The Global World of Indian Merchants, 1750–1947: Traders of Sind from Bukhara to Panama* (Cambridge: Cambridge University Press, 2000).

Mazlish, B. and Buultjens, R. (eds), *Conceptualizing Global History* (Boulder, CO: Westview, 1993).

McNeill, W. H., *The Rise of the West: A History of the Human Community* (Chicago, IL: University of Chicago Press, 1963).

Novick, P., *That Noble Dream: The 'Objectivity Question' and the American Historical Profession* (Cambridge: Cambridge University Press, 1988).

Otto, Bishop of Freysing, *The Two Cities: A Chronicle of Universal History to the Year 1146 AD*, trans. C. Christopher Mierow (New York: Columbia University Press, 2002).

Pomeranz, K., *The Great Divergence: China, Europe, and the Making of the Modern World Economy* (Princeton, NJ: Princeton University Press, 2000).

Ponting, C., *A Green History of the World: The Environment and the Collapse of Great Civilizations* (Harmondsworth: Penguin, 1989).

Richards, J. F., *The Unending Frontier: An Environmental History of the Early Modern World* (Berkeley, CA: University of California Press, 2003).

Spengler, O., *The Decline of the West*, trans. C. F. Atkinson, 2 vols (New York: Alfred A. Knopf).

Spier, F., *The Structure of Big History: From the Big Bang until Today* (Amsterdam: University of Amsterdam Press, 1996).

Vico, G., *The New Science of Giambattista Vico*, trans. T. G. Bergin and M. H. Fisch (Ithaca, NY: Cornell University Press, 1984).

Voltaire, *The Philosophy of History* (London: Vision, 1965).

von Ranke, L., *The Secret of World History: Selected Writings on the Art and Science of History*, trans. and ed. R. Wines (New York: Fordham University Press, 1981).

Wallerstein, I., *The Modern World-System: Capitalist Agriculture and the Origins of the European World-Economy in the Sixteenth Century* (New York: Academic Press, 1974).

Wells, H. G., *The Outline of History, Being a Plain History of Life and Mankind* (London: George Newnes, 1920).

White, H., *Metahistory: The Historical Imagination in Nineteenth-Century Europe* (Baltimore, MD: Johns Hopkins University Press, 1973).

Wright, R., *The Moral Animal. Why We Are the Way We Are: The New Science of Evolutionary Psychology* (New York: Vintage, 1994).

Wright, R., *Nonzero: The Logic of Human Destiny* (New York: Vintage, 2001).

4
scales

david christian

'Universal history comprehends the past life of mankind, not in its particular relations and trends, but in its fullness and totality.'

Leopold von Ranke[1]

The issue of scale is extremely important in historical teaching and research, yet historians have not given it the consideration it deserves.[2] The issue has certainly not been discussed as much as other familiar topics such as the problem of 'objectivity' or 'how historians use sources' or whether or not historians can and should make moral judgements.[3] Yet no historian interested in world history can ignore the problem of scale, because world history requires us to think about the past on scales that challenge some basic conventions of modern historical scholarship.

It may be easiest to consider the issue by thinking of history writing as the construction of diagrams or 'maps' of the past.[4] Maps, like diagrams, are different from the objects they describe. A map that was on the same scale as the real world wouldn't be much use because, to find out what was a mile away from you on the map, you'd have to walk as far as you would in the real world.[5] Maps are helpful precisely because they are normally on smaller scales than the real world.[6] Maps, like diagrams, compress information. But to do this they have to select, excluding most of the real world, and including only what is important for their particular purposes. This process of choosing what is and what is not important forces mapmakers (and historians) to think carefully about the questions they are asking, and the sort of knowledge they want to convey. It also gives mapmakers (and historians) great power, because it means they can shape the questions that other people ask, as well as the images of the world that other people carry around in their heads. And those images matter. Anyone who has been seriously lost knows that having a good map (that is to say, a map that describes the right things because it is at the right scale) can be a matter of life or death.

As mapmakers know, the questions you can answer depend very much on the scales of the maps you construct. A street map contains different information from a world map because it is on a different scale and answers different questions. A world map cannot possibly show every street in every town and city on earth. On the contrary, on a world map, cities such as New York or Beijing, that might take up an entire A to Z Guide, will appear as no more than a dot. However, on the world map you will also be able to see the position of the oceans, the polar caps and the continents. Different scales show different things, in history as well as in cartography.

Unlike mapmakers, though, historians have to worry about scales in time as well as in space. They may choose to write about the past of a particular village or an entire continent or even (in the case of some world history texts) of the entire world. They may choose to write about a single decade, or a few hundred years, or even (in world history) of the entire period during which humans have been on earth. The choices they make determine the sort of history they write, so historians ought to think as hard as mapmakers when choosing the scale of their 'maps of the past'. Yet in practice, this is not what has happened. Instead, certain scales have come to seem natural and 'appropriate', while others have been ignored. In a lecture given in Australia in 1968, just one year after a referendum had given full citizenship to Aboriginal Australians, the anthropologist W. E. H. Stanner asked why so much modern historiography has been blind to the history of indigenous peoples. Why do indigenous peoples, whose ancestors have often inhabited their homelands for thousands of years, get ignored on most modern maps of the past? Stanner argued that:

> inattention on such a scale cannot possibly be explained by absent-mindedness. It is a structural matter, a view from a window which has been carefully placed to exclude a whole quadrant of the landscape. What may well have begun as a simple forgetting of other possible views turned under habit and over time into something like a cult of forgetfulness practised on a national scale. We have been able for so long to disremember the aborigines that we are now hard put to keep them in mind even when we most want to do so.[7]

As this example suggests, certain scales can become so familiar and so habitual that historians forget how much they exclude. Through this slow, institutionalized forgetting, many important questions, themes and insights have vanished from our modern accounts of the past.

These problems are particularly important within world history. The goal of world history is to see beyond the particular states, empires and cultures that have dominated history writing in the past century and a half. As Patrick Manning puts it, world history is 'the story of past connections in the human community. World history presumes the acceptance of a human community – one riven sometimes by divisions and hatreds but unified nonetheless by the nature of our species and our common experience.'[8] World History is as interested in the 'world maps' as in the street maps of conventional historiography. So one of the major challenges World history faces is to overcome the bias of most historians against large-scale accounts of the past. I will argue that most historians, like those referred to by W. E. H. Stanner, have fallen into the habit of 'framing' the past in only a few conventional ways. This has limited our understanding and narrowed our vision of the past. World historians are well placed to open up new windows on the past and help us see human history in new ways.

universal histories

The restricted vision of the past that dominates modern historical scholarship is curious because, as far as we know, most human communities viewed the past through windows of many different sizes. All human communities that we know of have constructed accounts of the past, and most have treated these accounts with great seriousness. Like maps, stories of the past told you where you were and how you fitted into the world, so they provided powerful ways of achieving a sense of identity. Traditional accounts of the past are often referred to today as 'creation stories' or 'creation myths', because, when seen in the glare of modern science, much of what they say can be shown to be incorrect. But this is no reason to underestimate their significance. In their own time and place, the dreamtime stories of Aboriginal Australians, like the *Histories* of Herodotus or the 'Genesis' story in the Judaeo-Christian-Islamic tradition, were believed to be accurate because they had the 'feeling' of truth, just as modern science does in the early twenty-first century. Because they felt true, traditional creation stories shaped how millions of people lived and behaved and perceived the world over many thousands of years.

Traditional accounts of the past usually worked at many different scales. Cycles of creation stories might contain stories about one's own family and ancestors, or one's own people and neighbouring peoples. But they also included stories about the creation of the land, the earth and the entire universe. In other words, like a modern atlas, they contained maps of the past at many different scales, allowing you to figure out your place in the immediate historical 'neighbourhood' but also in the larger 'world maps' of time and space. The task of historians, then, was to link the personal and the universal, to make apparent the unity of the past at all scales. As Diodorus of Sicily wrote more than 2000 years ago:

> just as Providence, having brought the orderly arrangement of the visible stars and the nature of men together into one common relationship... so likewise the historians, in recording the common affairs of the inhabited world as though they were those of a single state, have made of their treatises a single reckoning of past events....[9]

Within most religious traditions even today, such universal maps of the past remain very important. They are also important within modern science. Ever since the 'Scientific Revolution' of the seventeenth century, scientists have looked for large, all-encompassing accounts of reality. Indeed, within modern cosmology, it is fashionable, even today, to talk of the search for a 'General Unified Theory', a theory that would explain all aspects of physics and cosmology.[10] For a long time, historians also tried to construct 'universal' accounts of the past. The modern 'scientific' historical profession is often traced to the era of the 'Enlightenment' in the eighteenth century, and in that era, most historians assumed that they should try to construct histories of the entire past alongside histories of particular peoples or communities. Giambattista Vico, Johann Gottfried Herder, Immanuel Kant, G. W. F. Hegel, all took it for granted that history should aspire to some degree of universality. As the epigraph to this chapter suggests, even the great German historian Leopold von Ranke, who is often thought of as the pioneer of sharply focused archive-based historiography, was committed in principle to the idea of universal history.

The challenge of constructing a coherent 'world map' of the past survived into the nineteenth century. The sociologist Auguste Comte attempted to construct a unified account of human history, and so did Karl Marx, the founder of modern 'scientific' socialism. Marx also saw a natural link between his work and that of Darwin, for Darwin's work provided the foundations for a coherent account of the history of life on earth.[11] The search for a universal history was linked, in the minds of many historians (including Comte and Marx), to the search for general laws of history. In his *History of Civilization in England* (first published in 1857), Henry Thomas Buckle wrote:

> In regard to nature, events apparently the most irregular and capricious have been explained, and have been shown to be in accordance with certain fixed and universal laws. This has been done because men of ability, and, above all, men of patient, untiring thought, have studied natural events with the view of discovering their regularity; and if human events were subjected to a similar treatment, we have every right to expect similar results.[12]

the retreat from universal history

In the twentieth century, the hope of constructing a universal history based on general laws of some kind disappeared almost entirely, except in the communist world, where Marx's own work kept the project alive.[13] Elsewhere, those who attempted universal histories, such as H. G. Wells or Arnold Toynbee in the English-speaking world, were often regarded with disdain by professional historians.[14] Today, most monographs, most research projects, and most of the graduate programmes that induct people into the history profession, operate within a conventional range of scales that professional historians regard as familiar, normal and appropriate. These range from a few years in the history of a small community, to the histories of entire nations over several centuries. Why is this particular range of scales so dominant? Is it because these are the best scales – perhaps the 'natural' scales – for good history writing? Or are they familiar simply because they are the scales historians feel most comfortable with? Is there something fundamentally wrong about the large scales? Or is it just that modern historians aren't used to dealing with them?

There are many reasons why this limited range of scales is so dominant today, and all are linked to the complex processes by which the modern, 'scientific' history discipline emerged in the nineteenth century. None of them suggest that there is anything intrinsically unsound about the large scales; but they do help explain why professional historians began to ignore the large scales of universal history.

The first important reason is linked to the methods of research that came to dominate the modern history profession. Modern historians, like scientists, take great care to ensure the accuracy of the information they use, and they do so by observing well-established research procedures. Many of these arose in nineteenth-century Europe. German historians such as Leopold von Ranke played a crucial role in the emergence of history as a modern, 'scientific' field of scholarship. They argued that 'scientific' history writing had to be based primarily on the thorough but critical study of written records from the past. There was much truth in this, and the careful use of archives in the last century or so has generated a huge amount of carefully tested information about the past. Unfortunately, the tradition of archival research also helped narrow the frames through which historians view the past, for most of the records that historians found in the archives were concerned with matters of politics, administration and economics, so historians relying on archival sources tended to focus mainly on political history. That ensured that the timescales they used would be those familiar to politicians, scales of a few years and (in the case of the most far-sighted of politicians) perhaps a few decades. They studied the emergence of modern states, such as the French or American revolutions, the major wars, or the major changes in economic history such as the Industrial Revolution. Or they focused on the history of ancient states with literate officials who could generate written documents. The archives provided a window on the past through which it was easy to see modern states and some ancient states; but much harder to see the people they ruled and almost impossible to see those who were illiterate and did not produce written records of any kind.

Nineteenth-century historians also bequeathed a second important convention to modern historians: a concern with the nation state. The nineteenth century was an era of intense nation-building, and the era in which mass education became normal for the first time in human history. Nation states were naturally interested in ensuring that their citizens learned about the nation of which they were citizens, so that the earliest school syllabuses tended to be dominated by national histories, by histories of Britain, Germany or the US. Historians responded in kind, by writing histories of particular nations. Nationalist history stretched the temporal scales of historical scholarship, for most national traditions could be shown to have deep roots in the past. Yet it narrowed the spatial focus of historians, for its natural unit of study was a particular nation state (such as Britain or Germany) or, at best, a cluster of similar or related states (such as 'Europe'). There can be no doubt about the importance of nation states in modern history, but it is also true that many human communities have not lived within states, and the modern focus on nation states has tended to marginalize such communities.

A third important influence was the blizzard of information that descended on researchers in most fields of scholarship in the nineteenth and twentieth centuries. Faced with so much information, specialists in field after field had to grab the information that was closest to hand. This forced them to specialize. The humanities split from the sciences. The study of human societies split into history, anthropology, sociology, archaeology and prehistory; and each discipline, in its turn, spawned many subdisciplines, each studying a single piece of the jigsaw. The process has continued to the present day. Human history was eventually carved up between so many different subdisciplines that it became impossible to see its underlying coherence. The emerging structures of research were well suited to the challenge of bringing more and more precise information into the field of view; but they neglected the challenge of synthesis across and between disciplines and subdisciplines. Historiography became more and more bitsy, and large questions of meaning began to vanish from the historians' field of vision. By the early twentieth century, most professional historians had abandoned the pursuit of large general laws, and the discipline concentrated, instead, on the task of collecting carefully tested data about the human past. A French historian, Gabriel Monod, expressed this sceptical attitude in a talk given at the First International Congress of Historians in 1900:

> We want nothing more to do with the approximations of hypotheses, useless systems, theories as brilliant as they are deceptive, superfluous moralities. Facts, facts, facts – which carry within themselves their lesson and their philosophy. The truth, all the truth, nothing but the truth.[15]

By the early twentieth century, even those who continued to pay lip service to universal history did not try to write universal histories.[16] In practice, history writing and research at large scales disappeared from the practice of the history profession. Historians retreated into archival research, focusing on the task of generating a larger and more precise body of information than had been available to earlier generations of historians, and concentrating on problems that could be answered through the detailed study of archival records and that had some bearing on the history of the modern nation state. So powerful were these conventions that they acquired, like traditional creation stories, the force of truth. Historians began to feel in their bones that history could only be written on certain familiar scales, that there was an appropriate level of detail or 'graininess' in good history writing, while attempts to write history on large scales could only result in empty generalities.

The history profession has paid a high price for ignoring the large scale. History based mainly on written evidence automatically excluded or marginalized the illiterate, which is to say, all those who lived in the palaeolithic or neolithic eras, the vast majority of people even within agrarian civilizations, an even larger number of those living outside agrarian civilizations, almost all women, and an only slightly smaller fraction of men. Except in very recent periods, when the range of information to be found in archives broadened, most archive-based history focused on the few humans who left written records, which means, in effect, tiny elite groups dominated overwhelmingly by elite males. When they appeared at all, other groups were usually seen through the eyes of the literate minority. By no definition can such history be described as the study of the past of 'humanity'. The history profession's focus on the nation state also narrowed the field of vision, by marginalizing those who were either unimportant within states or never lived within states. Paradoxically, as history became more 'scientific', its field of vision narrowed and it ignored more and more of the past. Like ants on an elephant, we seem to have no way of seeing the whole beast.

the revival of the large scale

In the late twentieth century historians in many parts of the world began to move beyond the conceptual frames of nationalist historiography. Social historians attempted to describe the worlds of non-elite groups, as did historians interested in the colonial and postcolonial world. Historians of gender attempted to explore the largely neglected world of women, both within the elite world and amongst non-elite groups. As historians shifted their focus away from the nation state, it became apparent that they would also have to move beyond an exclusive reliance on archival research simply because most archival records were the products of elite groups and their officials and servants. So historians began to approach their sources in new ways, finding new ways of reading traditional sources, or picking up on the methods of anthropologists (in oral history) or even archaeologists. But new approaches to the past had to fight for legitimacy within the history profession, and this often steered them back towards the temporal and spatial scales of traditional historiography, even if their questions, and their research techniques were new. Much of the new social history was still framed as the social history of this or that nation or region; and much the same can also be said about much women's history. Such approaches, though they opened up large questions about the past, did not necessarily encourage historians to approach the past on larger scales.

Gradually, though, some historians began to rediscover the large scale. In the communist world, the influence of Marx ensured that questions about the overall shape of human history had never entirely vanished, though the Cold War also ensured that Soviet historiography would have little impact on the west. In France, the *Annales* School of historians showed an unusual interest in large-scale accounts of the past. Best known outside of France is the work of Fernand Braudel, who argued forcefully for the study of historical patterns such as those shaped by geography, patterns that changed very slowly and could be appreciated only by studying large time periods. Braudel wrote:

> the way to study history is to view it as a long duration, as what I have called the *longue durée*. It is not the only way, but it is one which by itself can pose all the great problems of social structures, past and present. It is the only language binding history to the present, creating one indivisible whole.[17]

The emergence of 'world history' in North America has pushed historians even more powerfully towards larger scales. The rise of world history in North America owed much to the work of three remarkable historians all based in Chicago: Marshall Hodgson, Leften Stavrianos and William H. McNeill.[18] Marshall Hodgson wrote a synoptic history of the Islamic world, demonstrating its centrality in the history of the Eurasian landmass.[19] Though prolific, his influence was limited by the fact that he died at the age of 46, leaving most of his work still unpublished. Leften Stavrianos wrote several pioneering world histories, but it was William McNeill who was to have the greatest impact. McNeill's study, *The Rise of the West*, first published in 1963, transformed attitudes to world history amongst professional historians because, despite its huge scale, it was as thoroughly researched, and as coherent as the best history writing on more conventional scales. It was reviewed very positively and soon became a bestseller. Philip Curtin, a historian of Africa based at Madison, Wisconsin, also had a significant impact on the field, and his students have been amongst the most influential of a later generation of world historians.[20]

Despite this body of work, world history took a long time to establish itself, even within North America. Part of the problem was that the narrow time scales of modern historical scholarship had congealed within the institutional structures of the history profession. They were embedded in patterns of training, research and publication. History programmes were generally advertised as national or regional in their focus, while journals and job advertisements followed a similar pattern. Meanwhile, the rite of passage into the profession through doctoral programmes required sharply focused archival research as proof of one's potential as a historian. Those who ignored these conventions did so at their peril, so historians interested in world history have struggled to persuade their colleagues of the importance, even the legitimacy, of large-scale accounts of the past.

Finding the core concepts and questions for a world historical approach to the past has proved equally difficult. The nation state will certainly not provide the main focus for world history. But what *is* the natural focus for such a field? In a retrospective essay on *The Rise of the West*, McNeill described how he chose as his central theme interactions between distinct 'civilizations'. McNeill had been inspired, in part, by the work of Arnold Toynbee. But while Arnold Toynbee's monumental *Study of History* tended to treat each of the many civilizations it described as if it were an autonomous entity, almost like an empire or a nation state, McNeill made the strategic decision to focus on the relations between civilizations, on the grounds that these provided the primary motor of historical change:

> it seemed obvious to me in 1954 when I began to write *The Rise of the West*, that historical change was largely provoked by encounters with strangers, followed by efforts to borrow (or sometimes to reject or hold at bay) especially attractive novelties. This, in turn, always involved adjustments in other established routines. A would-be world historian therefore ought to be alert to evidence of contacts among separate civilizations, expecting major departures to arise from such encounters whenever some borrowing from (or rejection of) outsiders' practices provoked historically significant social change.[21]

The theme of intercivilizational exchanges and contacts has inspired an entire generation of scholarship in world history. Yet in retrospect, it is apparent that such questions were still being shaped, indirectly, by the agendas of traditional nationalist historiography, for they still assumed that the basic units of history were particular nations or civilizations or regions. Was world history no more than the sum of many national or regional histories? Or could it aspire to a more unified account of human history as a whole? The trouble was that the windows through which civilizational world history viewed the past were still too small to embrace humanity as a whole.

For many world historians, the concept of 'world-systems' seemed to offer a more promising conceptual focus for world history than 'civilizations' or regions. World-system approaches to world history were inspired by the work of Immanuel Wallerstein, and in particular by *The Modern World-System*, whose first volume appeared in 1974.[22] By a 'world-system', Wallerstein meant a large region of the world, whose separate societies were bound together not by an overarching imperial authority, but mainly by market exchanges. Wallerstein claimed that such a system first appeared only with the rise of capitalism from the late fifteenth century. Previously, large areas had been integrated mainly through the creation of large empires. That the market should integrate what had previously been integrated only through the direct use of power, he saw as one of the distinguishing marks of the capitalist world.[23] He argued, further, that economic relations within the world-system created a hierarchy of powerful core regions, which controlled weaker, subordinate peripheries. Since he wrote others have argued that there were earlier world-systems. Janet Abu-Lughod has written of a thirteenth-century world-system extending from China through the Islamic world to Europe.[24] Other writers have pushed the idea back even further in time.[25] Andre Gunder Frank and Barry Gills have argued that world-systems can be identified, certainly in the Afro-Eurasian region, at least 4000 years ago. More recently, Christopher Chase-Dunn and Thomas Hall have argued that world-systems existed even in regions without state structures, such as northern California before European colonization.[26] There has even been vague talk of a palaeolithic 'world-system'.[27] Such approaches suggest that the binding of distinct societies and cultural zones into a larger unity through the exchange of goods and ideas is not a property unique to the capitalist world. Stretched in this way, it seemed that the notion of a world-system might well provide a more coherent framework for the study of world history than concepts such as civilizations or states. This is exactly what Frank argued in an influential essay called 'A Plea for World System History'. Frank suggested that the concept of evolving world systems might provide the 'simple, all-encompassing, elegant idea' that world history needed to provide its conceptual foundation.[28]

The notion of world-systems, in various forms, has proved immensely influential in recent discussions of world history. But it has not really achieved the conceptual centrality that Frank hoped for. Part of the problem may be that, though the concept embraces large regions and has great explanatory power, it is still, like the concept of 'civilizations', exclusive. It excludes those who never belonged to world systems; so it may still consign many human communities to the margins of world history. Once again, the scale is not quite large enough to embrace humanity as a whole.

In a recent short essay, William McNeill has argued that ecological questions may offer the best way of identifying the deeper unity of world history. By ecological questions, he means 'asking what it was, in successive ages, that was conducive to human survival and the expansion of our collective control and management of the world around us'.[29] The advantage of such questions, of course, is that, unlike questions about civilizations or world systems, they do not commit us to particular time scales or to the study of particular types of human communities. On the contrary, they are questions that are raised by all periods of human history, and all human communities, including those of the palaeolithic and other communities that did not generate archival records. They are questions about the trajectory of human history as a whole, so they point the way to a unified history of humanity, and one that helps us see human history as part of processes such as natural selection or climatic or geological change, processes that occur on even larger scales than those of human history. One of the most spectacular illustrations of how environmental questions can push historians towards the large scale is Alfred Crosby's *Ecological Imperialism* (1986). Crosby began with a sharply focused research project on aspects of what he has called 'the Columbian exchange': the exchange of peoples, animals, crops and diseases as a result of the bridging of the Atlantic ocean at the end of the fifteenth century.[30] But in order to appreciate the full implications of these global ecological exchanges, the myriad ways in which humans and the domesticates surrounding them have spread and mingled throughout the world in recent centuries, Crosby carries us back more than 200 million years to geological timescales. At these scales, continental plates ferried whole biota from region to region, so that they engaged in migrations and minglings similar to those that modern humans achieve using human communications technologies. What the reader gains by moving up and down the timescales in this way is a vivid understanding of the ecological significance of modern human migrations; and of the ways in which human history repeats, but also diverges from, older patterns of symbiosis and competition. Crosby helps us see surprising similarities, but equally important differences between human history and geological history. Above all, by contrasting the leisurely timescales of plate tectonics with the more hectic pace of human history, he illustrates the astonishing acceleration in ancient processes caused by our own species of animal. A number of other historians have also written accounts of world history that have focused on human relations not only to each other, but also to the natural world.[31]

In 2003, William and John McNeill published a world history that explored how interconnections between human communities have generated the innovations that make the history of our species so unique. They did so using the metaphor of a web.[32] *The Human Web* develops the theme of human interconnectedness, which has been present in all of William McNeill's work, but its central metaphor helps us focus less on the communities that are linked by the web than on the web itself. By doing so, it helps us see that the interconnections between human communities may be more important than any particular society or community in all eras of human history. Interconnectedness may indeed be what world history is really about, in the palaeolithic era as much as today, because interconnectedness (through language) is what distinguishes the human species from all other species on earth.

In the 1990s, there emerged attempts to look at the past on scales even larger than those of human history, through the project of 'big history'.[33] Several big history courses emerged, in Australia, the US and the Netherlands, all attempting to see what the past looked like when viewed on multiple scales up to those of the Universe as a whole. In 1996, Fred Spier, of the University of Amsterdam, wrote the first book-length study of the implications of big history, and in 2004, I published the first book-length survey of the past on the multiple scales of big history.[34] From one point of view, courses in big history can be regarded as a violent attempt to break out of the conventions about scale that have dominated historical scholarship in the last century. (Like ants on an elephant, we may need to move far away from the beast in order to see it more clearly.) But they were also attempts to reconnect history to the natural sciences from which it had become increasingly separated since the nineteenth century.[35] Remarkably, at the point where big history meets world history, there is a surprising amount of agreement about the core concepts that are needed. While John and William McNeill have argued that world history is essentially about the webs of interconnection that have linked human societies, Fred Spier has argued that big history is essentially about 'regimes', or large and more or less stable patterns that exist at many different scales, from those of cosmology to those of human history. The McNeills' use of the metaphor of a 'human web' may well turn out to be one of the better ways of describing the distinctive 'regimes' of world history. I have argued in *Maps of Time* (2004), that it is 'collective learning', or the unique ability of humans to share learned information with precision and in great detail, that accounts for the power of the webs of interconnection that link all humans.[36] Unlike all other animals, humans can share what they learn with enough precision to ensure that new information gets passed on from community to community and from generation to generation. From the palaeolithic to the present day, so much new information has been caught in the webs of human culture that humans have acquired unprecedented power to control and reshape their world. Here, in the meeting of very large-scale views of the past with more conventional approaches to the past, history may eventually find a way of helping us see how human history is linked to the larger histories of the earth and the universe.

The very large scales of big history have the further advantage that, like the creation stories of most traditional societies, they encourage historians to return to traditional questions about the relationship between human history and the history of the earth and the universe. What is it that is distinctive about history? What does it mean to be human? These are all questions that ought to concern historians whatever their training, because they are questions about what history is and what makes the study of the past of human beings a distinctive field of scholarship. They are also questions that lead directly to deeper issues about the significance of human history. Is human history unique? How likely is it that something like human history is repeated elsewhere within the Universe? We have no definitive answers to such questions, but even the hints that are available have a lot to tell us about the deeper meaning of the study of our own species.[37]

In all these different ways, world historians are slowly rediscovering the ability to move through multiple scales, a skill that historians seemed to lose for a time as they struggled to find their place in the world of modern science. As world history develops we may see history return to the idea of a universal history that links the pasts of all communities on earth and once again links human history to the histories of the earth and the cosmos.

the difficulty of large-scale history

For many historians, the nagging question remains: is it really possible to write about the past on the large scales of world history or big history? This is a question that arises naturally given the training that most professional historians have in detailed archival research. Writing a PhD dissertation is daunting enough if your research covers two or three years in the history of a major government institution (as mine did). It is even more daunting to teach courses covering the history of a large country such as Russia or the United States over one or two centuries. So how is it possible to teach the history of all human beings over many thousands of years, or to teach on the even larger scales of big history?

These are serious and important questions. Of course, it is true that no teacher of world history can know all 'the facts'. Nor can they visit all the 'archives', and even if they could, they would miss the most important things, for most humans during most of human history could not write or read. But the truth is that these difficulties appear on all historical scales. It is just that on the conventional scales there are familiar and accepted ways of dealing with them. Most history teachers at some time in their career teach about the history of entire societies or regions (such as the US or Europe) over a century or more of its history. It goes without saying that they do not know all the facts, they have not visited all the libraries or read all the books that would be needed to understand the lives of the many millions of people who lived in these societies. What they do is to read a combination of specialist studies and synoptic works that condense other specialized studies; then they generalize on the basis of their reading. Extracting large, tentative generalizations on the basis of a huge amount of empirical work is what goes on in all scientific endeavours, and historians are no different in this. Even writing the history of a particular village over 100 years is a project fraught with difficulties. The problems do not necessarily get worse on large scales, though they may take different forms. On the scale of 100,000 years, archives (the traditional foraging ground for professional historians) don't provide the appropriate intellectual nourishment. On these scales, the basic raw materials are provided by the works of other historians or by researchers in related fields such as archaeology and anthropology. On even larger scales, the works of biologists or geologists may provide the information that is needed. Specialists in these fields are more familiar than most historians with the types of objects that appear on larger scales, and with the approaches and methods needed to deal with them. Just as world maps generalize from local maps, and local maps are embedded in world maps, so world history will generalize on the basis of histories constructed at smaller scales, but will also provide a context within which to better understand problems on smaller scales. World history is as doable as any other type of history; we just have to develop the methods and conventions needed to do history at large scales. And despite the many difficulties, it is worth doing because what can be seen at large scales are objects and problems (such as the distinctiveness of our species, *Homo sapiens*, or the uniqueness and importance of human webs of interconnection) that cannot be seen at smaller scales. The wide-angle lens of world history allows historians to see new things about the human past.

different ways of framing the past

As this suggests, the rediscovery of the large scale does not mean we can now forget about the smaller scales that historians have traditionally explored. On the contrary, large-scale accounts of the past have been built on the basis of small scale accounts. At the same time, small-scale accounts of the past can be illuminated by large-scale accounts, in history as in geography. Indeed, there have been many fine works of scholarship in world history which moved from sharply focused questions to large generalizations about world history, and back again, illuminating both the large scale and the small scale as they did so. Eric Wolf's *Europe and the Peoples Without History* (1982) showed that, though they had often been ignored by conventional historiography, the many peoples in the world who lacked literacy and written histories, from indigenous Americans to the peoples of Siberia, have nevertheless played a vital role in the creation of the modern world. Sydney Mintz's classic study of the history of sugar in the modern world explored what sugar meant to individual households and consumers, and also what it meant on global markets. What world history can offer is an enhanced ability to look at the past on multiple scales. So it may help to end by listing some of the more important scales through which historians can view the past, and some of the questions and themes that come into prominence at each scale.

1. *The scales of 'microhistory'*: Particular individuals or events or communities. Microhistories are the streetmaps of modern historiography. They focus on particular individuals or communities, normally within time spans close to that of a human lifetime. They can help us keep a sense of the texture and complexity of the past, reminding us of the limits of all large generalizations. But the small scale can also illuminate the large scale. As Carlo Ginzburg has shown in his classic study of the cosmology of a sixteenth-century Italian miller, or Emmanuel Le Roy Ladurie in his study of religious conflicts in a medieval French village, or Natalie Zemon Davis in *The Return of Martin Guerre* (1983), evidence about the life of a particular individual or community can illuminate more general structures of thought and social life. In the same way, a streetmap can show patterns of community that are replicated in hundreds and thousands of other streetmaps. The approach of microhistory has been particularly

effective at recovering the past of groups that have been ignored by archive-based history. This is particularly true of the history of women, which is why so much of the history of gender has attempted to reconstruct the lives of women and men through recreating the lives of individuals who lived unspectacular, conventional lives.[38]

2. *The conventional scales of modern national historiography*: Decades to a few centuries. The conventional scales of most modern historical research and teaching range from a few decades to a century or two. The entities that stand out most crisply at this scale are ethnic and national. Nation states and their rulers tend to hog the stage, and the people they ruled provide little more than a backdrop. In a world dominated politically by the nation state, it is right that we should explore the role of states in shaping the modern world. But as we have seen, an exclusive focus on the nation state can hide many important themes and topics. To focus on the state is also to focus on what divides humans from each other rather than on their common history, for, as Ross Poole has argued: 'A national identity is always a form of difference and thus a form of exclusion.'[39]

3. *The global history scale*: 500 years. Within contemporary world history, the study of the last 500 years is emerging as a strategic subfield in its own right. Sometimes work at this scale is referred to as 'global history'.[40] Fernand Braudel and Immanuel Wallerstein have done much to legitimize historical study at this scale. What is less obvious is the thematic unity of global history. It is inevitably dominated by the modern, European, world-system and the emergence of worldwide patterns of interaction, so it is the natural scale at which to study modernization and globalization. The problems that stand out most clearly at this scale are those that link or do not link individuals with modernity, or the West, and it is these themes that provide the fundamental dichotomies of modernization theory: tradition and modernity. It is no surprise that in contemporary global history, the problem that stands out most clearly is the issue of Europe's role in the rise of the modern world.[41]

4. *The world history scale*: 5000 years. The 5000-year timescale dominates most modern World History textbooks, beginning with William McNeill's classic, *The Rise of the West* (1963). It brings into sharp focus the role of literate, agrarian civilizations, a type of human community that appeared for the first time about 5000 years ago. Modern world history, as exemplified particularly in the standard texts on the subject, tends to highlight the distinctive features of particular agrarian civilizations and the elite groups and ideologies that ruled

them. Prehistory is often blurred at this scale; and communities not based on agriculture, not organized within states, and without literacy can fall away to the margins.

5. *The human history scale*: 100,000 years–4 million years. This is the natural scale on which to explore the history of human beings as a unified species. Yet this scale has been surprisingly unimportant in recent works on world history. Even within most world history textbooks, the palaeolithic era normally plays an introductory role to the history of agrarian civilizations. That is a shame because this is the first scale at which it is possible to see what is distinctive about human beings as a whole. It is the scale on which to discuss what is shared by all human beings simply because they are human beings. This is also the scale which forces historians to begin a serious exploration of the relationship between history neighbouring disciplines such as biology and geology.

6. *The planetary scale*: 4.6 billion years. This is the scale at which to explore the human relationship with the biosphere. Like the first satellite images of the earth, which made such an impact in the 1960s, this scale highlights the place of human beings within the history of the biosphere. It highlights the unity of what James Lovelock has called 'Gaia', the large interrelated system of all living things that has shaped the surface of the earth for almost 4 billion years.[42] At a more practical level, this is a strategic scale at which to study issues of the human impact on the biosphere because on this scale we can explore how the human impact compares with other major impacts, such as those of asteroids or other new types of organisms. To date, most explorations of the past at this scale have been undertaken by geologists or biologists rather than by historians, which is a shame because historians have a distinctive set of questions to bring to such discussions, questions concerned above all with the distinctiveness of the role of human beings in the history of the biosphere and the earth.

7. *The big history scale*: 13 billion years. The most striking aspect of this scale is that it offers a sense of completeness. Only at these vast scales can we seriously explore the relationship between the personal, the human and the universal. So at this scale, we can help students understand how they, as individuals, fit into the larger scheme of things, according to modern scientific thinking. This scale can be humbling, but it can also induce a certain realism about the place of human beings in the universe, and about the nature of human history. As Mark Twain wrote: 'If the Eiffel Tower were now representing the

world's age, the skin of paint on the pinnacle-knob at its summit would represent man's share of that age; and anybody would perceive that that skin was what the tower was built for. I reckon they would, I dunno.'[43] At present, few historians have been tempted to explore the past on these scales, yet, as this chapter has already argued, in the past, the writing of 'universal history' seemed a natural task for historians.

conclusion: maps of the past at multiple scales

I hope the conclusion is clear. The potential of world history to transform modern historical thinking lies not just in its exploration of large scales. It lies, rather, in the fact that, to do world history, you have to learn to move through multiple scales in both time and space. By doing so, modern world history can help historians break out of the restricted range of scales that had become the norm within historical scholarship in the nineteenth and twentieth centuries. Modern historical scholarship can only be enriched by the multiple perspectives on the past offered by historical scholarship that moves as freely between the local community and the world as a whole, as geographical maps move from the street to the globe. Such a historiography can offer a richer and more rounded account of the past than any one scale on its own. And it can help historians move back towards the deep questions about meaning that lay at the heart of all traditional creation stories.

notes

1. Leopold von Ranke, as cited in Arthur Marwick, *The Nature of History* (London: Macmillan, 1970), p. 38. Ranke's 'Universal History' focused mainly on Europe, but his definition of the goal of history is remarkably close to that of modern world historians. See Marnie Hughes-Warrington, *Fifty Key Thinkers on History* (London: Routledge, 2000), p. 260.
2. For a recent discussion, see Pat Manning, *Navigating World History: Historians Create a Global Past* (New York: Palgrave Macmillan/St. Martin's Press, 2003), chapter 15.
3. Two classic discussions from the middle of the twentieth century are E. H. Carr, *What is History?* (Harmondsworth: Penguin, 1964) and Marc Bloch, *The Historian's Craft*, trans. P. Putnam (Manchester: Manchester University Press, 1992).
4. The metaphor of science in general as a sort of mapping is explored in J. Ziman, *Reliable Knowledge: An Exploration of the Grounds for Belief in Science* (Cambridge: Cambridge University Press, 1978), chapter 4.
5. The Argentine author Jorge Luis Borges once wrote of a fantastic realm in which 'the art of Cartography attained such Perfection that... the Cartographers

Guilds struck a map of the Empire whose size was that of the Empire, and which coincided point for point with it. The following Generations, who were not so fond of the Study of Cartography..., saw that that vast Map was Useless, and... they delivered it up to the Inclemencies of Sun and Winters. In the Deserts of the West, still today, there are Tattered Ruins of that Map, inhabited by Animals and Beggars.' Jorge Luis Borges, *Collected Fictions*, trans. A. Hurley (New York: Penguin, 1998), p. 325, cited from J. L. Gaddis, *The Landscape of History: How Historians Map the Past* (Oxford: Oxford University Press, 2002), p. 32.

6. Of course, in the study of tiny objects, the opposite may be true; chemists often draw diagrams of atoms which are billions of times larger than real atoms. The microscope, like the telescope, is designed to help us understand things by creating models or pictures of them on a scale that is appropriate for our senses.

7. W. E. H. Stanner, *After the Dreaming*, 1968 Boyer Lectures (Sydney: Australian Broadcasting Commission, 1969), pp. 24–5.

8. Manning, *Navigating World History*, p. 15.

9. Diodorus of Sicily, *The Library of History*, §1.1.3–4, as cited in Marnie Hughes-Warrington, 'Big History', *Historically Speaking*, 4(2) (2002) 17.

10. Stephen Hawking's bestselling *A Brief History of Time: From the Big Bang to Black Holes* (London: Bantam Books, 1988) provides one of the more accessible introductions to such theories; but, as he admits, we are not there yet; see his later book, *The Universe in a Nutshell* (New York: Bantam, 2001).

11. Marx was enthusiastic enough about Darwin's writings to have sent him a signed copy of *Capital* in 1873, though it is probably not true, as some have claimed, that he thought about dedicating his work to Darwin. See Tom Bottomore et. al. (eds), *A Dictionary of Marxist Thought*, 2nd edn (Oxford: Blackwell, 1991) p. 131.

12. Cited in Robert L. Carneiro, *Evolutionism in Cultural Anthropology* (Boulder, CO: Westview Press, 2003), p. 13, from Henry Thomas Buckle, *History of Civilization in England*, vol. 1 (London: John W. Parker and Sons), p. 6.

13. Marx's own work focused mainly on the modern era and the emergence of capitalism. But he wrote many notes and shorter pieces on early phases of history and many of these were used by Engels in a short, synoptic study of human history that was to have a colossal influence in the twentieth century: F. Engels, *Origin of the Family, Private Property and the State*, ed. E.B. Leacock, introduction by M. Barrett (Harmondsworth: Penguin, 1985).

14. H. G. Wells, *The Outline of History: Being a Plain History of Life and Mankind* (Garden City, NY: Garden City Publishers, 1920); *A Short History of the World* (Harmondsworth: Penguin Books, 1922); A. J. Toynbee, *A Study of History*, 12 vols (London: Oxford University Press, 1934–61).

15. Cited from J. Appleby, L. Hunt and M. Jacob, *Telling the Truth about History* (New York: W. W. Norton, 1994), p. 75.

16. Examples are E. H. Carr and Marc Bloch. Though neither attempted universal histories, both took it for granted that history must attempt, in some fashion, to embrace the entire past of humanity. Bloch wrote in a posthumous work on history: 'Historical research will tolerate no autarchy. Isolated, each will understand only by halves, even within his own field of study; for the only true history, which can advance only through mutual aid, is universal history.'

Bloch, *The Historian's Craft*, p. 47. Carr quotes Acton, who described 'universal history' as 'that which is distinct from the combined history of all countries', and adds: 'It went without saying for Acton that universal history, as he conceived it, was the concern of any serious historian.' Carr, *What is History?*, p. 150.

17. F. Braudel, *On History* (Chicago, IL: University of Chicago Press, 1980), p. viii, from the 1969 Preface to a collection of his historiographical essays. His major works exemplified this approach by studying extremely stable patterns in economic, social and material life; see *Civilization and Capitalism, 15th-18th Century*, 3 vols (Glasgow: William Collins, 1981–82) and *The Mediterranean and the Mediterranean World in the Age of Philip II*, trans. S. Reynolds, 2 vols (Glasgow: William Collins, 1972–73).

18. W. H. McNeill's classic world history is *The Rise of the West* (Chicago, IL: University of Chicago Press, 1963); reprinted 1991, with a retrospective essay, '*The Rise of the West* after Twenty-five Years'. On Hodgson, see M. S. Hodgson, *Rethinking World History: Essays on Europe, Islam, and World History*, ed. Edmund Burke III (Cambridge: Cambridge University Press, 1993). L. S. Stavrianos, *Lifelines from our Past: A New World History* (New York: M. E. Sharpe, 1989) gives a feeling for Stavrianos' approach to world history. For an overview of the early history of world history in North America, see G. Allardyce, 'Toward World History: American Historians and the Coming of the World History Course', *Journal of World History*, 1(1) (1990) 23–76, reprinted in R. E. Dunn (ed.), *The New World History: A Teacher's Companion* (New York: Bedford/ St. Martin's, 2000), pp. 29–58. See also Manning, *Navigating World History*, chapters 2 and 3.

19. M. G. S. Hodgson, *The Venture of Islam: Conscience and History in a World Civilization*, 3 vols (Chicago, IL: University of Chicago Press, 1974).

20. On Curtin's influence, see C. A. Lockard, 'The Contributions of Philip Curtin and the "Wisconsin School" to the Study and Promotion of Comparative World History', *Journal of Third World Studies*, 11(1) (1994) 180–2, 199–211, 219–23.

21. McNeill, *Rise of the West*, 1991 edn.

22. I. Wallerstein, *The Modern World-System I: Capitalist Agriculture and the origins of the European World-Economy in the Sixteenth Century* (New York: Academic Press, 1974); on Wallerstein's impact, see the brief discussion in Manning, *Navigating World History*, pp. 61–5.

23. Wallerstein, *The Modern World-System I*, p. 16.

24. J. L. Abu-Lughod, *Before European Hegemony: The World System AD 1250–1350* (New York: Oxford University Press, 1989).

25. M. Rowlands, 'Centre and Periphery: A Review of a Concept', in M. Rowlands, M. Larsen and K. Kristiansen (eds), *Centre and Periphery in the Ancient World* (Cambridge: Cambridge University Press, 1987), pp. 1–11; A. G. Frank and Barry Gills, *The World System: From Five Hundred Years to Five Thousand* (London: Routledge, 1992).

26. For a brief survey of world-systems theories, see Dunn, *The New World History*, Part Five, 'World Systems and World History'; for a fuller survey, see S. K. Sanderson (ed.), *Civilizations and World Systems: Studying World-Historical Change* (Walnut Creek, CA: Sage, 1995); see also Wallerstein, *The Modern World-System*; Frank and Gills, *The World System*; C. Chase-Dunn and T. D.

Hall, *Rise and Demise: Comparing World Systems* (Boulder, CO: Westview Press, 1997).

27. Clive Gamble and Olga Soffer refer critically to discussions which treat the societies of the late palaeolithic as parts of an 'exclusive but disjointed world system' of the late palaeolithic; Gamble and Soffer, 'Pleistocene Polyphony: The Diversity of Human Adaptations at the Last Glacial Maximum', in C. Gamble and O. Soffer (eds), *The World at 18,000 BP*, 2 vols (London: Unwin Hyman, 1992).

28. A. G. Frank, 'A Plea for World System History', as cited in Dunn, *The New World History*, p. 258.

29. W. H. McNeill, 'An Emerging Consensus about World History', *World History Connected* 1(1), online at <http://worldhistoryconnected.press.uiuc.edu/1.1/mcneill_print.html>, §4.

30. A. W. Crosby, *Ecological Imperialism. The Biological Expansion of Europe, 900–1900* (Cambridge: Cambridge University Press, 1986); see also *The Columbian Exchange: Biological and Cultural Consequences of 1492* (Westport, CT: Greenwood Press, 1972).

31. They include C. Ponting, *A Green History of the World* (Harmondsworth: Penguin, 1991); J. D. Hughes, *An Environmental History of the World: Humankind's Changing Role in the Community of Life* (London: Routledge, 2001); John R. McNeill, *Something New Under the Sun: An Environmental History of the Twentieth-Century World* (New York: W. W. Norton, 2000); J. Richards, *The Unending Frontier: An Environmental History of the Early Modern World* (Berkeley: University of California Press, 2003); and two books by a biologist, J. Diamond, *The Rise and Fall of the Third Chimpanzee* (London: Vintage, 1991); and *Guns, Germs and Steel* (London: Vintage, 1998).

32. J. R. McNeill and W. H. McNeill, *The Human Web: A Bird's-Eye View of World History* (New York: W. W. Norton, 2003).

33. For a brief survey, see Hughes-Warrington, 'Big History'.

34. Fred Spier, *The Structure of Big History. From the Big Bang until Today* (Amsterdam: Amsterdam University Press, 1996) is an attempt to identify the patterns that are apparent at all the many different scales of 'Big History'; David Christian, *Maps of Time: An Introduction to Big History* (Berkeley, CA: University of California Press, 2004) is one of the first modern attempts by a historian to view the past at all scales, using the knowledge of modern science and historiography.

35. The scientist and writer C. P. Snow described the gulf between the sciences and the so-called 'Humanities' in a famous lecture given in 1959: 'The Two Cultures and the Scientific Revolution', in C. P. Snow, *Public Affairs* (London: Macmillan, 1971), pp. 13–46.

36. See also D. Christian, 'World History in Context', *Journal of World History*, 14(4) (2003) 437–58.

37. Ibid.

38. Many examples can be found in one of the pioneering works of women's history: B. S. Anderson and J. P. Zinsser, *A History of their Own: Women in Europe from Prehistory to the Present* (New York: Oxford University Press, 2000).

39. R. Poole, *Nation and Identity* (London: Routledge, 1999), p. 42.

40. See B. Mazlish and R. Buultjens (eds), *Conceptualizing Global History* (Boulder, CO: Westview Press, 1993).

41. See, for example, the recent discussion in K. Pomeranz, *The Great Divergence: China, Europe, and the Making of the Modern World Economy* (Princeton, NJ: Princeton University Press, 2000).
42. On the 'Gaia' hypothesis, see J. C. Lovelock, *Gaia: A New Look at Life on Earth* (Oxford: Oxford University Press, 1979, 1987); and its sequels, *The Ages of Gaia* (Oxford: Oxford University Press, 1988); and *Gaia: The Practical Science of Planetary Medicine* (London: Unwin, 1991); other works at the planetary scale include L. Margulis and D. Sagan, *Microcosmos* (Berkeley, CA: University of California Press, 1987) and P. Cloud, *Cosmos, Earth and Man* (New Haven, CT: Yale University Press, 1978) and *Oasis in Space: Earth History from the Beginning* (New York: W. W. Norton, 1988).
43. Mark Twain, 'The Damned Human Race' in *Letters from the Earth*, ed. B. De Voto (New York: Harper & Row, 1962), pp. 215–16; cited in Margulis and Sagan, *Microcosmos*, p. 194.

recommended resources

Abu-Lughod, J. L., *Before European Hegemony: The World System AD 1250–1350* (New York: Oxford University Press, 1989).

Allardyce, G., 'Toward World History: American Historians and the Coming of the World History Course', *Journal of World History*, 1(1) (1990) 23–76, reprinted in R. E. Dunn (ed.) *The New World History: A Teacher's Companion* (New York: Bedford/St. Martin's, 2000), pp. 29–58.

Anderson, B. S., and Zinsser, J. P., *A History of their Own: Women in Europe from Prehistory to the Present*, rev. edn (New York: Oxford University Press, 2000).

Appleby, J., Hunt, L., and Jacob, M., *Telling the Truth about History* (New York: W. W. Norton, 1994).

Bentley, J. H. 'Cross-Cultural Interaction and Periodization in World History', *American Historical Review*, 101 (1996) 749–56.

Bloch, M., *The Historian's Craft*, trans. P. Putnam (Manchester: Manchester University Press, 1992).

Bottomore, T., et. al. (eds), *A Dictionary of Marxist Thought*, 2nd edn (Oxford: Blackwell, 1991).

Braudel, F., *The Mediterranean and the Mediterranean World in the Age of Philip II*, trans. S. Reynolds, 2 vols (Glasgow: William Collins, 1972 [1949]).

Braudel, F., *On History* (Chicago, IL: University of Chicago Press, 1980).

Braudel, F., *Civilization and Capitalism, 15th–18th Century*, 3 vols (Glasgow: William Collins, 1981–82).

Calder, N., *Timescale: An Atlas of the Fourth Dimension* (London: Chatto & Windus, 1983).

Carneiro, R. L., *Evolutionism in Cultural Anthropology* (Boulder, CO: Westview Press, 2003).

Carr, E. H., *What is History?* (Harmondsworth: Penguin, 1964).

Chase-Dunn, C., and Hall. T. D., *Rise and Demise: Comparing World Systems* (Boulder, CO: Westview Press, 1997).

Christian, D., 'The Case for "Big History"', *Journal of World History*, 2(2) (1991) 223–38.

Christian, D., 'World History in Context', *Journal of World History*, 14(4) (2003) 437–58.

Christian, D., *Maps of Time: An Introduction to Big History* (Berkeley, CA: University of California Press, 2004).

Cloud, P., *Cosmos, Earth and Man: A Short History of the Universe* (New Haven, CT: Yale University Press, 1978).

Coatsworth, J. H., 'Welfare', *American Historical Review*, 101(1) (1996) 1–17.

Crosby, A. W., *Ecological Imperialism: The Biological Expansion of Europe, 900–1900* (Cambridge: Cambridge University Press, 1986).

Davis, N. Z., *The Return of Martin Guerre* (Cambridge, MA: Harvard University Press, 1983).

Diamond, J., *The Rise and Fall of the Third Chimpanzee* (London: Vintage, 1991).

Diamond, J., *Guns, Germs and Steel* (London: Vintage, 1998).

Dunn, R. E. (ed.), *The New World History: A Teacher's Companion* (Boston, MA: Bedford/St Martins, 2000).

Engels, F., *Origin of the Family, Private Property and the State* (Harmondsworth: Penguin, 1985).

Frank, A. G., 'A Plea for World Systems History', *Journal of World History*, 2(1) (1991) 1–28.

Frank, A. G., and Gills, B., *The World System: From Five Hundred Years to Five Thousand*, (London: Routledge, 1992).

Gaddis, J. L., *The Landscape of History: How Historians Map the Past* (Oxford: Oxford University Press, 2002).

Gamble, C., and Soffer, O., 'Pleistocene Polyphony: The Diversity of Human Adaptations at the Last Glacial Maximum', in C. Gamble and O. Soffer (eds), *The World at 18,000 BP*, 2 vols (London: Unwin Hyman, 1990).

Ginzburg, C., *The Cheese and the Worms: The Cosmos of a Sixteenth-Century Miller*, trans. J and A. Tedeschi (Baltimore, MD: Johns Hopkins University Press, 1980).

Green, W. A. 'Periodization in European and World History', *Journal of World History*, 3(1) (1992) 13–53.

Hawking, S., *A Brief History of Time: From the Big Bang to Black Holes* (London: Bantam Books, 1988).

Hawking, S., *The Universe in a Nutshell* (New York: Bantam, 2001).

Hodgson, M. S., *The Venture of Islam: Conscience and History in a World Civilization*, 3 vols (Chicago, IL: University of Chicago Press, 1974).

Hodgson, M. S., *Rethinking World History: Essays on Europe, Islam, and World History*, ed. Edmund Burke III (Cambridge: Cambridge University Press, 1993).

Hughes, J. D., *An Environmental History of the World: Humankind's Changing Role in the Community of Life* (London: Routledge, 2001).

Hughes-Warrington, M., *Fifty Key Thinkers on History* (London: Routledge, 2000).

Hughes-Warrington, M., 'Big History', *Historically Speaking*, 4(2) (2002) 16–17, 20.

Le Roy Ladurie, E., *Montaillou: Cathars and Catholics in a French Village, 1294–1324*, trans. B. Bray (London: Scolar, 1978).

Livi-Bacci, M., *A Concise History of World Population* (Oxford: Blackwell, 1992).

Lockard, C. A., 'The Contributions of Philip Curtin and the "Wisconsin School" to the Study and Promotion of Comparative World History', *Journal of Third World Studies*, 11(1) (1994) 180–223.

Lovelock, J. C., *Gaia: A New Look at Life on Earth* (Oxford: Oxford University Press, 1979).

Lovelock, J. C., *The Ages of Gaia* (Oxford: Oxford University Press, 1988).

Lovelock, J. C., *Gaia: The Practical Science of Planetary Medicine* (London: Unwin, 1991).

McNeill, J. R., *Something New Under the Sun: An Environmental History of the Twentieth-Century World* (New York: W. W. Norton, 2000).

McNeill, J. R., and McNeill, W. H., *The Human Web: A Bird's-Eye View of World History*, (New York: W. W. Norton, 2003).

McNeill, W. H., *Mythistory and Other Essays* (Chicago, IL: Chicago University Press, 1985).

McNeill, W. H., *The Rise of the West*, rev. edn (Chicago, IL: University of Chicago Press, 1991).

McNeill, W. H., 'History and the Scientific Worldview', *History and Theory*, 37(1) (1998) 1–13.

McNeill, W. H., 'An Emerging Consensus about World History', *World History Connected*, 1(1) (2003), online at <http://worldhistoryconnected.press.uiuc.edu/1.1/mcneill_print.html>.

Manning, P., *Navigating World History: Historians Create a Global Past* (New York: Palgrave Macmillan/St. Martin's Press, 2003).

Margulis, L., and Sagan, D., *Microcosmos: Four Billion Years of Microbial Evolution*, (Berkeley, CA: University of California Press, 1987).

Marwick, A., *The Nature of History* (London: Macmillan, 1970).

Mazlish, B., and Buultjens, R. (eds), *Conceptualizing Global History* (Boulder, CO: Westview Press, 1993).

Mintz, S. W., *Sweetness and Power: The Place of Sugar in Modern History* (New York: Viking, 1985).

Northrup, D., 'When Does World History Begin? (And Why Should We Care?)', *History Compass*, online at <www.history-compass.com/Pilot/world/World_WhyArticle.htm#top>.

Pomeranz, K., *The Great Divergence: China, Europe, and the Making of the Modern World Economy* (Princeton, NJ: Princeton University Press, 2000).

Ponting, C., *A Green History of the World* (Harmondsworth: Penguin, 1991).

Poole, R., *Nation and Identity* (London: Routledge, 1999).

Richards, J., *The Unending Frontier: An Environmental History of the Early Modern World*, (Berkeley, CA: University of California Press, 2003).

Rowlands, M., 'Centre and Periphery: a Review of a Concept', in M. Rowlands, M. Larsen and K. Kristiansen (eds), *Centre and Periphery in the Ancient World* (Cambridge: Cambridge University Press, 1987).

Sanderson, S. K. (ed.), *Civilizations and World Systems: Studying World-Historical Change*, (Walnut Creek, CA: Sage, 1985).

Snow, C. P., 'The Two Cultures and the Scientific Revolution', in *Public Affairs* (London: Macmillan, 1971), pp. 13–46.

Spier, F., *The Structure of Big History. From the Big Bang until Today* (Amsterdam: Amsterdam University Press, 1996).

Stanner, W. E. H., *After the Dreaming*, 1968 Boyer Lectures (Sydney: Australian Broadcasting Commission, 1969).

Stavrianos, L. S., *Lifelines from our Past: A New World History* (New York: Pantheon, 1989).

Stearns, P. N., 'Periodization in World History Teaching: Identifying the Big Changes', *The History Teacher*, 20 (1987) 561–80.

Stokes, G., 'The Fates of Human Societies: A Review of Recent Macrohistories', *American Historical Review*, 106(2) (2001) 508–25.

Toynbee, A. J., *A Study of History*, 12 vols (London: Oxford University Press, 1934–61).

Wallerstein, I., *The Modern World-System I: Capitalist Agriculture and the Origins of the European World-Economy in the Sixteenth Century* (New York: Academic Press, 1974).

Wells, H. G., *The Outline of History: Being a Plain History of Life and Mankind* (Garden City, NY: Garden City Publishers, 1920).

Wells, H. G., *A Short History of the World* (Harmondsworth: Penguin Books, 1922).

Ziman, J., *Reliable Knowledge: An Exploration of the Grounds for Belief in Science* (Cambridge: Cambridge University Press, 1978).

5
beginnings and endings
craig benjamin

The fundamental question of where to begin and end any piece of historical writing is not confined solely to practitioners of large-scale history.[1] All histories are the product of selective judgement, no matter how objectively the historian might approach his or her particular task, and this is particularly so when it comes to the question of where a history should begin and end. To the ancient historian intent upon producing a study of the civilizations of Mesopotamia, for example, the standard starting point has traditionally been with the appearance of the first cities of the Tigris and Euphrates deltas late in the fourth millennium BCE. But the emergence of these cities should more accurately be seen as just another, almost inevitable stage in a continual process towards urbanization that began with the adoption of agriculture by semi-sedentized communities in the Fertile Crescent of South Western Asia some six or seven thousand years earlier. A more accurate account of the emergence of these early states, then, would need to explain why certain human communities abandoned hunter-gatherer lifeways and adopted domestication and sedentism sometime in the tenth millennium. At the other end of the study, the Mesopotamian specialist is faced with the equally troubling dilemma of where to conclude, for does the history of any particular region ever really end? Mesopotamia was under the control of a vast array of rulers and states, from Sargon to Hammurabi, from the Sumerians to the Assyrians. Later still the region came under Achaemenid control, then Alexander and the Seleucids, later the Parthians and the Romans. Any particular ending chosen by the historian is the product of a carefully reasoned but ultimately arbitrary exercise of selective judgement, which essentially suggests that, although the progress of history is generally more fluid and seamless than our easy compartmentalization of it might suggest, the historian has decided for

90

a variety of reasons to tap into the stream at one point, and exit at another. These same sorts of problems are equally relevant to students of all historical eras, geographies and genres.

Nowhere, however, is the exercise of this judgement more obvious than in the work of world historians. Decisions taken about the overall shape and intent of a work, for example, are often evident in the choice of a title. It does not take insightful historiographical analysis to realize that Oswald Spengler probably had a different intention in writing *The Decline of the West* to that of William McNeill when he wrote *The Rise of the West*. Similarly, as will be explored in Chapters 6–9, decisions about which cultures or even whole civilizations to include, leave out, or treat in a piecemeal way give a clear indication of the particular focus or 'centricity' of the author. Decisions about beginnings and endings have also varied, with the history of world history writing being characterized in part by periods of temporal expansion and contraction. The intention of this chapter is to explore some of the practical and philosophical dimensions of the selection of beginnings and ends through a chronological survey of ancient and modern world histories and to show how decisions made by individual world historians were and are often as much a product of prevailing and inescapable cultural attitudes or general philosophical intentions, as of any subjective orientation.

expansion and contraction: a history of world history writing

Although the principal aim of Herodotus was to write a history of the Greeks, he significantly expanded his scope to include as much of the world that surrounded Greece as possible. And although his main subject was the war between the Greeks and the invading Persians, he sought the origins of that conflict as far back in history as his resources would reasonably allow him to go, exploring not only the role of the Phoenicians in the abduction of Io, but also the abduction of Helen and the resulting Trojan Wars several centuries earlier. When compared to Thucydides' account of the Peloponnesian Wars, for example, Herodotus' choice of a beginning seems extraordinarily early, and when coupled with the fact that his study concluded in his immediate present, suggests an acute awareness of the connectedness of events in history, and the broad flow of historical processes within which the Persian War was just another chapter.[2]

Similarly expansive is the writing of the Han Chinese historian, Sima Qian. Sima Qian inherited from his father the task of writing the first ever complete narrative history of China, and ultimately compiled a massive 130-chapter manuscript known today as the *Shiji*, or *Records of the Grand Historian*.[3] Even in the second century BCE, China already had the longest continuous recorded history of any state on earth, and the task of writing an inclusive narrative account from the beginning must have been daunting to say the least. He chose to commence with the ancient, semi-mythical sage rulers of China, including the Emperor Yu, founder of the first dynasty of China, the Xia. He went on to trace the rise and fall of the Xia, and its successors the Shang and Zhou dynasties. He then described the division of the powerful Zhou into a number of warring states, and the rise to power of the short-lived Qin Dynasty, before concluding his study with an in-depth (and personally dangerous) analysis of the Han Dynasty up until the reign of his own emperor, Wudi (140–87 BCE).

The incorporation of religion as the central concern of most historians in the late-Classical and early 'Middle Ages' eras also fostered historiographical expansion. That is, religious historians argued that human history needed to be interpreted as a search for, or an abandonment of, a particular god or gods, be it Yahweh, the Christian God or Allah. The religiously focused universal histories they produced were also two-directional, suggesting that human history was not random and chaotic, but headed in a clear direction from a specific beginning to an ultimate – generally apocalyptic – end. Obviously, this conception of purposeful, directional history had a powerful impact on the question of where such histories should begin and end. For Christian universal historians the starting point for their works was determined by the Old Testament, which provided the essential chronological framework for history. But even so, the specific purposes of individuals shaped their decisions. For example, in the climate of a widespread condemnation of the failure of Christianity to protect Rome from the sack of Alaric and the Visigoths, Paulus Orosius felt compelled to 'speak out in opposition to the empty perversity of those who, aliens to the City of God, are called pagans'.[4] His beginning and end points followed on from that purpose. He was critical of Greek and Latin historians for choosing to begin their works with the civilizations of Mesopotamia, specifically the Assyrians:

> Since nearly all men interested in writing, among the Greeks as among the Latins... have made the beginning of their writing with Ninus, king of the Assyrians, because they wish it to be believed in their blind opinion that the origin of the world and the creation of mankind were without beginning...[5]

For Orosius there had been a definite start to the history of humankind, and that was the creation of Adam and Eve by God. But as one of his intentions was to 'set forth all the records available' of 'shameful deeds', it was inevitable that Orosius' first chapter would begin with the emergence of sin.[6] Nor was Orosius faced with a particularly difficult problem when it came to ending his history. The sack of Rome by Alaric had sent shock waves through the Roman world. Under the pagan gods, critics of Christianity argued, Rome had never been violated, whereas the Christian God had proven incapable of protecting the city and state from barbarians. Orosius himself had been forced to flee to the relative calm of North Africa in the wake of the Visigoth invasion. Like his mentor St Augustine, who wrote *The City of God*, Orosius felt impelled to answer the criticism by continuing his account of human history up until the immediate present, in the hope of justifying the adoption of Christianity as the state religion of Rome.

Orosius' decisions about the temporal parameters of world history were influential in medieval historiography. An excellent example of Orosius' impact can be found in Bishop Otto of Freysing's *The Two Cities: A Chronicle of Universal History to the Year 1146 AD*. Despairing of the civil unrest of his own times, Otto's history was cast as a tragedy that traced the descent of the earthly City of Man (Babylon) into the mire of sin, and compared it with the shining City of God (Jerusalem).[7] To conclude his account, Otto extended history into the distant future. This was an eschatological perspective, seeking evidence either of an ultimate reuniting of the earthly and heavenly cities, or more probably the working out of God's final judgement on humanity. Such an apocalyptic tone is evident in chapter titles such as 'Of the coming and persecution that will occur under him'; 'Of the destruction of the world by fire'; 'Of the final judgement and its terrors'; and 'On the destruction of the wicked city'. Once again, with such a clear purpose, Otto's selection of a beginning and ending was largely circumscribed.

Christian universal historians made a significant contribution to the evolution of the historiography of world history. R. G. Collingwood has noted the emergence of a genuine universality in the sense that all peoples were involved in the working out of God's plan, not just those of the Graeco-Roman tradition. This realization demanded a genuine inclusiveness, a real 'history of the world, a universal history whose theme shall be the general development of God's purposes for human life',[8] and that in turn suggested a beginning and end well beyond the particularism of Greek and Roman history. In general, contemporary historians of other religious traditions, particularly Islam, shared a similar sense of inclusiveness, as the works of Abu Ja'far al-Tabari and Ibn Khaldun demonstrate.

Al-Tabari was a prolific writer best known for his extraordinary *History of Prophets and Kings*. His work was guided by a constant concern to trace the unbroken line of transmission of the sayings of the Prophet Mohammed, and this sacred purpose clearly prescribed the beginning and end to his history. Drawing on a range of evidential sources, including the Bible, Greek, Roman, Persian and Byzantine documents, al-Tabari traced the relationship between man and Allah, from the emergence of Iblis/Satan and the creation of Adam through to his own times, and expounded a view of history as an organic and continuous process of cultural transmission. Four hundred years later, Ibn Khaldun (1332–1395 CE) produced the *Muqaddimah* ('Introduction to History'), a history of human social organization.[9] This intention might suggest a history that would commence with the earliest human communities, but Khaldun was also interested in climate and geography, and so, following on from his historiographical introduction, he looked to the natural world and its relationship with human origins. Khaldun concluded the *Muqaddimah* with a series of essays on human philosophy, scientific inquiry, literature and the development of languages. His is thus a complete universal history in which all the various 'arts of man' and the influences that act upon them are included, from the natural sciences to ethics, from the royal dynasties to human social organization, and from the modern scientific account of the geographical origins of the planet to the finest achievements of contemporary poets.

When nineteenth-century historians like Jules Michelet and Jakob Burckhardt used the word 'Renaissance' to describe the emergence of secular humanism in sixteenth-century Western Europe, they believed they were capturing attempts to revive the cultural and philosophical attitudes of the ancient Greeks and Romans. The idea of a rebirth or rediscovery in the writing of history, however, is misleading because medieval historians had remained aware of the shape and content of Classical history, even though this had been subordinated to their religious purposes. Furthermore, the evolution of a more secular 'humanist' approach to history writing in the Renaissance, which influenced views of the parameters of world history, did not occur overnight. The Spanish humanist Juan Luis Vives (1492–1540), for example, began his account of the history of history writing with the exploits of Moses, but he still chose the Book of Genesis over the histories of the Greeks as his preferred source of evidence. Other writers, like Niccolò Machiavelli (1469–1527), managed to shift the emphasis of their works away from religion towards more earthly issues. In *Discourses on Livy*, Machiavelli attempted to apply the prevailing appreciation of ancient 'Culture' to the task of instructing princes and other rulers of Italian city states in the Classical arts of leadership.[10] His work thus opens with the origins of cities and republics, in a manner that united historical analysis with urban geography and political science. Machiavelli's choice of beginning – and the sort of evidence he incorporated – was determined entirely by his specific purpose, which in his case happened to be secular and didactic.

French universal historians of the Renaissance and Reformation had an entirely different aim again, being more interested in the application of 'scientific' principles and methodologies to the writing of history, and this again had implications for the choice of beginning and end points. In his *Method for the Easy Comprehension of History*, for example, Jean Bodin attempted to codify historiography by providing a comprehensive, chronological list of 282 histories and historians, along with a guide to the proper order for reading them.[11] He worked his way methodically from ancient Greek and Roman historians (including Herodotus, Dionysius, Polybius) through to late-Roman Christians (like Eutropius and Eusebius), to the chroniclers of the Middle Ages (including the Venerable Bede), and concluded with historians of the Renaissance. Bodin also saw it as essential to move from the big picture to the most detailed, and this influenced his choice of beginning and ending, writing:

> As they err who study the maps of regions before they have learned accurately the relation of the whole universe and the separate parts of to each other and to the whole, so they are not less mistaken who think they can understand particular histories before they have judged the order and sequence of universal history and of all times, set forth as it were in a table.[12]

Like Bodin, Bishop Jacques Bossuet was also systematic in his *Discourse on Universal History*, arguing that correctly ordered history could provide 'a guiding line to all the affairs of the world'.[13] As a Christian yet also a humanist, Bossuet attempted to incorporate both perspectives into his analysis: he opens with Adam and Noah; moves through the Fall of Troy, the Building of Rome and the Birth of Jesus Christ; and concludes with Constantine and Charlemagne.[14]

By the eighteenth century, Western Europe had entered a period of global cultural and economic domination that has largely continued until the present day. As a result of the global expansion of European power, many of the intellectuals of Europe felt compelled to construct an ideology that explained and justified European superiority. This resulted in a fundamental change in the purpose of European historiography, and also an intensification of the 'scientific' methodology that had emerged during the Reformation, both of which are reflected in responses to the question of where such accounts should commence and conclude. Giambattista Vico produced several important works of historiography, most notably the *Scienza Nuovo* (*The New Science*). Amongst his contemporaries, it was commonly held that the evolution of 'civilized practices' in the world was, as Leon Pompa has argued, 'a consequence of the fact that the various nations of the world had had a single historical origin'.[15] But rather than a common origin, Vico perceived a more fundamental commonality of essential nature, so much so that '[i]f the various historical nations were left to develop without external interference, they would necessarily develop certain common characteristics in their social, economic and cultural conditions at correspondent points of their histories'.[16] In Book Two of the *The New Science*, Vico argued that one aspect of this commonality of nature was that 'all histories of the Gentile nations have had fabulous beginnings'. In order for the new science of history to clearly comprehend these fabulous origins, the beginning of each 'national' analysis was with the science of 'mythology, or the interpretation of fable'.[17] The investigation of mythology necessitated an examination of three essential institutional constants – religion, marriage and the burial of the dead – that emerged early in the lifecycle of all cultures, and which, if properly and 'scientifically' understood, would reveal the eternal principles and essential common nature of all societies.

The French philosopher Voltaire also had something to say about the proper beginning for a work of universal history in *The Philosophy of History* (the introduction to *Essai sur les Moeurs et L'Espirit des Nations*). To his view, it was necessary to establish the physical conditions that had allowed for the ultimate emergence of civilized society. He thus began by 'examining whether the globe, which we inhabit, was formerly the same as it is at present', before considering the former great extent of the oceans, and the many changes the surface of the earth had apparently undergone.[18] Although suggesting that 'this little globe of ours undergoes perpetual changes', he drew the line at mountain building, however, arguing that he 'dare not... aver that the sea has formed or even washed all the mountains of the earth'.[19] What most interested Voltaire was the evolution of the human spirit, which had, he believed, reached its ultimate stage in the Enlightenment, and so this formed the end point of his work.[20] Voltaire's contemporary, Nicolas de Caritat Condorcet was also interested in the origins and evolution of the human spirit, both to explain its current 'enlightened' state, but also to indicate how it should be cultivated for the future.[21] His history was thus open-ended.

A leading thinker of the German Enlightenment, Johann Gottfried Herder was opposed to historical generalizing practiced by the French. What was important for Herder was the essentially unique quality of individual peoples, nations and historical events. For Herder, each nation had its own 'centre of happiness within itself, just as each sphere has its own centre of gravity',[22] and this was best understood through an analysis of the *Volkgeist* of particular states and peoples. So for Herder, the starting point for any historical analysis was not the enlightened state of reason and high culture achieved by the educated elite during his own age, but the literature, art, folklore and religion that were all manifestations of the basic spirit of the whole people, the *Volk*.

The dominant historiographical issue in eighteenth- and nineteenth-century Germany historiography, however, was the confrontation between philosophy and history and the principles of a 'science' of history. In his early writings, for instance, Leopold von Ranke was adamant that the study of history could only begin with human documents.[23] Unlike Ibn Khaldun or Voltaire, von Ranke had neither the time for, nor an interest in, the geophysical circumstances of history. He wrote:

> One should exclude entirely that which usually is taken over in world history from geological deduction and form the results of natural history about the first creation of the world, the solar system and the earth. By our method we find out nothing about these topics; it is permissible to confess our ignorance.[24]

Nor did von Ranke have much time for myth, backhandedly disagreeing with Herder about the evidential role of myth and legend in a proper understanding of the origins of a people or nation: 'As for myths, I do not want to deny categorically that they contain perhaps an occasional historical element.'[25] Above all, von Ranke recognized the primacy of the written word, and thus the vast millennia of human existence that preceded the emergence of writing were dismissed as essentially unknowable:

> In the abstract, history would embrace all of the life of mankind appearing in time. But too much of it is lost and unknown. The first period of its existence as well as the connecting links are lost without any hope of ever finding them again.[26]

Of course, von Ranke could scarcely have imagined the role that palaeontology, archaeology, radiometric dating and DNA analysis would come to play in unlocking the secrets of prehistory, but his insistence upon documents as the only acceptable form of evidence was a powerful and inhibiting influence upon decisions about the parameters of world history in the nineteenth and twentieth centuries.

Immanuel Kant and G. W. F. Hegel were even more restrictive, showing an interest in human activities only when rationality began to emerge. Hegel wrote, for instance:

> The spreading of peoples over the earth, their separation from each other, their comminglings and wanderings, remain involved in the obscurity of a voiceless past. They are not acts of will becoming self-conscious – of Freedom mirroring itself in a phenomenal form, and creating for itself a proper reality. Not partaking of this element of substantial, veritable existence, those nations... never advanced to the possession of a *history*.[27]

As they saw rationality as an exclusively Western activity, those outside of Europe became 'the peoples without history'.

When novelist H. G. Wells turned his hand to history, he hoped to redress the narrow rationalist Eurocentrism of world history by writing a genuinely inclusive work that would 'bring it within the normal limitations of time and energy set to the reading and education of an ordinary citizen'.[28] With a passionate interest in science, it is no surprise that he commenced his history with a detailed account of the physical origins of the planet, and life upon it. The opening chapters attempt to explain the world 'in space and time', the beginning of life, and the 'ages' of fish, coral swamps, reptiles, birds and mammals. The evolution of hominids (or 'sub-men') and early human thought processes are considered as a necessary prelude to a detailed, large-scale study of human history, from the origins of agriculture to World War I. Another product of the war was Oswald Spengler's *The Decline of the West*. Written in the midst of poverty and despair in Munich, Spengler's work concluded with a consideration of his own age, which he termed 'Faustian' because it was characterized by the limitless ambition of its people, who would apparently sell their own souls for material wealth and military conquest. By ending his world history with this stinging rebuke of contemporary Western culture, Spengler captured the mood of the day and his work thus became a commercial success.

Like Spengler, Arnold Toynbee also had ambivalent feelings about contemporary Western culture. Taking as his starting point Western (and specifically British) civilization, Toynbee attempted to trace its origins as far backwards in time as possible. In doing so, Toynbee discovered that, far from being easily divided into a number of compartments or eras, human history was essentially seamless and continuous. In a very real way, he seemed to be arguing, there had never been a 'beginning' (although there might ultimately prove to be a cataclysmic end) to human history:

> This conclusion follows from the fact that, in the process of tracing the history of our western society backwards towards its origins, we strike upon the last phase of another society of the same kind, the origins of which evidently lie considerably further back in time. This conclusion regarding the age and origins of the Western Society carries with it a corollary regarding the continuity of history.[29]

Halfway through writing his twelve-volume *A Study of History*, Toynbee changed his mind and disagreed with Spengler about the ultimate decline and collapse of Western culture, suggesting instead that the future would herald the emergence of utopian universal churches.

By the time Toynbee wrote the concluding volumes of *A Study of History*, world history had blossomed into a number of different subgenres, many of them now firmly located in the United States. World-system and dependency theorists, for instance, argued that the rise of the West was best explained not by internal characteristics, but by colonial exploitation. The best-known exponent of world-system theory is Immanuel Wallerstein. Wallerstein defined a world-system as 'not a system "in the world" or "of the world". It is a system that "is a world"'.[30] For world-system theorists there was clearly no debate about the end of their histories. By the late twentieth century the world-system had become truly global, in that it really did encompass the whole world. But the question of where to begin was (and is) hotly debated, because the way in which one defines a 'world-system' has significant ramifications for determining when the first world-system emerged. Wallerstein argued for a starting point around 1450, Abu-Lughod for the thirteenth century,[31] Andre Gunder Frank and Barry Gills for 3000 BCE,[32] and Christopher Chase-Dunn and Thomas Hall for 7000 BCE.[33]

Also influential in North American scholarship were William McNeill, Marshall Hodgson and Philip Curtin. Paul Costello describes William McNeill as 'perhaps the most powerful voice in the promotion of the idea of world history as a means to a global consciousness'.[34] Influenced initially by Toynbee and Spengler, McNeill soon abandoned the idea of cyclical patterns of rise and fall in civilizations, and instead attempted to trace a unified and continuous pattern of cultural growth, interrupted by occasional ecological disasters and manmade catastrophes. When his classic work *The Rise of the West* was published in 1963, Toynbee's influence, and McNeill's concept of civilizational continuity and interruption, led him to a beginning dated to the emergence of the early civilizations. However, McNeill traced the origins of Mesopotamian culture not from the first city states, but from the adoption of agriculture. He argued that the development of agricultural technologies like the plough and irrigation allowed for the accumulation of surpluses, so that as human communities grew in size and concentration, 'managerial leaders' emerged in the guise of early kingships. After following the continuous growth and development of civilizations (essentially four of them) through the ancient and late Classical eras, McNeill pursued Western expansion (despite periodic interruptions by disease) and concurrent Eastern contraction through to the world wars of the twentieth century.

Like many other world historians before him, McNeill's analysis was futurological. He speculated for instance, that Cold War bipolar tensions would probably be resolved by the emergence of a 'single world sovereignty', either as a result of war or by the convergence of American and Soviet culture.[35] He also warned that the elites of the new world order would be swayed by 'bureaucratic self-interest' that would result in the creation of 'elaborate rules and precedents', which would be used to discourage disruptive scientific innovations and social change.[36] William McNeill has continuously modified and adapted his views on world history over the past four decades, but decisions he made in the 1960s concerning where to begin and end the highly influential *Rise of the West* have shaped the writing of world history in North America ever since.

One of McNeill's colleagues at the University of Chicago was Marshall Hodgson, who became the shaping voice of Islamic world history in the United States. As early as 1944 Hodgson despaired of the prevailing Eurocentrism in world history, and demanded a more equitable inclusion of Asian history. He argued: 'The history of Chinese culture... is very nearly as important, from an international point of view, to modern world humanity as is the history of Europe. Yet when we read "world history" we read chiefly of Europe.'[37] Hodgson was critical of so-called world histories that 'mention China in one or two chapters, whereas they spend all the rest of their time in Europe'.[38] Thus for Hodgson, world history had to begin with the great (and more ancient) civilizations of

China and India, rather than the development of 'Western' culture from the ancient Greeks. Hodgson's three-volume masterpiece, *The Venture of Islam*, attempts to put his historiographical philosophy into practice by offering a large-scale examination of the development of Islamic and Afro-Eurasian civilizations, from the beginning of regnal records until the mid-twentieth century.[39]

Founder of the 'Wisconsin School', and an African historian by training, Philip Curtin pioneered comparative world history based on the African diaspora and the interregional exchanges of the Atlantic region.[40] His aim was not so much to survey a large temporal sweep of world history, but rather to answer the question 'How did the world come to be as it is?' by treating topics selectively, with examples detailed enough to be comprehensive.[41] In *The Rise and Fall of the Plantation Complex*, for example, Curtin examined the relationship between plantations, sugar and slavery in the West Indies and the Southern states of the US. Although he dated the emergence of the plantation complex to 1800, his beginning point was considerably earlier, in the 'plantations that began growing cane sugar in the eastern Mediterranean at the time of the European Crusades to the Levant'.[42] Curtin then followed the evolution and global spread of the plantation complex until its dismantling following the emancipation of slaves throughout the tropical world. In other words, although the spatial and temporal scope of his particular study was far less ambitious than that of McNeill or Hodgson, Curtin's beginning point for an essentially nineteenth century phenomenon was located some eight centuries earlier, and his end was effectively the moment at which the complex disappeared.

Another strong stream of world history writing in the twentieth century arose in concert with the natural sciences. In the twentieth century, science was increasingly 'historicized' as changes and origins were debated for life on earth, the planet itself, the solar system and indeed the entire universe. The almost quintessential example of this trend was Stephen Hawking's attempt to describe the emergence of time at the birth of the universe.[43] The implications of the marriage of the natural sciences and world history for decisions about beginnings and endings have been on the one hand predictable, and on the other quite staggering. For example, ecological historians like Brian Fagan, in books such as *The Little Ice Age* (2000) and *Floods, Famines and Emperors* (2001) have used geophysical and climatological data to trace the effects of recent climate change (the 'little ice age' of 1300–1850 CE) and longer-term climatic cycles (for example, El Niño) on human history. Alfred Crosby has considered the success of European people, seeds and germs in colonizing the planet, and in so doing extended the beginning of his analysis as far back as the origins of the human race, their animals, pathogens and weeds.[44] And Australian Tim Flannery, in *The Eternal Frontier* (2001) commences his study of the environmental evolution of North American flora and fauna at the moment a great asteroid slammed into earth some 65 million years ago.

An even more dramatic example of the trend towards both a non-anthropocentric historiography, and the expansion of the temporal dimensions of world history, is the work of Lynn Margulis and Dorion Sagan. In *Microcosmos* (1987) they point out that the evolution of life on earth has traditionally been studied only as a prologue to humans, the 'supreme' beings of the planet.[45] But arguing against this, they suggest that far from being special, apart and supreme, humans are in fact composed of billions of microbial organisms, and that the emergence of the human species (and hence the beginning of human history) needs to be traced back to the evolution of bacterial cells like prokaryotes, which will continue to exist long after our species has become extinct:

> There is no evidence that human beings are the supreme stewards of life on earth, nor the lesser offspring of a superintelligent terrestrial source. But there is evidence to show that we are recombined from powerful bacterial communities with a multibillion-year-old history. We are part of an intricate network that comes from the original bacterial takeover of the earth... They may well survive our species in forms of the future that lie beyond our limited imaginations.[46]

Though world environmental historians tend not to begin as far back as Margulis and Sagan, their works reach much further into the future.[47] Quite often, the future of world environmental histories is dystopian, and Marnie Hughes-Warrington has argued that it might be a secular substitute for the eschatological focus found in the work of early Judaeo-Christian universal historians.[48]

While most world historians would feel uncomfortable looking back to the origins of life or even the universe, many current world history textbooks pay some attention to hominid evolution. With few exceptions, though, surveys are piecemeal or cursory.[49] David Northrup makes the obvious point that 'historians have not been in the vanguard of reclaiming prehistory and in North America they are scarcely to be found at all'.[50] Some world historians have welcomed the involvement of evolutionary biologists in explaining human evolution, although they tend to leave Darwinian evolution behind once language has evolved, and articulate instead a cultural evolutionary theory. For a small but growing band of twenty-first-century historians, however, the union of the historical sciences and human history ought to be much tighter. They have written histories that tell the biggest story of all: that of the origins and evolution of all life on earth, of the planet and solar system, and of the entire universe, from its moment of birth to its ultimate death. This subfield of world history – big history – is made up of a varied group of practitioners. The best known of them, David Christian, a Russian specialist by training, found himself intrigued by the same question that has plagued all world historians since ancient times: 'Where does human history begin, and why?' Eventually he was led, almost against his will, back to the Big Bang, that moment of ultimate origination some 13.7 billion years ago:

> To understand the history of human beings, you must understand their relationship to other living organisms. That means understanding how life itself appeared, evolved and diversified over some 4 billion years. To understand the earth on whose surface life appeared and evolved, or to understand the sun that supplied the energy needed for life to sustain itself, you have to understand how the solar system was conceived, nourished and born as the offspring of our galaxy, the Milky Way. To understand the Milky Way, you need to understand how it was born from the very early Universe. In other words, we cannot really understand human history until we see that human societies are one small component of much larger systems.[51]

At the other end of his work, Christian takes his readers into the distant future, offering a detailed account based on the latest scientific evidence about the ultimate fate of the universe. To him, the limits of world history are the limits of scientific evidence.[52] Obviously then, one of the most significant historiographical contributions of big history has been to push the temporal boundaries of historical inquiry to extraordinary limits. Where H. G. Wells appeared radical in beginning *The Outline of History* with the geological origins of the earth, David Christian starts with the origins of the universe itself. And where early Christian or more recent environmental historians project their accounts towards an apocalyptic future, Christian takes his readers hundreds of millions of years forward in time to the slow, heat-death of a lifeless universe.

David Northrup has recently suggested that the approach of big history has serious implications for the history profession in general, pointing out that, although he and many other world history teachers have reservations about the sort of time scales big historians consider, 'the proposal has the great virtue of provoking a serious re-examination of the proper beginning point for history'.[53] Marnie Hughes-Warrington goes further, arguing that big history has the potential to shake traditional world history writing to its very foundations, because it has made available a range of lenses with which to view the past and future, not just the standard 'viewing of individual actions' or the 'nation-state' lens. The 'wide-angle' and 'landscape' lenses of big history help us see, for the first time, the emergence of patterns in human behaviour over vast temporal timescales. It is, she writes, 'like stepping back from a detailed inspection of the rocks and dust of traditional history, and being rewarded with a view of the Nazca Lines of Peru'.[54]

conclusion

From Herodotus to David Christian, world historians have wrestled with the problem of where to begin and end their accounts. The resolution of that problem has in the main been the result of decisions made by individual historians, based on the methodological and ideological purposes of their work. But historians do not work in a vacuum, and more often than not the cultural and philosophical environment in which they lived is also a shaping force. Ancient world historians like Herodotus and Sima Qian broke out from the limits of prevailing historiographical norms when they expanded the temporal and geographical limits of their analyses to include information about the whole 'world' as it was known to them. On the other hand, Judaeo-Christian and Islamic universal historians of the Post-Classical era wrote from deep within a prevailing set of cultural assumptions when they offered purposeful, directional histories that extended from the divine origins of the human species to some ultimate apocalyptic fate. Over time, world historians found themselves treading a fine line between the sacred explanation of human affairs and more secular, systematic, quasi-scientific explanations, all the time driven by a didactic impulse to promote history as a form of political and moral instruction.

By the Enlightenment, European global dominance more or less insisted upon the production of Eurocentric histories that somehow justified the purposeful tracing of world history from some primeval age of darkness through to the glorious pinnacle of Western civilization achieved in eighteenth-century Europe. This idea was further emphasized by German philosophers a century later, who traced the evolution of rationality and economic activities from prehistoric families to the future.

By the twentieth century, writers like Spengler and Toynbee encouraged even more interest in the future as well as the past, by making it clear that it would be the product of dangerous and destructive activities in the near past and present. Interestingly, smaller-scale historians have never apparently felt similarly entitled to make predictions about the future, even when the depth of their knowledge about a particular society, event or nation would surely allow them to do so. It is hardly surprising, therefore, that Karl Popper was so scathingly critical about some world historians. In *The Poverty of Historicism*, Popper launched an attack on all forms of social engineering aimed at altering the future (including National Socialist and particularly Marxist revolutionary prophesy), proposing instead a more manageable form of 'piecemeal social engineering'. His aim was to enhance human control over always fallible and potentially disastrous forays into the future, and in so doing he contrasted the apparent paucity of historical prophecy with that of scientific prediction. For Popper the prediction of social events, that is, social change, would always be severely limited by the potential impact on society of unforeseeable new knowledge.[55]

Popper's condemnation of historians who concerned themselves with the future would find almost universal agreement from most twenty-first-century professional historians. With the exception of environmental and big historians, virtually all world historians – let alone those working on the smaller scale – have not only withdrawn from offering considerations of the future, but disdainfully view such attempts as amateurish and even embarrassing. Even a casual glance at any of the very worthwhile, standard world history textbooks most commonly being used in universities today confirms this conclusion.[56] As someone who has taught big history to undergraduates in two continents for the past six years, this seems extraordinary given that there is actually a great deal we can say about the future with a fair degree of certainty. Student exam questions such as 'Do you think a study of history on the scale of big history permits historians to consider the future?' elicit responses that confirm not only the right of historians to do this, but even their obligation, given that world historians are perhaps more fitted than anyone to observe the likely unfolding of large-scale trends and processes.

At the other end of their accounts, today's world historians have also adopted a safety first, conservative approach to the question of beginnings. David Northrup sets the tone for this when he argues that 'human history is different in a fundamental way from natural history. Human history began at the point when cultural change shot past biological evolution as the primary force shaping humankind's relations with the rest of the world'.[57] But even if Northrup is right, when exactly was that moment when humans stepped out of the biosphere that surrounds them? What evidence can we point to which shows conclusively that human evolution had become cultural rather than biological? Cave art? Ritualized burial? The migrations of *Homo erectus*? Most world histories deal with, at best, 42,000 years of history, and the first 30,000 of those are barely considered at all. Nor is this a perspective limited to American world historians. English author John Roberts, in the *Penguin History of the World* (1988), makes these underlying anthropocentric assumptions explicit when he asks:

> When does history begin? It is tempting to reply 'In the beginning', but like many obvious answers, this soon turns out to be unhelpful. As a great Swiss historian once pointed out in another connexion, history is the one subject where you cannot begin at the beginning. If we want to, we can trace the chain of human descent back to the appearance of vertebrates, or even to the photosynthetic cells which lie at the start of life itself. We can go back further still, to the almost unimaginable upheavals which formed this planet and even the origins of the universe. Yet this is not 'history'. Commonsense helps here: history is the story of mankind, of what it has done, suffered or enjoyed.[58]

What is surely beyond dispute is that mainstream world history writing has settled for a conservative, traditional and anthropocentric set of assumptions that articulate a clear starting point to history, and a disengagement of human history from that of the environment in which it has unfolded. For this reason, big history and world scientific histories remain at the margins of world history historiography in the early twenty-first century.

Leaving this historiographical situation to one side, there is no denying that regardless of their personal attitudes and the prevailing intellectual milieux, world and universal historians have been responsible for a dramatic extension of our conception of the timescales of human history. There is of course no correct answer to the question, 'When does human history begin'?, nor yet any way of knowing with certainty how it will ultimately end, but in being prepared to dramatically extend the parameters of both past and future chronologies, often to quite extraordinary lengths, world historians have forced us to question the very meaning of what it is to be human, and what it is that distinguishes human history from that of our biosphere, planet and universe. It remains a fundamental question that historians of the future will have to grapple with just as doggedly as those of the past, but the developing relationship between scientific and historical knowledge may ultimately result, not only in a clearer understanding of human origins and destinies, but also in a fundamental redefinition of what it means to be human.

notes

1. I would like to express my thanks to Marnie Hughes-Warrington, the students of HIST359 at Macquarie University, Australia, and my own students at Grand Valley, who stimulated much of my thinking in this chapter.
2. See for example Herodotus, *The Histories*, trans. A.D. Godley, Loeb Classical Library (London: Heinemann, 1966) 1.1.3.
3. Sima Qian, *Records of the Grand Historian: Han Dynasty II*, trans. B. Watson, rev. edn (New York: Columbia University Press, 1993).
4. Paulus Orosius, *Seven Books of History Against the Pagans*, trans. J. Deferrari (Washington, DC: Catholic University of America Press, 1964), p. 4.
5. Ibid., p. 5.
6. Ibid.
7. Otto, Bishop of Freysing, *The Two Cities: A Chronicle of Universal History to the Year 1146 AD*, trans. C. C. Mierow (New York: Octagon, 1966), p. 95.
8. R. G. Collingwood, *The Idea of History*, ed. W. J. Van der Dussen, rev. edn (Oxford: Oxford University Press, 1993), p. 49.
9. Ibn Khaldun, *The Muqaddimah*, trans. F. Rosenthal (Princeton, NJ: Princeton University Press, 1958), p. 11.
10. N. Machiavelli, *Discourses on Livy*, trans. H. C. Mansfield and N. Tarcov (Chicago, IL: University of Chicago Press, 1996), p. 5.
11. J. Bodin, *Method for the Easy Comprehension of History*, trans. B. Reynolds (New York: Octagon, 1966), p. 20.
12. Ibid., p. 26.
13. Bishop Bossuet, *Discourse on Universal History*, trans. E. Forster (Chicago, IL: University of Chicago Press, 1976), p. 4.
14. Ibid., p. 5.
15. L. Pompa, *Vico: A Study of the 'New Science'* (Cambridge: Cambridge University Press, 1975), p. 2.
16. Ibid.
17. G. Vico, *The New Science*, trans M. H. Fisch and T. G. Bergin, rev. edn (Ithaca, NY: Cornell University Press [1744], 1984), pp. 202, 361.
18. F. M. A. Voltaire, *The Philosophy of History*, trans. anon. (London: Vision, 1965), p. 1.
19. Ibid., p. 3.
20. Ibid.
21. A.-N. de Condorcet, *Sketch for a Historical Picture of the Progress of the Human Mind*, trans. J. Barraclough, in P. Gardiner (ed.), *Theories of History* (New York: Free Press, 1959) p. 52.
22. J. G. Herder, 'Yet Another Philosophy of History', in *Against Pure Reason: Writings on Religion, Language and History*, trans. and ed. M. Bunge (Minneapolis, MN: Augsburg Fortress, 1993), p. 43.

23. L. von Ranke, 'On the Character of Historical Science', in *The Theory and Practice of History*, ed. G. G. Iggers and K. Von Moltke (Indianapolis, IN: Bobbs Merrill, 1973), p. 37.
24. Ibid., p. 45.
25. Ibid.
26. Ibid.
27. Ibid.
28. Ibid.
29. A. Toynbee, *A Study of History*, vol. 1 (London: Oxford University Press, 1934), p. 43.
30. I. Wallerstein, 'The Timespace of World-Systems Analysis: A Philosophical Essay', *Journal of Historical Geography*, 23 (1972) 294.
31. Janet Abu-Lughod, *Before European Hegemony: The World System, AD 1250–1350* (New York: Oxford University Press, 1989).
32. A. G. Frank and B. K. Gills, *The World System: Five Hundred Years or Five Thousand?* (London: Routledge, 1992).
33. C. Chase-Dunn and T. Hall, *Core/Periphery Relations in Precapitalist Worlds* (Boulder, CO: University of Colorado Press, 1991).
34. P. Costello, *World Historians and their Goals: Twentieth Century Answers to Modernism* (De Kalb, IL: Northern Illinois University Press, 1994), p. 183.
35. W. H. McNeill, *The Rise of the West: A History of the Human Community* (Chicago, IL: University of Chicago Press, 1963), p. 868.
36. Ibid., pp. 875–6.
37. M. G. S. Hodgson, *Rethinking World History: Essays on Europe, Islam and World History*, ed. E. Burke III (Cambridge: Cambridge University Press, 1993), p. 35.
38. Ibid.
39. M. G. S. Hodgson, *The Venture of Islam*, 3 vols (Chicago, IL: University of Chicago Press, 1975–77).
40. For an excellent assessment of the work of Philip Curtin, see C. Lockard, 'The Contributions of Philip Curtin and the "Wisconsin School" to the Study and Promotion of Comparative World History', *Journal of Third World Studies*, 11(1) (1995) 59ff.
41. P. Curtin, 'Depth, Span and Relevance', *American Historical Review*, 89 (1984) 4.
42. P. Curtin, *The Rise and Fall of the Plantation Complex: Essays in Atlantic History* (Cambridge: Cambridge University Press, 1990), p. ix.
43. S. Hawking, *A Brief History of Time* (London: Bantam Books, 1988).
44. A. Crosby, 'Ecological Imperialism', in *Germs, Seeds and Animals* (London: M. E. Sharpe, 1994), pp. 32ff.
45. L. Margulis and D. Sagan, *Microcosmos: Four Billion Years of Microbial Evolution* (Berkeley, CA: University of California Press, 1986), p. 27.
46. Ibid., p. 36.
47. See C. Ponting, *A Green History of the World* (Harmondsworth: Penguin, 1993).
48. Marnie Hughes-Warrington, Lecture 12, HIST359: World Histories, Macquarie University, 2002.
49. See J. Bentley and H. Ziegler *Traditions and Encounters: A Global Perspective on the Past*, 2nd edn (New York: McGraw-Hill, 2002), pp. 8–13; P. Brummett

et al., *Civilization, Past and Present*, 10th edn (New York: Longman, 2003), pp. 6–7; and A. Esler, *The Human Venture. From Prehistory to the Present*, 5th edn (Upper Saddle River, NJ: Pearson Education, 2004), pp. 7–16.

50. D. Northrup, 'When Does World History Begin? (And Why Should We Care?)', *History Compass*, 2003, online at <www.history-compass.com/Pilot/world/World_WhyArticle.htm>.

51. David Christian, 'This Fleeting World', unpublished ms., 1999, p. 3. Published as D. Christian, *Maps of Time* (Berkeley, CA: University of California Press, 2004). See also 'The Case for "Big History"', *Journal of World History*, 2(2) (1991) 223–38.

52. E. Chaisson, *Cosmic Evolution* (Cambridge, MA: Harvard University Press, 2001).

53. Northrup, 'When Does World History Begin?'

54. Marnie Hughes-Warrington, 'Big History', unpublished ms.

55. K. Popper, *The Poverty of Historicism* (London: Routledge, 1986). Popper expanded on his ideas in *The Logic of Scientific Discovery: The Open Universe* (London: Routledge, 1988).

56. See any of the texts cited above at note 49.

57. Northrup, 'When Does World History Begin?'

58. J. Roberts, *The Penguin History of the World* (Harmondsworth: Penguin, 1987), p. 19. To balance the more limited perspective of European world historians like Roberts and G. Barraclough (*Turning Points in World History* (London: Thames & Hudson, 1979)), consider C. Cipolla's astonishing early Malthusian study of human populations in *The Economic History of World Population* (Harmondsworth: Penguin, 1962).

recommended resources

Abu-Lughod, J. L., *Before European Hegemony: The World System, AD 1250–1350* (New York: Oxford University Press,1989).

Bentley, J., *Shapes of World History in Twentieth-Century Scholarship* (Washington, DC: American Historical Association, 1996).

Barraclough, G., *Turning Points in World History* (London: Thames & Hudson, 1979).

Bentley, J. and Zeigler, H., *Traditions and Encounters: A Global Perspective on the Past*, 2nd edn (New York: McGraw-Hill, 2002).

Bodin, J., *Method for the Easy Comprehension of History*, trans. B. Reynolds (New York: Octagon, 1966).

Bossuet, Bishop of Meaux, *Discourse on Universal History*, trans. E. Forster (Chicago, IL: University of Chicago Press, 1976).

Brummett, P. et al., *Civilization Past and Present*, 10th edn (New York: Longman, 2003).

Chaisson, E., *Cosmic Evolution* (Cambridge, MA: Harvard University Press, 2001).

Chase-Dunn, C. and Hall, T., *Core/Periphery Relations in Precapitalist Worlds* (Boulder, CO: University of Colorado Press, 1991).

Cipolla, C., *The Economic History of World Population* (Harmondsworth: Penguin, 1962).

Christian, D., 'The Case for "Big History"', *Journal of World History*, 2(2) (1991) 22–38.

Christian, D., *Maps of Time* (Berkeley, CA: University of California Press, 2004).

Collingwood, R. G., *The Idea of History*, ed. W. J. Van der Dussen, rev. edn (Oxford: Oxford University Press, 1993).

Costello, P., *World Historians and their Goals: Twentieth Century Answers to Modernism* (De Kalb, IL: Northern Illinois University Press, 1994).

Crosby, A., *Germs, Seeds and Animals* (London: M. E. Sharpe, 1994).

Curtin, P., 'Depth, Span and Relevance', *American Historical Review*, 89(1) (1984) 1–9.

Curtin, P., *Cross-Cultural Trade in World History* (Cambridge: Cambridge University Press, 1984).

Curtin, P., *The Rise and Fall of the Plantation Complex: Essays in Atlantic History* (Cambridge: Cambridge University Press, 1990).

de Condorcet, A.- N., *Selections from Sketch for a Historical Picture of the Progress of the Human Mind*, trans. J. Barraclough, in P. Gardiner (ed.), *Theories of History* (New York: Free Press, 1959).

Diamond, J., *Guns, Germs and Steel* (London: Vintage, 1998).

Esler, A., *The Human Venture: From Prehistory to the Present*, 5th edn (Upper Saddle River, NJ: Pearson, 2004).

Frank, A. G. and Gills, B. K., *The World System: Five Hundred Years or Five Thousand?* (London: Routledge, 1992).

Hawking, S., *A Brief History of Time* (London: Bantam Books, 1988).

Hegel, G. W. F., *The Philosophy of History*, trans. J. Sibree (New York: Dover, 1956).

Herder, J. G., 'Yet Another Philosophy of History', in *Against Pure Reason: Writings on Religion, Language and History*, trans. and ed. M. Bunge (Minneapolis, MN: Augsburg Fortress, 1993).

Herodotus, *The Histories*, trans. A. D. Godley, Loeb Classical Library (London: Heinemann, 1966).

Hodgson, M., *The Venture of Islam*, 3 vols (Chicago, IL: University of Chicago Press, 1975–77).

Hodgson, M., *Rethinking World History: Essays on Europe, Islam and World History*, ed. Edmund Burke III (Cambridge: Cambridge University Press, 1993).

Hughes-Warrington, M., 'Big History', *Historically Speaking* 4(2) (2002) 16–17, 20.

Ibn Khaldun, *The Muqaddimah*, trans. F. Rosenthal (Princeton, NJ: Princeton University Press, 1958).

Kant, I., 'Idea of a Universal History from a Cosmopolitan Point of View', in *On History*, trans. L. W. Beck (New York: Macmillan, 1963).

Machiavelli, N., *Discourses on Livy*, trans. H. C. Mansfield and N. Tarcov (Chicago, IL: University of Chicago Press, 1996).

Margulis, L. and Sagan, D., *Microcosmos: Four Billion Years of Microbial Evolution* (Berkeley, CA: University of California Press, 1986).

Marx, K., *Selected Writings*, ed. D. McLellan (Oxford: Oxford University Press, 1977).

McNeill, J., *Something New Under the Sun* (New York: W. W. Norton, 2000).

McNeill, W. H., *The Rise of the West: A History of the Human Community* (Chicago, IL: University of Chicago Press, 1963).

Northrup, D., 'When Does World History Begin? (And Why Should We Care?)', *History Compass*, online at <www.history-compass.com/Pilot/world/World_WhyArticle.htm>.

Orosius, Paulus, *Seven Books of History Against the Pagans*, trans. J. Deferrari (Washington, DC: Catholic University of America Press, 1964).

Otto, Bishop of Freysing, *The Two Cities: A Chronicle of Universal History to the Year 1146 AD*, trans. C. C. Mierow (New York: Octagon, 1966).

Pompa, L., *Vico: A Study of the 'New Science'* (Cambridge: Cambridge University Press, 1975).

Ponting, C., *A Green History of the World* (Harmondsworth: Penguin, 1993).

Popper, K., *The Poverty of Historicism*, rev. edn (London: Routledge, 1986).

Popper, K., *The Logic of Scientific Discovery: The Open Universe* (London: Routledge, 1988).

Roberts, J., *The Penguin History of the World* (Harmondsworth: Penguin, 1987).

Sima Qian. *Records of the Grand Historian: Han Dynasty II*, trans. B. Watson, rev. edn (New York: Columbia University Press, 1993).

Spengler, O., *The Decline of the West*, trans. C.F. Atkinson (New York: Alfred Knopf, 1926).

Spier, F., *The Structure of Big History* (Amsterdam: Amsterdam University Press, 1996).

Stearns, P. et al., *World Civilizations: The Global Experience* (New York: Pearson-Longman, 2004).

Toynbee, A., *A Study of History*, vol. 1 (London: Oxford University Press, 1934).

Vico, G., *The New Science*, trans. M. H. Fisch and T. G. Bergin, rev. edn (Ithaca, NY: Cornell University Press, 1984).

Voltaire, F. M. A., *The Philosophy of History*, trans. anon. (London: Vision, 1965).

von Ranke, Leopold, 'On the Character of Historical Science', in *The Theory and Practice of History*, ed. G. G. Iggers and K. Von Moltke (Indianapolis: Bobbs Merrill, 1973).

Wallerstein, I., *The Modern World System: Capitalist Agriculture and the Origins of European World-Economy in the Sixteenth Century* (New York: Academic Press, 1974).

Wells, H. G., *The Outline of History* (London: George Newnes, 1920).

6
shapes

marnie hughes-warrington

At the end of Johan Galtung and Sohail Inayatullah's edited work *Macrohistory and Macrohistorians* there is a fascinating collection of pictorial representations of various world historical theories.[1] Sima Qian's and Lovelock's theories are rendered by the creator of the appendix, Daniela Minerbi, as curvy; Hegel's, Comte's, Marx's and Gramsci's as step-like; Sorokin's as spiky, and Steiner's as a series of necklaces with dangling pendants. Though it was probably assumed by the editors that the diagrams would be viewed as ancillary to the text, the text need not be read in order to make sense of Minerbi's project. For though idiosyncratic and perhaps even mistaken – surely, for example, Vico's theory should look like a spiral – she has rendered in images what we take for granted in words: that world histories are narratives of differing shapes.

Writing world history – and indeed any form of history – entails countless decisions. This is because the past does not present itself in a form that is ready made for interpretation and telling. As we have seen, there is no necessary or absolute beginning, end or size to any event that happened in the past. Nor is there any one necessary or absolute way of describing it or ordering it. A fact only becomes an historical fact, Carr once argued, when it is deemed significant by selection, interpretation and ordering:

> The facts speak only when the historian calls on them: it is he who decides to which facts to give the floor, and in what order or context.[2]

For example, most world histories are presented in Western chronological order. But need they be? To Arnold Toynbee, the answer was yes. He wrote that the historian must:

adapt the mode of his thinking and of his experience to the movement, in the time stream, of the events that he is trying to convey... human affairs actually present themselves incessantly on the move. They cannot be described or analysed truly to life in any other mode.[3]

There are, however, non-chronological world histories and world histories that portray parts of the past synchronically, in cross-section, rather than sequentially: for example, Sima Qian's *Shiji* and John Wills' *1688: A Global History*. The dominance of chronological world histories is thus clearly a matter of cultural convention rather than logical necessity. But temporal order is not all there is to historical meaning. Even a series of historical events in chronological order, can be given different meanings and significance through emphasis. Take five events that appear in most world history textbooks, for example:

(a) Evolution of the hominids
(b) Origins of agriculture
(c) Emergence of states
(d) Global exploration and trade
(e) Western industrialization.

Now think about them as follows:

   A, b, c, d, e
   a, B, c, d, e
   a, b, C, d, e
   a, b, c, D, e
   a, b, c, d, E.

The use of capital letters here indicates the imputation of explanatory force to an event either because it is seen as a cause explaining the structure of the series or as a symbol 'of the plot structure of the series considered as a story of specific kind'.[4] Thus if an historian emphasizes A (Evolution of the hominids) it might be seen as shaping or even determining everything that follows. If an historian emphasizes E (Western industrialization), on the other hand, the preceding events might be presented in such a way as to suggest that they led to it. Emphasis might be apparent from the amount of space given to the discussion of an event or period or the favouring of particular kinds of evidence, as with, for instance, the disproportionate space given to the discussion of post-eighteenth-century economic developments in many world histories today. But emphasis might also be signalled through the repeated use of particular concepts, including spatial and temporal ones. Histories, Hayden White writes, are thus 'not only about events but also about the possible sets of relationships that those events can be demonstrated to figure'.[5]

In my example so far, I have employed a highly simplistic model of storytelling, in which 'narrative' is construed as a linear progression of logically connected events. This would be in keeping with the discussions on narrative that dominated Anglo-American historiography in the 1960s and 1970s.[6] Since that time, though, the 'linguistic turn' in historiography has fostered a greater appreciation of the complexity of narrative structure. In some works, for instance, intended emphases might clash with less intended ones, generating sub- and perhaps even contrary narratives. A good example is the UNESCO *History of Humankind*, which despite being advertised as a corrective to a Eurocentric view of world history promotes just that view through the use of, among other things, the BC/AD dating system, Western names for the continents and oceans and Western notions of the nation state.[7] Similarly, as will be argued in Chapter 9, world historians might have created spaces for women in their narratives, but the conceptual frameworks they fit them into are more often than not products of a masculinist ordering of the world.

Unfortunately, there is not much in recent historiographical scholarship that can help us to better understand the narrative shapes of world histories. Surveys of world histories tend to offer brief intellectual biographies and plot summaries of post-fifteenth- or even post-nineteenth-century works. More detailed analyses, like Paul Costello's *World Historians and their Goals*, are restricted to twentieth-century works.[8] This privileging of modern world histories reinforces a pervasive metanarrative of Western historiographical professionalization. Patrick Manning's *Navigating World History*, for instance, presents a modernization narrative in which historiographical legitimation is achieved by the field through the embrace of 'professional' concepts, methods and analytical frameworks.[9] Likewise, in *Shapes of World History in Twentieth-Century Scholarship*, Jerry Bentley celebrates the appearance of a 'more analytical and professional world history' and in 'The Changing Shape of World History', W. H. McNeill has taken the emergence of professional organizations such as the World History Association as evidence of the liveliness of the field.[10] The persistent hold of this metanarrative has meant that pre-nineteenth-century works tend to be treated in terms of their relation with present day world historical research and writing. Judgements of works as 'lacking' or as 'embryonic' prevail and serve to shore up a comfortable view of twentieth-century historiographical evolution and even 'efflorescence'.[11]

At work here is what Herbert Butterfield would call historiographical 'Whiggism', or Georges Canguilhem 'the virus of the precursor'. As they and Gaston Bachelard and Michel Foucault have argued, we ought not assume that history is continuous or evolutionary.[12]

Historians do not expect to find much worthy of study beyond a narrow canon of pre-nineteenth-century philosophies of history and universal histories. Combine this with the general neglect of world history narratology and the result is that the impression of the field as providing only one kind of story – a linear, speculative, triumphalist account of the 'rise of the West' – goes relatively unchallenged. This view is captured well by Raymond Grew, who writes that in popular tradition:

> World history provides the framework for a continuous narrative, one that starts with the pulse of civilisation beating to the rhythm of riparian agriculture along the Tigris and Euphrates, then moves through the classical world and across two millennia until Europe's power and influence extend across the globe. The civilisations not on this direct line, however much admired, are presented initially as separate stories but differ most from the main narrative in always coming to an end, each giving way to the next until all become part of the world the West has won.[13]

World histories are also cast as sites not of historical information but of redirection; they are narratives that provide no satisfaction in themselves but only as introductions to other, more specialized, that is, small-scale narratives. Historians only write world histories on the way to specialized narratives, or when their reputation is sufficient that they have nothing to lose.

in search of narratology

If all of these assumptions about world histories were true, then there would be little need for this chapter. As historians, though, we should not settle for assumptions, and must look instead for guidance from historiographical research on narratives. F. R. Ankersmit, Lionel Gossman, Stephen Bann, Robert Berkhofer, Dominick La Capra, Hans Kellner, Nancy Partner, Linda Orr and Paul Ricoeur have all analysed rhetorical strategies in history, but Hayden White's writings are regarded as seminal. White has argued that historians bestow meaning upon the past through the use of figurative language:

All historical narratives presuppose figurative characterisations of the events they purport to represent and explain. And this means that historical narratives, considered purely as verbal artefacts, can be characterised by the mode of figurative discourse in which they are cast... [History] is made sense of in the same way that the poet or novelist tries to make sense of it, ie. by endowing what originally appears to be problematical and mysterious with the aspect of a recognisable... form. It does not matter whether the world is conceived to be real or only imagined; the matter of making sense of it is the same.[14]

White's final claim is, as we shall see in Chapter 8, hotly disputed. But his accounts of the figurative forms of histories – particularly in *Metahistory* – warrants further investigation here. In *Metahistory*, White suggests that historical narratives are constructed out of 'argument modes' (formism, organicism, mechanism, contextualism), 'emplotment modes' (romance, comedy, tragedy, satire), 'ideological modes' (anarchism, conservatism, radicalism, liberalism) and 'tropes' (metaphor, metonymy, synecdoche, irony). By a 'formist' argument, White means the works of historians who, like antiquarian collectors, aim to identify and depict the uniqueness and vividness of ideas and events in their chosen field of study in a precise and detailed way. Contextualists, on the other hand, believe that ideas and events are best understood in context, leading to a view of history as a succession of discrete periods, trends or movements. Organicist historians are even more integrative, considering different trends, periods or movements as reflecting or expressive of a single macrohistorical process, such as development, modernization or the realization of an ideal like freedom (as in the writing of Hegel). Finally mechanist historians search for laws 'by which the events in the historical field can be reduced to the status of manifestations of impersonal causal agencies'.[15] Emplotment refers to the process of bestowing a plot or story type. Historians, White argues, tend to emplot the past in four main modes. In romance, individuals, groups or even all of humanity achieve release from or transcendence of the situations they find themselves in. Satire is the opposite of romance, conveying the message that individuals or groups are ultimately captive in some way. In comedy, hope is held out for release or transcendence and setbacks are seen as ultimately beneficial; and in tragedy, setbacks are accepted with resignation.[16] Ideology colours histories too, with historians imputing their beliefs about the desirability and pace of social change and temporal location of a utopian ideal. Conservatives are the most suspicious of change to the status quo, writing history as the progressive realisation of the social and political structure that prevails in their time. Anarchists, by contrast, are the most socially transcendent, writing about the past in the hope for a better future, while liberals and radicals are located more towards the centre of White's ideological spectrum.[17]

While any combination of the modes described so far may be used, White claims that particular stylistic constellations operate and have been (consciously or unconsciously) favoured by historians at different times. So for example on the basis of his study of the writings of the nineteenth century historians Hegel, Michelet, Ranke, Tocqueville, Burkhardt, Marx, Nietzsche and Croce, he has identified the following correlations:

Emplotment	Explanation	Ideology
Romance	Formist	Anarchist
Comedy	Organicist	Conservative
Tragedy	Mechanistic	Radical
Satire	Contextualist	Liberal

These correlations, he further argues, are shaped by four tropes or conventions of figurative, linguistic representation: metaphor, metonymy, synecdoche and irony. In metaphor, a descriptive name is transferred to another object; for example, 'humanity is a parasite'. In metonymy, part of the past is substituted for a larger part or the whole: for example, the use of 'industrialization' as equivalent to 'modernization'. In synecdoche, an attribute is used to describe a quality thought to belong to the totality: for example that all history is the history of freedom (Hegel) or of class struggle (Marx). And in irony, the intended meaning is the opposite of the language used to describe it: for example, when I declare 'humanity is *so* civilized', I can either mean it or mean its opposite.

White's theory of historical narratives is not meant to be exhaustive. He is careful to note, for instance, that the sixteen rhetorical conventions identified by him are not the only ones available. His modes are, like the three forms of time identified by Braudel, points of activity on a spectrum.[18] Nor does his work extend to the analysis of subnarratives, despite how influential they can be in the determination of meaning. To these limitations we can add other criticisms. Mark Salber Phillips, for example, has argued that White's account of nineteenth-century historical writing in *Metahistory* is undermined by his use of twentieth-century rhetorical modes.[19] W. H. Walsh was right to argue that historians are entitled to employ anachronistic concepts – for example 'revolution' or 'renaissance' – to facilitate an understanding of a constellation of events, but on what grounds do they do so? Similarly, on what grounds do they decide that differences among phenomena – including narratives – are such that they cannot be grouped under a single mode?[20] Is what White calls the 'historical imagination' responsible for the formation of historical narratives and historiographical metanarratives? If so, does rhetorical convention determine historical meaning entirely? Is White's 'historical imagination', like Derrida's 'imagination', a hall of mirrors from which we cannot escape?[21] This is again an issue that will be further considered in Chapter 8. Other commentators have been unsure as to the mental and social status of tropes: do they operate unconsciously or consciously? Additionally, they have questioned whether the different tropes can be clearly distinguished from one another, how tropes relate to the other modes and whether irony is a 'super-trope', shaping the others or even undercutting them.[22] Finally, it has been noted that White's study of historical writings focuses almost entirely on philosophical works by male writers and neglects more 'literary', 'sentimental' and even 'mundane' works.[23]

This last criticism is important, for it throws into doubt a twofold conclusion that might be made about world histories on the basis of *Metahistory* and the 'rise of the professional West' metanarrative of historians of world histories described above. To White's view, since the nineteenth century, formist and contextualist arguments have been favoured over synecdochical and organicist or mechanistic ones, these two being appraised as digressions from academic history into the pejoratively named 'speculative philosophy of history'.[24] Combine this conclusion with current histories of world histories, and it is hard to avoid the conclusions that first, pre-twentieth-century world history writing was characterized by organicist and mechanistic modes of argument and second, that professionalization entailed a shift away from these modes. If White, Bentley, Manning, Costello and McNeill had selected different world historical narratives for their surveys, however, would this twofold conclusion still hold?

world history narratives

It would not be possible to offer an all-encompassing account of world historical narratives in the space of this chapter. I have therefore opted to present eight examples, the rationale for which I will explain after they have been examined: Herodotus' *Histories* (c. 431–404 BCE), Diodorus of Sicily's *The Library of History* (60–30 BCE), Sima Qian's *Shiji* (104–97 BCE), Ibn Khaldun's *Kitab al-'Ibar* (c.1375–1406), Christine de Pizan's *The Book of the City of Ladies* (1405), John Millar's *Origin of the Distinction of Ranks*

(1777), Lydia Maria Child's *History of the Condition of Women in Various Ages and Nations* (1835) and Mike Davis' *Late Victorian Holocausts: El Niño Famines and the Making of the Third World* (2001).

Herodotus is commonly described as the 'father of history' and among world historians, he is also credited for having discovered 'history as a method for understanding the world as a whole'.[25] His *Histories* describes the rise and expansion of the Persian Empire and its defeat by the Greek city states in 490 and 480 BCE. But it also includes over 200 digressions, ranging from single lines to 28 *logoi* or detailed ethnographic expositions. So while one part of the text diachronically relates contemporary history and is tied together chronologically and sometimes even causally, the other synchronically relates contexts and customary activities. Until the mid twentieth century, commentators assumed that the *logoi* were part of a separate work conceived by Herodotus at a different time and with different aims in mind. More recently, writers such as Lattimore, Immerwahr, Lateiner and Munson have stressed the overall unity of the work.[26] They have argued that Herodotus employed *logoi* rhetorically as part of a narrative technique called anaphoric ring composition: he would start with a diachronic account, digress to a synchronic exposition and then alert his readers that he was returning to the diachronic account. This structure clearly underpins books two and three, where the recording of Cambyses' intention to invade Egypt is followed by a digression into the geography and ethnology of Egypt and then returns to relate the details of Cambyses' invasion. To what end the technique was used is a matter of dispute: Lateiner, for example, has argued that

> Ethnographic information in the *Histories* is neither shapeless nor only there to charm; rather it is documentation deployed to assert an historical thesis, namely that mankind has benefited from ethnic and political separation and self-determination.[27]

This assessment bestows too much unity on the text, for the *logoi* suggest multiple themes. Lateiner's assessment, for instance, ignores Herodotus' use of *logoi* to establish a connection between gender and world order. It is thus perhaps best to stick with a more general conclusion, that the *logoi* were used to introduce, expand and refine the auditor's or reader's understanding of concepts that underpin the Persian narrative.

Looking below the level of the whole narrative, and thus beyond the limits of White's theories, we can discern other rhetorical techniques and experiments of note. While the whole narrative is marked by cycles, on the level of sentence structure, Herodotus frequently employed parataxis:

simple linear connectives. Further, Fehling has advanced the controversial thesis that many of Herodotus' source citations – for example, 'the Greeks say' – should be regarded not as connections to evidence but as rhetorical devices that follow fixed patterns.[28] There is much more to the *Histories*, therefore, than a single mode of argument, emplotment or even ideology can capture.

As with Herodotus' *Histories*, Diodorus of Sicily's 40-volume *Library of History* moves from year to year in a predominantly chronological fashion. The more ambitious scope of his project, though – to provide a unified 'account of all the events which have been handed down to memory and took place in the known regions of the inhabited world' – required a different narrative arrangement to that of Herodotus.[29] In Diodorus' writing, the notions of an unbroken narrative thread and weaving a story are important.[30] But to achieve that cohesion, careful organization was needed:

> We could censure the art of history because in life many actions happen at the same time, but those that must record them must interrupt the narrative and parcel out different times to simultaneous events, contrary to nature, with the result that the written record mimics the events, but lacks the true arrangement.[31]

Diodorus' first solution to the problem of organization was to write a synchronic history for each year of the period from the Trojan War to 60 BCE, moving in turn through events which took place in Greece, Sicily, Africa and Italy. So, for example, in his account of the events for the year 314 BCE, he first outlines the manoeuvres of Antigonus and Cassander in Greece, moves on to document the conflict between Agathocles and the Sicilian city of Acragas and then gives an update on the Samnite war in Italy.[32] His second solution was to apply the principles of 'brevity', 'due proportion' and the 'measurement' and 'demarcation' of times. This led him to curtail geographical and ethnographic digressions of the sort used by Herodotus to great effect and to return relentlessly to his temporal thread.[33] Finally, he held the work together by the use of cross-references, the measured use of *oratio obliqua* (created or embellished speeches) and prooemia (introductory prologues) in which he foreshadowed the key moral, didactic and historiographical issues of each book.[34]

Diodorus' narrative arrangement has been thoroughly criticized, with Oldfather complaining, for instance, that it made it impossible for him to 'write either a readable story or an accurate history'.[35] Such complaints, however, fail to give Diodorus due recognition for an ingenious experiment with narrative conventions designed to solve the problems brought on by an expanded definition of history's object of study. Where once it had been sufficient to pursue a more or less narrow narrative of action in Greece, history now needed to comprehend a whole range of experiences outside. As a result, Greek events – once the whole frame of historiography – now figured as one thread in a multiplicity of woven plots. Overall, the *Library* promotes a moderately critical assessment of Imperial Rome, but the fragmentary nature of the sections of the book dealing with it make it impossible to state with any confidence that Rome is the unifying thread of the work.[36] Thus while the work is universal in scope, we cannot be sure that a unified, organicist, narrative was part of it. The extant work is more suggestive of formist argument. As it is, we cannot conclude with any certainty what rhetorical modes operated in the work.

Whereas Diodorus' work emphasizes what Jaroslav Prusek calls the *ununterbrochener Fluss* (unbroken flow) of a chronological narrative, the Han historian Sima Qian's *Shiji* emphasizes *Treppenabsatz* (segmented progress) in its narrative. As Prusek argues:

> The Chinese historian does not work up his sources into a chronological flow, he does not combine the facts he has found in successive chains, he does not fictionalise them, but he arranges them in certain categories.[37]

Like Diodorus, when Sima Qian set out to write a history of his world, he found the traditional historical narratives – collections of speeches, chronicles and anecdotes arranged by place – inadequate. As I suggested in Chapter 1, in response, he devised a synchronic structure for his history, divided into basic annals, chronological tables, treatises, hereditary houses, and categorized biographies. The structure of the *Shiji* is not well known to English-language readers, as most studies of it focus on the author and his context or textual provenance and the English translation offers a rearrangement of his claims into linear, chronological order. So for example, in their study of Sima Qian as a 'macrohistorian', Chang Xie and Sohail Inayatullah say nothing of the structure of his work and assume that the narrative takes the shape of a curvy chronological line, writing that 'the two thousand years covered... [move] with a ceaseless rhythm of rising and falling political fortunes'.[38] As Grant Hardy has shown us, though, such a tidy reckoning of the *Shiji* is not possible.[39]

The *Shiji* opens with 'basic annals', in which he offers an increasingly detailed chronology – dated by regnal years – of the major events from the legendary Five Emperors to the reign of Emperor Wu in his own times. In 'Chronological Tables' he again covers the same period, but he presents his information in the form of nine tables. All of the tables consist of a grid with time (of varying duration) along one axis. The other axis is put to more varied use, divided into segments showing the family connections of emperors, major events in each of the different states and then kingdoms, individuals enfeoffed, chancellors, generals and censors. Many of the intersecting spaces on the grid are filled with brief notations. Hardy has also noted that upside down print was used in the final table to denote deaths and dismissals.[40] Section three, the 'treatises' constitutes eight historical and technical essays on a wide range of topics from ceremonies to hydrography. In section four, 'hereditary houses', Sima Qian returns again to a chronological account of Chinese history to his own day, but the focus is on events in the families of feudal lords. Accounts of particular events are presented more than once to indicate family overlaps and the influence of an event elsewhere: for example, the assassination of Duke Yin of Lu in 712 BCE is mentioned seven times. Finally in section five, 'categorized biographies', Sima Qian offers a part-chronological and part-thematic collection of biographies that vary in length, detail and in the degree of quotation use. So for example, chapters 86–120 include a roughly chronological account of notable individuals and groups in the Han dynasty, barbarian peoples and their leaders and 'assassin retainers, compassionate officials, Confucian scholars, cruel officers, local bosses, imperial catamites, jesters, diviners and businessmen'.[41] Now if the five sections were not complex enough, Sima Qian also uses smaller-scale rhetorical strategies, such as copying from earlier sources, flashbacks, summaries, dialogue and evaluative comments embedded in dialogue and descriptions of actions to enhance either the explanatory clarity or aesthetic effect of his narrative.[42]

Little wonder then that there are so few close studies of even major parts of the work. And it is little wonder too given the inconsistency of his comments and even accounts of particular events across the five sections.[43] The *Shiji* is not a world history by organicist or mechanistic argument. It is, like the extant copy of Diodorus' *Library*, a formist work, but is far less cohesive. Further, it shows no trace of a unified mode of emplotment or even ideology. If Diodorus was a weaver of history, Sima Qian was a tangler, the creator of a metonymic microcosm or a model of the world that as Hardy puts it 'intentionally replicates, though to a lesser degree, the confusing inconsistencies, the lack of interpretative closure, and the bewildering details of raw historical data'.[44]

Issues of cultural translation also affect understandings of the world historical narrative of Ibn Khaldun. Ibn Khaldun's *Muqaddimah* (*Introduction to History*) is commonly separated from the *Kitab al-'Ibar* (*Universal History*) of which it was originally a part.[45] The former is judged to be a fine example of a philosophy of history, whereas the latter is regarded as a more mundane collection of historical information. Consequently, the majority of the *Kitab al-'Ibar* has been ignored by translators and historiographers. Recently, however, Abdesselam Cheddadi has demonstrated through his translation of parts of the *Kitab al-'Ibar* (with the *Muqaddimah* reincorporated) that the work possesses narrative unity.[46] To Cheddadi's view, the aim of the *Muqaddimah* is *ta'rikh*. *Ta'rikh* means literally 'the assignment of a date, the process of dating'.[47] Early contributions to the genre of *ta'rikh* were chronologies and annals. By the time Ibn Khaldun wrote, however, predecessors such as al-Tabari and al-Mas'udi had expanded the genre so that it came to refer to chronological, encyclopaedic accounts of the known or meaningful world. Ibn Khaldun, in turn, modified the genre again, loosening the prevailing *isnad* method – replicating information handed down through an unbroken chain of transmitters – and basing his study on the unit of *umma* or nations.

Book one of the *Kitab al-'Ibar* (the *Muqaddimah*) is encyclopaedic in scope and style. It opens with an account of the physical environment and its influence on the activities of people. This is followed by a lengthy account of the factors that explain the various states of nations, in particular, two types of social forms: *'umran badawi* (rural, Bedouin or nomadic life) and *'umran hadari* (urban, sedentary life). To his view, the mainspring of the change from *'umran badawi* to *'umran hadari* and the ultimate decline of the latter is the disappearance of *'asabiya* or 'group feeling'. The book concludes with a thematic survey of the commercial, philosophical, scientific and artistic activities of urban nations at their peak. In this way, Ibn Khaldun establishes the framework for the information in the remainder of his work: a history of the nations of the Maghrib, the belt of territory from Tripolitania and Southern Tunisia to the Sous of southern Morocco, from the eleventh to the fourteenth century.

To Ibn Khaldun's contemporaries, the *Kitab al-'Ibar* was a work of high literary quality and was judged to be 'more brilliant than well-strung pearls and finer than water fanned by the zephyr'.[48] Rhetorically, the work is characterised by long, involved sentences, a redundancy of expression designed to help readers understand the large range of terms used and the frequent use of threefold *parallelismus membrorum*, or groups of three sentences of parallel construction that present antitheses or complementary extensions to an idea. These features, as Rosenthal has noted, are difficult to translate into readable English.[49] Additionally, a reader's impression of Ibn Khaldun's narrative varies according to whether they consider the *Muqaddimah* on its own or as part of the *Kitab al-'Ibar*. On its own, the *Muqaddimah* resembles an organicist or even mechanistic philosophy of history, with the linear argument of a work like Hegel's *Philosophy of History*. Reunite it with the *Kitab al-'Ibar*, however, and the shape of the narrative changes, for the philosophical framework is set up only to be diffused in the parallel narratives of the nations of the Maghrib. Overall, the work is still organicist or mechanistic, but such descriptions hardly do justice to the parts of the whole, which we know are beyond the explanatory reach of White's scheme.

Roughly contemporary with Ibn Khaldun's *Kitab al-'Ibar* is Christine de Pizan's *The Book of the City of Ladies* (*Livre de la Cité des Dames*), a reworking of the conceptual and structural norms of earlier universal and biographical catalogue writings by male authors. The *City* in de Pizan's title, for instance, is evocative of Augustine's *City of God*, and both texts are united in their interest in the deeds of people 'who deserved to reign with God'.[50] Like Augustine's work, de Pizan's *City* is structured according to a hierarchy of virtue that sees saintly women ranked above good wives and female warriors. In distinction from Augustine, though, de Pizan stresses woman's common humanity with man in spiritual and mental terms and ability to be man's companion in society.[51] Furthermore, de Pizan does not act as a detached narrator who recounts exempla for her readers' edification. Rather, through the use of the narrative frame of a dream vision, she places herself in her history and shows her readers that they, like her, can emulate the deeds of virtuous ladies. As Brown-Grant has argued, de Pizan's 'readers can choose to copy her lead and so "write" themselves, metaphorically, into the *Cité* [*City*]'.[52]

When discussing the role of men in the history of civilization, de Pizan looks to contemporary events and echoes the late medieval view of society's decline and decadence.[53] When discussing the contributions of women, however, she looks to events over the long term and observes progress. Women are credited with the invention of the letters of the alphabet, arms and agriculture and the development of cities and education. They are also expected to make valuable contributions to society in future – mostly through their companionship with men. Men, on the other hand, are portrayed as increasingly willing to slander women and as connected with the decadent institutions of the Church and State. De Pizan's work is thus characterised by two gender narratives of differing time scales and modes of emplotment (male: organicist-tragedy-anarchist; and female: organicist-romance-anarchist). White's theory, we recall, does not encompass twofold narratives, nor does it accommodate the role of gender in the shaping of rhetoric. Again, therefore, we see a rhetorical construction too complex for White's model.

Conventional historiography, with its almost exclusive attention to the activities of men, was of little help in supplying the evidence and even the narrative structure needed by de Pizan in *City*. John Millar too, found little that could help him to assemble and present his investigation into the 'obvious and common improvements which gradually arise in the state of society' in *Origin of the Distinction of Ranks* (1771).[54] He writes:

> With regard to the facts made use of in the following discourse, the reader, who is conversant in history, will readily perceive the difficulty of obtaining proper materials for speculations of this nature. Historians of reputation have commonly overlooked the transactions of early ages, as not deserving to be remembered; and even in the history of later and more cultivated periods, they have been more solicitous to give an exact account of battles, and public negotiations, than of the interior police and government of a country.[55]

To complete his conjectural, comparative study of 'interior police and government', Millar had to look to travel literature, ethnography, antiquities, laws and poetry. These sources influenced the organization of his book. From legal and ethnographic scholarship and the writings of Hume and Kames, for instance, he adopted the notion that peoples' rights emerged historically in the context of families.[56] His study is thus arranged in the order he perceived to be the natural history of society, a history constituted by the cumulative development of larger and more civilized forms of community. *Origins* begins with a discussion on the relations within families, which includes an extended examination of 'the rank and condition of women in different ages' and the powers of fathers over children. Millar's interest in women is as a barometer of civilization, for in his view the shift to a polished civilization is characterized by the transformation in their treatment from slaves and sexual idols to friends and companions in the private sphere of the home. He then extends his examination beyond the private sphere, offering a comparative account of the relationships of power and subordination in tribes and states with sovereigns. Moving on, Millar considers the influence of the arts and polished manners on government in contemporary Europe before concluding with a consideration of the authority of a master over his servants. Millar's work is organicist and progressive, and thus might be aligned with Hegel's *Philosophy of History*. We must be wary of concluding that they are alike in narrative form, however, for while Hegel offers a linear, chronological history in which the torch of freedom is passed from civilization to civilization, Millar's narrative is characterized by the near-circular movement from private sphere to public sphere and back again. Additionally, Millar subordinates chronology to his social evolutionary framework: he thought it appropriate, for instance, to connect information on contemporary Africa with that on the ancient history of Europe.

The subordination of time to place is even more marked in Lydia Maria Child's *History of the Condition of Women, in Various Ages and Nations* (1835). Although Child formulated her categories of analysis on the basis of works like Millar's and William Alexander's *The History of Women, From the Earliest Antiquity, to the Present Time* (1779), she expanded their coverage by looking to travel literature for more information on non-Western societies. Furthermore, as her chapter headings clearly suggest, her narrative was organized by space rather than time: for example, 'Asia', 'Europe', 'America', and the 'South Sea Islands'. This allowed Child to examine the place and treatment of women within specific cultures.

Reflecting contemporary stereotypes and lacunae in evidence, Child's work diachronically relates European history and synchronically relates contemporary contexts and customary activities in non-European locations. For instance, in the section on Africa, present-tense ethnography is substituted for history:

> The African women separate the seeds from cotton by rolling it with a thick iron spindle... The Kaffer women make baskets of a strong reedy grass, the workmanship of which is so clever that they will contain water... The African women are so passionately fond of dancing, that wherever the itinerant minstrels appear, they flock around them, and encourage them by songs, while they beat time by clapping their hands.[57]

Unlike many of her peers, though, Child did not assume a unified African culture and stressed regional differences in physical appearance, activities and artefacts. Child accommodated African variations because in the *History* she steadfastly refused to deduce organicist or mechanistic theories from the facts she assembled. The 1835 edition lacks even an introduction or preface. This was noted by Sarah Josepha Hale, who in her review of the work complained that 'from her we did anticipate somewhat more of the philosophy of history.... . In the few general remarks she has ventured, there is so much good sense, that we only regret in these volumes she should have transcribed so much, and written so little'.[58] The preface Child added to the 1845 edition, confirmed that she saw it as a formist rather than an organicist work:

> This volume is not an essay upon women's rights, or a philosophical investigation of what is or what ought to be the relation of the sexes. If any theories on this subject are contained in it, they are merely incidentally implied by the manner of stating historical facts. I have simply endeavoured to give an accurate history of the condition of women, in language sufficiently concise for popular use.[59]

Many of Child's other writings are concerned with liberation from slavery, and it is true that her interest in that cause influenced her choice and presentation of materials in *The History*. As a theme, however, it does not loom large enough to warrant being called a narrative thread. The strongest single message of the *History*, then, as Child suggests, is that there is no single essentialist narrative that can be used to celebrate or confine women.

Finally, we come to Mike Davis' *Late Victorian Holocausts: El Niño Famines and the Making of the Third World* (2001). Between 30 and 50 million people died worldwide after droughts in 1876–79, 1888–91 and 1896–1902. That death toll, Davis claims in *Late Victorian Holocausts*, was as high as it was in part because of the 'conscription' of colonies into a British-centred world economy during El Niño episodes.[60] Putting climate and empire together, Davis concludes that El Niño entered into 'sinister partnership' with a world market founded on the principles of Smith, Bentham and Mill.

Organizationally, Davis' work consists of multiple, intertwined narratives. It opens with an account of former US President Ulysses S. Grant's social and gastronomic tour around the world in 1877, which seemed by coincidence to follow the trail of a 'monster' that left in its wake severe drought in Egypt, India and China.[61] Held in microcosm in this narrative is the 'fatal meshing' of empire and capitalism and the extreme weather of El Niño episodes that drives Davis' impassioned critique of the rise of Western capitalism.[62] In support of his thesis, Davis shifts from micronarrative to the parallel histories of the Sertão in Northeastern Brazil, the Deccan in India and the Northern Chinese provinces of Shandong, Henan and Shanxi. These are written at the scale of what Davis, with a nod to Braudel and Labrousse, calls *'conjuncture'*: history that examines medium-term economic trends such as recessions. In part three, he recounts the emergence of scientific theories about what came to be called the El Niño Southern Oscillation, before drawing science and history together in a final section that traces the longer-term emergence of a world marked by the inequality of nations.

Ever present in the work is El Niño, not only a climatic phenomenon, but also a powerful rhetorical site for metaphor, gendered language and moral judgements. Traditionally, the concept of El Niño has been used to describe the periodic warming of the waters off the coast of Ecuador and Peru which brings years of plenty to some and deprivation to others. To Davis, as for other contemporary El Niño historians though, the phenomenon is gendered masculine and connected solely with destruction. But in a departure from his contemporaries, Davis portrays it as a henchman for the capitalist West that leaves its 'messy fingerprints' over sites of human misfortune.[63] El Niño serves to subjugate the 'rest' to the West, but it also serves as the medium through which Davis condemns the West.

On White's model, Davis' work is clearly organicist and metaphorical, for his evidence points towards a macrohistorical process: the emergence of a 'developing', 'developed' world divide. Yet no commentators have identified Davis' work as a speculative philosophy of history, and they would be unlikely to do so. To White, all histories are philosophies of history because they are fashioned out of presuppositions. But as he has also noted, philosophies of history differ in degree of emphasis: philosophers of history like Hegel work to illuminate, question or defend the presuppositions that remain implicit in the works of historians like Davis.[64] The difference in emphasis between Hegel's and Davis' works is significant, but emphasis is not recognized in White's typology. Furthermore, Davis' work does not deliver the comic mode of emplotment or conservative ideology correlated by White to the organicist mode of argument. The work is, rather, satirical and anarchist, stressing the entrapment of many nations in a world capitalist economy of which Davis does not clearly approve. Finally, White's theory offers us nothing to account for Davis' gendering of weather.

getting the story of world history 'crooked'

Having now looked to the world historical narratives of Herodotus, Diodorus, Sima Qian, Ibn Khaldun, Christine de Pizan, John Millar, Lydia Maria Child and Mike Davis, it is time to offer a rationale for my selection. To begin, I would like to admit that I chose eight world historical narratives for no other reason than that is the same number of case studies in White's *Metahistory*. Further, I decided that a very different collection of examples to that of White was needed to test the twofold assumption that first, pre-twentieth-century world history writing was characterized by organicist and mechanistic modes of argument and second, that professionalization entailed a shift away from these modes. White's selection – Hegel, Michelet, Ranke, Tocqueville, Burkhardt, Marx, Nietzsche and Croce – is all male, all Western European and all nineteenth century. Furthermore, there would be little disagreement that the writers chosen all made a significant contribution to nineteenth-century historiography. I, on the contrary, opted to look at male and female writers from a broader temporal sweep and a broader range of cultural contexts. Furthermore, I deliberately selected some 'literary' and even 'mundane' world histories that are generally passed over in silence in surveys. For example, my only nineteenth-century selection – Child – is generally ignored in surveys of academic writing on the grounds that her work better fits the gendered diminutive of travel writing.

Eight is a small enough number of examples to illuminate both White's and my use of selective judgement, and more importantly for this chapter, a large enough number to illuminate the rhetorical shape of our efforts. White's examples support his organicist and perhaps even mechanistic argument about nineteenth-century historical narratives. It is an argument which sees – through the examples of Hegel and Marx – world history writing associated with organicist and mechanistic modes of argument. It is an argument that thus does not challenge the common historiographical assumption that prior to the twentieth century, world history writing was dominated and even limited by 'speculative' philosophies of history. Furthermore, White's selection of the nineteenth century affirms the common perception of that century as a time of historiographical significance. My examples, I believe, suggest a more formist argument: that there are a greater variety of approaches to the writing of world history prior to the nineteenth century than current scholarship acknowledges. Additionally, I identified a twentieth century organicist world history that few commentators would label a speculative philosophy of history. Moreover, I stressed the role of each of the surveyed writers as rhetorical innovators, indicating the solutions they proposed to a widened scope of inquiry or body of evidence or even a lack of documented 'historical evidence'. Finally, my narrative highlights rhetorical features that White's account ignores, particularly the limitations of evidence for making judgements about ancient works, the intersection of narrative and gender, the explicitness of philosophical presuppositions and the parts of a world historical narrative.

If we open up the range of historiographical evidence beyond the temporal and scholastic parameters usually settled for, it becomes apparent that there was more to world history writing than organicist and mechanistic modes of argument prior to the twentieth century. World historians adopted formist and contextualist modes of argument too. More importantly, though, they called upon and even invented a range of rhetorical devices that White's theory does not cover adequately. These devices are significant, for they are evidence of the active way in which writers fashioned their visions of the world. Knowledge of these innovations is also valuable, for it may lead us to revisit the common assumption that the twentieth century saw an efflorescence of world history writing.

In *Language and Historical Representation*, Hans Kellner argues that historians should try to 'get the story crooked'. 'Getting the story straight' presupposes that 'there *is* a "story" out there waiting to be told' and that it can 'be told straight by an honest, industrious historian using the right methods'. In getting the story crooked, on the other hand, historians 'foreground the constructed, rhetorical, nature of our knowledge of the past'. That is, they work to make the rhetorical decisions they make more apparent.[65] Kellner's argument applies to the authors of world histories, encouraging them to make it clear to their readers that they are not colourless ciphers but the fashioners of worlds that are shaped by, among other things, philosophical presuppositions, rhetorical necessity and fashion, power relations, culture and gender. The shaping influence of these factors will be examined in the next four chapters.

But Kellner's argument might also be applied to the writers of the history of world histories. Up to now, that history has been treated as a straight modernization story that ends on the high note of twentieth-century professionalization. I hope that some of the examples included in this chapter raise doubts about that story, showing us, first, that we might have given pre-twentieth-century world histories short shrift and second, that definitive organicist and mechanistic arguments are still present today. My collection of examples, though, is by no means exhaustive, and we will not get the measure of the influence of rhetorical fashion, philosophical presuppositions, power relations, culture and gender upon the narrative of world histories history until we know more of the history of the field of world history. That history is worth knowing and worth debating and getting crooked, I believe, because it might lead us to reflect on, appreciate and even challenge the presuppositions that shape current world history narratives.

notes

1. J. Galtung and S. Inayatullah (eds), *Macrohistory and Macrohistorians* (Westport, CT: Praeger, 1997), pp. 249–59.
2. E. H. Carr, *What is History?*, ed. R. W. Davies, rev. edn (Harmondsworth: Penguin, 1986), p. 11.
3. A. Toynbee, 'Narrative History: The Narrator's Problems', *Clio*, 4 (1975) 299–300.
4. Example adapted from H. White, *Tropics of Discourse: Essays in Cultural Criticism* (Baltimore, MD: Johns Hopkins University Press, 1978), pp. 93–4; quote at p. 94.
5. Ibid., p. 94. For a range of views on periodization in world history, see R. E. Dunn (ed.), *The New World History: A Teacher's Companion* (New York: Bedford/St. Martin's, 2000).
6. See for example A. Danto, *Analytical Philosophy of History* (Cambridge: Cambridge University Press, 1965); W. B. Gallie, *Philosophy and the Historical Understanding* (New York: Chatto & Windus, 1964); and M. White, *Foundations of Historical Knowledge* (New York: Harper, 1965).
7. See for example Georges-Henri Dumont's description of the UNESCO *History of Humanity* project at <www.unesco.org/culture/humanity/html_eng/projet. htm>.
8. P. Costello, *World Historians and their Goals: Twentieth Century Answers to Modernism* (De Kalb, IL: Northern Illinois University Press, 1994).
9. See for example P. Manning, *Navigating World History: Historians Create a Global Past* (New York: Palgrave Macmillan/St. Martin's Press, 2003).
10. J. H. Bentley, *Shapes of World History in Twentieth-Century Scholarship* (Washington, DC: American Historical Association, 1996), p. 2; and W. H. McNeill, 'The Changing Shape of World History', *History and Theory*, 34(2) (1995) 13–14.
11. A term favoured by world historians at present to describe the emergence of Europe, and earlier, Asian economies.
12. H. Butterfield, *The Whig Interpretation of History* (London: Bell, 1931); G. Canguilhem, *Ideology and Rationality*, trans. A. Goldhammer (Cambridge, MA: MIT Press, 1988); G. Bachelard, *The New Scientific Spirit*, trans. A. Goldhammer (Boston, MA: Beacon, 1984); and M. Foucault, *The Order of Things: An Archaeology of the Human Sciences*, trans. anon (New York: Vintage, 1973).
13. R. Grew, 'Review of *World Historians and Their Goals: Twentieth-Century Answers to Modernism*', *History and Theory*, 34(4) (1995) 371.
14. White, *Tropics of Discourse*, pp. 94–8.
15. Ibid., p. 66; see also H. White, *Metahistory: The Historical Imagination in Nineteenth-Century Europe* (Baltimore, MD: Johns Hopkins University Press, 1973), pp. 14, 64.
16. Ibid., p. 9.
17. Ibid., p. 69.
18. F. Braudel, *On History* (Chicago, IL: University of Chicago Press, 1980).
19. M. S. Phillips, *Society and Sentiment: Genres of Historical Writing in Britain 1740–1820* (Princeton, NJ: Princeton University Press, 2000), p. 9.
20. W. H. Walsh, 'Colligatory Concepts in History', in P. Gardiner (ed.), *The Philosophy of History* (Oxford: Oxford University Press, 1974), pp. 139–40.

21. J. Derrida, 'The Double Session', in *Dissemination*, trans. B. Johnson (London: Athlone, 1981).
22. For a clear summary of the reception of White's writings, see R. T. Vann, 'The Reception of Hayden White', *History and Theory*, 37(2) (1998) 143–61.
23. Phillips, *Society and Sentiment*, p. 10.
24. White, *Metahistory*, pp. 20–1.
25. H. Immerwahr, *Form and Thought in Herodotus* (Cleveland, OH: Western Reserve University Press, 1966), p. 5.
26. R. Lattimore, 'The Composition of the *Histories* of Herodotus', *Classical Philology*, 53 (1958) 9–21; Immerwahr, *Form and Thought in Herodotus*; D. Lateiner, *The Historical Method of Herodotus* (Toronto: University of Toronto Press, 1989); and R. V. Munson, *Telling Wonders: Ethnographic and Political Discourse in the Work of Herodotus* (Ann Arbor, MI: University of Michigan Press, 2001).
27. Lateiner, *The Historical Method of Herodotus*, p. 16.
28. D. Fehling, *Herodotus and his 'Sources': Citation, Invention and Narrative Art* (Leeds: Leeds University Press, 2000).
29. Diodorus of Sicily, *The Library of History*, trans. C. H. Oldfather (London: Heinemann, 1968), §1.9.1.
30. K. Clarke, *Between Geography and History: Hellenistic Constructions of the Roman World* (Oxford: Oxford University Press, 1999).
31. Diodorus of Sicily, *The Library of History*, §20.43–4.
32. Ibid., §19.66–72.
33. Ibid., §§1.9, 1.29, 1.41, 4.5, 13.84.
34. K. S. Sachs, *Diodorus Siculus and the First Century* (Princeton, NJ: Princeton University Press, 1990), chapter 4.
35. Oldfather, 'Preface', *The Library of History*, p. xviii.
36. Sachs, *Diodorus Siculus and the First Century*, pp. 117–21.
37. J. Prusek, 'History and Epics in China and the West', *Chinese History and Literature* (Prague: Academia, 1970), pp. 12, 18.
38. C. Xie and S. Inayatullah, 'Ssu-Ma Ch'ien: The Cycles of Virtue', in Galtung and Inayatullah, *Macrohistory and Macrohistorians*, p. 16.
39. G. Hardy, *Worlds of Bronze and Bamboo: Sima Qian's Conquest of History* (New York: Columbia University Press, 1999).
40. Ibid., p. 35.
41. Ibid., p. 38.
42. J. R. Allen, 'An Introductory Study of Narrative Structure in the Shi ji', *Chinese Literature: Essays, Articles, Reviews (CLEAR)*, 3(1) (1981) 31–66.
43. For example, *Shiji* 3.91, 4.111, 13.488–9, and 3.106 and 4.116; as cited in Hardy, *Worlds of Bronze and Bamboo*, pp. 46–7.
44. Ibid., pp. 47–8.
45. Franz Rosenthal notes that during Ibn Khaldun's lifetime, he developed a view of the first book of his *Kitab* as an independent work with the title *Muqaddimah*.
46. Ibn Khaldun, *Peuples et nations du monde. La conception de l'histoire. Les Arabes du Machreq et leurs contemporains. Les Arabes du Maghrib et les Berbères. Extraits des 'Ibar traduits de l'arabe et présentés par Abdesselam Cheddadi*, 2 vols (Paris: Sindbad, 1986).

47. R. Allen, *The Arabic Literary Heritage: The Development of its Genres and Criticism* (Cambridge: Cambridge University Press, 1998), p. 253.
48. As quoted in F. Rosenthal, *A History of Muslim Historiography*, 2nd edn (Leiden: E. J. Brill, 1968), p. 419 n.7.
49. F. Rosenthal, 'Translator's Introduction', *Muqaddimah* (Princeton, NJ: Princeton University Press, 1967), p. cxii.
50. S. L. Hindman, 'With Ink and Mortar: Christine de Pizan's *Cité des Dames*: An Art Essay', *Feminist Studies*, 19 (1984) 471.
51. R. Brown-Grant, *Christine de Pizan and the Moral Defence of Women: Reading Beyond Gender* (Cambridge: Cambridge University Press, 1999), p. 154.
52. Ibid.
53. J. B. Bury, *The Idea of Progress: An Inquiry into its Growth and Origins* (New York: Dover, 1932), pp. 20–2.
54. J. Millar, *The Origin of the Distinction of Ranks* (Bristol: Thoemmes, 1990, facsimile of 1804 edition), p. 12.
55. Ibid.
56. R. Olson, 'Sex and Status in Scottish Enlightenment and Social Science: John Millar and the Sociology of Gender Roles', *History of the Human Sciences*, 11(1) (1998) 82–3; and M. S. Phillips, *Society and Sentiment*, p. 186.
57. L. M. Child, *History of the Condition of Women in Various Ages and Nations* (Boston, MA: John Allen, 1835), vol. 1, pp. 251, 252, 255.
58. S. J. Hale, 'The History of the Condition of Women, in Various Ages and Nations. By Mrs. D. L. Child,' *American Ladies' Magazine* 8 (1835) 588; as quoted in C. L. Karcher, *The First Woman in the Republic: A Cultural Biography of Lydia Maria Child* (Durham, NC: Duke University Press, 1994), p. 224.
59. Child, *History of the Condition of Women*, vol. 1, preface.
60. M. Davis, *Late Victorian Holocausts: El Niño Famines and the Making of the Third World* (London: Verso, 2001), p. 9.
61. Ibid., p. 6.
62. Ibid., p. 12.
63. Ibid., p. 14.
64. White, *Metahistory*, pp. xi, 428.
65. H. Kellner, *Language and Historical Representation: Getting the Story Crooked* (Madison, WI: University of Wisconsin Press, 1989), pp. vii, 7, 24, 54.

recommended resources

'Metahistory: Six Critiques', *History and Theory*, 19(4) (1980).
Bentley, J., *Shapes of World History in Twentieth-Century Scholarship* (Washington, DC: American Historical Association, 1996).
Berkhofer, R. F., *Beyond the Great Story: History as Text and Discourse* (Cambridge, MA: Harvard University Press, 1995).
Brown-Grant, R., *Christine de Pizan and the Moral Defence of Women: Reading Beyond Gender* (Cambridge: Cambridge University Press, 1999).
Canary, R., and Kozicki, H. (eds), *The Writing of History: Literary Form and Historical Understanding* (Madison, WI: University of Wisconsin Press, 1978).
Costello, P., *World Historians and their Goals: Twentieth Century Answers to Modernism* (De Kalb, IL: Northern Illinois University Press, 1993).

Hardy, G., *Words of Bronze and Bamboo: Sima Qian's Conquest of History* (New York: Columbia University Press, 1999).

Kellner, H., *Language and Historical Representation: Getting the Story Crooked* (Madison, WI: University of Wisconsin Press, 1989).

Kraus, C. (ed.), *Limits of Historiography* (Leiden: E. J. Brill, 1999).

Lateiner, D., *The Historical Method of Herodotus* (Toronto: University of Toronto Press, 1989).

Manning, P., *Navigating World History: Historians Create a Global Past* (New York: Palgrave Macmillan/St. Martin's Press, 2003).

Munson, R. V., *Telling Wonders: Ethnographic and Political Discourse in the Work of Herodotus* (Ann Arbor, MI: University of Michigan Press, 2001).

Phillips, M. S., *Society and Sentiment: Genres of Historical Writing in Britain 1740–1820* (Princeton, NJ: Princeton University Press, 2000).

Robinson, C. F., *Islamic Historiography* (Cambridge: Cambridge University Press, 2003).

White, H., *Metahistory: The Historical Imagination in Nineteenth-Century Europe* (Baltimore, MD: Johns Hopkins University Press, 1973).

White, H., *Tropics of Discourse: Essays in Cultural Criticism* (Baltimore, MD: Johns Hopkins University Press, 1978).

White, H., *The Content of the Form: Narrative Discourse and Historical Representation* (Baltimore, MD: Johns Hopkins University Press, 1989).

7
centres and margins: the fall of universal history and the rise of multicultural world history

ricardo duchesne

The liberal idea that human history could be comprehended as a rational process, having an intelligible order, which could be described in terms of successive stages of cognitive/technical and moral knowledge, commanded wide credence in the West from the Enlightenment onwards until the 1960s. While there were many interpretations about the forces which governed the process of history, and the kind of stages one would expect to find, not many world historians doubted that it was their business to construct a *universal* scheme into which all of human history could be fitted. This directional view, it is true, sometimes came together with odious assumptions of racial hierarchy. 'We are fully authorized to say', wrote William Swinton in his *Outline of the World's History*, published in 1874, 'that the Aryans are peculiarly the race of progress.' Similarly, Philip Myers, in a popular high school textbook he wrote in 1889, offered a narrative of progress with racial references to the 'the White, or Caucasian race' as 'by far the most perfect type, physically, intellectually, and morally'.[1] Myers did remove these racist remarks from later editions, but the liberal idea that civilization was moving in a desirable direction continued to be heavily infused with imperious attitudes toward cultures and peoples believed to be outside the mainstream of cultural progression.

The idea of progress had indeed developed into much more than an explanation of world history; it spawned a Western arrogance that belittled the historical role of non-Western societies. As Marshall Hodgson lamented in the early 1950s, world history was 'essentially Western history amplified by a few unrelated chapters on other parts of the world'.[2] 'Prehistoric man' and some of the ancient civilizations – Mesopotamia, Egypt and Palestine – were sometimes treated fairly well, but once the story moved on to Greece, Rome and medieval Europe, the Near East tended to disappear from the texts, except for a brief section on the expansion of Islam between the eighth and the twelfth centuries. Indian, Chinese, Mesoamerican, and Sub-Saharan cultures were usually given little attention until Europeans came into contact with them in modern times. There was a triumphalist assumption that Western peoples were the truly progressive ones, and that Asians contributed little to human progress after the first millennium BCE. Western European civilization, having inherited the Judaeo-Christian vision of a universal brotherhood of men, the Greek ideal of a free citizen and the Roman legal tradition, was considered the 'mainstream' of world history.

It would be extremely tendentious and unfair, however, to assume that the conception of world history which Hodgson observed in the 1950s was simply the product of Western racial arrogance and ethnocentric malice. Let us not forget that the study of world history in the 1940s and 1950s was still in its beginnings. And yet, on the other hand, we can only marvel at the vast body of scholarship which had already been generated in earnest by Western-trained scholars on the cultures, traditions and histories of *all* the regions of the world during the first half of the twentieth century. A complete listing of these works would take the space available for this chapter![3] Even more remarkable perhaps is the fact that, by the early 1960s, scholars in the United States were already trying to deal with the problem of ethnocentrism in the study of non-Western cultures, and were loudly calling upon educators to integrate into world history the new findings and ideas of anthropologists, sociologists and 'area-studies' historians doing research in non-Western lands. Robert Crane, Fellow of the American Institute of Indian Studies, 1962–63, was already hoping that with 'a self-conscious awareness of the problem of ethnocentrism', it would be possible for historians to study different cultures in their own terms and not as 'replicas... of our own'.[4] Mark Krug, Associate Professor of Education in History at the University of Chicago, also condemned, in a publication of 1964, what he called the 'Europacentric' approach to world history which assumed 'that the Chinese, Indian, and Islamic civilizations attained a measure of historic importance only when they impinged upon the civilization of the West'.[5]

The more historians learned about other cultures and civilizations of the world, the more reasons they had to heed Hodgson's original voice. In 1962, Leften Stavrianos, a few years after he, too, had insisted in

1958 that 'world history is not European history', and that world history courses should be 'genuinely global' rather than about 'Europe and its world relationships', published a two-volume high school textbook, *A Global History of Man* and *Readings in World History,* under the idea that a world history course 'should include an overview of the entire history of man from a consistent global viewpoint'. The history of humans should not be taught 'merely by adding the study of non-Western civilizations to the study of Western history'. Only by grasping the whole of human history do the parts become 'meaningful and comprehensible'.[6] One year later, in 1963, William McNeill's book, *The Rise of the West: A History of the Human Community*, was out in print, and the thesis of this work was quite clear: the history of the world presented a panorama *not* of separate civilizations following their own rhythmic cycles, but of diverse cultures and civilizations in a state of constant interaction. While the civilizations in Mesopotamia, Egypt and Greece were different actors in world history,

> there has always been a process of cultural flow, and cultural stimulation between adjacent societies... the process of collision and contact, peaceful and warlike, between peoples of different cultures [has been] the central motor of historical change.

'The generation of new styles of life', McNeill added, 'seems to be related to the intensity of contact between people having alien ways of life.'[7]

The idea that world history and Western civilization were synonymous was no longer taken for granted by scholars in the United States in the 1960s but was veritably the subject of much criticism.[8] It would be an oversimplification as well to view the teaching of the 'Western Civ' course across American campuses in the years between and after the world wars as just a way for American educators to instil upon young students an ideology that pictured 'Western Civilization' as the only world history that mattered and which educated immigrants to believe that the United States, in its position of global leadership, was the only legitimate heir of the European democratic tradition and the legitimate military protector of the free world in the struggle against communism.[9] When we look at James Harvey Robinson's textbook, *An Introduction to the History of Western Europe*, published in 1902, and widely used in college classes, and his *An Outline of the History of the Intellectual Class in Western Europe* (1915), books which in Gilbert Allardyce's view prepared American educators 'intellectually for the coming Western Civ course' after World War I, one simply uncovers the optimistic, Whiggish idea that central to the narrative of world history is the progression of rationalism, science and liberal values. Robinson was much less an ideologue than a scholar interested in the origins of the liberal values of his own American civilization. He saw the seventeenth-century conflict between the English 'people' and their king as a watershed in the triumph of freedom against authoritarianism. Looking at the eighteenth-century Enlightenment, he saw a continuation, this time in France, of the struggle for 'freedom of the human mind'. Similarly, when James Harvey Robinson and Charles A. Beard joined together to write a new text in 1929, *The Development of Modern Europe*, they sincerely identified 'modern' history with the scientific struggle to liberate the mind from superstition and obscurantism. They also placed the Enlightenment in the centre of their story. J. B. Wolf (1964) has noted that both authors 'seem to have had few doubts about the eventual victory that would free the human mind from the tyranny of old and outmoded ideas'.[10] The text which Carl Becker wrote in 1931 for high school students, *Modern History: The Rise of a Democratic, Scientific, and Industrialized Civilization*, which went through numerous editions, also emphasized the great issues and transformations of the past which had pushed forward the torch of progress; it was a book unafraid to raise big questions about 'what history is about' – all in a straightforward manner as if the rational directionality of history needed no explanation. The same optimism is apparent in a recommendation Beard made in 1934 for more European history in secondary schools, in a report of the Commission on the Social Sciences, where he identified the 'study of the evolution of Western Civilization' with the study of 'the development of democratic ideals and practices', 'the accumulation and spread of knowledge and learning' and 'the advance of science and technology'.[11]

As McNeill was later to recall, the 'great idea' which led to the creation of the Western Civ course was the idea of European history as the history of liberty.[12] This was in fact a major organizing idea of world history books published in the first half of the twentieth century – of H. G. Wells' *Outline of History* (1920), of James Henry Breasted's *Ancient Times, A History of the Early World* (published in 1916 and largely rewritten in 1935), of M. Rostovzeff's *A History of the Ancient World* (first written in Russian between 1921 and 1923), of Christopher Dawson's *The Age of the Gods: A Study in the Origins of Culture in Prehistoric Europe and the Ancient East* (1928), and of V. Gordon Childe's popular books, *Man Makes Himself* (1936) and *What Happened in History* (1942). All these works, in their own respective ways, presented human history as a directional process of cumulative learning, not only in the dimension of technically useful knowledge but also in the dimension of moral-practical ideas. Their basic message, even if not always stated in explicit terms, was that world history was a *universal* learning process, a process which could be reconstructed on the basis of distinct eras and *successive* stages. It was a West-centred message no doubt, but one which tried, as much as the sources available at the time allowed, to understand the contributions of non-Western cultures. Each of these works contained detailed sections on all the major civilizations of the ancient world. Breasted, in no uncertain terms, observed that 'while Europe still lay in Stone Age barbarism the peoples of the Ancient Near East gave the world for the first time a whole group of further inventions [in addition to those of prehistoric peoples] surpassed in importance only by those of the modern world', in the practical arts, in the use of the potter's wheel, the potter's furnace, the earliest metalwork and the art of hollow casting, glass-making, paper-making and other industries. They also made essential contributions in writing, in poems and historical works, in mathematics and astronomy, and in the earliest belief 'in a sole God and *his fatherly care for all men*'. But the 'East' had not yet 'gained the idea of a free citizen', and 'had made little inquiry into the natural causes of such things' as storms and eclipses, they 'suffered from a lack of freedom of the mind'. While the Greeks and the Romans carried the learning process forward, Breasted appreciated the later contributions of non-Western cultures to this universal process: the Muslims 'developed a civilization far higher than that of the Franks, and indeed the highest of that age in Europe, [they] were the leading students of science, astronomy, mathematics, and grammar'.[13]

Rostovzeff's two-volume work, *A History of the Ancient World*, is a true masterpiece. First written in the Russian language, translated into English in 1925, and revised in 1929 after 'important new discoveries' in excavations in Egypt, Mesopotamia, Syria and Asia Minor, this book presented a picture of successive ancient civilizations spreading 'by degrees over the world', each civilization reaching a 'zenith of cultural creation' followed by a period of stagnation and decline. But in terms of human (ancient) history as whole, the decline was temporary, for the foundations of the old civilizations served as a basis for the start of another creative civilization. If the

> Greeks were especially remarkable for the power of their creative spirit... it must be remembered that the lofty creation of Greece was developed from the culture attained by the ancient East; that Greek civilization became world-wide as the result of a *fresh and prolonged contact with*

the Eastern cultures, after the conquest of the East by Alexander the Great.

What enabled Europe later to start their civilization, 'not from the lowest stratum of prehistoric life but from a comparatively high level', was the fact that Rome inherited, transformed and passed on 'the civilization *of the East* and of Greece' to Europe.[14]

The subject of these books was not always the West. If our contemporary multicultural readers feel that Rostovzeff's 'East' is too narrow in its focus on the Near East, they can read H. G. Wells' classic *The Outline of History,* being truly what the subtitle says, 'a plain history of life and mankind'. The book gave more attention to Europe, but it dedicated many sections to India and China, and contained full chapters on the Islamic and the Mongol empires. Wells was so impressed by the 'urbanity, the culture, and the power of China under the early Tang rulers' that he felt compelled to pose the 'grand problem' we now wrongly associate with the Sinologist Joseph Needham:

> The Chinese knew of gunpowder in the sixth century, they used coal and gas heating locally centuries before these things were used in Europe; their bridge-building, their hydraulic engineering were admirable; the knowledge shown in their enamel and lacquer ware is very great. *Why did they never organize the system of record and cooperation in inquiry that has given the world modern science?*

The labours of specialists had not yet provided enough sources for Wells to offer an answer, and rather than meeting this question with the customary 'platitudinous answers' he found in other writers, he reminded readers that China never experienced a permanent decline in creativity as had ancient Greece and Rome when they decline never to rise again, or the Arabs 'who blazed like a star for half a dozen generations after the appearance of Islam' but never achieved the same. While China was not as progressive as Europe was *after* 1500, it did experience throughout its long history 'several liberalizing movements'.[15] All in all, Wells had a progressive vision of the overall course of human history. He was disillusioned by the 'disaster' and 'slaughter' of World War I, but still believed that

> it was possible [at least until the year 1914] to view the history of the world as a progress, interrupted but always resumed, towards peace and freedom. In most of the states of the world political and parliamentary

freedom was extending, personal rights were more protected, liberty of thought and of speech was expanding, and states were beginning to be less irresponsible in their foreign policy.

Childe, a Marxist who accepted and, in the tradition of Friedrich Engels, espoused the nineteenth-century evolutionary idea of stages of Savagery, Barbarism and Civilization, also saw a progressive improvement in the history of technology stemming from the expansion in the store of human knowledge. This expansion in technology was for him the underlying foundation of most progress in other spheres of social life, art, politics, ethics and philosophy. Childe on the other hand recognized that environmental differences were too great in the earliest centres of civilization to expect parallel sequences of progress. He thought that diffusion, or contact between cultures, was a major factor in the process of change. He also recognized that the long progressive career of humans was discontinuous. But when he looked at history as a whole – universal history – he saw a cumulative pattern: 'The upward curve', he concluded in *What Happened in History*, 'resolves itself into a series of troughs and crests. But... no trough ever declines to the low level of the preceding one; each crest out-tops its last precursor.'[16] In a short philosophical essay Childe published in 1947, *History*, as 'Volume Six of the series Past and Present, Studies in the History of Civilizations', he stated in a matter of fact way that the main business of the world historian was 'to yield a science of progress', 'to disclose an order in the process of human history'. Aware as he was that the path of human history was 'distinctly erratic', he thought it was still possible for the scholar to recombine and rearrange enough facts from the historical and archaeological records to show that world history in general did exhibit 'an orderly sequence', a 'continuous linear sequence' of improvements.[17]

In the *Age of Gods*, back in 1928, Christopher Dawson had already presented an even more sophisticated account of cultural change. While 'it is impossible', he said, 'to deny the reality and importance of cultural progress', this progress 'is not a continuous and uniform movement, common to the whole human race... It is rather an exceptional condition, due to a number of distinct causes.' The adaptation of a people to their 'original environment without the intrusion of human factors from outside' brings social change but it generally exemplifies the case of primitive peoples who barely change. Moving to a new geographical environment and having to readapt to it, is what encourages cultural change of at least the 'simplest type'. But the 'most important of all the causes of cultural change', he explained, was 'the case of two different peoples, each with its own way of life and social organization, which mix with one another usually as a result of conquest, occasionally as a result of peaceful contact.' We think it was McNeill, but Dawson long ago hypothesized that interaction between different cultures was the chief motor of historical change. 'It is the origin of practically all those sudden flowerings of new civilization, which impress us as almost miraculous.' Dawson thought that the mere borrowing of some foreign cultural element was an important common occurrence which demonstrated the 'close interdependence of cultures', but added that such borrowing did not automatically encourage social progress. Real world historical change – 'intense cultural activity' – comes when an old advanced culture is reawakened or fertilized through a vital 'organic process of fusion' with a new people, or when 'the creative activity of a new people [is] stimulated by contact with the old autochthonous culture'.[18] Thus, the Mycenaean culture which gradually replaced and fused with the old Minoan civilization, and which was a 'new type of warlike society which arose from the contact between the invading Indo-European peoples and the Archaic Culture of the Near East', was in turn later fused with a new wave of Indo-European tribal peoples, a wave which would have resulted in the 'complete barbarization' of the Greek mainland world, and not the rise of Hellenic civilization, were it not for the creative survival of the now older Mycenaean culture and the creative adaptation of the new invaders to the old traditions of the Mediterranean cultures. Let us be clear: Dawson understood that *external* contacts and borrowing were not enough; the change, if it was to be 'fully progressive', had to 'come from *within*', from the creative activity of cultures stimulated by their fusion with other cultures.[19]

These early world histories gave readers the feeling that, in the overall drama of human history generally, there was a meaningful pattern in the direction of higher levels of technical knowledge, material well-being, and moral-practical insights. In their very preoccupation with Western civilization as the 'high history' of mankind, they cultivated an understanding of history that was *transcultural* in the sense that successive, *connected* cultures were interpreted as steps in a *single universal* process.[20]

This progressive, optimistic vision continued to find its way in world history books right into the 1960s, through the time that world historians were increasingly writing from a more world-oriented perspective. It was certainly articulated in UNESCO's *History of Mankind: Cultural and Scientific Developments, Vol. 1: Prehistory and the Beginnings of Civilization*, published in 1963. This massive volume of 873 pages in small print was intended specifically to shed light on mankind's 'cultural and scientific development', starting with the prehistory of the peoples of Asia, Africa and America – 'all alike discussed' – and ending with the Bronze Age civilizations of the world. It gave 'equal time' to the history of the world's cultures and yet did not hesitate to trace the 'expansion of human consciousness' and the higher stage of cultural development achieved by the upper palaeolithic cultures over the middle palaeolithic cultures – higher because 'the latest Palaeolithic hunters had at last succeeded in bringing speech to a point where the precise naming of things and the elementary discussion of ideas had become possible'. It spoke of the 'continuous improvement of material equipment' by the palaeolithic and neolithic cultures and showed how these cultures laid the foundation on which later civilizations were to be built.[21] It contrasted the 'barbarism of the Neolithic period' with the birth of urbanized life, and it went into great detail describing 'the immense progress in culture and in technical knowledge' achieved by 'mankind' during the Bronze Age.[22] By studying 'the interrelations, across time and space, of ideas, values and techniques', this book sought to offer a true universal history, 'a history of human thought which is the product of the thought of mankind', a history of Egypt, Mesopotamia, China, India, and Phoenicia which is the history of 'the advance of man in general'.[23]

This idea of progress was also visible in McNeill's *Rise of the West*, a book generally considered the most complete recounting of the whole history of mankind at the time, but which nonetheless argued that the predominant development of history after 1500 was the ascendancy of Western culture. McNeill, always careful not to offer pat answers about the nature of human history, seemed confident enough, particularly as he looked at the dazzling political and scientific changes of modern Europe, to say in the last part of this highly spirited book: 'Progress there has most certainly been in science and technology; progress also, it seems to me, in many important aspects of human relations.'[24] Less hesitant in its appreciation of human progress, was Fernand Braudel's *A History of Civilizations*, originally published in 1963 in France as part of *Le Monde actuel: Historie et civilisations*. This may seem surprising since commentators have generally downplayed the liberal theme of progress in Braudel's books. While Braudel saw the history of civilizations as 'the history of continual and mutual borrowing over many centuries', he also believed that every civilization was 'very different' and that in the march of human progress each civilization had played its own unique role. This difference came out of different 'material and biological conditions [which] always help determine the destiny of civilizations', and out of different cultural origins and different geographical links to the world. If China and Black Africa were relatively isolated, Islam was an 'intermediary' civilization linking the Far East, Europe and Black Africa. And Europe was the only civilization 'linked in all directions to the seven seas'. If China was a continuous civilization – 'imagine the Egypt of the Pharaohs miraculously preserved' – Europe and Islam were 'derivative civilizations' built on the civilizations which 'preceded it in the Near East'. If Islam rose and then declined, the 'West' experienced 'breaks with the past and the birth of new civilizations', from Greece to Rome to Christian Europe through Islam to Renaissance Europe. If Islam was 'the most brilliant civilization in the Old World' between the eighth and twelfth centuries, and China was ahead of the West in science and technology 'until at least the thirteenth century', Europe 'took up the torch' of progress in the fourteenth century.

Since the time of its origins in Greek culture, 'the tendency of Western civilization', Braudel observed, 'has been towards rationalism' – not only towards rationalism but towards greater freedom.[25] Echoing the 'great idea' of Western Civ courses, Braudel enthusiastically explained that the growth of liberty was 'one of the secrets that explain[ed] Europe's progress': from the development of towns 'marked by unparalleled freedom', through franchises or corporate groups which could regulate their own affairs independently of the state, to the 'intellectual ferment' of the Renaissance which 'preached respect for the greatness of the human being as an individual', and of the Reformation which 'laid the bases for freedom of conscience', through the 1789 Declaration of the Rights of Man which stated that all Frenchmen were citizens with equal liberties, to the revolutions of 1848 which established the principle of universal suffrage.[26]

But just as this world-oriented and universal vision of world history was gaining ground, it came under fierce attack in the 1960s.[27] In the context of the Soviet socialist experiment, the threat of nuclear destruction, the Vietnam War, the growing (relative) gap between poor and rich nations, and the creation of pan-Arab and pan-African identities, the notion that Western Europe and the United States, as liberal-democratic cultures, were at a higher stage of development, and that poorer nations were simply lagging behind on a linear path of progress, seemed both naive and ethnocentric. Surely there were always voices of discontent against earlier Whiggish and Enlightenment notions of progress and human 'perfectibility', from Jean-Jacques Rousseau's (1712–1978) argument that the happiest period of the human race ended with civilization, through Robert Malthus' (1766–1834) observation that population would always tend to outrun our ability to produce enough food, to Friedrich Nietzsche's (1844–1900) complaint that since the 'last great age' of the Renaissance history appears as 'a development in decline'. But it was really from the 1960s onwards that the very notion of progress and the idea of directionality in history came under sustained criticism by scholars interested in the causes of persistent poverty in the Third World. Critics such as Samir Amin, Andre Gunder Frank and Walter Rodney charged that Western 'progress' was really a process by which Europe and the United States had enriched themselves through the exploitation of Africa, the Americas and Asia.[28] They insisted, moreover, that it was wrong to treat the history of Western societies as worlds unto themselves, and repudiated the idea that European civilization generated out of its own cultural attributes the capacity to out develop the rest of the world. It was, rather, the systematic conquest and destruction of the Incas and the Aztecs, and the extraction of gold and silver from the Americas in the sixteenth century, that boosted the fortunes of Europe to begin with, including the brutal importation of African slaves to work in sugar, tobacco and cotton plantations in the Americas from about 1600 until 1850.

These radical critics, however, better known as 'dependency' theorists, were not really world historians as much as pioneers of 'development studies', and the subject of their attacks were not the liberal world histories produced in the West, but a group of social scientists writing under the rubric of 'modernization theory'. The years of high popularity of modernization theories were the 1950s and the 1960s when Talcott Parsons, Neil Smelser, Daniel Lerner, Richard Bendix, Samuel Huntington and Walt Rostow published some of their most influential works.[29] By academic profession these scholars, too, were not world historians but sociologists and political scientists. They did, however, draw heavily on nineteenth-century Classical evolutionary theory and its assumption that the whole of human history had a form, a *universal* pattern, or meaning underlying the multitude of seemingly accidental and unconnected events. They believed that long-term trends were clearly evident in human history, from traditional to modern societies, from relationships based on ascription to relationships based on personal effort and merit, from focus on groups and collectivities to focus on autonomous individuals, from patrimonial adjudication and enforcement to universally applicable laws and rights. While modernization theorists were aware that not all societies had followed the same evolutionary path, they believed that the overall course of human history had resulted in the betterment of human life. They were optimistic that rich liberal-democratic nations could accelerate the development of poor traditional societies through programs of population control, technology transfers, investment capital in the form of foreign aid, and diffusion of liberal attitudes and entrepreneurial skills.

But the modernizing efforts of Western elites did not create the results they had anticipated, at least in the short term. Poverty persisted or even deteriorated in many newly independent countries in the Third World, and in the 1970s dictatorial regimes, rather than democracies, appeared to be gaining ground in much of Latin America, added to which were recurrent national and local wars, swelling populations, increasing social inequalities, and ethnic factionalism in most of Africa and the Middle East. Social life in the advanced nations did not seem so rosy either, as numerous pathological side-effects seemed to be coming out of modernization itself, such as increasing delinquency, urban decay, breakdown of community bonds, pollution and economic dislocation. Just as important perhaps was the accusation that modernization theory was ethnocentric, in that it elevated the historical experience of the Western advanced nations to the level of universal truth, as the only true model to be followed by 'less developed' nations, without asking whether other nations would want to follow their own paths rather than the path of Western rationalism, secularism and liberalism.[30] This charge of ethnocentrism eroded the confidence of modernization theorists who basically agree with the relativistic assumptions of their critics that there were no value-neutral grounds on which they could defend Western values. Modernization theory itself had drawn heavily from Max Weber and had accepted his sceptical argument that ultimate principles and moral values, as opposed to empirical or technocratic problems of efficiency, were not amenable to rational evaluation. Even though there was considerable evidence that in some Third World countries education was expanding, per capita GNP was growing and infant mortality was dropping – in Singapore, Hong Kong, Taiwan and South Korea, as well as Brazil, Mexico and Argentina – the influence of modernization theory declined sharply over the 1970s.[31]

Meanwhile, the anti-imperialist world outlook of dependency theory was no longer confined to a few academicians but gained a popular following among young sociologists and political scientists. Much as dependency theory was carefully criticized for ignoring factors inside Third World countries like political corruption, gender inequality, concentration of farmland in a few families, the 1970s saw an enormous mass of anti-imperialist literature. This was the context for the publication of Immanuel Wallerstein's multivolume work, *The Modern World-System*, a work which came to exercise a long-lasting, powerful effect on the writing of world history.[32] Although Wallerstein added little to the old dependency argument that the world economy was structured in such a manner that the development of the core societies occurred at the expense of the peripheral societies, his global or 'world-system' perspective was certainly a new contribution to the theory of historical change 'in emphasizing', in the words of Roland Robertson, 'the idea that the world is a systemic phenomenon and that much of what has been traditionally analysed by social scientists in societal, or more broadly, *civilizational* terms can and should be relativized and discussed along *global-systemic* lines.'[33]

Wallerstein distinguished three major stages in history. He called the first the stage of 'mini-systems', in which relatively small, self-sufficient economic regions with a single cultural outlook dominated. These mini-systems, small in space and short in duration of time, existed all through the long eras of hunter-gatherer, horticultural and early agricultural societies. Their basic economic logic was one of 'reciprocity' in exchanges. He called the second the stage of 'world-empires' (ancient Egypt, the Ottoman Empire, the Mughal Empire) in which large, comprehensive political and military systems incorporating a considerable number of earlier mini-economic networks dominated the dynamics of world historical change. These 'world-empires' were multiethnic entities embracing major parts of the world, all tied together through wide networks of exchange, founded on an agricultural economy and supported by means of strong military and political rule, coercive taxation and conquest. The third stage of the 'world economy' originated in the sixteenth century when Europe's merchant economy expanded throughout the globe and created a 'new division of labour' based primarily on economic-market exploitation rather than political-military domination. This is the stage when modern capitalism was born, when the whole globe was gradually incorporated into a single, so-called 'modern world-system' of economic interdependencies. It is a stage in which all peripheral or less developed societies of the world are eventually drawn into the dominant capitalist system, to support the leading economic societies of the West, by providing inexpensive labour, easy access to raw materials and vast markets for manufactured goods.[34]

As Jerry Bentley has pointed out in his *Shapes of World History in Twentieth-Century Scholarship*, the world-system approach of Wallerstein, a professor of sociology, 'deeply influenced the way historians, anthropologists, and scholars in other disciplines [understood] the dynamics of modern world history'. The essential message of his approach was that 'modern world history made sense only in the context of Western imperial and colonial hegemony'.[35] It rejected the idea that world history could be seen as a series of stages involving the progressive realization of freedom. The attack on the possibility of a universal history, however, was not the work of any one person or school of thought. It was the work of many elite groups, of feminists, cultural relativists, postmodernists, critical theorists, Foucault-inspired new historicists and deconstructors; many of whom, I should add, were individuals acting in the service of morally valuable aims. The interrelations of postmodernism and world history and gender and world history will be examined in Chapters 8 and 9. But there are two philosophical outlooks which deserve further reflection. The first is the 'negative philosophy of history' of Max Horkheimer and Theodor Adorno, expressed most forcefully in their influential book, *Dialectic of Enlightenment*, which they published in 1947. The second is the cultural relativism which grew out of the field of anthropology in the early twentieth century and which by the 1980s had come to capture the social sciences and the humanities throughout the institutions of higher learning.

The *Dialectic of Enlightenment* turned the nineteenth-century liberal idea of human progress on its head: the history of Western civilization was a history of regress. The book sought to explain how Nazism and the Holocaust had been possible in Western Europe, how modern science, technology and instrumental reason had been employed in the service of fascism, and how Western culture had brought 'mankind into a new kind of barbarism'.[36] It was a total, sweeping critique of the Occidental tradition of reason. It traced the increasing power of instrumental reason – the domination over one's own nature, the domination of outward nature and the domination of labour through factory organization – back to the 'turning points' of Western civilization: from the 'enlightened character of Homer', to the Renaissance and the Enlightenment, to the mass culture industry and the capitalist bureaucratic state. Much as 'bourgeois' ideology postulated the idea of a free and humane social life, the political domination of humans was at the base of modern Galilean and Newtonian science. Calculability, efficiency, and impersonality were the basic characteristics of this pattern of domination. To the extent that nature was perceived by Westerners as neutral, disenchanted, with no intrinsic qualities, it was open to manipulation, alteration and destruction.

The radical critique of Western civilization contained in the *Dialectic of Enlightenment*, and numerous other writings by Adorno and Horkheimer, including Marcuse's celebrated books, *Reason and Revolution* (1941), and *One Dimensional Man* (1964) – which claimed that bourgeois society threatened the very existence of 'human reality' and that a 'total and radical revolution' was both necessary and defensible – did not have a direct impact on the writing of world history, but it did capture the political imagination of students and intellectuals in the 1960s and 1970s, and became a key component in the formation of the New Left. In many parts of the world, radical protest movements against imperialism, the private exploitation of scarce resources and Western modernization found much inspiration in the writings of the 'Critical' school.[37]

But in the long run the most devastating attack on the idea of a universal history *originated* out of the pen of an indefatigable worker named Franz Boas. Known for his accomplishments as a teacher, administrator, researcher, founder and president of societies, editor, lecturer and fieldworker, and as the author of half a dozen books and over 700 articles (!), Boas has been claimed by Margaret Mead as 'the man who made anthropology into a science' and by Marvin Harris as 'one of the most influential figures in the history of the social sciences'.[38] Although Boas did not use the term 'cultural relativism', the main idea of his classic work, *The Mind of Primitive Man*, published in 1911, was that Western culture (and the 'White race') should not be seen as superior just because it had 'advanced far beyond the stages' on which other cultures were still living. The idea of directionality in history and the tendency to view Western culture as the highest achievement of mankind created the inevitable impression that primitive cultures were inferior.

> The superiority of our inventions, the extent of our scientific knowledge, the complexity of our social institutions, our attempts to promote the welfare of all members of the social body, create the impression that we, the civilized people, have advanced far beyond the stages on which other people linger, and the assumption has arisen of an innate superiority of the European nations and of their descendants... Since the intellectual development of the White race is the highest, it is assumed that its intellectuality is supreme and that its mind has the most subtle organization'[39]

This was no doubt a powerful critique against the snobbish evolutionary definition of progress which dominated, for example, the writings of Herbert Spencer (1820–1903), and which indeed constituted the framework for the racist ideas of A. Gobineau. This critique soon gained popularity within the field of cultural anthropology which by its very nature calls on field workers to imagine unfamiliar cultural traits from the point of view of *them* rather than *us*.

Mead, Boas' most celebrated student, was very clear about the meaning of Boasian relativism: 'it stood against any grading of cultures in hierarchical systems which would place our own culture at the top and place other cultures of the world in a descending scale according to the extent that they differ from ours'.[40] While there were still anthropologists like Leslie White who continued through the 1940s and 1950s to defend 'neoevolutionist' ideas of historical directionality, by the early 1960s this relativism had gained much favour within the social sciences and humanities at large. In 1963, for example, Lucian Pye, a political scientist studying development, was already writing that 'a generation of instruction in cultural relativism has had its influence, and social thinkers are no longer comfortable with any concept which might suggest a belief in "progress" or "stages of civilization"'.[41] We saw before, too, how historians like Krug and Stavrianos were trying in the early 1960s to think of new ways of teaching and writing world history without a 'Western-European ethnocentric bias', and how modernization theory seemed unable to respond to the charges of ethnocentrism. But these charges were only the beginning of what Allan Bloom was to observe later in the mid-1980s: 'there is one thing a professor can be absolutely certain of: almost every student entering the university believes, or says he believes, that truth is relative'.[42] Not only the notion of scientific truth but also the very ideals of Western democratic-liberalism had been relativized. Tracing the full flowering of cultural relativism, its textured combination with postmodernism, multiculturalism, world-system theory, together with the rise of new academic disciplines such as women's studies, black history, Chicano studies, and Asian studies, not to mention the increasing proportion of citizens in Western countries claiming their ethnic background as 'Chinese', 'South-Asian', 'Black', 'Arab/West Asian', 'Filipino', 'Southeast Asian', 'Latin American', 'Japanese', 'Korean' or 'Other' is too difficult a task for one chapter.[43]

One thing seems certain: by the 1970s world historians had generally lost faith in Western civilization ideas and had given up the old liberal interpretation of the meaning and course of human history. In 1974, when McNeill published his little book *The Shape of European History,* parts of which he presented to a session of the Eleventh International Congress of Anthropological and Ethnological Sciences (September 1973) under the encouragement of Sol Tax, Professor of Anthropology at the University of Chicago, he observed that 'few living historians accept' the 'no longer very convincing idea' that 'Europe's history is the history of liberty'.[44] In searching for another organizing vision that would give meaning to the whole of European history, McNeill adopted the anthropological notion of 'cultural pattern', which he defined as 'repeatable behaviour recognizable in the lives of relatively large numbers of men, often millions or hundreds of millions'. This bland, structuralist definition of culture was specifically set against the traditional emphasis on the elite culture of the West. It was a definition which minimized rational patterns of behaviour in favour of unconscious behaviours performed by anonymous faces on a regular basis. It was a definition which suited anthropologists who spent a good part of their research lives with peasants and tribesmen. When European history was seen in this way, from the standpoint of the daily lives of ordinary people, it did not appear particularly unique. If it still seemed 'worthwhile' to study it, McNeill concluded, it was because of the predominant role of European industrial and military power in world affairs in recent centuries.[45]

This was just the beginning of McNeill's self-corrections away from the idea that a history of *The Rise of the West* could be subtitled *A History of the Human Community*. In a self-critical article he published in 1995, 'The Changing Shape of World History' – which continued an earlier self-appraisal he published in 1990 in the inaugural issue of the new *Journal of World History* – he proudly told his readers how he had gradually come to accept a slightly revised version of Wallerstein's world-system analysis together with a new ecological perspective which placed microparasites rather than ideas at the centre of global history. He felt he had not gone far enough in *The Rise of the West* in his emphasis on interactions between civilizations. He had restricted his study of interactions to geographical regions like the Near East rather than focusing on interactions across the entire world. In writing *The Pursuit of Power* (1982), and researching the strong effects Chinese commercial expansion had on the European economy after 1000 CE, he realized 'that a proper world history ought to focus *primarily* upon changes in the ecumenical world system'.[46] The very idea that civilizations were distinctive cultural entities which, despite their interactions, could be appraised in the same way that an art critic evaluated styles of art was no longer tenable. The civilizations of the past were too 'internally confused and contradictory' and 'no single recognizable style of life' could be attributed to any of them. What was common to them all – and what indeed should be 'the proper definition of a "civilization"' – was the 'common subjection' of people to powerful rulers.[47]

If this definition seems like a late appreciation of Marx, it was more likely a Maoist dismissal of high culture. The moral and religious patterns that distinguished a civilization's elite, McNeill intimated, were in truth ideologies of oppression which the rulers themselves disregarded since their real interests were plundering, taxing and reaping profits unjustly, although the principal religions of the core regions of the world system – Christianity, Confucianism, Buddhism and Islam – did soften somewhat the suffering which accompanied the imperial subordination of less powerful cultures. Tracing the cultural/biological and economic/ technological expansion of the ecumenical world system through the expansion of new communications networks into previously isolated peoples and cultures should be the task of the world historian. Hopefully this new shape of world history writing, McNeill concludes, 'can play a modest but useful part in facilitating a tolerable future for humanity'.[48] But it is difficult to see how, after thousands of years of civilized history, a new world history that recognizes no progress can create a better future.

As McNeill was revising his ideas, the author of world-system theory, Wallerstein, was hard at work writing essays (mostly through the 1980s which he published in 1991 in a book, *Unthinking Social Sciences*) turning his critique of modern Western imperialism into a complete rejection of the assumptions underlying the concept of 'development'. This concept, which social scientists had inherited from the nineteenth century, was highly misleading and unacceptable because it falsified the dominant historical trend of the modern world – or so Wallerstein claimed. By its very definition, it explained change as if it proceeded by means of the gradual unfolding of internal potentialities within societies or civilizations. It assumed, as McNeill put it elsewhere, that changes within civilizations were 'autocatalytic'. The main role in the dynamics of society, Wallerstein insisted, was played by global factors and influences. The drive for change came from intersocietal contacts, competition, conflict and conquest. Societies were not autonomous and did not evolve according to their own specific tendencies since they were primarily created by 'world-scale processes'. This concept of development also had to be abandoned because of its intimate association with the notion of progress and the idea that history had moved in a better direction. The later stages of the 'world-system' could hardly be defined as improvements compared with earlier stages when egalitarian 'mini-systems' prevailed. The issue of progress must be treated as historically contingent and culturally relative.[49]

By the 1990s the influence of cultural relativism was powerful enough that when Stephen K. Sanderson decided in his book *Social Transformations, A General Theory of Historical Development* (1995) to revive and defend the nineteenth-century evolutionary theory of history, he did so by rejecting completely the idea that social evolution had generally been progressive. 'There is nothing inherent in the concept of evolution that requires anyone to assume that it must be linked with progress.' Synthesizing the anthropological findings of Marvin Harris and Mark Nathan Cohen, the evolutionary sociological ideas of Gerhard Lenski, and the world-system perspective of Wallerstein, Sanderson argued, to the contrary, that 'throughout most of world history social evolution has been largely regressive'.[50] Upon examining the material standard of living, the quality of work and the human workload, the degree of social and economic equality, and the extent of democracy and freedom, Sanderson concluded that hunter-gatherer societies were the most progressive of all societies. While he recognized that with the rise of industrial capitalism the standard of living of the people of advanced societies had improved, and some gains had been achieved in less-developed countries in recent decades, he still pointed out that the absolute number of people living in abject poverty in the world had increased, and that the gap between developed and less-developed countries had steadily widened. He did not deny that individual autonomy and freedom had increased in modern capitalist societies, compared to agrarian civilizations, but still insisted that hunting and gathering bands and horticultural tribes were 'the truest democracies', and that primitive peoples enjoyed about the same if not greater freedom.[51]

This attack against the idea of human progress in general, and the ideals of Western civilization in particular, coincided with the spread of world history courses across high schools, colleges and universities in the United States. When world history curricula finally flourished in the 1980s and 1990s, and Western Civ courses faded from prominence, they did so indeed by repudiating the very idea of 'the West' as a unique civilization. Ross Dunn, Jerry Bentley, Patrick Manning, David Christian and others who took over the cause of world history in the 1980s, and founded the World History Association (1982), the *World History Bulletin* (1983), the *Journal of World History* (1990) and promoted PhDs in world history, all came to the conclusion that the great events of European history could only be explained within the wider context of interrelated events happening all around the world. The 'West' did not exist except by reference to the 'World'. Whether they call their approach 'big history', 'world-system history', 'worldcentric history' or 'historyforusall', they generally agree that all large-scale transformations in human history should never be attributed to intracivilizational processes and foundational traits, because all the peoples of the world have been shaped by their participation in the world and their relation with other civilizations and cultures. They all agreed that world history should be defined as the study of past 'connections in the human community', 'the story of the 'common experience' of the human species. If some, like Bentley and Andre Gunder Frank, extended backward in time Wallerstein's world-systemic approach by emphasizing mass migrations, imperial accumulation and long-distance trade in premodern times, others, like Clive Pointing and Christian, drew attention to the common physical and biological nature of humanity, the propensities and desires of the human species, the universal ecosystem of the earth and the ways in which people have been interdependent with all other forms of life. If McNeill and Dunn focused on transhemispheric intercommunicating zones, Alfred Crosby (beginning with the publication of his *Columbian Exchange* in 1972) illustrated the ways in which plants, animals and diseases had moved across continents beyond the boundaries of nations and civilizations.[52]

There is no denying that this emphasis on the interactions of communities and cultures in the past has produced indispensable insights about the worldwide impact of not only modern but premodern forces and movements. The trend toward a more even-handed evaluation of non-European voices and the history of women and minority groups also deserves to be celebrated. It is after all a trend in character with the universal ideals of human rights and dignity evolved by European civilization. But it is my view that a narrow-minded, anti-Western ideology has taken hold of much of world history writing in recent decades, a new orthodoxy which espouses, as a matter of political principle, the idea that there has been no cultural progression in history. It is an ideology that rejects the very notion of a unique 'Western civilization' by people who feel that, as McNeill has observed, 'the historical heritages of every people of the earth are of equal value, even if, or *especially if they were mistreated by European imperialists in the recent past*'.[53] It is an ideology that encourages students to place the intellectual achievements of all cultures on the same moral and rational level, and discourages the so-called 'triumphalist' idea that Western civilization has made the major contributions to the ideals of freedom, democracy and reason. The 'frames of meaning'– to use the phrase of the anthropologist Clifford Geertz, one of the most influential writers of our time – in which people everywhere live out their lives are equally valid and authentic in their own terms.[54] Dare anyone argue that the modern philosophy of Leibniz, Kant, and Hegel was more profound and self-aware than the mythical beliefs of the Zulus and the Papuans, for they will be decried as 'profoundly contemptuous', ethnocentric, parochial and politically retrograde. Far more attractive are stories which hold that many interconnected regions of Afro-Eurasia had roughly the same potential for modernity, and that only a sequence of accidental/imperial factors account for Europe's sudden (and recent) divergence from the rest of the world.[55]

I am not arguing that Afrocentrics and the like have taken over world history. The ideological multiculturalism of world historians today has become almost second nature and no longer finds expression in overzealous books such as Kete Molefi Asante's *The Afrocentric Idea* (1987). It now comes in moderate, politically temperate writings such as Bentley's 1996 *Shapes of World History in Twentieth-Century Scholarship*. This work may very well be read as a fair treatment of the unfolding of world history as a 'professional' field of study in the second (but not the first) half of the twentieth century. Bentley does not make the predictable attacks of world-system theorists against the 'modernization school of history', but carefully points out that Rostow, Cyril Black and Bendix 'made contributions of large significance for the effort to understand the dynamics of modern world history'. He also pays attention to reappraisals by modernization historians such as E. L. Jones who came to reject the earlier 'ethnocentric assumption' that intensive economic growth was a peculiarly Western phenomenon, and recognizes that Jones placed 'the European experience in [a] global context by comparing it with those of other societies'.[56]

But this is the world historiography of the past, the Garden of Eden lies in the future, and in the end Bentley's ideological intentions become apparent. When he states at the beginning of the book that 'world history represents a particularly appropriate means of recognizing the contributions of all peoples to the world's common history', we should take him at this word.[57] This statement by itself, of course, sounds benign enough. Why be against a conception of world history which calls for the inclusion of the achievements of all peoples? Why continue to neglect the history of those who were on the margins of the major civilizations? Because what Bentley actually promotes as the world's common history is not just the positive idea that all the world's peoples deserve serious consideration but primarily the negative idea that there was nothing distinctive about the European Renaissance, the Reformation, the Scientific Revolution, the Enlightenment or the French Revolution, since these transformations were fundamentally determined by world-historical processes. He also cultivates the anti-Western idea that the single most important phenomenon of modern world history is the imperialist expansion of Europe against the development of societies situated in the periphery.

It is not that Bentley is more sympathetic towards 'dependency and world-system analyses' than he is to modernization theory. It is that Bentley's historiographical outlook is guided fundamentally by Wallerstein's belief 'that modern world history makes sense only in the context of Western imperial and colonial hegemony'. While Bentley does say that world-system analyses 'have probably not delivered the last word on the most useful approach to the study of world history' – which is really no criticism at all – and recognizes that these analyses have tended to ignore the role of culture, religion and moral values, he still accepts the premise that modern world history should be about, in the world of Michael Adas, the series editor and author of the foreword to Bentley's book, 'bringing the experience of the "people without history" into the mainstream of teaching and scholarship [and] of relating the development of Europe to that of the rest of the world, or of challenging the mainstream myth of [Western] exceptionalism.'[58]

Thus, much as Bentley chastises world-system theory for focusing too much 'on the interests and activities of Western capitalists' and overlooking 'the roles played by peoples in the satellites or periphery as participants in the making of the world's history', he accepts their basic ideology that the main characteristic of European modernity is the creation of a worldwide capitalist system of surplus extraction.[59] Bentley is hardly unique in this. Dunn has observed that when the first volume of Wallerstein's work *The Modern World-System* was published in 1974 it 'excited' many historians who were just beginning to promote world history courses on college campuses.[60] At first, not everyone was sure how to apply Wallerstein's analysis of the origins and dynamics of the modern capitalist system to global developments before 1500 CE. In a 1981 article, Craig Lockard opined that the world-system approach was 'the most exciting and influential' one for global historians seeking to explain transcontinental developments, but he also observed that this approach had not yet 'penetrated the pages of world history textbooks'.[61] By the late 1980s, however, after scholars had found enough time to improve, revise, and enlarge Wallerstein's approach, his concept of 'world-system', in the words of Dunn, proved to be a 'multifunctional tool' which could be used to comprehend all sorts of interactions and exchanges among all the regions of the world even in premodern times.[62]

But no team depends on one player, and Manning may be right when he estimates in his historiographical book, *Navigating World History*, that Philip Curtin and Crosby, together with Wallerstein, made the 'most lasting contributions' to the development of the idea that world history is 'the study of connections between communities and between communities and their environments'. There is no need to be distracted by the friendly word 'community' and its apparent lack of connection with Wallerstein's system of exploitation: the contribution of Curtin's work on the Atlantic slave trade has been all about *connecting* the history of Africa to other regions of the world, and arguing that the accumulation of wealth in the Atlantic world rested heavily on the enslavement of millions of Africans. Curtin has also adopted a world-scale frame for investigating the history of European colonial migration, trade, and disease. Crosby, for his part, has concentrated on the 'ecological imperialism' of Europe and the movements of diseases, plants, and animals across the Atlantic after 1492.

These scholars have had an undeniable influence on the writing of 'new' world history. Look at the books Bentley examines from the 1980s and early 1990s: they are almost all about how Europeans came to establish economic, cultural and ecological hegemony over the rest of the world and how non-European cultures sometimes 'succumbed' to European 'numbers, weapons, and disease' but sometimes fought heroically against European 'deculturation'. Bentley actually gives special attention to Curtin's and Crosby's books as seminal contributions to our understanding of the establishment of European hegemony in the modern world. He describes other books influenced by the idea of 'cross-cultural interaction and diffusion', such as Daniel Headrick's *The Tools of Empire: Technology and European Imperialism in the Nineteenth Century*; *The Tentacles of Progress: Technology Transfer in the Age of Imperialism, 1850–1940*; *The Invisible Weapon: Telecommunications and International Politics, 1851–1945* – all of which, according to Bentley, 'explore the technological dimension of European imperialism' and 'how Europeans rapidly extended their influence throughout the world during the age of the new imperialism'.[63] Even books on the histories of tiny islands, informed by anthropological and ethnohistorical insights, such as Greg Dening's *Islands and Beaches: Discourses on a Silent Land: Marquesas, 1774–1800*, and David Hanlon's *Upon a Stone Altar: A History of the Island of Pohnpei to 1890*, are celebrated as global in scope inasmuch as they explain how 'Europeans approached the islands in large numbers equipped with firearms, alcohol, and exotic diseases' and how the cultures of these islands were destroyed by European settlements, weapons and diseases. Works on the encounter between Europeans and the indigenous peoples of North America are also listed as insightful studies of a hemispheric encounter which 'brought demographic collapse, ecological imbalance, dependence on trade goods from abroad, heightened intertribal tensions, psychological despair, alcoholism, and deculturation'.[64]

The list goes on, and there are many similar ones mentioned by Manning in *Navigating World History*, a book which traces recent trends in world history writing and which is likely to be adopted as a required reference book for students. Manning's book, in fact, goes further than Bentley's in its refusal to even want to discuss books which examine 'the rise of the West'. He much prefers books which link Africa to other regions of the world. This bias, in my view, is less a result of Manning's 'role as a historian of Africa' than his belief that 'the place of African societies in the worldwide system of slavery' stands as the paradigmatic case of world historical connections. Although Manning likes to repeat that what matters to him are historical 'connections' rather than issues of 'Western dominance', Europe generally enters into his historiographical screen when it dominates, enslaves and infects other societies. What he really dislikes are stories which attribute Europe's dominant position in the Atlantic world to internal factors and civilizational traits. Europe's lead in overseas trade and new industrial technologies must be seen as products of Europe's 'connections' to Africa and the Americas, and Africans must be seen as equal partners in the making of industrial Europe.

And yet the works of Curtin, Crosby and Wallerstein (and Frank) which Manning so admires for their sensitivity to 'connections' are actually about European 'dominance'. They all present a view of Africans as passive victims of European imperialists rather than as equal partners in the creation of the Atlantic slave system.[65] But I gather it is better to contradict oneself than to recognize that the 'process of acquisition of slaves', as John Thornton carefully documented in his book *Africa and Africans in the Making of the Atlantic World, 1400–1800,*

> had long been used in African societies, that African political systems placed great importance on the legal relationship of slavery for political purposes, and that relatively large numbers of people were likely to be slaves at any one time, [and that] the process of acquisition, transfer, and sale of slaves was under the control of African states and elites.[66]

Thornton's book was constructed explicitly against the Eurocentric idea that the Atlantic world was a creation of the Europeans alone, an idea which he detected in dependency theory and world-system analysis. In Manning's world history the only connections that can be condemned are Western ones, and so he prefers to propagate the idea that the African experience of slavery and underdevelopment was '*largely imposed from outside* the community'.[67] This is hardly a view in tune with the idea of cross-cultural *interactions*.

This discursive shift away from the great themes of freedom and rationality which students learned from the traditional Western Civ courses and which world historians still accepted in the 1960s was perhaps the most important event in twentieth-century historiography.[68] It is tempting to conclude that this liberal idea of progress was rightfully abandoned because it was massively contradicted by the facts of the twentieth century – the century of two global wars, of Auschwitz, of Hiroshima, of the Great Depression, of Korea and Vietnam, of Chernobyl, of ozone layer depletion and of AIDS. Believing that history has progressed in the direction of higher levels of scientific knowledge and economic productivity is one thing, but it is another to argue that it has progressed in the direction of higher levels of happiness, morality and freedom. Rousseau may be right that the farther humans have travelled from a primitive way of life, the more they have been exposed to the calamities of warfare, moral decrepitude, inequality and slavery. Sanderson may also be right that in the economic evolution of societies there has not been a corresponding and proportional increase in the material well-being of humans. Yet, in truth, the idea of progress should not be read as implying that there is an increase in well-being, or decrease in suffering, at each stage. The idea of progress should be moderately conceived in the way of Voltaire (1694–1778) who did not indulge in utopian speculations about the future but simply celebrated the progression of the human spirit from savagery, superstition and theocracy. If Voltaire believed that life in the Paris or London of his day was preferable to life in the Garden of Eden, he also recognized that the improvement of human reason was frail and precarious and that progress could be followed by decay and regress.[69]

The idea of progress is actually incompatible with the belief that human nature is good and that all is for the best in this world. As we learn from Bernard Mandelville's provocative book, *The Fable of the Bees* (1723), the innocence of manners of people living an Arcadian existence cannot be reconciled with the 'wordly greatness' of civilizations. A society of people living peacefully in a friendly and easy style would be the safest and happiest but it would also be a non-historical or stagnant society. The force which makes progress possible in history, as Turgot, Kant and Hegel all realized, is not some initial state of human wisdom and enlightenment but the 'tumultuous and dangerous passions' of pride, ambition and greed. These are the passions which drove humans to leave the Garden of Eden and which 'nature' used to promote the material and intellectual advancement of the human species. Humans were not rational and free at the beginning of history.[70] As Hegel liked to remind his readers, God himself ratifies the prophesy of Satan after Adam has eaten the forbidden fruit: 'Look, Adam has become like one of us, and knows what is good and evil.'[71] If Adam and Eve were happy in Paradise, they had not yet discovered the *reason* why they were happy, why something was just, good or courageous. It is self-consciousness as *reason* that comes on the scene with the ancient Greeks. The detachment of consciousness from its immediacy in the traditions and customs of society was a critical step in the progression of humanity. Modern life is progressive insofar as it is based on a wholly critical, self-reflexive culture, that is, a culture in which the norms and principles of life are not given by external, uncriticized forces but are justified by appeal to rational debate and to the capacities for free agency presupposed in such appeals.

The task of world historians who claim as their scope the globe and not just regional connections should be to explain the succeeding forms of rationality and the progressive realization of the social conditions for the full equality of freedom. It is not a proper objection to this task to argue that it results in a 'Westward distortion' of world history because of its preoccupation with Western values. World history is 'connected' but different nations and regions are connected in different degrees. There was in fact a greater diversity of peoples, civilizations, languages and customs merged in the ancient Near East and in the Mediterranean world than in any other ecumenical region of the world. The Eurocentric view that civilization began in Mesopotamia and Egypt and then progressed successively to Greece and Rome and finally to Europe was from the beginning based on the supposition that cultural progression resulted from intense cultural interaction. The task now is to show that the rise of the West involved far more interactions with the world's peoples than had been thought in the past. Affirming the uniqueness of Western civilization does not imply affirming its isolation but its greater interactions with different cultures of the world.

notes

1. Swinton and Myers are cited in G. Allardyce, 'Toward World History: American Historians and the Coming of the World History Course', reprinted in R. E. Dunn (ed.), *The New World History: A Teacher's Companion* (New York: Bedford/ St. Martin's, 2000 [1990]), p. 35.
2. M. G. S. Hodgson, 'Hemisphere Interregional History as an Approach to World History', reprinted in Dunn, *The New World History*, pp. 113–14.
3. See S. Engle (ed.), *New Perspectives in World History* (Washington, DC: National Council for the Social Sciences, 1964), which is a compilation of historiographical studies by specialists on all the main regions of the world.
4. R. Crane, 'India', in Engle, *New Perspectives in World History*, p. 386.
5. M. Krug, 'The Proper Study of World History', in Engle, *New Perspectives in World History*, p. 549.

6. L. Stavrianos, 'The Teaching of World History', reprinted in Dunn (ed.), *The New World History*, and 'A Global Perspective in the Organization of World History', in Engle, *New Perspectives in World History*, pp. 616–20, where Stavrianos discusses his two-volume work.

7. These words, expressed by W. H. McNeill, are cited by Krug in 'The Proper Study of World History', pp. 547–51.

8. Another historian stressing the need for teaching world history as the interaction of civilizations rather than as the study of disparate civilizations, and calling upon Western historians to take seriously 'the views of Asians and Africans themselves', and to approach the era of European hegemony 'without false pride', was M. D. Lewis in 'How Many Histories Should We Teach? Asia and Africa in a Liberal Arts Education', reprinted in L. Stavrianos (ed.), *The Epic of Modern Man, A Collection of Readings* (Englewood Cliffs, NJ: Prentice Hall, 1966). Another effort at broadening the curriculum to include sources on non-Western civilizations was V. M. Dean and H. D. Harootunian (eds), *West and Non-West, New Perspectives, An Anthology* (New York: Holt, Rinehart & Winston, 1963).

9. This view is expressed in a moderate way by G. Allardyce in 'The Rise and Fall of the Western Civilization Course', *American Historical Review* 87 (1982) 695, who points out that this course was a 'product conditioned by... a time when Americans envisioned themselves as partners with the Europeans in a great Atlantic civilization'. But this view is pushed too far by Roxann Prazniak when she explains the content of the course itself in terms of the political requirements of American imperialism and the Cold War, in 'Is World History Possible?', in A. Dirlik, V. Bahl, and P. Gran (eds), *History After Three Worlds* (Lanham, MD: Rowman & Littlefield, 2000).

10. J. B. Wolf, 'The Early Modern Period, 1700–1789', in S. Engle, *New Perspectives in World History*, p. 215.

11. Beard's words are cited in Allardyce, 'The Rise and Fall of the Western Civilization Course', p. 709.

12. Ibid., p. 696. See W. H. McNeill's *The Shape of European History* (New York: Basic, 1974, p. 3) which makes the same point.

13. J. Breasted, *Ancient Times, a History of the Early World* (Boston, MA: Ginn 1944 [1935]), pp. 279–81, 790. These are not isolated passages, in page after page Breasted expresses a deep, sincere admiration for the remarkable cultural accomplishments of Sumerian, Babylonian, Egyptian and Persian civilizations.

14. M. Rostovzeff, *A History of the Ancient World* (Oxford: Oxford University Press, 1945 [1925]), pp. 2–11. Emphasis added.

15. H. G. Wells, *The Outline of History* (London: George Newnes, 1920), pp. 464–6. Wells also wondered, 'why did the Chinese never discover America or Australia' despite their 'considerable overseas trade' during the period of the 'cultured Mings' (1368–1644)?

16. V. G. Childe, *What Happened in History* (Harmondsworth: Penguin, 1964 [1942]), p. 292.

17. V. G. Childe, *History* (Harmondsworth: Penguin, 1947), pp. 3–14.

18. G. Dawson, *Age of the Gods* (New York: Howard Fertig, Inc., 1970 [1928]), pp. xii–xx.

19. Ibid., pp. 256, 360–1, 383.

20. To cite the concluding words of another inspiring work by J. Breasted, *The Conquest of Civilization*, first published in 1926 and then revised in 1938 and 1954: 'Today, still disclosing the successive stages of the long human career, the stone first-hatchets lie deep in the river gravels of Egypt and France; the furniture of the pile-villages rests at the bottom of the Swiss lakes; the majestic pyramids and temples announcing the dawn of civilization rise along the Nile; the silent and deserted city-mounds by the Tigris and Euphrates shelter their myriads of clay tablets; the palaces of Crete look out toward the sea they once ruled; the Hittite cities yield up the wonderful story of their newly deciphered writing; the noble temples and sculptures of Greece still proclaim the new world of beauty and of freedom first revealed by the Greeks; the splendid Roman roads and aqueducts assert the supremacy and organized control of Rome; and the Christian church spires proclaim the new ideal of universal human brotherhood. These things continue to reveal the age-long course along which the developing life of man has moved; and in thus following his conquest of civilization, we have been following a *rising trail.*' See *The Conquest of Civilization* (New York: Harper and Brothers, 1954 [1926]), p. 650.

21. UNESCO, *History of Mankind: Cultural and Scientific Developments, Vol. 1: Prehistory and the Beginnings of Civilization* (Paris: UNESCO, 1979 [1963]), pp. 820, 104, 111, 351.

22. Ibid., pp. 359, 834.

23. Ibid., pp. xiii, xiv, 829.

24. W. H. McNeill, *The Rise of the West* (Chicago, IL: University of Chicago Press, 1963), p. 729. He writes further in the same page: 'However weak the reed, human reason has yet a rapier point....'

25. F. Braudel, *A History of Civilizations* (New York: Penguin, 1995), pp. 8, 42, 73, 168, 23.

26. Ibid., pp. 307, 315–16, 325, 329–31. Given this history, Braudel thought it was 'both fair and appropriate' for the Western world, during the Cold War conflict of ideologies, 'to call itself "the free world"' (p. 315).

27. There were many other world history textbooks published or redesigned in the 1960s which continued to articulate the idea of progress in the context of at a less Eurocentric narrative. The two-volume text, *A History of the World* (Chicago, IL: Rand McNally, 1960), by C. Starr, C. Nowell, B. Lyon, R. Stearns and T. Hamerow contained chapters and sections on the cultural achievements of all the world's people, although most of the book was still dedicated to the progress of Western civilization. Thomas P. Neill's *Story of Mankind* (New York, 1968) also devoted more attention to Western civilization, but it did at least 'assume a unity in the story of mankind that is based on its common origin, its common destiny, its common human nature, and its occupancy of a common globe' (p. 6). In his foreword to the English edition of the *Larousse Encyclopedia of Ancient and Modern History* (Feltham: P. Hamlyn, 1963), Arnold Toynbee had this to say: 'In this work, Western writers and editors have made a valiant effort to transcend the parochial Western point of view and to present the history of mankind as the sum of all the efforts of all sections of the human race... [T]he *Larousse Encylopedia* has earned the right to its title. It has made a notable new departure in giving non-Western contributions to mankind's culture a place in the sun' (p. 11). E. M. Burns'

and P. L. Ralph's *World Civilizations, Their History and Their Culture* (New York: W. W. Norton, 1974), was 'thoroughly revised' in the fifth edition of 1974 to include materials and recent historical research on the history of Africa, China, Japan and the Indian subcontinent. This was all done, let me emphasize, in a text in which the 'basic philosophical interpretation underlying the narrative is the conviction that most human progress thus far has resulted from the growth of intelligence and respect for the rights of man' (pp. xxv–xxvi).

28. S. Amin, *Accumulation on a World Scale: A Critique of the Theory of Underdevelopment* (New York: New York University Press, 1970); A. G. Frank, *Capitalism and Underdevelopment in Latin America* (New York: Penguin, 1967); A. G. Frank, *Latin America: Underdevelopment or Revolution* (New York: M. R. Press, 1969); W. Rodney, *How Europe Underdeveloped Africa* (Kingston, Jamaica: Vincent Harding, 1972).

29. T. Parsons, *Societies: Evolutionary and Comparative Perspectives* (Englewood Cliffs, NJ: Prentice Hall, 1966); N. Smelser, *Social Change in the Industrial Revolution* (London: Ashgate, 1959); D. Lerner, *The Passing of Traditional Society* (New York: Free Press, 1958); R. Bendix, *Nation Building and Citizenship* (Berkeley, CA: University of California Press, 1964); S. Huntington, *Political Order in Changing Societies* (New Haven, CT: Yale University Press, 1968); W. W. Rostow, *The Stages of Economic Growth: A Non-Communist Manifesto* (Cambridge: Cambridge University Press, 1960).

30. See M. Kesselman, 'Order or Movement? The Literature of Political Development as Ideology', *World Politics* 26 (1973) 139–54; Howard Wiarda, 'The Ethnocentrism of the Social Science: Implications for Research and Policy', *Review of Politics* 43 (1981) 163–97.

31. As early as 1973, the Marxist B. Warren published 'Imperialism and Capitalist Industrialization', where he persuasively showed , through the use of a large amount of data, that capitalist development was rapidly taking place in some Third World countries, see *New Left Review* 81 (1973) 3–44. P. Berger's *The Capitalist Revolution: Fifty Propositions about Prosperity, Equality, and Liberty* (New York: Basic Books, 1986) used the experience of East Asian industrialization as a refutation of dependency theory.

32. I. Wallerstein, *The Modern World-System I: Capitalist Agriculture and the Origins of the European World-Economy in the Sixteenth Century* (New York: Academic Press, 1974); *The Modern World-System II: Mercantilism and the Consolidation of the European World-Economy, 1600–1750* (New York: Academic Press, 1980); *The Modern World-System III: The Second Era of Great Expansion of the Capitalist World-Economy, 1730–1840s* (New York: Academic Press, 1989).

33. R. Robertson, 'Globality, Global Culture, and Images of World Order', in H. Haferkamp and N. J. Smelser (eds), *Social Changes and Modernity* (Berkeley, CA: University of California Press, 1992), pp. 395–411. Emphasis added.

34. In the last chapter of the *Modern World-System I*, Wallerstein drew a clear distinction between world-empires and 'the modern world system' (pp. 346–57). But it is in his collection of articles in *Unthinking Social Science* (Philadelphia, PA: Temple University Press, 2001, pp. 231–2, 247–8), where he articulated the idea of three stages in history and spoke of 'mini-systems'.

35. J. H. Bentley, *Shapes of World History in Twentieth-Century Scholarship* (Washington, DC: American Historical Association, 1996).

36. M. Horkheimer and T. Adorno, *Dialectic of Enlightenment* (Berkeley, CA: University of California Press, 1980), p. xi.
37. Two excellent sources on the 'Critical' school as a whole and its impact on social science studies and radical politics are D. Held, *Introduction to Critical Theory, Horkheimer to Habermas* (Berkeley, CA: University of California Press, 1980), and M. Jay, *The Dialectical Imagination* (Cambridge, MA: Harvard University Press, 1973).
38. M. Harris, *The Rise of Anthropological Theory, A History of Theories of Culture* (New York: Rowman & Littlefield, 1971), pp. 250–89.
39. F. Boas, *The Mind of Primitive Man* (New York: Free Press, 1963 [1911]), p. 20. Boas was more concerned with the implication of racial superiority but his arguments can also be read as a warning against the arrogance of cultural superiority implied in the idea of historical stages.
40. Cited in R. Wright, *Nonzero: The Logic of Human Destiny* (New York: Vintage, 2000), p. 14.
41. L. Pye (ed.), *Communications and Political Development* (Princeton, NJ: Princeton University Press, 1963).
42. A. Bloom, *The Closing of the American Mind* (New York: Simon & Schuster, 1987), p. 25.
43. Another school which deserves attention, as Marnie Hughes-Warrington has reminded me, is the highly influential 'postcolonial' school engendered by Edward Said after the publication in 1978 of his best seller *Orientalism* (New York: Vintage, 1978), where he carried what he later characterized as an 'adversarial critique' of the 'essentialized' way European artists, painters, travellers and writers had portrayed non-Western cultures as the 'Other' ('illogical' and 'despotic') of everything that was thought to be progressive ('rational' and 'liberal') about the West. A discussion of this school, and others associated with it, such as the Subaltern Studies school, will have to be postponed. For the moment let me recommend Keith Windschuttle's 'Edward Said's Orientalism revisited', where he argues effectively that it was really Said who presented an essentialist account of Western civilization in his silent treatment of the majority of Western scholars who had long transcended the ethnic prejudices of the past in their diligent devotion to the understanding of the histories and traditions of the world's cultures. *New Criterion* 17(5) (1999), online at <www.newcriterion.com>.
44. W. H. McNeill, *The Shape of European History* (New York: Oxford University Press, 1974), p. 3.
45. Ibid., pp. 24–30, 176.
46. W. H. McNeill, 'The Changing Shape of World History', reprinted in Dunn, *The New World History*, p. 148.
47. Ibid., pp. 148–9.
48. Ibid., p. 157. It is interesting to note McNeill's recollection that when he was writing *The Rise of the West* he was under the influence of the evolutionary anthropologist Robert Redfield from whom he learned that historical change was 'largely provoked' by encounters between 'separate civilizations'. In other words, much as the young McNeill stressed interactions among cultures, he believed that changes in history came about as *distinctive* cultures tried to adapt to new ways coming from other cultures; he did not think that cultures were figments of the imagination and that the real stuff of history were communication networks without cultural boundaries.

49. I. Wallerstein, *Unthinking Social Science, The Limits of Nineteenth-Century Paradigms* (Philadelphia, PA: Temple University Press, 2001), pp. 2, 64–79, 253–4. In one of the essays in this book which Wallerstein wrote originally in 1987, he observed that the idea of progress was still quite dominant despite a few detractors. He hoped that world-system analysis would 'remove the idea of progress from the status of a trajectory'. I tend to think that by the late 1980s the idea of progress was already dead.

50. S. K. Sanderson, *Social Transformations* (Cambridge, MA: Harvard University Press, 1995), pp. 356, 336.

51. Ibid., pp. 337–56.

52. For an excellent collection of writings on recent trends in world history by all the above-mentioned historians and many others see Dunn, *The New World History*.

53. W. McNeill, 'History and the Scientific World View,' *History and Theory* 37(1) (1998) 6. Emphasis added.

54. See K. Windschuttle's 'The Ethnocentrism of Clifford Geertz' for a cogent and vibrant critique of cultural relativism and how it excited Geertz to write a description of the practice of the burning of widows 'as a spectacle of awesome beauty'! *New Criterion* 21(2) (October 2002), online at <www.newcriterion. com>.

55. These stories can be found in a recent wave of challenging works including R. Bin Wong's *China Transformed: Historical Change and the Limits of the European Experience* (Ithaca, NY: Cornell University Press, 1997); A. G. Frank's *ReOrient: Global Economy in the Asian Age* (Berkeley, CA: University of California Press, 1998); Kenneth Pomeranz's *The Great Divergence: China, Europe and the Making of the Modern World Economy* (Princeton, NJ: Princeton University Press, 2000); and J. Lee and W. Feng's *One Quarter of Humanity: Malthusian Mythology and Chinese Realities, 1700–2000* (Cambridge: Cambridge University Press, 2001). For a critical assessment of these books, see R. Duchesne, 'Between Sinocentrism and Eurocentrism: Debating Andre Gunder Frank's ReOrient', *Science and Society* 65(4) (2001–2); 'What is Living and What is Dead in Eurocentrism', *Comparative Civilizations Review* 47 (2002); 'The Post-Malthusian World Began in Western Europe in the Eighteenth Century: A Reply to Goldstone and Wong', *Science and Society* 67(2) (2003); 'Malthus and the Demographic Systems of Modern Europe and Imperial China: A Critique of Lee and Feng', *Review of Radical Political Economics* 35(4) (2003); and 'On the Rise of the West: Researching Kenneth Pomeranz's Great Divergence', *Review of Radical Political Economics* 36(1) (2004).

56. Bentley, *Shapes of World History in Twentieth-Century Scholarship*, pp. 9–12.

57. Ibid., p. 4.

58. Ibid., pp. 2, 12–15.

59. Ibid., p. 14.

60. Dunn, *The New World History*, p. 225.

61. C. Lockard, 'Global History, Modernization, and the World-System Approach', in Dunn, *The New World History*, pp. 233, 238.

62. Dunn, *The New World History*, p. 226. P. Stearns, in his 1987 article 'Periodization of World History Teaching', also refers to Wallerstein's model as 'one of the most fruitful general theories for world history.' In Dunn, *The New World History*, p. 371.

63. Bentley, *Shapes of World History in Twentieth-Century Scholarship*, pp. 16–17.

64. Ibid., pp. 21–3.
65. P. Manning, *Navigating World History* (New York: Palgrave Macmillan/St. Martin's Press, 2003), pp. xi, 3–6, 15. Emphasis added.
66. J. Thornton, *Africa and the Africans in the Making of the Atlantic World, 1400–1800* (New York: Cambridge University Press, 1998), p. 7.
67. Manning, *Navigating World History*, p. 159.
68. Not everyone of course stopped teaching Western Civ courses, or writing Eurocentric world histories. Two world histories published in the 1970s, *The Penguin History of the World* by J. M. Roberts (1976) and *A History of the World* (1979) by Hugh Thomas, devoted even less space to Asia and Africa than McNeill's *Rise of the West* and Braudel's *History of Civilizations*. Although Roberts expanded the areas dedicated to non-Western histories in later editions, he also added in the preface to the 1995 edition that he was even more convinced about 'the centrality of Europe's role in the making of the modern world' (Harmondsworth: Penguin, 1995, pp. xiii–xiv). And yet, what is illuminating about this attitude is that Roberts was also no longer convinced about the progressive role of the West, but felt that the only 'general trend' which could be observed in history was 'a growing unity of human experience' and 'a growing human capacity to control the environment'. While the West was the main source of this trend, he did *not* think it was possible to decide whether the European tradition was 'greedy, oppressive, brutal and exploitative', or 'objectively improving, beneficent and humane' (pp. 1098–109). Similarly, Thomas may seem too Eurocentric in his obvious identification with Western liberal values, but he also could not help writing 'it is obvious that it is western Europe with North America which, since the fifteenth century at least, *for good or evil*, has provided the world's dynamism' (New York: HarperCollins, p. xvii).
69. There may even be a 'limit' to the good that 'the industry of man' can bring to the 'felicity of man in general', as Denis Diderot (1713–1784) thought. On the origins and growth of the idea of progress in the writings of Enlightenment thinkers, see J. B. Bury's *The Idea of Progress* (New York: Dover, 1960 [1932]). This work still remains the best account of the history of this idea 'up to the time when it became a current creed' – as Bury thought it had in his own time.
70. Ibid. For a short but excellent discussion of Kant's essay 'An Idea for a Universal History from the Cosmopolitan Point of View', originally written in 1784, see R. G. Collingwood's *The Idea of History*, ed. W. J. Van der Dussen, rev. edn (Oxford: Oxford University Press, 1993), pp. 93–104.
71. This passage and other aspects of Hegel's philosophy of history are well examined in S. Rosen's *G. W. F Hegel, An Introduction to the Science of Wisdom* (New Haven, CT: Yale University Press, 1974), pp. 3–46. Kant had earlier made the similar argument that 'the history of nature begins with goodness, for it is the work of God; but the history of freedom begins with evil, for it is the work of man', as cited in Manfred Kuehn, *Kant, A Biography* (Cambridge: Cambridge University Press, 2002), p. 300.

recommended resources

Bentley, J., *Shapes of World History in Twentieth-Century Scholarship* (Washington, DC: American Historical Association, 1996).

Braudel, F., *A History of Civilizations* (Harmondsworth: Penguin, 1995).

Breasted, J. H., *The Conquest of Civilization* (New York: Harper and Brothers, 1954 [1926]).

Bury, J. B., *The Idea of Progress: An Inquiry into its Origin and Growth* (New York: Dover, 1960).

Childe, V. G., *What Happened in History* (Harmondsworth: Penguin, 1964 [1942]).

Duchesne, R., 'On the Rise of the West: Researching Kenneth Pomeranz's Great Divergence', *Review of Radical Political Economics* 36(1) (2004) [in press].

Dunn, R. (ed.), *The New World History: A Teacher's Companion* (New York: Bedford/ St. Martin's, 2000).

Frank, A. G., *Latin America: Underdevelopment or Revolution* (New York: M. R. Press, 1969).

Horkheimer, M., and Adorno, T., *Dialectic of Enlightenment* (Berkeley and Los Angeles, CA: University of California Press, 1980).

Manning, P., *Navigating World History: Historians Create a Global Past* (New York: Palgrave Macmillan/St. Martin's Press, 2003).

Roberts, J. M., *The Penguin History of the World* (Harmondsworth: Penguin, 1995 [1976]).

Rostow, W. W., *The Stages of Economic Growth: A Non-Communist Manifesto* (Cambridge: Cambridge University Press, 1960).

Wallerstein, I., *Unthinking Social Science, The Limits of Nineteenth-Century Paradigms* (Philadelphia, PA: Temple University Press, 2001).

Wells, H. G., *The Outline of History* (London: George Newnes, 1920).

Windschuttle, K., 'The Ethnocentrism of Clifford Geertz' *New Criterion* 21(2) (October 2002), online at <www.newcriterion.com/archive/21/oct02/geertz. htm>.

8
modern, postmodern, world

'... in all these fundamental positions of subjectivity, a different kind of I-ness and egoism is also possible... the insertion of the I into the we'.

Martin Heidegger[1]

In 1918, a decorated Austrian artillery officer called Ludwig Wittgenstein was taken prisoner by the Italian army. During his internment he completed one of the great philosophical works of the twentieth century, his *Tractatus Logico-Philosophicus*. The slender volume ranged over a broad array of topics, but great attention was placed on the philosophy of language. In this early piece, Wittgenstein explored the difference between saying and showing. Like his logician colleagues, he believed that only the logical propositions of science could make clear sense, but unlike them, Wittgenstein argued that what cannot be said may nonetheless be shown. Linguistic propositions, for example, can represent reality, yet they cannot represent the operation of representation itself. That operation can never be described, though it is often referenced. Wittgenstein illuminated the *limits* of language and indicated an unspeakable realm beyond it. Offering a glimpse of the otherwise nonsensical, he concluded this work of numerically sequenced steps by proposing that the reader 'must so to speak throw away the ladder, after he has climbed up on it'.[2] Wittgenstein later rejected much of what he had written under Italian guard, but his distinction between saying and showing endured. Yet for the academic work that premises itself on the logical ordering of statements, patterns and habits remain well grooved. The past weighs heavily on the present. In the discipline of history, few take seriously the questions concerning representation, and the problem of the linguistic limit rarely raises a stir. With unabated confidence in the power of language, most historians have not climbed Wittgenstein's ladder. Meanwhile, the actual process of history constantly steps ahead of us. History moves forward, complicated and different, and with each new configuration, historians must recharge or reassess their perspective.

In recent years, historical thought has been recharged and reassessed in two important and challenging ways. From within the discipline, world history has demanded an opening of topics and questions away from the solipsism of 'Western Civilization'. World history has sought to include others, and further, to understand the various world regions, including Europe, within broad social and ecological networks of interconnection and exchange. The other challenge to historical thought has come from postmodernism, a general category of ideas with no particular disciplinary home. Interestingly, postmodernism has also argued that Europe has overextended itself. It has asserted that European modes of thought regard themselves as natural, and therefore superior, to all others. Like world history, postmodernism has endeavoured to decentre European presumptions about itself. But in general, whereas world history has ventured to change the *content* of historical scholarship, postmodernism has undertaken to change the *thinking* behind such scholarship. Despite their cotemporaneous emergence and despite the resemblance of their agendas, the differences between world history and postmodernism have overwhelmed their similarities. Except for an occasional expression of opposition, scant dialogue has occurred between the two positions.[3]

This chapter aims to show both the common set of concerns and the distinct strategies of world history and postmodernism. It details the Eurocentric bases of world-historical thought, but argues as well that the postmodern critique of history is itself nested within a condition that postmodernism must consider historical. Postmodernism resides in an irresolvable tension between its programme and its own historical circumstance: the position has emerged from the perception of a world-historical development, but its sceptical turn undermines the possibility of representing that condition. The resulting impossible predicament is the basis of postmodern historiography. The chapter evaluates 'the modern', world history and the place of Europe, postmodernism and its historical condition, and the postmodern historiography of subaltern studies.

'the modern'

For the last several decades, 'postmodernism' has been vigorously discussed within and across several academic disciplines. Its meaning has varied in these different contexts, and there has been little agreement concerning its significance, applicability or value. Such instability has perhaps contributed to the concept's success. Without an enforceable definition, 'postmodernism' remains analytically flexible, much like the descriptor 'globalization'. Unlike 'globalization', however, the multiplicity of postmodern positions mirrors the general indeterminacy and uncertainty that most of its proponents associate with the term. Much of the problem in defining 'the postmodern' follows from the centuries-old debate, still unresolved, over what precisely constitutes 'the modern'. To arrive at some understanding of 'the postmodern' it is necessary to clarify its point of departure.

Though a term of everyday use, 'the modern' is a historical concept that marks the present as qualitatively distinct from the past. According to the intellectual historian Reinhart Koselleck, a self-conscious notion of living in the modern emerged only at the end of the seventeenth century after decades of European religious wars and the emergence of the state system. Polities faced an entirely new and unknown future. Previous methods for understanding the passage of time, such as eschatology, classical example, astrology and rational prognosis, had conceived the future in terms of an already known past. Within such frameworks, time had been regarded as a neutral medium for human activities. But into the eighteenth century, the increasing complexity and acceleration of an oncoming future gave time a cognitive dimension of its own. 'The modern' was thus used to detach the present from the past as the present uniquely encountered its own uncertain future. Under this condition, long-standing techniques for recording the movement of time became obsolete. Annals and chronicles told aggregate stories in neutral time and were incapable of grasping the new complex relation of past, present, and future. Furthermore, with every new future, the entire past would be seen from a new perspective, requiring fresh interpretation. 'History' as a distinct mode of thought was born along with its twin, 'the modern'. 'History' began as an attempt to understand human activity within the uncertainty of 'modern' time. As the past appeared evermore foreign and other, and as the future appeared ever closer and more present, history sought to master the experience of time, not through a simple recording of events, but through a thematic, narrative *reconstruction* of temporal complexity.[4]

One of the most important unknown futures that came into view during the eighteenth century concerned the European relation to the rest of the globe. By mid-century, as Europeans increasingly saw themselves interconnected to distant locales, commentators began to call for a more encompassing *world history*. Methodologically though, the relevant factors involved in intercontinental history were well beyond the actual experience of most writers. World history thus confirmed and further propelled the move away from the annal and toward thematic systematizing. In addition, this high degree of requisite abstraction enabled world history to absorb the various peoples of the globe into its singular narrative. Radically different cultures and understandings of time were historicized within a European set of meanings. This globe-spanning narration was accomplished by transforming spatial differences into temporal differences, by regarding contemporary non-Europeans as holdovers from a previous time.[5] By placing the earth's people into a chronological order of development, Europeans nullified existing differences under the single rubric of 'world history'. It is from here that the modern notions of 'progress' emerged, oftentimes justifying European domination over allegedly 'backward' or 'undeveloped' peoples. Postmodernism has often been described as the closing curtain on precisely this belief in progress.[6] It is important to note, however, that the concepts of development and progress, as applied to different peoples, would not be possible without the overcoming of difference along the *single* index of historical measurement. Just as historical thought attempted to master the new uncertainty of time, the expanded concerns of world history sought to master the European confrontation with human diversity. Both relied on a notion of 'the modern', the marker of present time.

In its understanding of itself, 'the modern' was (and is) a recognition of difference – the difference of non-modern times and non-modern peoples. But simultaneous to this differentiation, 'the modern' creates conceptual *unification* at a higher level of abstraction, what it calls 'history'. By the middle of the eighteenth century, European affairs, both at home and abroad, shattered the received understanding of neutral time. As the present entered into a precarious future, knowledge, order and political strategy demanded the reconstruction of a newly complex and uncertain time.

world history and the place of europe

This definition of 'the modern', what the art historian T. J. Clark called 'a way back to totality',[7] was at its core an ordering of the world through historical knowledge. Immanuel Kant attempted a philosophical consummation of this project in an essay of 1784, 'Idea for a Universal History from a Cosmopolitan Point of View'. Not normally one of Kant's leading themes, 'world history' in this essay expresses the human understanding of nature's plan for a global 'civic union' – as based on a particularly European form of law.[8] Hegel extended this style of speculation with a philosophical system more attentive to the problem of historical change itself. For Hegel, history is a dialectical progress of forces and counter-forces that increasingly raises the level of human consciousness and human freedom. Unlike Kant, whose history emphasized a Europe-centred *cosmopolitanism*, Hegel reactivated the unilinear narrative to rank in time the world's geographically separated peoples. In the appendix to his famous *Lectures on the Philosophy of World History*, Hegel defined Africa as a 'primitive... unhistorical continent, with no movement or development of its own'. Similarly, indigenous Americans are 'like unenlightened children', whose dying off in the millions is an inevitable result of their 'purely natural culture... [in] contact with more advanced nations'.[9] World historical reflection again embodied a political condition of its time. Anticipating Hegel's lecture by just a few years, US Secretary of War William H. Crawford had said of indigenous Americans, 'They cannot much longer exist in the exercise of their savage rights and customs. They must become civilized, or they will finally... become extinct.'[10]

Hegel's white-supremacist views of world history became standard fare as Europeans intensified their global colonial endeavours throughout the nineteenth century. Industrial power and the accelerating influence of science appeared to substantiate both the modern sense of temporal disjuncture and the superiority of European civilization.[11] Social applications of Darwinian theory did the same. Among historians though, the demands of ongoing disciplinary professionalization undermined to a degree the speculative, non-empirical claims of world-scale studies.[12] In addition, state competition and the rise of nationalism following Napoleon condensed the historical object of study. Von Ranke postulated that world historical events occur in the external relations of nations. Though the goal of historical scholarship 'remains the conception and composition of a history of mankind', it is from 'the conflict between the different national groups [that] Universal History comes into being'.[13] Given the increasing power of European states over other peoples, subsequent world histories considered the Europeanization of the world as the key to understanding the past. With due regard to evidence and method, historical writing remained, in the manner of Hegel, decidedly Eurocentric and triumphal into the twentieth century.[14]

World War I delivered a sharp blow to these kinds of European imaginings. The war squandered the wealth garnered during the late imperial period and wasted tens of millions of lives, maimed and killed. Art movements like 'Dada' now spoofed the pretence of European superiority. At the same time, Oswald Spengler's *The Decline of the West*[15] bespoke for many the anxiety concerning Europe's future. Spengler understood world history in civilizational terms, and in an application of 'organic' metaphors familiar since romanticism, he described civilizations in patterns of ascendancy and degeneration. Though Spengler emphasized 'the West', his system of nature-bound lifecycles dethroned Europe from the almost transcendent vanguard status enjoyed since Hegel. Largely influenced by these civilizational schematics, Arnold Toynbee issued his massive work *A Study of History*[16] in twelve volumes from 1934 to 1961. Toynbee was considerably more ecumenical than his predecessor, including substantial material on non-European traditions. This followed from his agenda to write a history for the age of world unification, in which disparate civilizational histories were reportedly now merging into a single history of the world.[17] Toynbee's attempt to fold the European story into a larger world history greatly offended the Dutch academic Pieter Geyl, who called it nothing less than 'treason [and]... blasphemy against Western Civilization'. In somewhat more sober tones, Geyl also objected to the speculative and minimally empirical methodology of this revived Kantian project.[18] Another commentator noted that Toynbee remained too entrenched in conventional beliefs concerning non-Europeans to write adequately a history of the world.[19] From this second perspective and contrary to Geyl's Euro-patriotism, it was precisely the ongoing and intensifying linkages between world regions, especially after 1945, that created the demand for a material, rather than philosophical, history of the world.

The work of William McNeill, starting with *The Rise of the West* of 1963, foregrounded material connections and dynamics between different locales.[20] Unlike the Rankean tradition, he did not focus singularly on national competition, but rather on cultural diffusion and influence. McNeill's many publications are perhaps the founding texts of contemporary English-language world history. Yet despite his attempt to overturn the Eurocentric presumptions of previous efforts, his work came under attack expressly on these grounds. His university colleague Marshall Hodgson pointed, for example, to period markers that reinscribe European emphasis and centrality. Above all, he critiqued McNeill's diffusionist approach that unwittingly understates the broad, extra-European complex *within which* social interactions could occur.[21] Similarly drawing on the commonalities of a large Afro-Eurasian context, J. M. Blaut went on to argue that diffusionism, McNeill's among others, reveals a European colonial mentality at the heart of modern historical practice. Blaut remarked that 'rise of the West' type histories prop up a series of 'myths' about inherently European qualities – technological expertise, social structure, rational thought, among others – to explain the success of modern Europe, a position of dominance better accounted by the story of its colonialism. By 'myth', Blaut meant a falsehood concerning cultural origins maintained by political power.[22] But declaring a view to be a myth is also a deployment of power; it attempts to dismiss a rival position by claiming possession of an otherwise obvious and neutral truth. Thus Geyl's Euro-patriotism, the precise opposite of Blaut's anti-colonialism, can also endeavour to push aside opponents with the denunciation of 'myth'.[23]

This problem of what constitutes truth recently emerged as a key issue within world-historical studies. R. Bin Wong and Kenneth Pomeranz showed that the so-called 'historical record' crucially depends upon the perspective of initial research questions. For example, explanations of modern economic and industrial expansion radically shift when Chinese history is given its own trajectory instead of being treated as a laggard version of Europe. Careful assessment of eighteenth-century China overturns long-held and still popular assumptions about Europe's uniquely dynamic economy. Categories of analysis themselves, such as 'state' or 'market', already bias analysis toward a European standard and a European teleology. Wong and Pomeranz have attempted to understand the past as best as possible, but have improved Blaut's anti-Eurocentrism by hesitating to assert knowledge claims as absolute, position-free statements of fact.[24] In a similar vein, world-system theory has acknowledged that its narrative of the past is itself within a historically contingent social system. The overall project has drawn much of its theory from Marx, but rejects both the normative Hegelianism and positivist economism found in the Marxist canon. 'There are no detached observers in world-systems study', one of its leading theoreticians explained.[25] From this perspective, neither the European teleology that Blaut attacked nor his counter-claim of absolute fact remains tenable. According to Immanuel Wallerstein, this very split between moral philosophy and objective science is itself the core of a European epistemology that professes position-free and value-free knowledge claims. Like Wong and Pomeranz, world-system theory has thus pursued empirical evaluation while critically assessing European categories of analysis. Yet this approach has also been attacked. With a Geyl-like defence of the 'European tradition' and its universal rationality, the Marxist sociologist Gregor McLennan has argued that such anti-Eurocentrism cannot shed its dependence on European modes of thought. Wallerstein responded that the contradiction is inescapable under current conditions of European (conceptual) domination, but that this does not preclude a simultaneous effort against it. For Wallerstein, the goal of scholarship remains the 'reconstruction of knowledge', a history beyond both moral teleology and positivist fact.[26]

postmodernism and its world-historical condition

From its start in the late seventeenth century, the 'modern' has referenced an intellectual or discursive strategy to eliminate the complexity of difference under a European-defined totality. A new experience of time marked the 'modern', which in distinguishing itself in this way simultaneously created the perspective of 'history' as the ordering of differential time. One of the most important of new experiences was the worldwide projection of European power. The world's various peoples were ordered, like time itself, into a single narration of 'world history'. Manifest differences between contemporary peoples were set into a chronological progression that stretched from a primeval jungle to Hegel's lecture hall. In world history, as in history generally, the notation of difference simultaneously served to fashion unity at a higher level. During the twentieth century, world-historical studies began to question this singular narrative of European centrality. World history took seriously the problems of historical differentiation with respect even to the categories of its own analysis. The project did not question the notion or value of history itself, however; it remained 'modern' by pursuing what Wallerstein called 'reconstruction'. Postmodernism is the suspension of this belief in the value of reconstruction. Postmodernism argues that differences are too great to be absorbed by the single register of historical time. Its authors vary in their approach to the problem, but postmodernism asserts that simply adjusting analytic categories does not sufficiently dismantle the Euro-supremacy of historical thought itself.

It was, not surprisingly, Toynbee who introduced the English term 'post-Modern' to describe Europe's 'spiritual crisis' of diminishing 'self-assurance' after World War I.[27] But Toynbee did not reflect this crisis back into his own narrative construction, written of course under the European rubric of 'history'. In the 1970s, 'postmodernism' re-emerged among critics of architecture and art, but developed an international currency and broad socio-theoretical applicability with Lyotard's *The Postmodern Condition* of 1979. Lyotard defined postmodernism as 'incredulity toward metanarratives', by which he meant teleological stories that guide or structure explanations of social reality. He was principally concerned with the metanarrative of progress, dependent of course on a historical framework.[28] He explained postmodernism as the consequence of capital and informational flows that have moved beyond political or institutional control. The mobility and complexity of this new transnational society has broken individual subjectivity away from large civic formations such as states, parties and traditions. Instead, personal identity has fractured into a series of aggregated, different, and constantly changing local meanings. These dispersed and otherwise incommensurable clusters of meaning, strewn across the social field, have upended the authority of singular and unifying metanarratives. 'Consensus', Lyotard wrote, 'has become an outmoded and suspect value.'[29] Lyotard's double focus on language and society became a common methodological move beginning in the 1980s. Cultural studies, for example, emphasized social heterogeneity against dominating, universalizing narratives. But as many commentators were quick to point out, the story of the end of the metanarrative was itself a metanarrative. Lyotard challenged the presumption of world history but could not disentangle himself from its explanatory power.

The hallmark of Lyotard's 'postmodernism' was its attention to (narrative) language. Several other important French theorists were grouped, in the English-speaking world at least, under his postmodern label. Though they did not always share Lyotard's concern with defining a new era, they were absorbed, nearly entirely, by the problems of linguistic representation. Addressing history directly, Michel Foucault critiqued its 'uniform model of temporalization... [its] single system of differences'. History collapses different meaning-systems, or what he called 'discursive practices', under its own 'totalization' or reconstruction. One particular discursive practice is in other words granted universal explanatory power. Similarly, Michel de Certeau argued throughout several works that historical scholarship resided in an irresolvable dilemma between narrative and epistemology. Historians distinguish their texts from fictions, but they cannot separate the object of their analysis – the past – from the narrative production of their own text. Roland Barthes also noted sceptically that the historical fact can only exist in language, and yet this fact alleges to copy, 'purely and simply', another kind of existence, entirely outside of language. The representation of past reality was thus for Certeau and Barthes a rhetorical performance. Barthes called it 'no more than the signifier of the speech act as act of authority'. Certeau elaborated: 'the discourse gives itself credibility in the name of reality which it is supposed to represent, but this authorized appearance of the "real" serves precisely to camouflage the practice which in fact determines that appearance.'[30]

Finally, the most intensive concentration on language-representation came from Jacques Derrida. In his first major work, a reading of Edmund Husserl's *Origin of Geometry*, Derrida noted that something could enter into historical narration 'only if it has become an absolute object, i.e. an ideal object which, paradoxically, must have broken all the moorings which secured it to the empirical ground of history'.[31] In other words, for history to have any sense at all, the uniqueness of the past must be generalized into some kind of communicable meaning which – in its communicability – violates the past's requisite particularity or difference. Few historians regard their work as non-empirical projections of an ideal, but without this 'absolute object', the past becomes incomprehensible, its residues utterly mute. The most common example of this 'ideality' is surely the historian's use of the date, which paradoxically communicates the past to the present as knowable while marking the past as distinctly other. Derrida writes, 'A date is mad because it is never itself or what it says it is, it is always more or less than what it is. What it is is either what it is or what it isn't.'[32] From Derrida's perspective, the writing of history inescapably enters into its own contradiction.

Unlike Lyotard, Derrida did not, and could not, ground his analysis in social causes and contexts. But even here, at the extreme edge of the postmodern critique of history, Derrida did offer something of a periodization for his position. It emerged, he wrote, when European culture could no longer confidently consider itself 'the culture of reference'.[33] At that world-historical moment, the conceptual presumptions of European thought became destabilized. Derrida did not consider this to have been simply a logical or philosophical problem, but an overall dislocation of European culture in political, economic, technical as well as discursive registers. Yet the conditions of Derrida's (anti-)method prevented him from historicizing these features. Reflecting on the problem of historical representation, he instead periodized several key 'names' to indicate the decentring of European thought. The first is Nietzsche. In an early and now well-known essay, 'On the Uses and Disadvantages of History for Life' (1874), Nietzsche launched a postmodern critique of historical metanarrative and totalization. He railed against the 'universal empire of history', which, in its reconstruction of the past, overcomes and absorbs all difference and thereby bloats itself into the goal of all existence and all time. 'Overproud European of the nineteenth century, you are raving!' he slammed. For Nietzsche, historical discourse reveals, in ironic opposition to itself, that representation has entered into crisis. Modernity is a 'cosmopolitan carnival of gods, arts, and customs', a complex of divergent meanings, signs and values, which the historian reassuringly orders into a single story, a 'world exhibition'. But this international and transnational convolution of culture relativized the European perspective. The European story is now just one of many; the 'world exhibition' actually undermines the historian's own claim to knowledge. History, or rather world history, reveals itself as 'only an occidental prejudice'.[34]

Nietzsche had already taken a more radical turn the year before in the essay 'On Truth and Lying in an Extra-Moral Sense'. Here the attack is not just against historical scholarship, but the entire concept of 'truth' itself. The essay opens with a 'fable' of '"world history"': an animal invented knowledge and then thought itself the centre of the universe. 'World history' gets scare-quotes to parody modernity's 'raving' elevation of itself into the source of the world's meaning and the world's 'truth', yet 'world history' drives Nietzsche's critique. 'What is truth? a mobile army of metaphors, metonyms, anthropomorphisms, in short, a sum of human relations which were poetically and rhetorically heightened, transferred, and adorned, and after long use seem solid, canonical, and binding to a nation.' Nietzsche defined truth as an aesthetic projection *onto* the world of a human perception *of* the world. Furthermore, a truth-claim's original, particular, emplaced perspective becomes obscured by its historical accretion to a transcendent principle that unifies a community. Truth guarantees the 'caste system and sequence of rank'; it grounds both social organization and conceptual order, disclosed to be two sides of the same coin. Though Nietzsche's use of 'nation' is not entirely clear (in one example he cites Rome), he showed that the historical formation of different truth-communities – different polities, different languages – undermines the basis of any pre-textual 'truth'. Nietzsche relativized all social formations and all universal claims to knowledge through a world-historical reflection that attempts to destroy itself and its own epistemology.[35]

The second name Derrida cites is Heidegger (the third is Freud, who will be not be discussed here). Like Nietzsche and influenced by him, Heidegger sought to dismantle European presumptions of knowledge. He called for the 'destruction' of Europe's theoretical tradition. Heidegger was largely concerned with what he called an 'authentic' way of life.[36] This has become difficult, he argued, because of the mushrooming success of European universalism. Science treats nature as a series of equations, technology annihilates distance, and history translates experience into chronology. 'The fundamental event of the modern age is the conquest of the world as picture.'[37] This refers not to any picture of the world, but to the world understood as a picture, to a representational universalism that has itself become universal. Heidegger described this dilemma of contemporary modernity in historical language: as the global domination of European concepts and practices, 'the world-historical moment of the planetary'.[38] Yet as historical scholarship is itself an expression of the modern, examining the European tradition from a world-historical perspective only redoubles the straightjacket of uniformity. Instead, the European presumption must be critiqued from within, 'this hardened tradition must be loosened up, and the concealments which it has brought about must be dissolved'.[39] For Heidegger, it is only the internal interrogation and disassembling of European theory that makes possible a 'transition' out of our historical epoch and toward a new beginning.[40]

Nietzsche, Heidegger and Derrida – the most important authors in the postmodern turn – focused their critiques on historical thought, and with it, the European ideal of universal 'truth'. All three nested their position within a particular historical relation between Europe and the world. Yet following their critique, they could not write 'world history' to explain it. They all acknowledged this contradiction. They marked themselves within a European epistemological tradition that they could not escape but that in their estimation was losing its conceptual balance into an unknown future. Nietzsche wrote:

> Among Europeans today there is no lack of those who are entitled to call themselves homeless in a distinctive and honourable sense... We are children of the future, how could we be at home in this today? We feel disfavour for all ideals that might lead one to feel at home in this fragile, broken time of transition.[41]

The future beyond 'truth' can be anticipated, but not yet practised, while the past and its ideals cling to the present. Contradiction is thus itself the sign of the present, the era of transition. Caught homeless between European 'truth' and its anticipated passing, the contradiction of the postmodern position is insurmountable for reasons that are themselves historical. What then distinguishes this contradiction from those these authors critiqued? The distinction is in the direction of the project's reflection. These authors were not looking to stabilize themselves – in the manner of historical narrative – through a *reconstruction* of complexity and difference. They sought instead to reclaim complexity and difference through a *deconstruction*[42] of their own European conceptual apparatus.

The postmodern strategy detailed here is historical and anti-historical at the same time. In the work of these authors, this contradiction is not conceptually managed, but emphasized. This contradiction exposes the otherness of time and place normally absorbed by the discourse of knowledge and mastery. But for many, discursive auto-critique is an insufficient tool of analysis. Cardinal emphasis on language, according to this view, is a blanket abstraction concealing the social distribution of power and privilege. Foucault's description of his work as a 'discourse about discourses'[43] denies analytic place to what by most standards comprises empirical reality. The feminist philosopher Susan Bordo argued that modernist objectivity – 'the view from nowhere' – had been replaced by a saturating language criterion that now constitutes a 'view from everywhere'. She criticized the institutional practice of postmodern knowledge production as metatheoretical discourse detached from 'concrete others'.[44] Her counter-position stressed differences, not as a function of language, but of empirically determinable social relations. Even sympathetic readings of deconstruction noted that internal critique of the 'Western' tradition recasts Asia into a bloodless other. In *Of Grammatology* for example, Derrida delimited 'the West' through a mistaken distinction between its phonetic writing and the supposedly ideographic system of the Chinese. The book's translator Gayatri Spivak called it 'reverse ethnocentrism', while another supporter of Derrida noted, 'he attributes imagined, fantastical qualities to the East without paying attention to its *reality*'.[45] Part of this demand for more detailed social specificity was taken up within postmodernism itself. In his later work, Michel Foucault increasingly configured the problem of discourse in relation to questions of power. Yet here too, 'the West' appears overdrawn. In the first volume of his *History of Sexuality*, Foucault explored sex-discourse in nineteenth-century Europe, detailing its power to organize society and control individuals through internalized norms. In a largely appreciative text, Ann Laura Stoler wrote that Foucault's explanation of this modern European subject formation missed entirely the colonialism at its core. She argued that the bourgeois subject and its social order relied on racial discourse and coercive systems of colonial labour. The modern European history of sexuality could not properly be distinguished from the 'discursive and practical field of empire'.[46] For practitioners of historically situated analysis, Derrida's derision of empiricism as 'philosophical nonsense'[47] leaves unattended the 'reality' of domination, especially as administered by Europe. The object of historical analysis is in this way caught between an account of power and the deconstruction of the analytic object itself.

postmodern world historiography

With the rise of postmodernism, this impasse generally split along disciplinary lines. Literary studies emphasized discursive contradictions, while historians generally ignored the epistemological complications evidenced by the postmodern critique. For historians, this has come without surprise. According to Rebecca Spang, the impasse would place historians in 'the impossible position' of having to assess both historical events and the limits of historical discourse.[48] Nonetheless, some historians like Spang have attempted to take seriously this double demand. Postmodern historiography can be defined as the work emerging from this impossible protocol. Joan Scott, for example, in her essential volume *Gender and the Politics of History*, presented a history of nineteenth-century France while simultaneously dismantling, both historically and historiographically, the concepts 'man', 'woman', 'gender' and 'work'. In a subsequent study on the history of French feminism, she showed that feminist women have insisted on equal status with men but necessarily through a differentiating category called 'women'. These women represent the kind of work Scott conducts; they have 'only paradoxes to offer'. But this paradox, or impossibility, does not entail political resignation or the substitution of aesthetics for knowledge, as critics like Bardo have charged. Rather, the paradox of the category 'woman' reveals the 'constitutive contradictions' of the social structures in which women have lived and against which they have fought.[49] In a similar strategy of paradox, subaltern studies has worked within and against the universal of 'Europe' and its 'world history'.

In logic, 'subaltern' refers to the subset of a universal. Subaltern studies began in 1980s India as an attempt to write the Indian past against the teleological, normative and universalizing presumptions of European history. The subaltern studies group considered that Indian history had hitherto overemphasized nation-state formation at the expense of local peoples, their perspectives, their experiences, and their resistance to colonialism and national elites. Such standard stories described India as approaching the European ideal of nation-state modernity. Simply shifting the focus of research to the indigenous would not be enough, however. The discipline of history is itself a conceptual framework derived from Europe. Every history in this regard resides in Europe. One of the movement's leading proponents, Dipesh Chakrabarty, summed up the predicament that faces all non-European and world histories:

'Europe' remains the sovereign theoretical subject of all histories, including ones we call 'Indian,' 'Chinese,' 'Kenyan,' and so on. There is a particular way in which all these other histories tend to become variations on a master narrative that could be called 'the history of Europe'. In this sense, 'Indian' history is itself in a position of subalternity.[50]

The founder of the subaltern studies group Ranajit Guha offered the tangible case of eighteenth-century British colonial administration. The East India Company commissioned historical scholarship to help organize its knowledge of the indigenous cultures and customs affecting colonial commerce and polity. Such histories were expressions of colonial power in which the non-historical cultures of India were translated into a conceptual apparatus then used to control the local population. These texts then become both the model and the evidentiary basis, the 'archival documents', used to understand the 'Indian' past.[51] This attention to the European imprint on all histories was of course not new. The keenest attempts in the mid-twentieth century to initiate a world-historical project, such as those of Hodgson and Barraclough, recognized that 'history' was a European category of understanding.[52] But subaltern studies has looked to move beyond this concession and into the 'impossible' space of critical history.

Subaltern studies focus largely on the conceptual horizon of historical actors. People rarely experience their lives in the ways historians explain them. Even histories of daily life are rationalized into a narrative of explication and chronology distinct from actual practice and self-understanding. This disjuncture becomes especially apparent in the evaluation of religion and superstition. In the case of Indian history, many Hindus experienced gods and spirits as real. This was an interpretation of reality, or a conceptual horizon, which contributed to the construction and cohesion of self and community. In such circumstances, the secular calendar of the historian is an imposed and alien time-world. Religion can of course be documented, but its own non-historical consciousness is erased by translation into the historical terms of modern Europe. Conversely, the goal of subaltern studies is to mark the limits of this historical representation and indicate those places that – outside of 'history' – fracture the universal claim of Europe. According to Chakrabarty's postmodern historiography, 'there is no getting away from the historical understanding of time. The point is to de-naturalize it.'[53] In Chiapas Mexico, for example, rebellion throughout the twentieth century was not fought solely on economic terms, but as a battle of 'the soul'. The defence of *el poblado* has blurred the historian's normal analytic categories by describing the people, the land and the past. This indigenous resistance, in the interpretation of Adolfo Gilly, signifies an 'enchanted world' outside the universal measures of money, territory and history.[54] Walter Johnson similarly interpreted African-American slave rebellions against the US national narrative of ever-greater inclusion.

Slaves rose up within distinct imaginative frameworks: as Africans, as Jacobins, as millennial Christians.

> The term 'slave revolt' is less a description of these events than the naming by one side – the winning side – of a bloody conflict characterized by the clash of alternative understandings of exactly what it was that was at stake in the Americas.[55]

Johnson argued that the 'neutral' reconstruction of historical time obscures the distinct temporality, the distinct meaning-world, within which slaves lived and fought. History thus preserves violations of the past by reiterating the European organization of time. Yet alternative slave temporalities can show from within this narrative of 'American history' the crack in its teleology. These postmodern historical works recognize the methodological complicity of their endeavour so as to indicate simultaneously those traces of life and thought outside the European conceptual horizon. Guha succinctly described this goal: 'we shall try and think World-history in terms of what is unthinkable within its boundaries'.[56]

In its foundation, world history, like history generally, emerged from the perception of an unknown future. It marked its present as distinct from its past by the new relation to this future. But the differentiation of past from present was at the same time their reunification at a heightened level of abstraction. The movement of time, no longer presumed to be orderly, was conceptually reconstructed under the rubric called history. Postmodernism showed in several ways that this reconstruction was self-contradictory. It reversed history by starting with abstraction so as to arrive at differentiation; it deconstructed history under the difference of time. But postmodernism could not explain itself without historical language. It recognized that the present was inflected by the epistemology of the past. In this sense, postmodernism was *more historical* than historical discourse. On the other hand, the latter was thus free to continually reinvent itself along the exigencies of new conditions. In its recent form, world history has interrogated the abstract universality of its own concepts. World history and postmodernism face each other across the line of reconstruction/deconstruction, but they share the goal of 'provincializing Europe'. Wong and Pomeranz relentlessly fracture teleological narratives, and Chakrabarty and Johnson still write history. In different ways, they recognize the limits of historical language. With that, their historical writing can indicate, if not describe, the realm of

other logics. We cannot kick away the ladder. We can critically historicize
the operations of history.

notes

1. M. Heidegger, 'The Age of the World Picture', in W. Lovitt (ed.), *The Question Concerning Technology, and Other Essays* (New York: Harper & Row, 1977), p. 152.
2. L. Wittgenstein, *Tractatus Logico-Philosophicus* (New York: Harcourt, Brace, and Co., 1922), §6.54.
3. See the contrasting essays by J. H. Bentley, 'World History and Grand Narrative', and A. Dirlik, 'Confounding Metaphors, Inventions of the World: What is World History For?', in B. Stuchtey and E. Benedikt (eds), *Writing World History 1800–2000* (Oxford: Oxford University Press, 2003).
4. R. Koselleck, *Futures Past: On the Semantics of Historical Time* (Cambridge, MA: MIT Press, 1985).
5. Ibid., especially '"Neuzeit": Remarks on the Semantics of the Modern Concept of Movement', pp. 247–53, as well as R. Koselleck, 'The Eighteenth Century as the Beginning of Modernity', in *The Practice of Conceptual History: Timing History, Spacing Concepts* (Stanford, CA: Stanford University Press, 2002), pp. 154–69.
6. G. Therborn, *European Modernity and Beyond: The Trajectory of European Societies, 1945–2000* (London: Sage, 1995).
7. T. J. Clark, *Farewell to an Idea: Episodes from a History of Modernism* (New Haven, CT: Yale University Press, 1999), pp. 11–12.
8. I. Kant, 'Idea for a Universal History from a Cosmopolitan Point of View', in *On History*, trans. L. W. Beck (New York: Macmillan, 1963), pp. 1–17.
9. G. W. F. Hegel, *Lectures on the Philosophy of World History: Introduction, Reason in History* (Cambridge: Cambridge University Press, 1975), pp. 178, 190, and pp. 165, 163.
10. P. Weeks, *Farewell My Nation: The American Indian and the United States, 1820–1890* (Wheeling, NC: Harlan Davidson, 1990), p. 13.
11. M. Adas, *Machines as the Measure of Men: Science, Technology, and Ideologies of Western Dominance* (Ithaca, NY: Cornell University Press, 1989).
12. G. Barraclough, 'Universal History', in H. P. R. Finberg (ed.), *Approaches to History: A Symposium* (Toronto: University of Toronto Press, 1962), pp. 83–109.
13. L. von Ranke, 'A Fragment from the 1860s', in F. Stern (ed.), *The Varieties of History: From Voltaire to the Present* (New York: Vintage Books, 1972), p. 61; L. von Ranke, *Universal History, the Oldest Historical Group of Nations and the Greeks* (New York: Charles Scribner's Sons, 1884), p. xiii.
14. See, for the German case, L. Dehio, 'Ranke and German Imperialism', in Dehio, *Germany and World Politics in the Twentieth Century* (London: Chatto & Windus, 1959), pp. 38–71.
15. O. Spengler, *The Decline of the West* (New York: Alfred A. Knopf, 1980).
16. A. Toynbee, *A Study of History*, 12 vols (London: Oxford University Press, 1934–61).

17. A. Toynbee, 'The Unification of the World and the Change in Historical Perspective', in Toynbee, *Civilization on Trial* (New York: Oxford University Press, 1948), pp. 62–125.

18. P. Geyl, *Debates with Historians* (London: B. T. Batsford Ltd, 1955), pp. 162, 178.

19. M. G. S. Hodgson, *Rethinking World History: Essays on Europe, Islam, and World History* (Cambridge: Cambridge University Press, 1993), pp. 78, 93.

20. W. McNeill, *The Rise of the West: A History of the Human Community* (Chicago, IL: University of Chicago Press, 1991).

21. Hodgson, *Rethinking World History*, pp. 91–4, 293–6.

22. J. M. Blaut, *The Colonizer's Model of the World: Geographical Diffusionism and Eurocentric History* (New York: Guilford Press, 1993), pp. 57–8.

23. P. Geyl, *Use and Abuse of History* (New Haven, CT: Yale University Press, 1955), pp. 75–8.

24. R. B. Wong, *China Transformed: Historical Change and the Limits of European Experience* (Ithaca, NY: Cornell University Press, 1997); K. Pomeranz, *The Great Divergence: Europe, China, and the Making of the Modern World Economy* (Princeton, NJ: Princeton University Press, 2000).

25. T. K. Hopkins, 'The Study of the Capitalist World-Economy: Some Introductory Considerations', in Hopkins et al. (eds), *World-Systems Analysis: Theory and Methodology* (Beverly Hills, CA: Sage Publications, 1982), p. 33.

26. I. Wallerstein, 'Eurocentrism and Its Avatars: The Dilemmas of Social Science', *New Left Review*, 226 (1997) 93–107, quote from p. 106; G. McLennan, 'The Question of Eurocentrism: A Comment on Immanuel Wallerstein', *New Left Review*, 231 (1998) 153–58, quote from p. 157; see also I. Wallerstein, 'Questioning Eurocentrism: A Reply to Gregor McLennan', *New Left Review*, 231 (1998) 159–60, as well as these themes developed in further detail, I. Wallerstein, *Social Sciences in the Twenty-First Century*, Fernand Braudel Center, 1999, <http://fbc.binghamton.edu/iwunesco.htm> [12 December 2003].

27. A. Toynbee, *An Historian's Approach to Religion* (London: Oxford University Press, 1956), p. 150; on the Spanish language precursor 'postmodernismo', P. Anderson, *The Origins of Postmodernity* (London; Verso, 1998), pp. 4, 20.

28. J.-F. Lyotard, *The Postmodern Condition: A Report on Knowledge* (Minneapolis, MN: University of Minnesota Press, 1984), p. xxiv; see also J.-F. Lyotard, 'Universal History and Cultural Difference', in A. Benjamin (ed.), *The Lyotard Reader* (Oxford: Basil Blackwell, 1989), pp. 314–23.

29. Lyotard, *The Postmodern Condition*, p. 66; the problem of incommensurability became the focus of his subsequent volume, *The Differend: Phrases in Dispute* (Minneapolis, MN: University of Minnesota Press, 1988).

30. M. Foucault, *The Archaeology of Knowledge* (New York: Pantheon Books, 1972), pp. 200, 205; R. Barthes, 'The Discourse of History', in Barthes, *The Rustle of Language* (New York: Hill & Wang, 1986), pp. 138, 139; M. de Certeau, 'History: Science and Fiction', in *Heterologies: Discourse on the Other* (Minneapolis, MN: University of Minnesota Press, 1986), pp. 199–221; see also de Certeau, *The Writing of History* (New York: Columbia University Press, 1988).

31. J. Derrida, *Edmund Husserl's Origin of Geometry: An Introduction* (Lincoln, NE: University of Nebraska Press, 1989), pp. 63–4.

32. J. Derrida, 'Shibboleth', in G. H. Hartman and S. Budick (eds), *Midrash and Literature* (New Haven, CT: Yale University Press, 1986), p. 330.
33. J. Derrida, 'Structure, Sign, and Play in the Discourses of the Human Sciences', in Alan Bass (ed.), *Writing and Difference* (Chicago, IL: University of Chicago Press, 1978), p. 282.
34. F. Nietzsche, 'On the Uses and Disadvantages of History for Life', in *Untimely Meditations* (Cambridge: Cambridge University Press, 1983), pp. 99, 108, 83, 66.
35. F. Nietzsche, 'On Truth and Lying in an Extra-Moral Sense', in S. L. Gilman et al. (eds), *Friedrich Nietzsche on Rhetoric and Language* (New York: Oxford University Press, 1989), pp. 246, 250, 251.
36. M. Heidegger, *The Question Concerning Technology and Other Essays* (New York: Harper & Row, 1977), p. 22 [German pagination], for 'authentic', passim.
37. Heidegger, 'The Age of the World Picture', in *Being and Time*, (New York: Harper & Row, 1972), p. 134.
38. M. Heidegger, 'On the Question of Being', in *Pathmarks* (Cambridge: Cambridge University Press, 1998), p. 309; for a brief on this history, see Heidegger, *Discourse on Thinking* (New York: Harper & Row, 1966), p. 50.
39. Heidegger, *Being and Time*, pp. 178, 22 [German pagination].
40. M. Heidegger, *Nietzsche*, 2 volumes (San Francisco, CA: Harper & Row, 1979), vol. 2, p. 182.
41. F. Nietzsche, *The Gay Science, with a Prelude in Rhymes and an Appendix of Songs* (New York: Random House, 1974) §377.
42. For Derrida's review of this term, see J. Derrida, 'Deconstructions: The Impossible', in S. Lotringer and S. Cohen (eds), *French Theory in America* (New York: Routledge, 2001), pp. 15–31.
43. Foucault, *The Archaeology of Knowledge*, p. 205.
44. S. Bordo, 'Feminism, Postmodernism, and Gender-Scepticism', in L. J. Nicholson (ed.), *Feminism/Postmodernism* (New York: Routledge, 1990) p. 140.
45. G. C. Spivak, 'Translator's Preface', in Jacques Derrida, *Of Grammatology* (Baltimore, MD: Johns Hopkins University Press, 1976), p. lxxxii; R. Chow, 'How (the) Inscrutable Chinese Led to Globalized Theory', *Publications of the Modern Language Association of America* 116(1) (2001) 70. Emphasis added.
46. A. L. Stoler, *Race and the Education of Desire: Foucault's History of Sexuality and the Colonial Order of Things* (Durham, NC: Duke University Press, 1995), p. 194.
47. Derrida, *Edmund Husserl's Origin of Geometry*, p. 152, n.184.
48. R. L. Spang, 'Paradigms and Paranoia: How Modern is the French Revolution', *American Historical Review*, 108(1) (2003) 147.
49. J. W. Scott, *Gender and the Politics of History* (New York: Columbia University Press, 1999); J. W. Scott, *Only Paradoxes to Offer: French Feminists and the Rights of Man* (Cambridge, MA: Harvard University Press, 1996), p. 18.
50. D. Chakrabarty, *Provincializing Europe: Postcolonial Thought and Historical Difference* (Princeton, NJ: Princeton University Press, 2000), p. 27.
51. R. Guha, *Dominance without Hegemony: History and Power in Colonial India* (Cambridge, MA: Harvard University Press, 1997), pp. 152–212; on reading such documents against the grain, see R. Guha, *Elementary Aspects of Peasant Insurgency in Colonial India* (Delhi: Oxford University Press, 1983).

52. Hodgson, *Rethinking World History*, pp. 72–94; Barraclough, 'Universal History', pp. 93–7.
53. D. Chakrabarty, 'Marx after Marxism: History, Subalternity and Difference', *Meanjin* 52(3) (1993) 431.
54. A. Gilly, 'Chiapas and the Rebellion of the Enchanted World', in Daniel Nugent (ed.), *Rural Revolt in Mexico: U.S. Intervention and the Domain of Subaltern Politics* (Durham, NC: Duke University Press, 1998), pp. 263, 320.
55. W. Johnson, 'Time and Revolution in African America: Temporality and the History of Atlantic Slavery', in T. Bender (ed.), *Rethinking American History in a Global Age* (Berkeley, CA: University of California Press, 2002), p. 160.
56. R. Guha, *History at the Limit of World-History* (New York: Columbia University Press, 2002), pp. 7–8.

recommended resources

Chakrabarty, D., *Provincializing Europe: Postcolonial Thought and Historical Difference*, Princeton Studies in Culture/Power/History (Princeton, NJ: Princeton University Press, 2000).
Derrida, J., 'Structure, Sign, and Play in the Discourses of the Human Sciences', in *Writing and Difference*, ed. A. Bass (Chicago, IL: University of Chicago Press, 1978), pp. 278–93, 339.
Foucault, M., *The Archaeology of Knowledge*, trans. A. M. Sheridan Smith (New York: Pantheon Books, 1972).
Guha, R., *History at the Limit of World-History*, Italian Academy Lectures (New York: Columbia University Press, 2002).
Hegel, G. W. F., *Lectures on the Philosophy of World History: Introduction, Reason in History* (Cambridge: Cambridge University Press, 1975).
Heidegger, M., *The Question Concerning Technology, and Other Essays* (New York: Harper & Row, 1977).
Hodgson, M. G. S., *Rethinking World History: Essays on Europe, Islam, and World History* (Cambridge: Cambridge University Press, 1993).
Kant, I., 'Idea for a Universal History from a Cosmopolitan Point of View', in *On History*, trans. L. W. Beck (New York: Macmillan, 1963), pp. 1–17.
Koselleck, R., *Futures Past: On the Semantics of Historical Time* trans. K. Tribe (New York: Columbia University Press, 2004).
Lyotard, J.-F., *The Postmodern Condition: A Report on Knowledge, Theory and History of Literature* (Minneapolis, MN: University of Minnesota Press, 1984).
Lyotard, J.-F., 'Universal History and Cultural Difference', in *The Lyotard Reader*, ed. A. Benjamin (Oxford: Basil Blackwell, 1989), pp. 314–23.
Nietzsche, F. W., 'On the Uses and Disadvantages of History for Life', in *Untimely Meditations* (Cambridge: Cambridge University Press, 1983), pp. 57–123.
Nietzsche, F. W., 'On Truth and Lying in an Extra-Moral Sense' in *Friedrich Nietzsche on Rhetoric and Language*, ed. S. L. Gilman, C. Blair and D. J. Parent (New York: Oxford University Press, 1989), pp. 246–57.
Pomeranz, K., *The Great Divergence: Europe, China, and the Making of the Modern World Economy*, The Princeton Economic History of the Western World (Princeton, NJ: Princeton University Press, 2000).

Scott, J. W., *Gender and the Politics of History*, rev. edn (New York: Columbia University Press, 1999).

Stoler, A. L., *Race and the Education of Desire: Foucault's History of Sexuality and the Colonial Order of Things* (Durham, NC: Duke University Press, 1995).

Wallerstein, I., *Social Sciences in the Twenty-First Century*, available online at <http://fbc.binghamton.edu/iwunesco.htm>.

Wong, R. B., *China Transformed: Historical Change and the Limits of European Experience* (Ithaca, NY: Cornell University Press, 1997).

9
gender

judith p. zinsser

For conventional historians, 'gender' has been as revolutionary a concept as 'world' history. Both arose out of the radical questions of the 1960s and 1970s, when historians in many parts of the world, both women and men, began to question the traditional narratives. In Europe and the United States, they came to see history as the story of the political activities of 'white male elites'. They began to recast national and regional histories to include men of many classes and races. Some envisioned similarly dramatic changes to 'world history'. Writing from what they characterized as a truly global perspective, they melded national and regional histories together in new ways.[1] They identified global and comparative themes that would not privilege the European or North American role in events and that emphasized 'encounters' between cultures, each with a long, full historical reality. The history of Africa, for example, would not suddenly appear in the narrative as the story of European penetration and conquest. There would no longer be, in the words of the anthropologist and historian Eric Wolf, 'peoples without history'.

And then they discovered the omission of women. It is a fact worthy of Leopold von Ranke's most stringent guidelines about facts as the stuff of history that women are and have been half of humanity, and thus their past lives constitute half of what we have come to call 'world history'. Turning, however, to the index of an early world history survey, even by a leading authority, readers found the names of individual women particularly those who became political rulers, but neither they nor concerns traditionally associated with women, constituted anywhere near half of the content. It was two entries on 'wolves', then five or six on 'women'. In addition, even as the scholarship on women grew exponentially in the 1980s and 1990s, the world's women suffered the same neglect in all but a few of the monographs that became staples of

189

the new world history reading lists. This was true whether the classics had been written by men, or by the few women granted elite status, such as Lynda N. Schaffer and Janet L. Abu-Lughod. Both Schaffer's theory of 'Southernization' and Abu-Lughod's description of early trading networks altered the world history narrative, but it remained a narrative in which men were understood to be the only actors on the stage. Women's participation in these grand narratives was only hinted at when Margaret Strobel is credited for leading the way in a 'promising new approach', 'gender analysis'.[2]

In fact, the concept of 'gender analysis' was not really understood in those first decades of this new world history. Initially, all but a few world historians assumed that the inclusion of women in the narrative and 'gender analysis' were synonymous. This conflation of 'women' with 'gender' made it even more difficult for world historians to see the grave distortions inherent in their accounts of the past in a global context. The exploration of gender as a way of analysing the past arose out of feminist historians' efforts to alter their national and regional narratives. Natalie Zemon Davis and Joan W. Scott, both historians of France, pointed out that there was more to women's history than simply chronicling their activities and achievements.[3] They argued that there was a 'gender' component to all of history. Women, like men, did not act in isolation. The two sexes interacted throughout time. In addition, the physical differences between women and men had been given significance that affected every aspect of those interactions. To understand these interactions is to use gender as a category of analysis. Feminist historians, whether writing from a national, regional or global perspective, believe this kind of analysis to be as significant as any of the more traditional approaches such as economic, political, social and religious. Every major world culture has privileged and exaggerated the physical differences between women and men, and thus, as United States anthropologist Gayle Rubin pointed out, suppressed the natural similarities between the sexes.[4]

The consequences of this suppression have been the same throughout history and across regions, whether in south Asia, North Africa, or central America. Women and men have acted in a hierarchical relationship that gave men more power because of their sexual identity. This choice and its corollary, the creation of 'gender identities', the concepts of 'masculinity' and 'femininity', came to be considered as fixed realities. For example, learned men argued for centuries that the uterus made women incapable of learning and by implication that the penis enabled men in this endeavour. In addition, cultures made the choice to give greater value to all associated with the 'masculine', rather than to those activities and qualities associated with the 'feminine'. For example, the ability to reason, a quality of mind, and an activity, scholarship, belonged to men, those with a penis; the ability to nurture and the activity of maintaining the household, cooking and cleaning, belonged to women, those with a uterus. This focus in the world's societies on the combination of perceived and constructed sexual and gender difference led to the denigration of all things female and feminine, and came to justify the institutionalization of the subordination of women. Feminist world historians insist that this story of the 'gendering' of human experience in religious dogma, customs and laws, in economic and social practices, must be included as part of global narratives.

Joining these two conceptual frameworks, 'world' and 'gender' history is a multistep process that not all historians have felt able or willing to undertake. First, the history of women must be included. Second, the ways in which sexual difference and definitions of what is 'masculine' and 'feminine' have been created and given significance and power, must be identified. Third, the question of how, in cultures around the world, these differences determined and institutionalized attitudes towards women and men, their roles and appropriate behaviour, must be answered and its consequences described. Even so, a number of the leading male authorities in world history have taken these omissions seriously; for example, Kevin Reilly, in his textbooks and document collections and in the series he edits, has for many years promoted a more inclusive global history.[5] Michael Adas has commissioned pamphlets and reprinted articles on women and gender for his American Historical Association series for teachers, 'Essays on Global and Comparative History'.[6] Some even moved on to the incorporation of gender analysis in their own world history narratives. The appearance in 1998 of McGraw-Hill's *In the Balance: Themes in Global History* by Candice L. Goucher, Charles A. LeGuin and Linda A. Walton (1998), of a new edition of Anthony Esler's *The Human Venture from Prehistory to the Present* (2004), and of two thematic studies, one by Peter Stearns, and the other by Merry Wiesner-Hanks, both entitled *Gender in World History* (published in 2000 and 2001 respectively) suggested the beginning of a trend.

But McGraw-Hill now favours the more conventionally formulated *Traditions Encounters: A Global Perspective on the Past* by Jerry H. Bentley and Herbert F. Ziegler. Esler's is only one of three textbooks marketed by Pearson Education. Few instructors or researchers would rely on Stearns or Wiesner-Hanks' gender analyses instead of a traditional textbook. Secondary school teachers preparing their students for standardized, national or provincial tests dare not make innovative choices. College and university faculties tend to see their survey courses in similarly conventional terms. In the United States, for example, for those seeking to 'diversify' their curriculum by requiring students to study cultures other than their own, the need to include women and analyse the significance of gender is lost in the excitement of having students learn about African, Asian, Latin American and Caribbean men's history. Thus, while most would agree that the definition of what constitutes 'world history' has changed to include all of humanity, the reality remains fixed, overwhelmingly as male and apparently neuter, as national and regional histories once were. Women remain ancillary to the main story and gender analysis, if acknowledged, deemed complete with the mention of whichever groups of females have qualified for inclusion.

Why has world history proved so resistant to this dual trend in scholarship: the inclusion of women on the one hand, and the consideration of women and men from the perspective of gender, on the other? The answer is twofold. Practically speaking, as contemporary forms of world history evolved beginning in the 1970s, authors could draw on many topical and national surveys and specialized monographs about men's history. This was not the case for women's past. Only gradually over the next two decades did women's historians create syntheses of national and regional histories, and the thousands of monographs that now fill the pages of bibliographies for all areas of the world. There are institutional factors as well. Women scholars and writers have been, until the very recent past, marginalized within the historical profession, a group traditionally defined as male. These male historians controlled access to training, to employment, to money for research, to publication, to awards and promotions. Those women who chose to write women's history found themselves doubly marginalized, by their inappropriate choice of a career and by their decision to research topics considered inconsequential in the long sweep of men's history.[7] To identify themselves with world history could isolate them even more.

For world history, as reconfigured by male and female historians in the 1960s and 1970s, was in and of itself controversial. Even a bestselling textbook author like William McNeill had to prove that this was a legitimate approach to history. Specialist-oriented definitions of what counted as 'history' necessitated archives and carefully constructed, detailed analyses rather than the sweeping comparisons and identification of worldwide phenomena that characterized this radical vision of an interconnected global narrative. Such scepticism and the necessity of relying on secondary materials made 'world history' a teaching field long before leaders in the profession took the subject seriously as a research specialty, or even acknowledged that it was possible to do 'world' history. Few, if any, of these innovative male practitioners even considered adding women's experiences or the consideration of gender to an already overloaded history of billions of 'peoples' and 'civilizations' over the millennia. Finally, there have been what, for the lack of a better term, could be called ideological and methodological reasons for the exclusion of women and the consideration of gender in world history. Historical fallacies based on presumptions of objectivity and clear, unbiased choices allow world historians to believe that 'women are included', or to justify women's exclusion because the narrative must highlight only what is truly 'significant' in world history. Women did nothing 'significant' and so require no space in the narrative. Similar presumptions lead to a history where men exist in a vacuum of asexuality that precludes gender analysis. Men's roles and reasons for action are defined as natural, unaffected by male sexuality and unrelated to concepts of 'masculinity', the denigration of its opposite, 'femininity', and the subordination of the female half of humanity. Thus world historians have believed that they could easily dismiss any criticisms of the patriarchally directed narratives they had created.

Rhetorical strategies mask these underlying assumptions and thus the practice, so that even the well-meaning historian may not notice that half of the world's population has been consigned to paragraphs on 'family', 'population growth' (as if women created this phenomenon alone) and 'feminism'. In addition, by failing to recognize gender as a significant component of the hierarchies created and definitions of difference assigned throughout the human past, readers are presented with a history filled with a long series of what the intellectual historian Hilda Smith calls 'the false universal'. Terms such as 'peasants' or 'workers', that we are told include both sexes, in fact only describe the experience of one group, the male. To expand on Smith's concept, world historians, both women and men, have constructed a 'false universal' on a global scale.[8]

the practical and institutional obstacles

Beginning with Natalie Zemon Davis and Bonnie G. Smith, and most recently Mary Spongberg, women scholars have documented and analysed Western European and North American women's contributions to the writing of history.[9] Today, women's participation in historical scholarship is known to have been a worldwide phenomenon. There are dictionaries and encyclopaedias of their names, dates and achievements; for example,

Jennifer S. Uglow's *Continuum Dictionary of Women's Biography* (1989). Women authors are included in reference works specifically about history, such as D. R. Woolf's *Encyclopedia of Historical Writing* (1998), which gives biographical sketches of over sixty women historians from across the centuries. Ban Zhao (c. 50–c. 115 CE) succeeded her brother as court historian of the Later Han dynasty; Anna Comnena (1083–1153) wrote a biography of her father, the Byzantine Emperor, Alexius. Herrad of Landsberg (1167–1195), abbess of the Alsatian convent of Hohenberg, and her nuns created a universal history and encyclopaedia of all extant knowledge, the *Hortius deliciarum*.

Although most of these early authors told about the lives of men, as early as the fifteenth century, Christine de Pizan wrote a biographical compendium of exemplary women for her patrons at the royal courts of France and Burgundy. *The Book of the City of Ladies* (*Livre de la Cité des Dames*), completed in 1405, included women from the traditions of Christian universal history such as Eve, Sarah, the Virgin Mary, and the saints and martyrs; from the Classical past, such as Arachne and Medea; from traveller's narratives, such as the Amazons; and from Europe's past, the queens and princesses of France. With these biographies Pizan hoped to counter men's negative depictions of women and to prove that women had achieved in categories of endeavour usually reserved to men. In addition, her early feminist defence of women led her to reject the prevalent assumption of women's 'innate' inferiority, and to describe what would now be termed the gendered consequences of men's denigration of women. Grant women access to education, she argued, and women would learn and achieve just as men had.

Pizan was correct. Access to learning created women scholars, and thus female as well as male historians. In Europe and North America, for example, once given education, especially after the opening of university studies to women in the nineteenth and early twentieth centuries, privileged women wrote every kind of men's history: from the Englishwomen, Sylvia Thrupp's (b. 1903) and Helen Maud Cam's (1885–1968) studies of England's early economic and constitutional history, to the United States scholars, Nellie Neilson's (1873–1847) analysis of medieval English law and Lucy Maynard Salmon's (1853–1927) innovative redefinitions of social history. Some, like the historians of women's monastic establishments, Lena Eckenstein (d. 1913) in Germany and Eileen Power (1889–1940) in England, turned away from men's history for their specialized, archival research.[10] A few took a more global approach to women's history. In North America Lydia Maria Child (1802–1880) included examples from many cultures in her two-volume *Brief History of the Condition of Women in Various Ages and Nations* (1835). Mary Ritter Beard (1876–1958) in her *Woman as Force in History: A Study in Traditions and Realities* (1946), although mired in her investigation of seventeenth-century English law, hoped to prove Western women's achievements despite their legal disadvantages and disabilities. The French philosopher Simone de Beauvoir (1908–1986) investigated what she believed to be the culturally created origins of all women's subordination and its consequences in *The Second Sex* (*Le deuxième Sexe*) (1949). Her evidence came from studies of women on many continents.

Beauvoir's work, like Christine de Pizan's *Book of the City of Ladies*, formed part of a long-standing phenomenon of Western intellectual life that underlies all contemporary histories and all arguments about the significance of women's and gender history: what is known in European history as the *querelles des femmes*. The 'debate over women' has reappeared periodically in Western learned circles. Beginning in Europe's Renaissance in the early fifteenth century, it was both an intellectual exercise and a serious consideration of sexual differences and the relative intellectual capacities of women and men. By the sixteenth century the characterization of women that had occasioned the debate had the familiarity of a litany. In Europe's allegories the female personified Idleness, Wealth, Hate, Villainy, Covetousness, Avarice and Envy. A French, male Renaissance writer described women as 'vile, inconstant, cowardly, fragile, obstinate, venomous... imprudent, cunning... incorrigible, easily upset, full of hatred, always talking, incapable of keeping a secret, insincere, frivolous and sexually insatiable'. In one early version of the argument, a protagonist noted that women had not been included in the Eastern Roman Emperor Justinian's *Digest* of the laws and therefore killing them did not constitute murder.[11]

These condemnations of women led Maria de Zayas y Sotomayor (c. 1590–c. 1661), the Spanish humanist, to criticize the male: 'So many martyrs, so many virgins, so many widowed and chaste, so many that have died and suffered by the cruelty of men.' The sixteenth-century Venetian Lucrezia Marinelli, in her treatise entitled *The Excellence of Women Together with the Defects and Deficiencies of Men*, also turned the debate upside down and, in addition to extolling women's virtues, described men in unpleasant terms as avaricious, envious, proud, ambitious, cruel and tyrannical. The seventeenth-century Frenchwoman Charlotte de Brachart gave the reason for this male tyranny over women, 'these gentlemen would like to see us plain imbeciles so that we could serve as shadows to set off better their fine wits'. Marie de Gournay, the protégée of the French essayist Michel de Montaigne, believed that these arguments had coloured the new scientific studies of differences between the sexes, leaving women as a separate species, nature's mistake, fit only to 'play the fool and serve [the male]'.

For these sixteenth- and seventeenth-century women, the issue presented itself as whether or not females would be allowed to read, to study and to write just like their male contemporaries. Maria de Zayas delighted in books: 'whenever I see one, old or new, I put down the sewing cushion and do not rest until I've read it all'. In the long term, however, it was not statements about the joy of learning that permitted women access to the scholarly world, but rather affirmations that it would make them better Christians, and ultimately better obedient companions to their husbands and tutors to their sons, as Anna Maria van Schurman (1607–1678), the seventeenth-century Dutch scholar, argued in her treatise, *Whether the Study of Letters is Fitting to a Christian Woman*, which had appeared in Latin, French and English by 1659. Even the woman identified as Europe's first modern feminist, Mary Wollstonecraft (1759–1797), used this argument in the *Vindication of the Rights of Woman*. She wrote this justification of equal education for girls and boys in response to recommendations on public education made by Tallyrand to the new French Constituent Assembly in 1791. Better education, she explained, would so enlighten women that they would choose marriage and its responsibilities rather than having to be forced to accept this role because of the dictates of culture and women's disadvantaged economic and social circumstances.

Although the debate did not surface in Asian and African cultures until the late nineteenth and early twentieth centuries, during the first decades of their feminist movements, this did not alter its basic tenets or its origins in the traditions of earlier centuries. Just as in the Mediterranean world, the innate inferiority of women was linked to the female body. In the Vedic literature of Hinduism, all foetuses were assumed to be male, only to be turned female by malevolent spirits in the first months of a mother's pregnancy. Confucianism, as it evolved in East Asia, placed a woman in a hierarchy of relationships within her natal and marital family, subject to the three obediences: to her father, to her husband, and if widowed, to her son. Buddhism, like Judaism, Christianity and Islam, assumed the spiritual equality of females and males, but denigrated women physically. The female was sexual, dangerous, the temptation that would keep the more perfect male from achieving the most blessed states. Even as holy women, Buddhist nuns, like their Christian counterparts, rarely had the opportunity to act outside of men's control. For these presumptions about women's bodies, the imagined dangers inherent in their sexuality, the decisions about their intellectual inferiority, both occasioned and justified prescriptions about all women's proper roles and appropriate behaviour. In these circumstances and with these attitudes institutionalized in religious doctrine and practice, legal codes, economic regulations and social arrangements until the twentieth century, only a few Asian, African and Latin American women of the privileged classes and castes gained access to the reading, learning and writing that characterized the life of the learned man.

Beginning in the late fifteenth century, as Europeans first encountered and then established their hegemony over various cultures in Latin America and the Caribbean, Africa and Asia, the debate about women took new forms. Since the 1980s, increasing numbers of historians have described the interplay between male elites, each insisting that their policy towards women was different, and therefore better. In nineteenth-century Bengal, the British administrators saw themselves as 'liberating' the victims of male tyranny by abolishing child marriage, while at the same time legalizing prostitution in England and in their dominions with no similar concern about age. As the feminist scholar Gayatri Chakravorty Spivak explains it, 'white men saving brown women from brown men'.[12] Indian nationalists, in turn, enshrined their women as symbols of cultural superiority. Thus they opposed 'Western', 'British' attitudes and efforts to change the relations between women and their families, but advocated equal rights in Western terms for men.

The comparative and thematic study of women and gender across cultures and regions has, perhaps not surprisingly, been done by women's historians and feminist scholars in women's studies. In this, the pattern follows that of men's world history; the authors came to the global consideration of women's history and gender analysis out of their own regional specialty. As in the case of Europe and North America, these first histories of women from other continents emerged as part of the feminisms of the 1970s. In a sense, they formed only the most modern version of the *querelles des femmes*, now conducted in a transcultural, transnational context. To prove women's worth was a goal, whether articulated or not. For feminist scholars, to discover and to chronicle the history of women in one's region, one's class or caste, one's race and culture, one's religion, to write of women's interactions with each other and with men, meant the recapturing of those lost to history and thus of the heritage of women's presence and achievement. This heritage gave value to women and could be used to argue for full participation in all aspects of society. The four United Nations documents that evolved from the Decade for Women of 1975–85 include numerous provisions on the significance of women's education, of writing about women as valued and significant members of communities from the most local to the most international. This, the 'Programmes of Action' argue, is key to the realization of all women's equal and equitable participation worldwide.[13]

Today, more than enough exists on women, more than enough models of gender analysis in comparative and thematic contexts have been created for the historian seeking to write an inclusive world history. Cheryl Johnson-Odim and Margaret Strobel edited a series entitled *Restoring Women to History*, with volumes on women in Asia, Latin America and the Caribbean, the Middle East and North Africa, and Sub-Saharan Africa (1999). The American Historical Association sponsored a two-volume series, *Women's and Gender History in Perspective*, edited by Bonnie G. Smith with studies of women and gender from both a regional and topical perspective. The bibliographies of these series lead to the more specific histories of women and of gender in particular eras, national and regional contexts. There the world historian will also find gendered analyses of global themes such as revolution, industrialization, migration, nationalism, colonialism and imperialism, 'development' and 'globalization' – to name only a few.[14]

ideology, methodology and rhetorical strategies

As the feminist historian Gerda Lerner has noted, 'recorded history' is a 'cultural product', it reflects the present in its construction of our collective memory.[15] How then, having created these histories of women and gender, might they be joined to men's history to create a more universal history of humankind? How could women's experiences and an analysis of the workings of gender, whether in twelfth-century Kyoto or nineteenth-century Goa, be incorporated into the existing global historical frameworks? The simple answer is, they cannot. For conventional world history, just like the old-fashioned national and regional histories, is based on premises that mask, appropriate or minimize women's presence, contributions and achievements. Women and gender analysis, in a sense, are excluded by configuration and definition.[16]

Part of the problem lies in the frameworks for world history created by traditional historians of men's lives. One author's chronology, or 'periodization', as it is called in world history, created an era from 1400–1600, while another made it 1500–1800. Male historians have argued the merits of their divisions in the pages of the *Journal of World History* in its first years, and in other scholarly venues.[17] Others have highlighted global comparisons and interchanges between cultures, such as 'migration' and the introduction of new crops in the Caribbean and New Zealand. Grand themes forced rethinking of whole eras: Philip Curtin's 'great plantation complex' (1990), Immanuel Wallerstein's 'modern world-system' (1974–89), and William McNeill's 'plagues and peoples' (1976). But whether a global, comparative or thematic focus, these frameworks were presented from men's perspectives, grouped eras and centuries according to men's activities, and highlighted those events deemed of significance to men. For example, the availability of cheap, reliable contraception was more important to women than the signing of the Versailles Treaty in 1917 or the founding of the United Nations in 1945, both defining dates of twentieth-century world history. Migration has been experienced differently by women and men. Maternal mortality and selective female infanticide have caused more women's deaths than any plague.

Joan Kelly was the first feminist historian to note these gender-filled choices. Using the field of her specialization, the Italian Renaissance, she explained that although this era meant progress for certain groups and classes of men, it did not have the same effect for women. World history is simply the same gendered phenomenon on a grander scale.[18] The traditional periodizations made it possible to ignore women altogether. They created the appearance of a unitary reality that was in fact the partial view of the dominant group. Women were subsumed in 'a generalized unified conception that was at once represented in the idea of Man, but was always different from and subordinate to it'.[19] H. G. Wells, the early-twentieth-century English writer and perhaps the first of the modern proponents of 'big history', a conception of world history that begins with the formation of the universe, is a classic example of this kind of thinking. The chapter headings tell the story with 'false universals': 'The Neanderthal Men' give way to 'The Coming of Men Like Ourselves'. Wells offers a glimpse of 'small family groups of men' squatting 'in the open about the fire'. There is 'the Old Man and his women', the drudges who hunt for flints for his weapons and prepare the skins to keep his body warm. But even these ancillary, shadowy figures disappear in the world of the neolithic. In the last chapter Wells gives his predictions for the future, the 'next stage of history'. The 'lessons of 1914' are men's lessons; women never appear in his descriptions of the 'world state', a curiously neutered world where even men have lost their sex.[20]

Even at the beginning of this, the twenty-first century, the male and female authors of the standard world history narratives, though not so oblivious as Wells, privilege events and phenomena from men's, not women's perspectives, and present them without gender connotation, as if the events had been experienced in the same way by both sexes and were of universal, primary significance for women and men. For example, describing global phenomena of the eighteenth to twentieth centuries, world historians will write of industrialization as a major cause of change and not realize that for women, urbanization has been of far more consequence. The nineteenth-century legislative victory of 'free trade' was more transformative for well-to-do men in societies than it was for women of the same class. For them the often unremarked establishment of programmes for women's university and professional education had more significance. In the more recent decades, defining changes in local economies and in international trade are demarcated without noting the consequences to women; for example, women's loss of access to the land, now lost in descriptions of the shift in many newly liberated countries from subsistence farming to commercial agriculture. The many forms of state and international welfare programmes appear briefly in men's narratives. A few sentences enshrine the concept of 'male breadwinner', and give no indication of the gradual feminization of social welfare programmes and the feminization of poverty that continues to make them necessary: the ever-increasing numbers of women and their children barely subsisting in urban ghettos and refugee camps.[21]

For women to be included, not only must the traditional periodization be questioned, but also the categorization that underlies most historical narratives. Conventional categories, or divisions of facts such as 'political', 'social' and 'economic', must be broadened and extended to describe women's as well as men's activities and experiences. For example, political studies of the conquest of the Americas by the Spanish, of the first decades of contact between Europe and the Americas, overlook the key political roles women played as intermediaries, interpreting for leaders and negotiating between them.[22] World history textbooks and monographs may mention women's participation in the great revolutions and nationalist movements of the eighteenth, nineteenth and twentieth centuries, but not the equally significant ways in which their subsequent exclusion from the new governments belies any asexual definition of 'citizenship'. Marriage is not simply 'family history' as it appears in many textbooks, and thus insignificant in the sweep of global events from a social perspective, but the standard way in which political and economic elites in all cultures have created and maintained alliances and patronage networks. Marriage has constituted a key partnership within peasant communities by which men and women, each with gendered tasks and responsibilities, ensured survival through the millennia. Failure to include these aspects of women's history and these insights from gender analysis distorts world history narratives.

The category 'economic' and its terminology must also be dramatically expanded to reflect women's as well as men's productive role in every culture in every century. Perhaps the most obvious omission comes because of the standard definitions of 'labour'. As presented in conventional world histories, this has meant only activities that generated wages. Thus the economic activities of women were lost: in household production, in the informal sectors of modern economies, and in the double day of work for wages and unremunerated work for the family that has always characterized women's labour in every major culture. Significantly, throughout every region's history, the vast majority of women have performed untold hours of labour, usually in ways that have not been measurable in the male-oriented statistical categories unless given over to individuals, groups or commercial enterprises that charged for the services they provided, such as delivery of clean water and sewage removal, food catering, laundering and child care.

Nor do these standard accounts of global economies describe the cross-cultural gender aspects of women's and men's participation. For example, in the case of waged employment, when a significant number of women filled the ranks, as in secondary school teaching, this sector of the profession was devalued while those relatively closed to women, such as university professorships, were not. The definition of 'skilled' labour, in general has followed this pattern, always shifting away as the number of women doing the work increased. The histories of cloth manufacturing from the sixteenth to the twentieth centuries illustrate this phenomenon. The designation of 'skilled' weaver shifted from male to female and back again depending on the type of cloth and the amount of mechanization. Sometimes the same task with the same fabric would change from 'skilled' to 'unskilled' depending upon which sex was doing the weaving. When it came to supervisory roles in nineteenth- and twentieth-century textile factories, men, not women, were chosen regardless of their experience in the trade.[23] A gender perspective on the history of labour overall offers the following useful generalization for world historians: that the waged work open to women has paid the least wages, required the least education, was deemed the least 'skilled' and therefore was the easiest to eliminate. Given the numbers of women who have formed part of the waged and unwaged labour force, and their significance in the evolution of all kinds of economic change from the domestication of grains in the neolithic age to the generation of foreign exchange in twentieth-century export manufacturing, they warrant inclusion. The absence of their stories and the gender distinctions their presence reveals has been a serious oversight in modern world histories.

Omission can also occur in a more subtle fashion, by a skewed definition of a term that denigrates rather than eliminates women's contributions. 'Technology' is an easy example that begins with world historians' recreation of prehistoric eras. Despite current research, some leading world historians continue to suggest that only those 'tools' having to do with hunting constitute 'technology'. In fact, there is now considerable evidence of 'tools' for gathering, cooking and weaving. To find food such as roots, to prepare it to be edible, to scrape and prepare animal skins, to create the warp and woof of cloth seem in retrospect to have been as significant, if not more so, than the smoothing of flints for arrowheads and the occasional kill. The first spool and whorl to spin thread, however crude, indicated an understanding of circular motion that could easily have been adapted to the invention of the wheel. World historians often marvel at 'early man's' ability to predict the passing of the seasons, when women had within their bodies the mechanism for counting the lunar cycle. It is hard to believe that someone did not make this connection between the female menstrual cycle of twenty-eight days and the waxing and waning of the moon.

By definition, then, these traditional chronological and thematic frameworks, and the categories and terminology formulated and used by female and male world historians, masked most women's lives. These incomplete and gender-skewed global histories made visible only the women who acted as 'men', such as queens and empresses, writers and political activists, or the unnamed companions, such as the twelfth-century Mongol women who rode horseback and the eighteenth-century Ibo women captured and enslaved with others in their family. This naming of the exceptional and the anonymous grouping of women have their own adverse connotations. The exceptional woman – the queen of Kongo, the boddhisatva associated with compassion, the Prophet's wives and his daughter, the imperial Moghul concubine, the Japanese court writer, the political martyr in the French Revolution, the Chinese empress, the lesbian novelist in Paris – rather than giving a sense of women's history, effectively erases all but the woman named. In addition, the appearance of the exceptional woman performing like a man in a man's category of activity only emphasizes the relative insignificance and lesser value attached to what all of the other women in that time and place were doing.

Those unnamed women grouped together, even when separated out in their own sentences, become essentialized versions of all of their sex, no more real than would be groups of men presented in this way. The most misleading groupings usually come in sections with titles such as

'Families, Women and Minorities in...' as if 'families' and 'minorities' meant only men. Statements can erase all distinctions between women: 'Scattered generalizations may be made about women in these centuries.' Sentences that begin 'Women's roles in traditional tribal Africa...' imply that all else in the narrative concerns men with particular histories, while women can be lumped together regardless of age, class, ethnicity, race, religion, economic activity, and so on. Inadvertently, women fall into stereotypes that perpetuate the gendered demarcation of characteristics of masculinity and femininity, female and male roles, and appropriate behaviour for each sex. The eminent English world historian Arnold J. Toynbee, in his multivolume *Study of History* published in the 1940s and 1950s, took this to extremes. Any individual woman mentioned came with a stereotypical characterization: Olympias was Alexander the Great's 'noble' mother; Helen of Troy was a 'mischief maker'. Thriving civilizations, essentially the heroes of his narrative, took on 'masculine' characteristics. Failing ones, in contrast, were associated with the 'feminine', with the worship of female gods such as Isis and Ishtar, and with unlicensed sexuality.[24]

Female and male world historians now would never write like Toynbee, but too often still suggest familiar stereotypes. Women are victims of witchcraft persecutions, of footbinding. Harems foster intrigue. Prostitutes are diseased, concubines are odalesques; suffragists are English, feminists are dissatisfied suburban housewives in the United States. The false distinction between 'public and private spheres' with men active in the former and women in the latter, appears and thus identifies women as acting only within the household, as part of a family, defined by their relationships to men. Even those existing outside of this parameter – the French woman novelist or the Japanese geisha – are, because of their rejection of this spatial and physical set of relationships, a part of the essentialization: the novelist because of her decision to leave the family; the geisha by the selling of her culturally defined 'feminine' skills outside of marriage.

Some of the leading male world historians fall back on the most enduring stereotype of all, the image of women devoting all of their time and effort to birthing and caring for children, and little else. William H. McNeill, in his majesterial *A History of the Human Community* (1997, 5th edition), suggests that the 'Old Stone Age' set the patterns familiar to us into the present: the hunters' tasks required 'muscular strength and endurance'. Women's tasks in contrast 'consisted of steady work', including making baskets and the first experiments with the cultivation of food plants.

Everything else, every other sentence in this section on prehistory, concerns the advances McNeill attributes to men's ingenuity.

This kind of sexual stereotyping and the weighting of women's perceived sexual differences as the determining factor in their lives can also appear in more subtle ways. One male world historian, perhaps unaware of privileging physical stereotypes, suggested that the way to include women in global narratives is to consider them always in relation to their 'labour': reproductive, domestic and social. Like the Marxist women's historians who first made and later rejected a similar suggestion in the 1970s, he could not see how constraining such designations would be. Where are the women active in other areas of human endeavour such as religion and politics? What of their labour outside the home? To make this a 'gendered analysis' men would also have to be analysed in these categories, beginning with their role in reproduction. Or is men's 'labour' obviously the whole rest of the story, and thus not in need of specific identification?[25]

Some female and male world historians have tried to remedy these factual and analytical omissions by adding bits of women's activities to sections often designated as 'social history' or 'the history of daily life'. This practice suggests that empty spaces already existed in these categories for millions of new people, and that these imagined spaces, like those created for women's tripartite 'labour', could accommodate all women and all of their activities and achievements. This is certainly an improvement over earlier textbook practices when male world historians hoped to satisfy the demands of the new scholarship with a short sidebar, a single document or an illustration of a female figure – a Hindu goddess, for example.

Today the most common solution of the leading world historians has been the creation of an entire new section, or even a whole new chapter, devoted exclusively to women, usually over several centuries and across cultures. However, this comes in the midst of a number of chapters of more traditional men's history on, for example, 'Chinese and European Expansion' or 'Enlightenment and Revolution'. Addition is not transformation. The basic global story remains intact. In addition, this juxtaposition and separation has unintended effects. It indicates to readers that women are not part of the main narrative; that their place in world history is outside of, and in addition to the central, and by implication more significant, series of events. This effect is particularly noticeable, as is the implied conflation of women with gender, in Michael Adas' global history series, where there is a pamphlet for 'Islamic History as Global History' and one for 'Gender and Islamic History', another pamphlet for

'Interpreting the Industrial Revolution' and one for 'Industrialization and Gender Inequality'.[26]

Each of these strategies in their own way diminishes the significance of women and returns them to their ancillary status in the history of 'mankind'. Even more important, none of these apparent solutions addresses the problem of how to include a gendered analysis. They do the opposite, by suggesting that women carry all the 'gender'. The feminist world historian Merry Wiesner-Hanks reminded her readers of *Gender in History* of a saying popular in the 1960s: 'women have more gender, blacks have more race, but men have more class'. Thus Marxist historians wrote as if only men fell into classes, racial historians noted only black–white racial dichotomies, and only women were considered to have a sexually determined history.[27] Narratives augmented in this way imply that by mentioning women, the analysis of gender is complete. Ironically, in these ungendered narratives women become visible in the 'public sphere' of politics only when they are barred from it because of their sex. As the feminist historian Joan W. Scott has explained, the designation of 'sexual difference was, then, the effect, not the cause' of their exclusion.[28]

In addition, by leaving all the gender in the stories of women's lives, only they are sexual beings. To deny the sexuality of humanity, even if it is just men alone, has many consequences for a history. It means that the hierarchical definitions of masculinity and of its denigrated opposite, femininity, that have evolved in all major cultures, go unremarked. Gerda Lerner has argued that this set of gender relationships, called patriarchy, was the first form of social order based on dominance. Men first took control of women's lives and then made their subordination the model for all other kinds of dominant relationships, including the enslavement of other men. Historians perhaps will never know if this explanation is true, but they can document without equivocation that patriarchy, the pervasive institutionalization of these concepts of sex-based hierarchy, has defined relationships between men and women and between men and men as long as there have been written records.[29]

the future of world history

To meet the demands of feminist critics would require the transformation, not just the augmentation of world history narratives. As Kathleen Canning, the historian of Germany, has pointed out, women's history, and by extension gender analysis, are 'deconstructive' by definition. They decentre the former primary subject of the narrative, even while new subjects are being discovered and constituted themselves.[30] With so much research and analysis to draw upon, world historians must take up the task of reconstruction. The result will be a richer history of both women and men, of all human experience.

Omitting women perpetuates a grossly incomplete definition of just what world history is; omitting gender as an analytical tool removes a key set of relationships from history. At best these omissions create a curiously neutered, unsexed story of mankind. Men's 'riverine civilizations' rise and fall; animals are domesticated; armies of conquest march across the landscape; forces of globalization prevail. At worst, the omissions leave a world history in which Western definitions of the male and masculinity are the unspoken normative realities, and all else is by definition remarkable, different, and by implication aberrant. To give an idea of what it would mean to have women and gender as central to world history, imagine how the narrative would read with both men and women in need of sexual identification: Buddha, the male religious leader, Michelangelo, the man artist, and Nkrumah, the male Ghanaian leader.[31]

This reconstruction, however, would require more than just 'sexing' the participants. Merry E. Wiesner-Hanks, in her global survey, *Gender and History* (2001), has experimented with new organizations of the information about women and men. Men's periodizations are gone, traditional categories have been expanded and gender-rich topics determine the arrangement of the factual information. There is chronology, but within each section, rather than as the defining factor of the whole narrative. Some of the chapter headings would sound familiar, such as 'Economic Life', Religion', 'Political Life', but others highlight the shift in focus and the resulting transformation: an introduction on the origins of the fact and the ideology of patriarchy, chapters on 'Family', Ideas, Ideals, Norms and Laws', 'Education and Culture' and 'Sexuality'.[32]

Some world historians, as the separate sections within their surveys and monographs indicate, have accepted and used headings similar to Wiesner-Hanks'. Though lacking in gender analysis, these scholars would not argue over the significance of topics such as 'Family' and 'Education and Culture'. 'Sexuality' would be another matter, however. What would it mean to make transcultural studies of 'sexuality' part of the larger narratives? First, global historians would have to accept, as the feminist historian Marilyn Morris has argued, that sexuality has been as important as, say, climate or geography in determining human behaviour across centuries and continents. Second, it would mean understanding that the concept of 'sexuality', like 'femininity' and 'masculinity', is malleable, unfixed. Definition has meant delineation of reproductive opportunities and practices, decisions about marriage age and consent, about appropriate dress for each sex, about which sexual acts will be allowed and with whom. This definition has made 'heterosexuality' so pervasive in historical narratives that, like the 'false universal' of man, it is hardly visible. The feminist scholar Eve Sedgwick notes that under 'its institutional pseudonyms such as Inheritance, Marriage, Dynasty, Domesticity, Population, heterosexuality has been permitted to masquerade... as History itself'.[33] The addition of sexuality as a global theme would acknowledge, for example, that cultures throughout the full range of world histories have assumed and not condemned relationships between people of the same sex. What Western historians call 'Classical Greece' is but one example. Love between people of the same sex has been as much a part of South and West Asian culture as it has been of European and American. The Japanese samurai had his young male companion, just as did Europe's knights. Intimate friendships between women occurred in the small towns of New England and in the palace harems of the Ottoman sultans.[34]

To give more of an idea of this reconstructed narrative of world history, enhanced by inclusion of new kinds of information and new analytical approaches, let us turn to a global topic that has been assumed to be male and without gender connotation. 'Politics' fits that criteria. Imagine, for example, a global history of nation building in the nineteenth and twentieth centuries. This new history would begin by comparing the gendered images of 'the mother country', and progress to descriptions of how citizenship became masculine, male, defined against idealizations of the feminine, and the theoretical purity and incapacity of the female within the legally mandated male-dominated family. The maleness of citizenship might be taken literally, as in Britain until 1981 when nationality, like kingship according to France's Salic law, was passed through the semen of its males. A British woman who married a foreigner forfeited her citizenship and thus the rights of her child.

A history of this period in Argentina centred on the relationship between these gendered definitions of citizenship and government policies about prostitution and the control of all women's sexuality. A woman outside of the protected roles of wife, mother and daughter, such as the prostitute, was defined as foreign and dangerous, carrying all of the sexuality being denied women of this new nation. A study of Indonesian nationalism offers similar insights into the ways in which gender enhances our understanding of these formative eras. As in many colonial relationships, 'the self-conscious masculinity' of both the colonizers and the liberators plays out in their interchanges both peaceful and violent. As Frances Gouda explains, for Sukarno and his followers, 'the anticolonial struggle' was 'a mission of steadfast men to rescue the vulnerable mother country'. The Dutch male colonial administrators and military leaders saw it in similar terms, but for their own vulnerable mother country. In the post-World War II era one could describe nationalisms in gendered terms, as the result of 'masculinized memory, masculinized humiliation and masculinized hope'. Often leaders have made their women the literal carriers of all tradition and thus nascent national, ethnic and racial identity. Thus male-dominated governments in many parts of the world, even the most industrialized and apparently progressive in their views about gender relationships, have justified familiar patriarchal constraints on women's choices and activities in the name of preserving the essential nature of their national culture.[35]

To continue with another aspect of 'politics', imagine what would happen to a history of twentieth-century political activism if it became a global history of what women and men had hoped and managed to achieve? There would be new questions to answer. What prompts men and women to action? And of what kinds? How have activists been effective and how has the sex of the participants and their opponents been significant? The United States settlement house leader Jane Addams and her commitment to international peace, the example of Indian tribal women's efforts to thwart ecological devastation, and the United Nations Decade for Women come to mind as essential to any analysis of activism for peace, the protection of the environment and the history of human rights advocacy. The linkage between international temperance movements and those for suffrage is another obvious global manifestation of politics. Each of these aspects of the topic raise further questions: When have the dominant perceptions of appropriate 'feminine' and 'masculine' behaviour been relevant? What has been the relationship between gender and other categories of causation? Which takes priority and when?

Global studies of the AIDS epidemic and of the responses by governments and international organizations exist. Given the confusion of sexual identities, what unites the activists? What makes it possible for one group to have an impact and another not? How have images of masculinity and femininity been manipulated both by proponents and the governments they oppose? What is the relationship between circumstances and gender and sexual definitions of identity, proper roles and behaviour as causes of conflicts? The inclusion of women and a gendered analysis can illuminate the causes, course and consequences of actual revolutions as well. The Iranian scholar Valentine Moghadam has not only explained the underlying gender aspects of the fundamentalist revolutions in Iran and Afghanistan (the 'Westernization' of women in

Iran, opposition to legislation on dowry and marriage age in Afghanistan), but has also shown that Iranian women have been more successful than Afghani women at reclaiming their liberties, because of differences not in the practices of Islamic fundamentalism in the two countries but in the extent of land reform and thus the weakening of tribal and clan patriarchal authority.[36]

What happens if we use a gender perspective on that most indisputably global of world history political themes, war? Male and female scholars have documented that women always participate in the fighting, whether as soldiers in uniform or not. They may use weapons, they may perform support functions for their own troops or for the occupying force, they may act as spies and informers. Women, by their support activities either with the troops as 'camp followers' or in their cities, towns and villages, make the continuation of any conflict possible. Wives, mothers, daughters and sisters farm the land and supply the goods and ancillary services made necessary by the transformation of men from their previous occupation and responsibilities to those of the soldier. These facts can be documented across centuries and across cultures, whether it was a raid on a neighbouring settlement or a full-scale siege of a fortified town.

But documentation of women's participation does not transform this world history of warfare. Consider, also, the ways in which images of 'masculinity' and 'femininity' govern every aspect of war and of the ways in which sexual violence is used. How does warfare offer the fantasy of fulfilling a culture's ideals for men and women? Every culture's soldier is 'masculine', filled with those qualities that somehow emanate exclusively from those who possess a penis and testicles. To kill another 'man' is the ultimate test of 'manhood' in many cultures. To turn from armed conflict has been characterized as 'feminine', the ultimate show of weakness. Turning male sexuality into a weapon, raping the other men's women, has always been another proof of one man's superiority over another, whether in a sixteenth-century war between the Moghul emperor and a Gujarat prince or twentieth-century conflict between Serbs and Croats. In 1994, systematic rape of women in time of war was acknowledged in international law as a 'crime against humanity', indicating the importance of this recurring event in world history.

All history is, in a sense, political in that it captures and freezes particular ways of remembering events and of justifying attitudes and actions in the present and future. World historians have been particularly astute at pointing out this use of the past. They have questioned traditional premises of significance and inclusion. They have valued new kinds of evidence that gave voice to classes, races and ethnic groups previously kept silent. They have led the profession in writing new narratives that incorporate a multiplicity of cultural perspectives. What keeps women and gender at the margins of their histories? The monographs and surveys have been written chronicling women's lives and offering many ways of utilizing gender as an analytical tool. What is at stake now? Until world historians, female and male, include full descriptions of women's varied past and of the gendered reality of both sexes' lives, they will have failed in their stated goal to present the global narrative of all human experience.

notes

1. A distinction has sometimes been made between 'global' and 'world' history, but here the terms will be used interchangeably. See, on Bruce Mazlish's formulation of 'global' history, P. Manning, *Navigating World History: Historians Create a Global Past* (New York: Palgrave Macmillan/St. Martin's Press, 2003), pp. 14n, 171–2. See on the evolution of the modern field of world history, Manning's Chapter 3, 'Grand Synthesis, 1900–65', pp. 37–78, and J. H. Bentley, *Shapes of World History in Twentieth-Century Scholarship* (Washington, DC: American Historical Association, 1996). See also Chapters 2 and 3 in this volume.
2. For example, see the entry on 'World History' in the *Dictionary of Historical Writing*, ed. D. R. Woolf (New York: Garland Publishing, 1998), vol. II, pp. 970–1. See Schaffer's article 'Southernization', *Journal of World History*, 5 (1994) 1–21; J. L. Abu-Lughod, *Before European Hegemony: The World System AD 1250–1350* (New York: Oxford University Press, 1989); M. Strobel, *European Women and the Second British Empire* (Bloomington, IN: Indiana University Press, 1991).
3. N. Z. Davis, 'Women's History in Transition: The European Case', *Feminist Studies*, 3(3) (1976) 83–103; J. W. Scott, 'Gender: A Useful Category of Analysis', in Scott, *Gender and the Politics of History* (New York: Columbia University Press, 1988).
4. G. Rubin, 'The Traffic in Women', in *Toward an Anthropology of Women*, ed. R. Reiter (New York: Monthly Review Press, 1975), p. 179. See, on the ways in which physical differences have been exaggerated, for example, L. Schiebinger, *Nature's Body: Gender in the Making of Modern Science* (Boston, MA: Beacon, 1994); A. Fausto-Sterling, *Myths of Gender: Biological Theories About Women and Men* (New York: Basic Books, 1985).
5. The first document collection for women in world history, edited by S. S. Hughes and B. Hughes, *Women in World History*, appeared in Reilly's series (Armonk, NY: M. E. Sharpe, 1997), 2 vols. For a more feminist and thematic, rather than chronologically organized collection, see E. Delmotte et al., (eds), *Women Imagine Change: A Global Anthology of Women's Resistance from 600 BCE to the Present* (New York: Routledge, 1997).
6. Titles in the series are J. Tucker, *Gender in Islamic History*; M. Strobel, *Gender, Sex, and Empire*; L. A. Tilly, *Industrialization and Gender Equality*; S. S. Hughes and B. Hughes, *Women in Ancient Civilizations*.

7. For a description of the evolution of the historical profession in Europe and the United States as exclusively male, see B. G. Smith, *The Gender of History: Men, Women and Historical Practice* (Cambridge, MA: Harvard University Press, 1998); see J. P. Zinsser, *History and Feminism* (New York: Twayne, 1993) on the experiences of women historians and the emergence of women's history in the United States in the nineteenth and twentieth centuries; for the evolution of women's history on an international scale, see K. Offen et al., (eds), *Writing Women's History: International Perspectives* (Bloomington, IN: University of Indiana Press, 1991).

8. H. Smith, *All Men and Both Sexes: Gender, Politics, and the False Universal in England, 1660–1832* (University Park, PA: Pennsylvania State University Press, 2002).

9. N. Z. Davis, 'Gender: Women as Historical Writers, 1400–1820', in *Beyond Their Sex: Learned Women of the European Past*, ed. P. H. Labalme (New York: New York University Press, 1984), pp. 153–82; B. G. Smith, 'The Contribution of Women to Modern Historiography in Great Britain, France and the United States 1750–1940', *American Historical Review*, 89(3) (1984); M. Spongberg, *Writing Women's History Since the Renaissance* (New York: Palgrave Macmillan, 2002).

10. L. Eckenstein, *Woman under Monasticism* (New York: Russell & Russell, 1963 [1896]); E. Power, *Medieval English Nunneries* (Cambridge: Cambridge University Press, 1922).

11. There are many specialized histories of this debate; see, for example, the classic studies: R. Kelso, *Doctrine for the Lady of the Renaissance* (Chicago, IL: University of Illinois Press, 1956); I. McLean, *The Renaissance Notion of Woman: A Study of the Fortunes of Scholasticism and Medical Science in European Intellectual Life* (New York: Cambridge University Press, 1980) on characterizations of women; on women's responses, see for example, C. Jordan, *Renaissance Feminism: Literary Texts and Political Models* (Ithaca, NY: Cornell University Press, 1990). The writings of many of these women have now been translated and published in modern editions. See, for example, the series edited by A. Rabil Jr and M. L. King, 'The Other Voice of Early Modern Europe', published by the University of Chicago Press. For the general description summarized here, see B. S. Anderson and J. P. Zinsser, *A History of Their Own: Women in Europe from Prehistory to the Present* (New York: Oxford University Press, 2000), vol. 1, pp. 89–99.

12. See her essay, 'Can the Subaltern Speak?' in *Marxism and the Interpretation of Culture* ed. C. Nelson and L. Grossberg (Chicago, IL: University of Illinois Press, 1988).

13. United Nations, *Report of the Fourth World Conference on Women: Beijing, 4–15 September 1995* (New York: United Nations, 1996), Sales No. 96. IV.13, paragraphs 69–88 (pp. 26–34).

14. M. Strobel and C. Johnson-Odim (eds), *Restoring Women to History* (Bloomington, IN: Indiana University Press, 1999), with separate volumes on the Middle East and North Africa by G. Nashat and J. E. Tucker; on Asia by B. N. Ramusak and S. Sievers; on Latin America and the Caribbean by M. Navarro and V. S. Korrol with K. Ali; on Sub-Saharan Africa by I. Berger and E. F. White; B. G. Smith, *Women's and Gender History in Perspective* (Champagne, IL: University of Illinois Press, 2004) with one volume arranged by region and the other by

themes: 'family as world history', 'women and gender in Judaism, Christianity and Islam', 'nation', 'education and culture', 'race and ethnicity in women's and gender history', 'gender and work' and 'worlds of feminism'.

15. G. Lerner, *The Creation of Feminist Consciousness: From the Middle Ages to Eighteen-Seventy* (New York: Oxford University Press, 1993), p. 4.

16. Much of the thinking in this section has been influenced by D. H. Fischer, *Historians' Fallacies: Toward a Logic of Historical Thought* (New York: Harper & Row, 1970); D. Spurr, *The Rhetoric of Empire: Colonial Discourse in Journalism, Travel Writing, and Imperial Administration* (Durham, NC: Duke University Press, 1993).

17. See, for example, the essays by W. A. Green, J. H. Bentley and P. N. Stearns reprinted in R. E. Dunn (ed.), *The New World History: A Teacher's Companion* (New York: Bedford/St. Martin's, 2000), pp. 359–93.

18. See Joan Kelly's essay, 'Did Women Have a Renaissance?', in Kelly, *Women, History and Theory: The Essays of Joan Kelly* (Chicago, IL: University of Chicago Press, 1984); for a more recent discussion of periodization, see A. Vickery, '"Golden Age to Separate Spheres": A Review of the Categories and Chronology of Women's History', *Historical Journal*, 36 (1993) 383–414.

19. J. Flax as quoted in L. J. Nicholson, Introduction, in *Feminism/Postmodernism*, ed. L. J. Nicholson (New York: Routledge, 1990), p. 6. Scott, *Gender and the Politics of History*, p. 183. See also Lerner, who describes women as 'obliterated from sight, marginalized out of existence', *Feminist Consciousness*, p. 282.

20. See H. G. Wells, *The Outline of History: Being a Plain History of Life and Mankind* (New York: Macmillan, 1921), pp. 57–63, 1086–101.

21. Examples for this section come from a variety of world history textbooks, including three that are among the best in their coverage of women's lives: J. H. Bentley and H. F. Ziegler, *Traditions Encounters: A Global Perspective on the Past* (2nd edn, 2003); R. Tignor et al., *Worlds Together, Worlds Apart: A History of the Modern World from the Mongol Empire to the Present* (2002); P. N. Stearns et al., *World Civilizations: the Global Experience* (2004). For alternative ways of telling these stories, see for example, on Cairo and Nairobi, L. Abu-Lughod, *Writing Women's Worlds: Bedouin Stories* (Berkeley, CA: University of California Press, 1993); L. White, *The Comforts of Home: Prostitution in Colonial Nairobi* (Chicago, IL: Chicago University Press, 1990); on social welfare policies, see G. Bock and P. Thane (eds), *Maternity and Gender Politics: Women and the Rise of the European Welfare States 1880–1950s* (New York: Routledge, 1991); S. Koven and S. Michel (eds), *Mothers of a New World: Maternalist Politics and the Origins of Welfare States* (New York: Routledge, 1993); on development, see M. H. Marchand and J. L. Papart (eds), *Feminism/Postmodernism/Development* (New York: Routledge, 1995); M. H. Marchand and S. Runyan (eds), *Gender and Global Restructuring. Sighting, Sites and Resistances* (New York: Routledge, 2000). For the relationship between ecology and feminism, see, for example, M. Mies and V. Shiva, *Ecofeminism* (Highlands, NJ: Zed Books, 1993).

22. See F. Karttunen, *Between Worlds: Interpreters, Guides and Survivors* (New Brunswick, NJ: Rutgers University Press, 1994).

23. See, for a general description of this phenomenon, J. P. Zinsser, 'Technology and History, the Women's Perspective: A Case Study in Gendered Definitions', reprinted in Dunn, *The New World History*, pp. 462–9. On the history of the cloth industry, see, for example, J. Brown, 'A Woman's Place Was in the

Home: Women's Work in Renaissance Tuscany', in *Rewriting the Renaissance*, ed. M. Ferguson et al., (Chicago, IL: University of Chicago Press, 1986); F. Bray, *Technology and Gender: Fabrics of Power in Late Imperial China* (Berkeley, CA: University of California Press, 1997); L. Ferandes, *Producing Workers: the Politics of Gender, Class, and Culture in the Calcutta Jute Mills* (Philadelphia, PA: University of Philadelphia Press, 1997).

24. A. J. Toynbee, *A Study of History*, abr. D. C. Somervell (New York: Oxford University Press, 1946, 1957). See, for example, I, 455ff.; II, 77, 197–9, 143, 345–7, 373–5 for the general description of the characteristics of declining civilizations.

25. See Manning, *Navigating World History*, pp. 210–11. Joan Kelly considered this approach in her essay 'The Doubled Vision of Feminist Theory', in Kelly, *Women, History and Theory*.

26. See, for some of the more inclusive examples, K. Reilly, *Worlds of History: A Comparative Reader* (New York: Bedford, 2003). Note that Reilly does begin with selections on 'Prehistory and the Origins of Patriarchy'; A. M. Craig et al., *The Heritage of World Civilizations* (Upper Saddle River, NJ: Prentice Hall, 2002).

27. This is an adaption of the idea that women carry all the 'sex', a thesis first advanced by the feminist historian D. Riley, *'Am I That Name?': Feminism and the Category of 'Women' in History* (London: Macmillan, 1987); the quotation comes from Merry Wiesner-Hanks, *Gender and History* (Malden, MA: Blackwell Publishers, 2001), p. 91.

28. J. W. Scott, 'Feminist Reverberations', *Differences*, 15(5), (2004), p. 15.

29. See G. Lerner, *The Creation of Patriarchy* (New York: Oxford University Press, 1986), pp. 8–11. For an anthropological perspective on these relationships, see S. B. Ortner, *Making Gender: the Politics and Erotics of Culture* (Boston, MA: Beacon Press, 1996).

30. See K. Canning, 'Dialogue', *Journal of Women's History*, 5(1) (1993) 101–14.

31. Merry Wiesner-Hanks has noted the awkwardness of these designations and the impossibility of making it sound 'right' whether one uses 'man' or 'male' as the designating adjective. See Wiesner-Hanks, *Gender and History*, p. 9.

32. Peter N. Stearns in his *Gender and History* (2000) retains much of the standard chronology by discussing gender relationships as evidenced in encounters between peoples, encounters that form the organizing basis of a number of survey world histories.

33. On these ideas, see J. W. Scott, 'Introduction', *Feminism in History*, ed. J. W. Scott (New York: Oxford University Press, 1996); M. Morris, 'Sexing the Survey: The Issue of Sexuality in World History Since 1500', *World History Bulletin* 14 (1998) 11–20.

34. See, for example, R. Vanita (ed.), *Queering India: Same-Sex Love and Eroticism in Indian Culture and Society* (New York: Routledge, 2002); G. P. Leupp, *Male Colors: The Construction of Homosexuality in Tokagawa Japan* (Berkeley, CA: University of California Press, 1995); J. Boswell, *Gay People in Western Europe from the Beginning of the Christian Era to the Fourteenth Century* (Chicago, IL: University of Chicago Press, 1981).

35. See, on Argentina, D. Guy, *Sex and Danger in Buenos Aires: Prostitution, Family and Nation in Argentina* (Lincoln, NB: University of Nebraska Press, 1991); Frances Gouda, 'Militant Masculinity and Female Agency in Indonesian

Nationalism, 1945–9', in *Colonialism and the Modern World: Selected Studies*, ed. Gregory Blue et al., (Armonk, NY: M. E. Sharpe, 2002), pp. 200–16. The quotation is from Cynthia Enloe, *Bananas, Beaches and Bases* (Berkeley, CA: University of California Press, 1989), p. 44. The Norwegian historian Ida Blom, with a number of European colleagues, has edited a collection that studies the gendering of nationalism and how it played out in Europe and in Europe's empires. I. Blom et al. (eds), *Gendered Nations: Nationalisms and Gender Order in the Long Nineteenth Century* (New York: Berg, 2000). See also T. Mayer (ed.), *Gender Ironies of Nationalism: Sexing the Nation* (New York: Routledge, 2000). On world politics and gender, see V. S. Peterson and A. S. Runyan, *Global Gender Issues* (Boulder, CO: Westview Press, 1999).

36. V. M. Moghadam, 'Revolution, Religion and Gender Politics: Iran and Afghanistan Compared', *Journal of Women's History*, 10(4) 172–95.

recommended resources

Anderson, B. S., and Zinsser, J. P., *A History of Their Own: Women in Europe from Prehistory to the Present*, rev. edn, 2 vols (New York: Oxford University Press, 2000).

Commire, A., and Klezmer, D., *Women in World History*, 17 vols (New York: Yorken Publishers, 2000).

Davis, N. Z., 'Women's History in Transition: The European Case', *Feminist Studies*, 3 (1976) 83–103.

Delmotte, E., et al. (eds), *Women Imagine Change: A Global Anthology of Women's Resistance from 600 BCE to the Present* (New York: Routledge, 1997).

Greenspan, K., *The Timetables of Women's History* (New York: Simon & Schuster, 1994).

Hughes, S., and Hughes, B., *Women in World History*, 2 vols (Armonk, NY: M. E. Sharpe, 1997).

Lerner, G., *The Creation of Patriarchy* (New York: Oxford University Press, 1986).

Morris, M. 'Sexing the Survey: The Issue of Sexuality in World History Since 1500', *World History Bulletin*, 14 (1998) 11–20.

Ortner, S. B., *Making Gender: The Politics and Erotics of Culture* (Boston, MA: Beacon Press, 1996).

Scott, J. W., *Gender and the Politics of History*, rev. edn (New York: Columbia University Press, 1999).

Smith, B. G. (ed.), *Women's and Gender History in Perspective* (Champagne, IL: University of Illinois Press, 2004).

Strobel, M., and Odim-Johnson, C. (eds), *Restoring Women to History*, 4 vols (Bloomington, IN: Indiana University Press, 1999).

Uglow, J. S., *Continuum Dictionary of Women's Biography* (New York: Continuum, 1994).

Wiesner-Hanks, M., *Gender and History* (Malden, MA: Blackwell Publishers, 2001).

10
readers, responses and popular culture
marnie hughes-warrington

'... despairing that I would ever find a book that would answer my questions, I began to formulate the research agenda for a study I really wanted to *read*, not write. Here is the outcome of that study...'

Janet Abu-Lughod[1]

World histories are more than typographical marks on paper. They are also more than the property of authors who inscribe and fix meaning. They are, rather, sites of relation and even contestation among authors, editors, publishers, critics and readers. Traditionally, however, studies of world histories have been author- and text- oriented. This is due in no small part to the assumption of a proprietary relation between authorial intentions and experiences and textual meaning.[2] In recent years, 'intentionalist' intellectual histories have come under increasing challenge from literary theorists. One of the recurring themes in the writings of Roland Barthes, for example, is 'the death of the author': for him, authors are no more than conduits for larger socio-cultural forces, and readers impute meanings to texts regardless of author intention. Barthes writes:

> We know that a text is not a line of words releasing a single 'theological' meaning (the 'message' of the Author-God) but a multi-dimensional space in which a variety of writings, none of them original, blend and clash. The text is a tissue of quotations drawn from innumerable centres of culture.[3]

Within literary theory, Barthes' pronouncements have stimulated the emergence of reader and audience theory.

The terms 'reader theory' and 'audience theory' cover a disparate group of critics. There is, for instance, little agreement on whether the concept of 'the reader' incorporates 'narratees' (persons addressed by narrators), readers implied by a cultural context or a specific text that has gaps that need to be filled, intended readers or the presumed readers of theorists engaged in review and criticism.[4] There is, nonetheless, widespread acknowledgement that readers participate in the construction of meaning and that they are therefore a part of intellectual history. As Michel de Certeau argues, readers do not accept texts passively; indeed, textual meaning is impossible without them:

> Whether it is a question of newspapers or Proust, the text has a meaning only through its readers; it changes along with them; it is ordered in accord with codes of perception that it does not control. It becomes only a text in its relation to the exteriority of the reader, by an interplay of implications and ruses between two sorts of 'expectation' in combination: the expectation that organises a *readable* space (a literality), and one that organises a procedure necessary for the *actualisation* of the work (a reading).[5]

Recognizing readers has led to a reappraisal of texts. Writing in *S/Z*, for example, Barthes has suggested a distinction between *lisible* ('readerly') and *scriptible* ('writerly') texts. 'Readerly' texts elicit a more or less passive response on the part of readers through the use of familiar themes and rhetorical devices like footnotes or an omniscient narrator. They disguise their status as timebound cultural products and encourage readers to treat them as timeless, transparent windows onto reality. 'Writerly' texts on the other hand self-reflexively draw attention to the various rhetorical techniques that produce the illusion of realism and encourage readers to participate in the construction of meaning. They may also be polysemic, that is, capable of being read in multiple ways. Barthes clearly favours writerly texts, insisting that 'the goal of literary work (of literature as work) is to make the reader no longer a consumer, but a producer of the text'.[6] Similarly, Paul Ricoeur has written of a hermeneutic arc, where the 'world of the text' and the 'world of the reader' collide and coalesce; Umberto Eco has identified 'open' texts in which readers are invited to collaborate in the creation of meaning, and Michael Riffaterre has described the activities of 'superreaders', who seek meaning beyond superficial appearances.[7] All of these writers emphasize negotiated readings, but Eco and Stuart Hall have gone further, allowing for 'oppositional' or 'aberrant' readings in which readers depart from what authors or conventions expect.[8]

The reorientation of literary theory towards readings results in the decentring of meaning making and the opening up of new avenues of historiographical research, where historians seek the 'elusive quarry' of ephemeral reading acts, places and habits as well as or even in preference to author statements and experiences.[9] The difficulty of this task is clearly acknowledged by de Certeau, who argues:

> Far from being writers – founders of their own place, heirs of the peasants of earlier ages now working on the soil of language, diggers of wells and builders of houses, readers are travellers; they move across lands belonging to someone else, like nomads poaching their way across fields they did not write, despoiling the wealth of Egypt to enjoy it themselves. Writing accumulates, stocks up, resists time by the establishment of a place and multiplies its production through the expansionism of reproduction. Reading takes no measure against the erosion of time (one forgets oneself *and* also forgets), it does not keep what it acquires, or it does it so poorly, and each of the places through which it passes is a repetition of the lost paradise.[10]

The explosion and even fragmentation of sources of historical meaning also logically extends to the history of historical texts and casts into doubt the authority and permanency of intentionalist historiographical pronouncements. Greg Dening has suggested that the 'forms and structures' of histories vary according to different expressions and social contexts and Keith Jenkins has likened the act of reading a history to eating a piece of cake in different ways and places.[11] Neither Jenkins nor Hall, though, are happy for variations in readings to be without limit: meaning cannot be simply private and individual.[12] Jenkins has thus argued for variation within limits, claiming that agreed readings are anchored to prevalent sites of power. That is, some readings of particular histories dominate because they affirm the needs and aspirations of certain social groups. These sites of power are not necessarily the province of elites who use them to subordinate the masses, nor are they the sole property of readers. Rather, power is infused throughout the network of relations in societies.[13] In Jenkins' view, intellectual history – including the study of world histories – thus seeks to study the relations of power manifested in the construction of textual meaning by all groups who engage with world histories.

In this chapter, we will adopt this view and examine the relations of power between the writers, producers and readers of past and present world histories. We will see that while the authors of world histories have long acknowledged the role of readers in the making of meaning, they have nevertheless tried to maintain authority by prescribing manners or orders of reading. Such efforts do not deliver a controlling hand over world histories, though, for the forms of texts readers seek and publishers offer may shape meaning. Furthermore, readers may appropriate and even refashion the concepts, assumptions and styles of world histories in ways not foreseen by either writers or publishers, as a study of the 'future histories' of the science fiction writers Isaac Asimov and Ray Bradbury, Julian Barnes' *History of the World in 10½ Chapters* and Mel Brooks' film *History of the World Part I* will show. This is, I grant, a varied and even unusual collection of examples, but they were selected because they all demonstrate, first, the agency of readers; and second, that 'popular' and 'elite' culture are not discrete. This chapter should not be taken as exhaustive, but more as a sketch of topics that should be further researched and developed.

world histories: author(itie)s and readers

Although reader and audience theory are a comparatively recent addition to literary research, an awareness of the role in readers in constructing meaning is present even in the earliest world histories. Writing in a context dominated by oral culture, for example, Herodotus often employed the term *epilegesthai*, which means to read aloud for others and to oneself.[14] There is some evidence to suggest that silent reading was not unknown at the time that Herodotus wrote, but the lack of spaces between words and the absence of standardized spelling made vocalization a virtual necessity. Importantly, though, the term *epilegesthai* also implies that the text is incomplete until it is translated into sound. Reading, or more precisely auditing, is thus an essential part of the text. The text is therefore not a fixed entity, but a symbiotic relationship in which the writer depends on but uses readers as slaves to distribute ideas, even after the writer's death. Clearly, the submissive view of readers was problematic in a culture that connected citizenship with the absence of constraints. Reading was thus identified as an activity that might be left to slaves, or practised in moderation lest the reader identify too much with their role.[15]

Medieval writers also allowed for the contribution of readers in the meaning-making process of Christian hermeneutics. Gregory the Great likened reading to the process of better understanding a person through conversation and Augustine saw allegory as a gift of the Holy Spirit to stimulate a better comprehension of truth.[16] Hermeneutics clearly shaped the writing and reading of medieval universal histories: for example, in the prologue to *Seven Books of History Against the Pagans* (c. 417), Paulus Orosius positions himself as a reader-interpreter in relation to Augustine (who was himself a reader-interpreter of the Bible) but also as an author in relation to readers who will interpret him. A relational dynamic also underpins Otto of Freysing's extension of Augustine's and Paulus Orosius' interpretations in *The Two Cities: A Chronicle of Universal History to the Year 1146 AD.*[17] The network of relations implied in these texts is hierarchical, due to its basis in the sacred book of the Bible. Accordingly Orosius and Otto set themselves up as authorities to their readers but also efface themselves lest their authority be taken as greater than that of Augustine or the Bible. Christian hermeneutics thus implies a paradox: on the one hand it seems to emphasize the role of the reader as interpreter, but on the other, it also suggests that the value of the reader lies in their ability to accurately discern and understand the mind of the author.

A similar paradox underpins Classical Chinese thought. The connection of the concept of author or *zuo* with the *shengren* or the sage led Confucius and later authors such as Sima Qian to efface themselves through self description as 'transmitters'. Writing in the preface to his *Shiji* (107–c. 97 BCE), Sima Qian comments: 'My work is only a classification of the materials that have been preserved. Thus it is not innovation [*zuo*].'[18] And again in Islamic writings like Abu Ja'far al-Tabari's universal history *Tarikh al-rusul wa-l-Muluk* (*The History of the Prophets and Kings*, 911–23 CE) we find the structuring principle of *isnads*, which, we recall from Chapter 7, are unbroken lists of transmitters that are cited to demonstrate the connection of the author to the valid claims of earlier authorities. Truth is not to be found in documents, but in the connections between knowledgeable and righteous persons, including readers.[19] Lest it be concluded that all writers saw themselves as subordinate to earlier writers, though, we must note the existence of other texts, of which Ibn Khaldun's *Muqaddimah* (1377 CE) is a notable example, in which writers berated their predecessors for their historiographical sloppiness and shortsightedness. Whether critical or affirmative of earlier texts, authors held in common the view that reading a text required a grasp of the proper method of approach. In the Abbasid period (750–1258) as with the Ming Dynasty (1368–1644) and the age of Western scholasticism (c. 1100–c. 1300), heightened interest in the act of reading was conjoined with the goal of spelling out the proper manner and order in which it was to be performed.

The proliferation of publications in those times – and competing readings – made typographical standardization, canonization, summarizing and selection increasingly urgent. Western European producers of texts responded with the introduction of conventions such as paragraph marks, chapter titles, tables of contents and indices. But they also produced florilegia and anthologies designed to help readers to gain quick and sure access to significant and edifying information. Florilegia also provided women with opportunities for expression as reader-interpreters: in *Hortus deliciarum* (*Garden of Delights*, c. 1176–91), for example, Herrad of Hohenbourg's self-effacement as a little bee of God making honey out of the different flowers of scriptural, philosophical, scientific and cosmological writings nonetheless allowed her to advance a universal history.[20] These compilations functioned not only as time-saving keys to important and even fashionable knowledge, but also as manuals for reading. An exemplary work of this kind is Jean Bodin's highly influential *Method for the Easy Comprehension of History* (1566), which provides not an anthology, but instructions for readers to construct their own universal history out of accessible and reliable texts. Bodin was interested not only in what was read, but also the order in which it was read, arguing:

> It is not enough to have a quantity of historical works at home, unless one understands the use of each and in what order and manner each ought to be read. At a banquet, even if the seasonings themselves are most agreeable, yet the result is disagreeable if they are put together in a haphazard fashion; so one must make provision that the order of the narratives be not confused, that is, that the more recent portion be not assigned to an earlier place for reading or the central portion to the end. People who make this error not only are unable to grasp the facts in any way but even seriously weaken the power of their memory.[21]

Ordering and misordering therefore have serious consequences for the mind. To Bodin, the logical order of universal history was chronological, from the general to the specific and from Europe outwards to the rest of the known world.[22] Present-day readers would no doubt question the last two principles, but would probably agree that world histories make most sense when they are presented in chronological order. This principle, though, is similarly a cultural convention rather than a logical necessity, a point which is apparent when we call to mind the non-chronological ordering of Sima Qian's *Shiji* and the editorial decision to render the English translation intelligible in part through chronological ordering.[23]

Bodin's work reminds us that the order as well as the content of world histories is culturally embedded.

Bodin's invitation to readers to construct their own universal history out of provided materials was supported by the contemporary tendency to personalize manuscripts and printed books through the use of hand-painted decorations and even marginalia.[24] Printing thus did little to dent the appreciation of books as status symbols or as objects created for particular readers. It did, however, broaden the pool of readers. As Roger Chartier has shown, throughout early modern Europe, booksellers created a popular market for printed materials by lowering manufacturing and distribution costs and by selecting texts or genres that would appeal to a large number of readers. In chapbooks and the *Bibliothèque bleue* of France, 'popular' readers gained delayed and sometimes even simultaneous access to modified versions of texts circulated among literate elites.[25] In some of these popular works, world history was marshalled and adapted to meet style and size constraints, as with Joseph Swetnam's compact and bald pamphlet summation of the contribution of women to world history in the statement 'ever since [Eve] they are and have been a woe unto man and follow the line of their first leader'.[26] Thus while authors attempted to control the ways in which their works were read, different forms of world histories existed for different groups within societies. For the majority of people, for instance, world histories were predominantly oral and pictorial, being conveyed via rumour, the reading aloud of pamphlets, the proclamations of public criers, sermons, drama, street songs, public reading, images and public performances and spectacle. The 'ages of man' framework of many a medieval and early modern European universal history, for example, was rendered in paint and stone in public locations such as the Virgin portal of Notre Dame Cathedral in Paris.[27] Until more research is done, however, we can only guess at the reach and historiographical nature of what we might call 'popular' early modern world histories.

During the eighteenth-century Enlightenment, 'useful' reading – reading construed as an individual's moral duty – began to develop a strong profile. This form of reading proved particularly popular with bourgeois women, who were given access to works designed not to produce savants, but to describe a world order in which women were the domestic companions of men. Works intended to produce moral edification, however, still had to jostle for attention against travel stories and fables and even novels. William Alexander clearly acknowledged as much in the preface to *The History of Women, from the Earliest Antiquity, to the Present Time* (1835), arguing that while he limited the use of references in his text because that would have been 'perplexing to the sex', they needed something to steer them away from novels and romances, 'which greatly tend to mislead the understanding and corrupt the heart'.[28] The direction of young readers was pursued with the same level of commitment, for as it was suggested in a pamphlet by the Tract Society of New York from around 1820,

> Books of mere fiction and fancy are generally bad in their character and influence... Beware of the foul and exciting romance. Beware of books of war, piracy and murder. The first thought of crime has been suggested by such books.[29]

World histories, we must remember, have not always been written for adults; child readers might have been seen as a more receptive and malleable audience.

Useful reading provided a remedy to the 'narcotic' – as the philosopher Fichte described them – effects of a sentimental and escapist reading mania.[30] It was still insufficiently rigorous and critical, however, to take the majority of readers to the kind of understanding philosophers like Herder, Kant and Hegel saw as necessary to the practice of historical research and reading. Kant complained that the great majority of mankind – and all women – were under lifelong tutelage because they let books and others understand for them. Rather than being a 'method of educating toward independence' and 'enlightenment', contemporary reading practices fostered a 'condition of eternal dependency'.[31] Herder demanded of his readers that they 'must read and learn to see' by 'feeling themselves into' [*sich Einfühlen*] every part of the past.[32] Hegel steered away from the nebulous concept of *Einfühlen*, but still sketched out a developmental sequence of historical research and reading. In the preface to the *Philosophy of History*, he laid down his view of the direction and destination of all human history: 'The history of the world is none other than the progress of the consciousness of freedom.'[33] While Hegel detected evidence of the progressive revelation of freedom on a social level, he also found it at work in the development of historical scholarship from universal, pragmatic and critical through to fragmentary and philosophical approaches. At the heart of the activities of the philosophical historian is the reading and assessment of the fundamental presuppositions that give shape to human activity. The progress of freedom thus depends on the development of philosophical historical reading. Hegel's interest in the development of philosophical historical understanding and reading was echoed by later commentators and interpreters such as Benedetto Croce and R. G. Collingwood.[34]

Despite philosophical exhortations, nineteenth century readers increasingly consumed cheap novels. While print runs in the early years of the nineteenth century were on average from 1000 to 1500 copies, when 40,000 copies of Walter Scott's historical novel *Waverley* were sold in 1829 alone, the existence of a market for texts on a previously unsuspected scale was demonstrated. So influential was the example of Scott that even the physical form which had been convenient for *Waverley* became the default form in the nineteenth and the first half of the twentieth century. *Waverley* was originally published in the 'handsome' format of three volumes, for no other reason than that the length of the work and printing limitations and conventions dictated it. Most books that followed *Waverley*, including scholarly works like world or universal histories, were also published in three volumes, regardless of their length. This format suited booksellers and the proprietors of circulating or lending libraries well because returns were based upon volume numbers, not work numbers. A number of publishers also realized that cheap, monthly instalments could reach a wider public than a three-volume 'handsome' edition. French readers first encountered Marx's *Capital* in weekly instalments, published in 1872.[35] The readers of H. G. Wells' *The Outline of History* (1920) also had a choice between the lavishly illustrated two-volume edition and 23 cheap fortnightly parts.

The differences in appearance between these various editions cannot be assumed to be trivial. Fonts, headings and subheadings and illustrations can influence readers' experiences of a text. Consider, for example, the 'United States of the World' illustration by J. Horrabin that appears between pages 752 and 753 of the two-volume edition of *The Outline of History* and on the cover of part 24 of the fortnightly series (Figure 10.1). Many of the students I have guided through the study of Wells' writings are initially quite sympathetic to his notions of a united world state, but when they see the 'next stage' map become extremely critical. When asked to explain their reaction, they have reported that they read the first two words – 'united states' – and immediately associate them with 'Americanization', despite North America not being represented on the map. On second inspection, they express relief, because to their mind the labelling of the Australian continent indicates that it will not be subsumed. This is clearly an example of an aberrant reading that might be peculiar to a group of early-twenty-first-century Australian readers. There are hundreds of other figures in Wells' work that can be read conventionally – in line with the assumptions of the author, the illustrator and other historians, for instance – or in an aberrant fashion which might influence judgements about the text.

Figure 10.1 'The Next Stage'[36]

The various editions of world histories remind us that there was and is no universal reader of world histories. While the authors of world histories offered advice or even prescribed *a* manner and order of reading, the different forms and contexts in which their works appeared fostered multiple readings. This relationship between authors, publishers and readers – sometimes cohesive, sometimes conflicting – continues today. The producers of world history texts – print and electronic – face pressures from publishers about word length, the use of illustrations, supporting websites, CD ROMs and footnotes. A writer might have in mind a long, careful, well-referenced study but be required to modify it to better capture key markets, that is, first-year undergraduates. Similarly, a student might prefer to read comic strips but find that none of their university texts take that form. Readers and writers may not always feel that they get what they want, but the variety of publishing firms and publication media at least ensures that there is no single vision of what world history is or might be.

towards a reception history of world histories

It is clear that authors and their publishers have, in many times and places, acknowledged the role of readers – including themselves – in shaping the content and form of world histories. Furthermore, I have indicated that the readers of world histories may not always respond in ways that they are invited or even expected to. This idea requires further examination. Since the publication of Richard Altick's *The English Common Reader* in 1957, historians have come to realize that, as Stuart Hall puts it, 'modes of using and understanding print changed over time'.[37] Scholars have begun to sketch out 'reception' histories, particularly for early modern Europe, but works of universal and world history have been neglected within these. Additionally, as Jonathon Rose has argued, our understanding of past readers is hampered by at least five unquestioned assumptions we make about them:

first, all literature is political, in the sense that it always influences the political consciousness of the reader; second, the influence of a given text is directly proportional to its circulation; third, 'popular' culture has a much larger following than 'high' culture, and therefore it more accurately reflects the attitudes of the masses; fourth, 'high' culture tends to reinforce acceptance of the existing social and political order (a presumption widely shared by both the left and right); and, fifth, the canon of 'great books' is defined solely by social elites. Common readers either do not recognise that canon, or else they accept it only out of deference to elite opinion.[38]

Rose's observations are important: we must, for instance, seek evidence for the influence of Spengler's and Toynbee's writings beyond their sales figures, and not assume that their influence was solely political. Further, these observations all point to a more fundamental assumption: that readers are more or less passive recipients of whatever authors put into their texts. In his studies of British working-class readers, Rose has found evidence of readers responding to literature in ways that were unintended, such as developing ambitions that set them against the status quo and finding 'great books' without the guidance of educated opinion.[39] Janice Radway, too, in her study of the reception of romance novels found that – contrary to the assumption of feminist scholars such as Ann Douglas – female readers treated them as fables of female independence rather than submission.[40] And Lyons and Arnold have demonstrated how women's reading practices in the latter part of the nineteenth century diverged from educational aspirations for 'legitimate' reading.[41]

Rose, Radway, Lyons and Arnold were able to reach readers through the use of oral interviews and questionnaires. Historians working with periods beyond living memory are not so fortunate. It is of course not hard to imagine oppositional or aberrant readings of some world histories: for example, the descriptions of 'shameful deeds' in Lactantius' *Deaths of the Persecutors*, Paulus Orosius' *Seven Books of History Against the Pagans* or Bishop Otto of Freysing's *The Two Cities* might have been quite titillating for some readers. And Lydia Maria Child's *The History of the Condition of Women, in Various Ages and Nations* (1835) might have been assimilated to the gendered diminutive of travel literature by female readers as well as male historians. But imaginings and 'might have beens' offer little satisfaction for historians, who prefer historical readers to the hypothetical readers of many literary theorists.

In Robert Darnton's view, the experience of the bulk of historical readers 'lies beyond the range of historical research'.[42] This conclusion gives little credit to the many cultural historians – including Darnton himself – who have opened up many new vistas on the past through the recovery and reinterpretation of evidence. As writers such as Chartier and Carlo Ginzburg have shown, autobiographies, letters and diaries are a rich source of information: for example, the letters that constitute Jawaharlal Nehru's *Glimpses of History* offer an extended record of his reading and refashioning of, among other sources, H. G. Wells' *Outline of History*. Rich as these sources of evidence may be, however, they must be used in conjunction with other materials because their authors may not be representative and may misremember, disremember, embellish, refashion with hindsight and select and arrange events to produce a compelling story. Nehru will be considered by many historians to be a significant reader, given his role in Indian politics and the recognition of *Glimpses* as a work of world history. His refashioning of Wells, though, might be quite unlike that of a bourgeois woman or working man in the same or another culture. Having access to his reading of Wells does not entitle us to call it representative. Materials that may be used to provide a cross-check or to augment the evidence derived from memoirs may include correspondence, trial and governance transcripts, marginalia, graffiti, art, sculpture, library and bookseller records, clothing, the reports of educational bodies and other contemporary writings. These are the potential sources for a history of world history reading, a history that is yet to be written. In the remainder of this chapter I have a less ambitious aim, to catch a glimpse of how the conceptual frames and assumptions of world history were appropriated and refashioned in three twentieth-century examples: the 'future histories' of Isaac Asimov and Ray Bradbury, Julian Barnes' novel *History of the World in 10½ Chapters* and Mel Brooks' film *History of the World Part I*. This is, I acknowledge, a far from representative sample of twentieth-century reception sources, but my selection suffices to demonstrate a key point: while texts may differ in form, intended audience and function, their reader-authors all treat the conceptual frames and assumptions of world history and the boundaries commonly etched between elite and popular culture as malleable and even disputable.

future, fictional and filmic world histories

Science fiction has a history that arguably stretches back to Lucian, the second-century author of *True History* and *Icaromenippus*. And within that tradition, MacLeod has argued, history has provided 'an inexhaustible source of plots and an indispensable map of the ways in which societies work and how they can change'.[43] In the science fiction genre of alternate history, for instance, authors have written of how a slight change in the past might bring about a future different from the one we know (Ronald Clark's *Queen Victoria's Bomb*, 1967), time travellers who journey to the past to change the future (L. Sprague de Camp's *Lest Darkness Fall*, 1941) and how the present that we live in could be altered by a different past (Robert Harris' *Fatherland*, 1992).[44] Of more interest to us, though, is the science fiction genre of 'future history', in which writers postulate and explore detailed futures for earth, the galaxy and even the universe. Future history could be written on any scale, but most writers have followed Robert Heinlein – the progenitor of the term – in thinking in terms of hundreds and even thousands of years and beyond the bounds of the nation state.[45] His collection *The Man Who Sold the Moon* offers an annotated timeline for the period 1950–2600 which he subsequently filled out in the omnibus volumes *Orphans of the Sky* (1964) and *The Past Through Tomorrow* (1967). Other large-scale future histories include Isaac Asimov's *Foundation* stories (1942–93), James Blish's *Cities in Flight* trilogy (1955–62), C. M. Kornbluth's *Space Merchants* (1953), Arthur C. Clarke's *2001* series (1964–85), Ray Bradbury's *The Toynbee Convector* (1988) and Warren Wagar's *A Short History of the Future* (1999).

Histories – and more specifically world histories – directly inspired many of these works. Heinlein, for instance, acknowledged the influence of H. G. Wells, framing him as a universal historian who

is, so far as I know, the only writer who has ever lived who has tried to draw for the rest of us a full picture of the whole world, past and future, everything about us, so we can stand off and get a look at ourselves.[46]

Blish made conscious and detailed use of Spengler's *Decline of the West*; Asimov, Bradbury, Kornbluth and Clarke of Toynbee's *A Study of History*; and Wagar has acknowledged Wells, Toynbee, Immanuel Wallerstein, W. H. McNeill and Leften Stavrianos as sources.

These examples point to a largely unexplored aspect of both science fiction and world history criticism. Only a handful of papers have been written on the use of world histories in future history. Further, in all of these, the selected science fiction author is presented as at best the passive analogist, and at worst the naive distorter, of world historical conceptual frames and assumptions.[47] The historiographical shift to reader and response theory outlined in this chapter suggests that we might view the use of world histories by science fiction writers in a more positive way, as critical appropriation or even refashioning. There is not space to deal with all the future histories identified above, so I have opted for two, Asimov's *Foundation* stories and Ray Bradbury's *The Toynbee Convector*.

Asimov's *Foundation* future history began as a series of short stories for the magazine *Astounding Science Fiction*, and by the time of his death in 1993 had grown to five novels. Recent sales figures are not available, but Gunn notes that the series passed 2 million in 1978.[48] The story begins in 24520 CE on the planet Trantor, centre of a galactic empire that incorporates 25 million worlds inhabited by the descendants of humans. Ostensibly, the empire seems to be stable, but according to Hari Seldon, proponent of the theory of 'psychohistory', the empire will decline and fall and usher in 30,000 years of warfare and barbarity. Seldon proposes the establishment of two foundations, one of which will preserve and extend human knowledge in order to devise ways to shorten the period of future barbarism to a mere 1000 years. The first *Foundation* trilogy (*Foundation, Foundation and Empire* and *Second Foundation*) covers 400 years of the predicted barbarism and tells how the scientific foundation on the planet Terminus and then the second foundation on Trantor respond to a series of crises.

In shape, the *Foundation* trilogy clearly suggests the influence of the writings of Toynbee, among others. The Trantorian empire grows, responds to challenges but then atrophies. If the 'primitive society' of Terminus is to develop into an empire, it must be challenged. It is like, as Toynbee writes, 'a climber who has not reached the ledge above him where he may hope to find rest... for unless he continues to climb on upward until he reaches the next ledge, he is doomed to fall to his death'.[49] The major challenges Terminus faces are external: a lack of planetary resources and the expansionary designs of other local rulers and empire generals. The breakdown of the Trantorian empire, on the other hand, is due to internal problems: the idolization of bureaucratic institutions, smugness about past achievements and a loss of creativity.[50] And as with our world and times, there is a Toynbee-like figure – Hari Seldon – who predicts the demise of the present 'world' (in this case a galaxy).

Toynbee, we know, softened his claims about the imminent 'suicide' of the West halfway through the writing of his twelve-volume *A Study of History* and posited instead a future dominated by 'universal churches' that are characterized by selflessness and compassion. Asimov's analogical usage of Toynbee is not slavish, because the trilogy reflects no such turn to 'absolute spiritual reality'. Asimov might not have kept up with his reading of Toynbee beyond volume five, or indeed even volume one. He may not have read Toynbee directly, relying instead on commentators or even publicly assessible sources such as radio and magazine interviews. Or he could have read on beyond volume five and chosen not to follow Toynbee's shift. Regardless, he clearly made a decision about what in Toynbee's world history was useful to him.

Reader refashioning is characterized by selection, but it can also be characterised by contestation. Asimov's central figure of the Mule, I believe, presents us with an example of reader criticism. Up to the end of *Foundation*, all of the challenges and responses of the scientific foundation on Terminus are predicted successfully by Seldon and reported via recorded holograms. In *Foundation and Empire*, however, things begin to go astray. 'Psychohistory', Seldon makes clear on more than one occasion, utilizes the study of past human history on the level of groups – clans, cities, nations and the planet – to predict statistically likely actions by groups up to the galactic level. It does not study, and therefore is unable to predict, the actions of individuals. This limitation turns out to be crucial, for Seldon did not foresee the rise of The Mule, a mutant who uses his ability to control other peoples' thoughts and emotions to conquer worlds. 'Psychohistory' fails because it does not reach individuals, and individuals can make history. So too throughout the trilogy, significant challenges and responses originate from individuals such as Salvor Hardin, Hober Mallow, Bel Riose, Toran and Bayta Darell. Asimov may have used Toynbee, but it was a usage ultimately subordinated to the conventional historiographical assumption that individuals are the locus of historical meaning. To make his future history meaningful, Asimov thus looked to smaller-scale histories such as Gibbon's *Decline and Fall of the Roman Empire* for individuals.

Ray Bradbury's *The Toynbee Convector* provides us with another example of critical appropriation and refashioning. The story opens with

the reporter, Roger Shumway, travelling to La Jolla to interview Craig
Bennett Stiles on the centennial anniversary of his journey 100 years
into the future. During the interview, Stiles first reveals the name of
his time machine: the 'Toynbee Convector'. The name, Stiles explains,
commemorates

> 'The great Toynbee, that fine historian who said any group, any
> race, any world that did not run to seize the future and shape it was
> doomed to dust away in the grave, in the past.'
> 'Did he say *that*?'
> 'Or some such. He did. So, what better name for my machine eh?
> Toynbee, wherever you are, here's your future-seizing device!'[51]

One hundred years earlier, Stiles claimed that the Toynbee convector had
allowed him to witness a bright future for humanity, characterized by
environmental regeneration, peace, medical advances and wide-ranging
space travel. When the younger Stiles fails to materialize in the reported
place of his journey 100 years later, however, the older Stiles confesses
that he made up the story of his journey to the future, because

> 'I was born and raised in a time, in the sixties, seventies and eighties,
> when people had stopped believing in themselves. I saw that disbelief,
> the reason that no longer gave itself reasons to survive, and was moved,
> depressed and then angered by it.... the self-fulfilling prophecies were
> declared; we dug our graves and prepared to lie down in them.'
> 'And you couldn't allow that?' asked the young reporter.
> 'You know I couldn't.'[52]

Bradbury's naming of the time machine is ironic: Toynbee provides a
remedy to the doom forecasting that he clearly participated in. But more
interesting still is Stiles' revelation that the inspiration for the idea of a
time machine (albeit fake) came from 'an old and beloved book by H.
G. Wells'.[53] The way to a bright future lies not, ultimately, with *A Study
of History*. Nor does it lie with Wells' *The Outline of History*, even though
that work looked hopefully to the achievement of a united world state.
(Wells' state has in common with Stiles' the characteristic of peace. They
diverge, though, in their views of the environment, with Stiles predicting
respect and regeneration and Wells hoping for an 'exploitation of all
natural wealth'.[54]) Bradbury did not see the unity of past and future in
Wells' writing as Heinlein did: Wells was an historian and a science fiction
writer, and the latter rather than the former offers redemption. As with

Asimov's *Foundation* stories, then, the science fiction writer – both as author and character – provides a corrective to world historical visions, not a passive analogical reiteration.

Julian Barnes' work is even more ambitious, refashioning not a single world history but some of the key assumptions that underpin the whole field. Almost all of his *A History of the World in 10½ Chapters* is suggestive of an authoritative world history. All, that is, apart from the ½, and a quick perusal of the volume confirms the fractional, fragmented and idiosyncratic nature of Barnes' 'world'. Barnes' 'history' opens with Noah's Ark, a narrative that would not be out of place in Judaeo-Christian eschatological or redemptive universal histories. His is no reiteration of universal historiographical tradition, though, for Barnes presents the tale from the point of view of an uninvited woodworm. History, the woodworm complains, is shaped by the interests and aspirations of victors, 'chosen' survivors who 'gloss over awkward episodes' and have 'convenient lapses of memory'.[55] The worm feels no sense of obligation, asking us to trust its portrait of Noah and his family as petty, oppressive and power-hungry and the least offensive examples of a 'species whose creation did not reflect particularly well on its creator'.[56] Later chapters reinforce the woodworm's complaints about the arbitrariness of historical selection: a women believes herself to be drifting in a stolen boat with a cat after a nuclear apocalypse ('The Survivor'); a television historian must explain the role allotted to cruise ship passengers by the terrorists who hold them hostage ('The Visitors'); 900 'tourists' – refugees from the Nazi regime – on board the liner *St Louis* find nowhere to disembark and are threatened with return to Germany and accommodation in Dachau and Buchenwald ('Three Simple Stories'); a daughter undertakes a fatal pilgrimage to Mount Ararat, supposed resting place of Noah's Ark ('The Mountain'); and a former astronaut undertakes a similar pilgrimage and declares her bones to be those of Noah ('Project Ararat'). Bound together in one book, these fragments – fictional and historical – make up anything but the coherent narrative that we expect of world histories. The imagery of Noah's Ark is woven throughout the novel, but the repeated appearance of woodworms and Barnes' concluding opposition of love to history has a literally and figuratively destructive effect on the work.

Barnes' apparently random selection of world historical episodes and elision of fact and fiction parallels Michel Foucault's observation of the arbitrariness of the connection of words and things in *The Order of Things*:

This book first arose out of a passage in Borges, out of the laughter that shattered, as I read the passage, all the familiar landmarks of thought – *our* thought, the thought that bears the stamp of our age and our geography – breaking up all the ordered surfaces and all the planes with which we are accustomed to tame the wild profusion of existing things and continuing long afterwards to disturb and threaten with collapse our age-old distinction between the Same and the Other. This passage quotes 'a certain Chinese encyclopedia' in which it is written that animals are divided into: (a) belonging to the Emperor (b) embalmed (c) tame (d) sucking pigs (e) sirens (f) fabulous (g) stray dogs (h) included in the present classification (i) frenzied (j) innumerable (k) drawn with a very fine camel-haired brush (l) *et cetera* (m) having just broken the water pitcher (n) that from a long way off look like flies. In the wonderment of this taxonomy, the thing we apprehend... is the limitation of our own [system of thought], the stark impossibility of [us] thinking *that*.[57]

For Foucault as for Barnes, any definition of 'world' may make sense to one person but be nonsense for another: the word 'world' is a wholly arbitrary marker that bears no necessary connection with the physical object. World histories are thus, as Dirlik puts it, 'rhetorical constructions'.[58] A problem arises, Dirlik argues, when we forget to ask whether these rhetorical constructions might be otherwise. Written world histories, like novels and films, have a 'mythological' grounding: words, concepts and forms of periodization are repeated and 'naturalized' so that they appear to 'go without saying'. Barnes' novel, as with Foucault's writing, aims to expose the 'natural' as the constructed.[59]

Though far, *far* less erudite, Mel Brooks' film *History of the World Part I* (1981) works towards the same end. With Foucault's claims in mind, consider the list of sketches that constitutes the film:

Our hominid 'forefathers' stand and become 'man' to the soundtrack of *2001*; 'stone age man' invents artistic, matrimonial, burial and comedic practices; Moses takes delivery of 15 commandments and then drops one of the tablets; a stand-up philosopher (Comicus) performs in Caesar's Palace and has to escape from Rome after insulting the Emperor; Comicus acts as waiter to the Last Supper while Leonardo Da Vinci paints it; the Spanish inquisition is presented as a musical routine; French peasants so poor that they cannot afford a language (just an accent like Maurice Chevalier) foment a revolution against

Louis XIV; and part II is promised in which will appear Hitler on ice, a Viking funeral and Jews in space.

Given this apparently random montage of images – and the dreadful jokes – there is little chance that this film might be taken for a 'serious' world history by viewers. On the contrary, the film works to undercut world historical conceptual frames and assumptions through the comic treatment of naturalized filmic 'icons'. 'Icons', Baty argues, are 'the sites for repeated stagings of narratives, the sites on which the past, present, and future may be written'.[60] The classic analysis of a filmic icon is Barthes' 'The Romans in Films', where he identifies the 'insistent fringes' on the foreheads of all the Roman men in Joseph Mankiewicz's *Julius Caesar* (1953) as a site for and the sight of Roman-ness.[61] Other examples of 'icons' would be the mud that invariably appears in films set in the Middle Ages or the prominent yellow cloth stars in Holocaust films. *History of the World Part I* overflows with icons. Roman fringes abound, as does medieval and early modern mud. Intertextual references to Brooks' other films also jostle for attention. For example, in the musical 'Spanish Inquisition' sketch, Brooks uses the monks' habits expected of a medieval film but also an aquatic sequence to point to the aquatic musical films of the mid-part of the twentieth century (and perhaps even more specifically to *Jupiter's Darling*, 1955), and the light-hearted musical treatment of tragic history is suggestive of Brooks' earlier film *The Producers* (1968). Importantly, in this sketch, as with all the others, many of Brooks' jokes are the icons. We see the Roman fringe, and recognize its overuse in other historical films. 'What has gone without saying' comes to the forefront of viewer attention, and in this case, the icon 'overshoots the target and discredits itself by letting its aim appear clearly'.[62] That is, Brooks, like Barnes, self-reflexively draws attention to the various icons that have been used in other historical texts – including world histories by professional historians – and through mockery, unmasks them as rhetorical techniques that produce the illusion of realism. Brooks' film is unlikely to bring down the academy, but it might just lead viewers to laugh a little at any Western civilizations survey they might have encountered.

a history waiting to be read

In *The Idea of History*, R. G. Collingwood argues that nothing ought to be included in a history that has not been actively interpreted by an historian. To him, histories are not 'webs of imaginative construction stretched between certain fixed points provided by the statements of [historical] authorities', because the fixed points of the web relieve historians of responsibility or diminish their autonomy.[63] Having reached the end of this chapter, I wonder whether Collingwood's active view of history making might also be applied to readers. Through a varied range of examples, I have shown that readers do not treat world histories as inert matter, to be reiterated in ways expected by authors. Rather, we have glimpsed readers appropriating and moulding the conceptual frames of world histories to build their own visions of the world or to mock those of others. The key question that remains to be answered is whether readers have final authority over writers or vice versa. This is a question that has been much discussed by literary theorists, and many answers have been offered. I do not believe that a satisfactory answer can be given to this question, though, until we replace the hypothetical readers of literary theorists with historical readers. The history of the reading of world history has yet to be written, and I cannot wait to read it.

notes

1. J. Abu-Lughod, *Before European Hegemony: The World System AD 1250–1350* (New York: Oxford University Press, 1989), pp. x–xi.
2. For a critical reappraisal of intentionalist intellectual history, see D. Lacapra, 'Rethinking Intellectual History and Reading Texts', *History and Theory* 19(3) (1980) 254–8; and Lacapra, 'History, Language and Reading: Waiting for Crillon', *The American Historical Review*, 100(3) (1995), 799–828.
3. R. Barthes, 'The Death of the Author', *Image, Music, Text*, trans. S. Heath (London: Fontana, 1977), p. 146.
4. G. Prince, 'Introduction to the Study of the Narratee', in J. P. Tompkins (ed.), *Reader-Response Criticism: From Formalism to Post-Structuralism* (Baltimore, MD: Johns Hopkins University Press, 1980); W. Iser, *The Implied Reader: Patterns in Communication in Prose Fiction from Bunyan to Beckett* (Baltimore, MD: Johns Hopkins University Press, 1974); J. Culler, *Structuralist Poetics: Structuralism, Linguistics, and the Study of Literature* (London: Routledge & Kegan Paul, 1975); P. J. Rabinowitz, *Before Reading: Narrative Conventions and the Politics of Interpretation* (Columbus, OH: Ohio State University Press, 1998); and S. E. Fish, *Is There a Text in this Class?: The Authority of Interpretative Communities* (Cambridge, MA: Harvard University Press, 1980).
5. M. de Certeau, 'Reading as Poaching', *The Practice of Everyday Life*, trans. S. F. Rendell (Berkeley: University of California Press, 1984), pp. 170–1.
6. R. Barthes, *S/Z*, trans. R. Miller (New York: Hill & Wang, 1974), pp. 4–5.
7. U. Eco, *The Role of the Reader: Explorations in the Semiotics of Texts* (London: Hutchinson, 1981); M. Riffaterre, *Semiotics of Poetry* (Bloomington, IL: University of Illinois Press, 1978); P. Ricoeur, *Time and Narrative*, trans. K. Blamey and D. Pellauer (Chicago, IL: University of Chicago Press, 1984–8), vol. 3, pp. 157–79.

8. S. Hall, 'Encoding/Decoding', *Culture, Media, Language* (London: Hutchinson, 1980), pp. 128–38.

9. P. Burke, *Popular Culture in Early Modern Europe*, rev. edn (Aldershot: Ashgate, 1994), pp. 65–87.

10. De Certeau, 'Reading as Poaching', p. 174.

11. G. Dening, *Performances* (Melbourne: Melbourne University Press, 1996), p. 49; K. Jenkins, *Re-thinking History* (London: Routledge, 1991), p. 24.

12. Jenkins, *Re-thinking History*, pp. 24–5; Hall, 'Encoding/decoding', p. 135.

13. S. Hall, 'Old and New Identities, Old and New Ethnicities', in A. King (ed.), *Culture, Globalization and the World System* (London: Macmillan, 1991), p. 68; D. R. Kelley, 'Horizons of Intellectual History: Retrospect, Circumspect, Prospect', *Journal of the History of Ideas*, 48(1) (1987) 162–3.

14. Herodotus, *The Histories*, trans. A. D. Godley (London: Heinemann, 1926).

15. J. Svenbro, 'Archaic and Classical Greece: the Invention of Silent Reading', in G. Cavallo and R. Chartier (eds), *A History of Reading in the West* (Cambridge: Polity Press, 1999), pp. 38–46.

16. M. B. Parkes, 'Reading, Copying and Interpreting a Text in the Early Middle Ages', in Cavallo and Chartier, *A History of Reading in the West*, pp. 99–100.

17. Paulus Orosius, *Seven Books of History Against the Pagans*, trans. J. Deferrari (Washington, DC: Catholic University of America Press, 1964), pp. 3–5; Otto, Bishop of Freysing, *The Two Cities: A Chronicle of Universal History to the Year 1146 AD*, trans. C. C. Mierow (New York: Columbia University Press, 2002), pp. 93–7.

18. Sima Qian, *Shiji* (Beijing: Zhonghua shuju, 1972), x, pp. 3299; as quoted in M. W. Huang, 'Author(ity) and Reader in Traditional Chinese Xiaoshuo Commentary', *Chinese Literature: Essays, Articles, Reviews (CLEAR)*, 16 (1994) 43.

19. W. A. Graham, 'Traditionalism in Islam: An Essay in Interpretation', *Journal of Interdisciplinary History*, 23(3) (1993) 501–7.

20. Herrad of Hohenbourg, *Hortus deliciarum*, eds R. Green, M. Evans, C. Bischoff and M. Curschmann (London: Warbourg Institute, 1979), p. 4.

21. J. Bodin, *Method for the Easy Comprehension of History*, trans. B. Reynolds (New York: Octagon, 1966), p. 20.

22. Ibid., pp. 21–7.

23. Sima Qian, *Records of the Grand Historian*, part 1: Han Dynasty, Part 2: Qin Dynasty, trans. B. Watson (New York: Columbia University Press, 1993).

24. A. Grafton, 'The Humanist as Reader', in Cavallo and Chartier, *A History of Reading in the West*, pp. 189–96.

25. R. Chartier, 'Reading Matter and "Popular" Reading: From the Renaissance to the Seventeenth Century', in Cavallo and Chartier, *A History of Reading in the West*, pp. 272–4.

26. J. Swetnam, *The Arraignment of Lewd, Idle, Froward, and Unconstant Women or the Vanity of Them, Choose you Whether, with a Commendation of Wise, Virtuous, and Honest Women, Pleasant for Married Men, Profitable for Young Man, and Hurtful to None*, 1615, available online at <www.u.arizona.edu/~kari/querjs. htm>.

27. W. Hinkle, 'The Cosmic and Terrestrial Cycles on the Virgin Portal at Notre Dame', *Art Bulletin*, 49(4) (1967) 287–96. See also E. Sears, *The Ages of Man:*

Medieval Interpretations of the Life Cycle (Princeton, NJ: Princeton University Press, 1986).

28. W. Alexander, *The History of Women, from the Earliest Antiquity, to the Present Time; Giving an Account of Almost Every Interesting Particular Concerning that Sex, Among All Nations, Ancient and Modern* (Philadelphia, PA: J. H. Dobelbower, 1796, reprinted by AMS, 1976).

29. J. R. Townsend, *Written for Children* (Harmondsworth: Penguin, 1974), p. 49.

30. J. G. Fichte, as quoted in R. Wittmann, 'Was There a Reading Revolution at the End of the Eighteenth Century?', in Cavallo and Chartier, *A History of Reading in the West*, p. 300.

31. I. Kant, 'What is Enlightenment?', *On History*, trans. and ed. L. W. Beck (New York: Macmillan, 1963), pp. 3–10.

32. J. G. Herder, 'Yet Another Philosophy of History', *Against Pure Reason: Writings on Religion, Language and History*, trans. and ed. M. Bunge (Minneapolis, MN: Augsburg Fortress, 1993), p. 40.

33. G. W. F. Hegel, *The Philosophy of History*, trans. J. Sibree (New York: Dover, 1956), p. 19.

34. On 'historical reading', see R. G. Collingwood, *The Principles of History and Other Writings in Philosophy of History*, eds W. H. Dray and W. J. Van der Dussen (Oxford: Oxford University Press, 1999), pp. 48–54.

35. M. Lyons, 'New Readers in the Nineteenth Century: Women, Children, Workers', in Cavallo and Chartier, *A History of Reading in the West*, p. 314.

36. H. G. Wells, *The Outline of History* (London: George Newnes, 1920), pp. 752–3.

37. D. D. Hall, 'The History of the Book: New Questions? New Answers?', *Journal of Library History*, 21(1) (1986) 27.

38. J. Rose, 'Rereading the English Common Reader: A Preface to a History of Audiences', *Journal of the History of Ideas*, 53(1) (1992) 48.

39. Ibid.

40. J. Radway, *Reading the Romance: Women, Patriarchy, and Popular Literature* (Chapel Hill, NC: University of North Carolina Press, 1984).

41. M. Lyons and J. Arnold (eds), *A History of the Book in Australia 1891–1945: A National Culture in a Colonised Market* (St Lucia: University of Queensland Press, 2001).

42. R. Darnton, *The Kiss of Lamourette: Reflections in Cultural History* (New York: W. W. Norton, 1991), p. 212.

43. K. MacLeod, 'History in SF: What (Hasn't Yet) Happened in History', in A. Sandison and R. Dingley (eds), *Histories of the Future: Studies in Fact, Fantasy and Science Fiction* (Basingstoke: Palgrave Macmillan, 2000), p. 9.

44. H. Harrison, 'Introducing the Future: the Dawn of Science-Fiction Criticism', in Sandison and Dingley, *Histories of the Future*, p. 5.

45. R. A. Heinlein, 'Guest of Honor Speech at the Third World Science Fiction Convention, Denver, 1941', in Y. Kondo (ed.), *Requiem: New Collected Works by Robert A. Heinlein* (New York: Tom Doherty Associates, 1992), p. 207.

46. Ibid., p. 218.

47. See for example D. Suvin, 'On the Poetics of the Science Fiction Genre', *College English* 34(3) (1972) 379; R. D. Mullen, 'The Earthmanist Culture: *Cities in Flight* as Spenglerian History', in J. Blish, *Cities in Flight* (New York: Overlook Press, 1999), afterword; the differing treatments of Asimov in J. Gunn, *Isaac*

Asimov: Foundations of Science Fiction (Oxford: Oxford University Press, 1982), pp. 27–50; C. Elkins, 'Isaac Asimov's *Foundation* Novels: Historical Materialism Distorted into Cyclical Psycho-History', *Science Fiction Studies*, 8(3) (1976), online at <www.depauw.edu/sfs/backissues/8/elkins8art.htm>.

48. Gunn, *Isaac Asimov*, p. 28.
49. A. Toynbee, *A Study of History* (Oxford: Oxford University Press, 1934–61), vol. 3, p. 373.
50. Ibid., vols 1–2.
51. R. Bradbury, *The Toynbee Convector* (New York: Knopf, 1988), p. 13.
52. Ibid., pp. 17–18.
53. Ibid., p. 18.
54. Wells, *The Outline of History*, vol. 2, p. 754.
55. J. Barnes, *A History of the World in 10½ Chapters* (London: Jonathan Cape, 1989), p. 4.
56. Ibid., p. 8.
57. M. Foucault, *The Order of Things: An Archaeology of the Human Sciences*, trans. anon (New York: Vintage, 1970), p. xv.
58. A. Dirlik, 'Confounding Metaphors, Inventions of the World: What is World History For?', in B. Stuchtey and E. Fuchs (eds), *Writing World History 1800–2000* (Oxford: Oxford University Press, 2003), p. 97.
59. R. Barthes, *Mythologies*, trans. A. Lavers (London: Paladin, 1988), p. 145.
60. S. P. Baty, *American Monroe: The Making of a Body Politic* (Berkeley, CA: University of California Press, 1995), p. 60.
61. R. Barthes, 'The Romans in Films', *Mythologies*, trans. A. Lavers (New York: Vintage, 1972), p. 26.
62. Ibid.
63. R. G. Collingwood, *The Idea of History*, rev. edn., ed. W. J. Van der Dussen (Oxford: Oxford University Press, 1993), p. 242.

recommended resources

Barthes, R., *Image, Music, Text*, trans. S. Heath (London: Fontana, 1977).
Burke, P., *Popular Culture in Early Modern Europe*, rev. edn. (Aldershot: Ashgate, 1994).
Cavallo, G., and Chartier, R. (eds), *A History of Reading in the West* (Cambridge: Polity Press, 1999).
Darnton, R., *The Kiss of Lamourette: Reflections in Cultural History* (New York: W. W. Norton, 1991).
Dirlik, A., 'Confounding Metaphors, Inventions of the World: What is World History For?', in B. Stuchtey and E. Fuchs (eds), *Writing World History 1800–2000* (Oxford: Oxford University Press, 2003), pp. 91–134.
Jackson, H. J., *Marginalia: Readers Writing in Books* (New Haven, CT: Yale University Press, 2001).
Phillips, M. S., *Society and Sentiment: Genres of Historical Writing in Britain, 1740–1820* (Princeton, NJ: Princeton University Press, 2000).
Thompson, M., 'Reception Theory and the Interpretation of Historical Meaning', *History and Theory*, 32(3) (1993), 248–72.

11
the greening of world history

j. donald hughes

A rapidly increasing number of historians in the past few decades have become aware of the importance of the natural environment to human history, and have created a new set of interpretive tools within history. As a subject, environmental history is the study of how human beings and human societies have related to the natural world through time. As a method, it is the use of ecological analysis as a means of understanding human history. Environmental historians recognize the ways in which the living and non-living systems of the earth have influenced the course of human affairs. They also evaluate the impacts of changes caused by human agency in the natural environment. They think, or at least most of them do, that the idea of environment as something separate from the human, and offering merely a setting for human history, is misleading. Instead, whatever humans have done to the rest of the earth has inevitably affected themselves. The living connections of humans to the ecosystems of which they are part must be integral to the historical account. Humans operate within the principles of ecology, and must continue to do so as long as the species is to survive. That all human societies, everywhere and throughout history, have existed within and depended upon biotic communities is true of huge cities as well as small farming villages and hunter clans. The connectedness of life is a fact. Humans never existed in isolation from the rest of life, and could not exist alone, because they depend on the complex and intimate associations that make life possible. To a very large extent, ecosystems have influenced the patterns of human events. Consequently, environmental historians believe that the narratives of history must place human events within the context of local and regional ecosystems, and world history must in addition place them within the ecosphere, the worldwide ecosystem. It is clear, therefore, that environmental history is an integral and important

238

part of world history, a fact increasingly recognized by world historians in the last quarter of the twentieth century and at the beginning of the twenty-first century.

Like history itself, environmental history is also a humanistic inquiry. Environmental historians are interested in what people think about the natural environment, and how they have expressed their ideas of nature in literature and art. That is, at least in one of its aspects, environmental history can be a subfield of intellectual history. It never strays far from the question of how attitudes and concepts affect human actions in regard to natural phenomena. But it is an entirely valid part of the environmental historical enterprise to establish what the significant views were on the part of individuals and societies.

William Green included a valuable chapter on environmental history in his *History, Historians, and the Dynamics of Change*.[1] Green observes that no approach to history is more perceptive of human interconnections in the world community, or of the interdependence of humans and other living beings on the planet. Environmental history, he adds, questions and transforms traditional economic, social and political forms of historical analysis. The environment can no longer be seen only as the stage setting on which human history is enacted. It is even more than an actor; indeed, it comprises a major portion of the cast. More recently, John R. McNeill published a remarkably comprehensive historiographical overview of the entire field of environmental history in a special issue of the journal *History and Theory* which should be required reading for anyone interested in the field.[2] McNeill sees among the values of environmental history to mainstream history the recognition that nature, and therefore the context of human history, changes; and the vitality it offers to the historical profession as a vigorous and rapidly growing subfield.

A valuable contribution of environmental history to world history has been to turn the attention of historians to topical environmental issues that produce global changes, such as global warming, climatic trends including the El Niño/La Niña Southern Oscillation,[3] atmospheric pollution and damage to the ozone layer, the dangers of radiation spread by nuclear weapons testing and accidents at nuclear power facilities, worldwide deforestation, extinction of species and other threats to biodiversity, in particular the introduction of opportunistic exotic species to ecosystems far from their regions of origin, waste disposal and other problems of the urban environment, pollution of rivers and oceans, and the environmental effects of warfare including weapons and agents intended to impact the resources and environments of antagonists. It might seem that many of these problems are recent, but there is no doubt of their tremendous effect since the early twentieth century, and most of them had important antecedents in all of the previous historical periods.

The idea that human history is shaped by the human interaction with the physical environment also may be found in the writings of ancient historians. Herodotus, the first Greek historian whose works survive, took as his subject the entire world as it was known to him, and commented on the relationship of peoples and nations to the particular environments that surrounded them. For example, he made the famous statement, 'Egypt is the gift of the Nile.'[4] The most admired Greek historian Thucydides maintained that environment had important effects on history, including warfare. The thin, dry, unrewarding soil of Attica (the territory of Athens), he thought, had made that land unattractive to potential invaders and thus saved it from conquest and depopulation. Because its relative safety made it a refuge for victims of war from elsewhere, the numbers of people in it grew to exceed the capacity of the land to feed them, and Athens was forced to send out colonies to relieve population pressure.[5] Similar ideas appear in Diodorus' *The Library of History* and other ancient universal histories, and geographers of the known world such as Strabo. Other Greek writers such as Hippocrates and Theophrastus speculated on environmental influences in countries around the Mediterranean Sea and as far distant as India. The Greeks, however, knew only a portion of the globe – the parts of Europe, Asia, and Africa revealed by colonists, explorers and military expeditions like that of Alexander of Macedon. In the late Middle Ages, the great Arabic historian and traveller, Ibn Khaldun, noted that the desert environment of the Middle East helped to make the Arabs hardier and thus better warriors.

In the early modern period, especially from the seventeenth century onward, scientists, including physicians, who were sent out by colonial powers noticed environmental changes on oceanic islands and also in subcontinents such as India and South Africa – changes that were often so rapid that they could be chronicled within the span of a human life.[6] They recorded evidence of human-induced deforestation, extinctions, and climatic alterations including desiccation. Although they did not as a rule present their findings in formal histories, they provided impetus for the idea that humans have caused environmental alterations around the world, and that many of these changes represent damage, not advance in human ability to utilize nature. Alexander von Humboldt made a number of observations of this kind in his encyclopaedic work, *Kosmos*, and others of his writings.

Among modern authors who helped turn attention to environmental history is George Perkins Marsh, who served as ambassador from the US to Italy during the nineteenth century. His great work, *Man and Nature*, first published in 1864, was a worldwide survey of the ways in which humankind had disturbed nature's harmonies.[7] He observed that many human activities such as deforestation deplete the natural resources on which civilization depends. He suggested that this factor had contributed to the downfall of the Roman Empire and other organized societies. What was the cause of this disturbance? He concludes that for the most part it was 'the result of man's ignorant disregard of the laws of nature', along with war, tyranny and misrule, which contributed to that disregard.[8] The cause of causes, *causa causarum*, was the despotism of Rome and her successors, which saddled the peasantry with agricultural taxes, military conscription, forced labour on public works and onerous regulations. His familiarity with the Mediterranean countries, Europe and North America led him to emphasize those areas.

In the early and mid-twentieth century, the *Annales* School of historians and related scholars based in France emphasized the importance of geographical analysis, providing an impulse for the rise of environmental history in the remainder of the twentieth century. As part of an effort to broaden the horizon of history, they emphasized the importance of geographical settings, and provided a formative impulse for world environmental history. Lucien Febvre, in *A Geographical Introduction to History*, published in 1924, anticipated some of the most salient topics that would be explored, tracing the reciprocal influences of human societies and the environment on a global scale.[9] Febvre insisted that historians recognize the importance of the environment, and of geographical studies, in their field. His book is one of the most important texts leading to the recognition of environmental history as a subject and method. Febvre argues that the natural environment has an important relationship to human affairs. Critics of a geographical approach to history at the time charged that it made humans into the pawns or 'patients' of environmental forces. While Febvre insisted on the importance of the environment, he maintained that it did no more than establish 'possibilities' for societies. Humankind, he felt, had a broad range of choices within which freedom and creativity operated.

The growth of environmental history within the field of history in some ways parallels the growth of ecology within the sciences, and results in part from an appreciation by historians in the mid-twentieth century of a worldview informed by the insights of ecology. An international symposium at Princeton in 1955 chaired by Carl O. Sauer, Marston

Bates and Lewis Mumford included ecologists, historians and social scientists. Its proceedings, entitled *Man's Role in Changing the Face of the Earth*, were edited by William L. Thomas, Jr, and presented a seminal collection of essays spanning the geographical extent of the planet and the chronological sweep of human history, laying a foundation for later work bridging ecological science and history. An early example of this work was William Russell's *Man, Nature, and History*,[10] which stood almost alone as a text in the field in 1969. The Thomas volume has been emulated and in some ways surpassed by a systematic and authoritative collection, *The Earth as Transformed by Human Action: Global and Regional Changes in the Biosphere over the Past 300 Years*, edited by B. L. Turner II, William C. Clark, Robert W. Kates, John F. Richards, Jessica T. Mathews and William B. Meyer. The latter volume is, however, limited to the period since 1700.

Alfred Crosby's earlier work, including his ground-breaking *The Columbian Exchange*,[11] combined medical and ecological science and history to demonstrate the biological impact of the Europeans and their domestic animals and plants, and the diseases to which they had developed resistance, on the Americas. He then expanded his scope in *Ecological Imperialism*,[12] showing that the Europeans toted their 'portmanteau biota' to temperate neo-Europes in many hitherto isolated lands around the world, where they achieved demographic takeovers. Jared Diamond, a physiologist who is eclectic in his sources of evidence, has written *Guns, Germs, and Steel: The Fates of Human Societies*,[13] which treats the influence of geographical and biological factors on the history of human societies from the earliest times to the present in often ground-breaking ways.

Under the stimulus of rising environmental concern, the American Society for Environmental History (ASEH) was founded in 1976. Its journal, *Environmental Review*, subsequently retitled *Environmental History*, and its annual conferences, included papers on many areas of the world. A European Society for Environmental History (ESEH) was later organized. The journal *Environment and History*, published in England but with a strong interest in Asia, Africa and beyond, began in 1995. There is an environmental history quarterly in the Netherlands, *Stichting Net Werk*. A journal published in Belgium, *Jaarboek voor Ecologische Geschiednis*, concentrates on the environmental history of the Low Countries. Other periodicals that often open their pages to articles on world environmental history include *Capitalism, Nature, Socialism; Human Ecology; Écologie Politique; The Ecologist* (UK); *Environmental Ethics; Ecological Economics; Pacific Historical Review;* the *Journal of World History* and *Mountain Research and Development*. John McNeill has counted more than 50 historical journals that have published articles dealing with environmental history during the period from 1999 through to 2003.[14]

Historical geographers discovered that they shared a border with environmental history, a border that they crossed with impunity. Indeed, geographers have produced much fine world environmental history.[15] Among them is Ian Gordon Simmons, whose *Changing the Face of the Earth: Culture, Environment, History* is a succinct, technically based review of the subject.[16] Andrew Goudie's text, *The Human Impact on the Natural Environment*, demonstrates perennial value.[17] Antoinette Mannion wrote *Global Environmental Change: A Natural and Cultural History*.[18]

Attempts by historians to write environmental histories of the world have been few; not surprisingly, due to the relatively recent delineation of the field and the vastness of the subject. An early effort to write a global environmental history was Arnold Toynbee's *Mankind and Mother Earth*,[19] but it was unfinished at the time of the author's death, and suffers from several flaws, the most important of which is an extremely cursory treatment of modern history. Despite a promising title and a prefatory section that takes ecology seriously, it remains for the most part a conventional political-cultural narrative repeating observations made in his earlier works. It can be appreciated as a gesture, however. Late in life, Toynbee apparently recognized that his *Study of History* had failed to give ecological process the role it demanded, and the later book might be viewed as an incomplete attempt to remedy that defect.[20] Clive Ponting's *Green History of the World*, which attempts to trace environmental issues through history, begins with the problem of the destruction of the ecosystems of Easter Island as a parable for environmental history, and proceeds topically.[21] Although his style is journalistic and his documentation inadequate, Ponting touches on most of the salient themes and argues fervently for a declensionist view of ecological history. Stephen Boyden's *Biohistory* applies the insights of systems ecology to world history.[22]

Joachim Radkau provided a professional historical review of major themes in world environmental history in his *Natur und Macht: Eine Weltgeschte der Umwelt* (*Nature and Power: A World History of the Environment*), a major work thus far available only in German.[23] My book, *An Environmental History of the World: Humankind's Changing Role in the Community of Life*, combines a concise narrative with a series of case studies that offer analyses of important environmental developments in locations and time periods around the Earth.[24] My approach emphasizes the mutual relationships between human societies and the ecosystems of which they are part. Scandinavian historians recently have made contributions to the literature on world environmental history. Hilde Ibsen used the 'ecological footprint' concept to interpret the history of ecological interactions between human societies and their environments.[25] Sverker Sörlin and Anders Öckerman have written a useful survey of global environmental history in Swedish, mostly dealing with the modern period.[26] Sing Chew, a sociologist, wrote *World Ecological Degradation*, in which he maintains that the most powerful engines of destruction are three: capital accumulation, urbanization and population growth.[27]

A number of collections of articles on world environmental history have appeared. Due to the nature of the subject it is hardly surprising that authors from other disciplines appear among the historians. This is true of Lester J. Bilsky's *Historical Ecology: Essays on Environment and Social Change*,[28] which has pieces representing timeframes from the prehistoric through to the modern, and to some extent of Donald Worster's choice *The Ends of the Earth: Perspectives on Modern Environmental History*.[29] My collection, *The Face of the Earth: Environment and World History*,[30] contains only essays by historians. Like Worster's, it is predominantly but not exclusively modern in scope.

An exemplary work of global reach is John R. McNeill's *Something New Under the Sun: An Environmental History of the Twentieth-Century World*.[31] It is the first synoptic world environmental history of the twentieth century. McNeill traces the environmental and related social changes, unique in scale and often in kind, that characterize the period. Where a look at previous times is necessary to understand them, he provides the background. He explains that present culture is adapted to abundant resources, fossil fuel energy, and rapid economic growth, patterns that will not easily be altered should circumstances change, and the behaviour of human economy in the twentieth century has increased the inevitability of change. The engines of change are conversion to a fossil fuel-based energy system, very rapid population growth and a widespread ideological commitment to economic growth and military power. McNeill includes a perceptive section on world economic integration. John F. Richards has produced an extensive survey of the period between 1500 and 1800 in *The Unending Frontier: The Environmental History of the Early Modern World*. As the title suggests, he emphasizes frontiers as an environmental theme of the early modern period, and the choice is apposite, since frontiers are the places where environmental changes were occurring most visibly. For him the story of the early modern world is in some important respects a story of progress. He argues that the salient patterns of the period were the expansion of Europeans across much of the rest of the globe and an evolutionary progress in human organization that was characteristic not only of Europe, but also of India and East Asia. This substantial volume can stand beside McNeill's twentieth-century environmental history as a complementary work. The two together almost cover the modern world; what is still lacking is an environmental history of the nineteenth century to bridge the gap between them, a very important gap since it includes industrialization and the second wave of colonization and their huge effects on the world environment. A book that almost fills the gap, but too briefly, is Robert B. Marks' *The Origins of the Modern World*, which is valuable for another reason in that it places China, not the West, in the centre of modern world environmental history.[32] Each of the two authors (McNeill and Richards) notes that the world of the time he describes was unprecedented in terms of worldwide environmental changes caused by human economic activity, and both are right.

Another category consists of studies and collections that are global in scope, but deal with special topics. These include books on world forest history, such as Michael Williams' recent comprehensive work, *Deforesting the Earth: From Prehistory to Global Crisis*,[33] and the collections *Global Deforestation and the Nineteenth-Century World Economy*, edited by Richard P. Tucker and John F. Richards,[34] and *Tropical Deforestation: The Human Dimension*, edited by Leslie E. Sponsel, Thomas N. Headland, and Robert C. Bailey.[35] On the history of fire, Stephen J. Pyne's *World Fire: The Culture of Fire on Earth*[36] is an incisive counterpart to his studies of fire in several regions of the earth. On climate, there is the older work of the *Annales* historian Emmanuel Le Roy Ladurie, *Times of Feast, Times of Famine*.[37] Among studies of the environmental impacts of imperialism, the collection *Ecology and Empire: Environmental History of Settler Societies*, edited by Tom Griffiths and Libby Robin,[38] is well worth mention. There are histories of the environmental movement around the world, including John Young's *Sustaining the Earth*,[39] Carolyn Merchant's *Radical Ecology: The Search for a Livable World*,[40] John McCormick's *Reclaiming Paradise: The Global Environmental Movement*[41] and Ramachandra Guha's *Environmentalism: A Global History*.[42]

World environmental historians in the present global setting find themselves increasingly challenged by the need to explain the background of the world market economy and its effects on the environment. Supranational instrumentalities threaten to overpower conservation in a drive for what is called sustainable development, but which in fact envisions no limits to economic growth. There is a growing literature of criticism of this trend by environmental economists including Robert Costanza, Herman Daly,[43] Hilary French[44] and James O'Connor,[45] which can inform historians whose field of inquiry is the international landscape as they take a long-needed, hard look at the impacts of the free trade regime on human societies and the biosphere. This will continue to be a leading theme of environmental history in the twenty-first century.

The literature of regional, national and local environmental histories outside North America has become extensive during the past decade or two, and defies exhaustive inclusion in a chapter of this length.[46] But such studies constitute the foundation for precise world environmental history, since the global must be based firmly on the local. Some of this work is being done by North Americans and Europeans working on other parts of the world, such as the important studies by environmental historians in the Netherlands on Indonesia, especially those represented in the *Indonesian Environmental History Newsletter*, edited by David Henley at Leiden, which, as of this writing, unfortunately is ceasing publication. There is also a growing international coterie researching the environmental history of their own regions in Austria, Australia, Brazil, China, Finland, France, Germany, India, Italy, the Netherlands, New Zealand, Portugal, Russia, South Africa, Spain, Sweden, Switzerland and the United Kingdom. T. C. Smout, for instance, has written an environmental history of Scotland and Northern England.[47] It is to be hoped that other nations will be added to this list. An outstanding example of a study of one country, which can serve as a model for writers on the world environment, is *This Fissured Land: An Ecological History of India* by Madhav Gadgil and Ramachandra Guha.[48] The authors have set their study of the South Asian subcontinent within a compelling philosophy of world environmental history extending from prehistory to the industrial age. A useful contribution in the future would be the writing of world environmental histories by scholars outside Europe and North America, whose viewpoints would undoubtedly present challenging perspectives. Writing by Indonesians on the environmental history of the archipelago has made a small but encouraging beginning.[49]

More work is needed in chronological periods that have been somewhat neglected until recently. Generally speaking, this means anything before about 1800. The Middle Ages is represented by a small but growing and diligent group of scholars including Richard Hoffmann,[50] William TeBrake,[51] Petra van Dam,[52] Charles R. Bowlus,[53] Ronald E. Zupko and Robert A. Laures.[54] The field of Classical Mediterranean environmental history is represented by the fine work of Russell Meiggs,[55] Robert Sallares,[56] Thomas W. Gallant,[57] Günther E. Thüry,[58] Helmut Bender,[59] Karl-Wilhelm Weeber[60] and J. V. Thirgood.[61] I also claim a place within the last-named group.[62]

Environmental history has an increasingly prominent place in textbooks on world history. John McNeill asserts that the patterns of human environmental relations are the most important aspect of twentieth-century history,[63] and this is no less true of preceding centuries and millennia. Prior to the past decade, world history textbooks had given little attention to environmental issues except in their chapters on prehistory and on the late twentieth century. But at the present time environmental historians increasingly are listed among the co-authors, and there is evidence that their perspectives are now reflected across the entire timeframe of some (but not all) of these books that are so important to the undergraduate education of the student generation of the early twenty-first century.[64]

In the writing of environmental history in recent years there is less environmental advocacy than before. John Opie once called it 'the spectre of advocacy,' in that environmental historians were likely to be suspect within the historical community for promoting an environmentalist point of view.[65] Today, such mistrust is not greatly warranted. Environmental historians guard their objectivity (perhaps sometimes they overcompensate in their desire to avoid advocacy), and are just as likely to be critical of environmentalists as of their opponents. Still it is undoubtedly true that most environmental historians today are aware in a positive sense that their field has roots in common with the environmental movement, and as citizens share many of its goals. Opie also reminded his audience that advocacy has certain virtues, and that to avoid it completely may be to dodge important ethical questions. To be trenchant should not mean to be less committed.

Among the trends in the field of environmental history that seem likely to continue, professionalism has made great strides as it has in most other parts of the scholarly world. Environmental historians are more strictly historians, although more likely than other historians to engage in interdisciplinary studies. This is reflected in a higher degree of acceptance for the subdiscipline within the historical profession. It is to be hoped that acceptance will not lead to complacency. Reviving the effort that gave birth to environmental history may be difficult, since the disciplines involved in that effort include some that are located on opposite sides of the famous cultural gulf between the sciences and the humanities, but it is inescapable if environmental historians are to avoid being marooned on an island of specialization.

A charge often made against environmental historians is that of environmental determinism, which is the theory that history is inevitably guided by forces that are not of human origin or subject to human choice. Studies that emphasize the roles of climate and epidemic disease in particular have been subjected to this criticism. The basic conception of environmental history, however, is that of the interaction of human societies and the natural environment. The judgement as to which is more dominant or effective in the interrelationship of humans and nature has varied greatly among environmental historians. There is in fact a continuum of opinion on the subject among environmental historians from one extreme to the other. Near the environmental determinist end of the spectrum, for example, is Jared Diamond, whose background is in medicine and anthropology, but who nonetheless admits to being an environmental historian. In his noted work, *Guns, Germs, and Steel*,[66] he attributes the success or failure of some human societies in competition with others not to their inherent abilities but to the availability of physical resources including the arrangement of topography and especially the presence or absence of animals and plants receptive or resistant to domestication. This is not said to dismiss his work, which clearly argues the extent to which human societies are embedded in the natural matrix. In emphasizing the role of environment, he rejects the idea that some human groups are physically or intellectually superior to others. Human groups developed as they did by dealing creatively with the factors presented to them by their particular environments. His book is wide-ranging, clear, and deals intelligently with a number of disciplines. At the other end of the spectrum is William Cronon, who with other authors in the volume of collected essays that he edited, *Uncommon Ground: Toward Reinventing Nature*,[67] argued that untrammelled nature no longer exists because humans have completely reshaped the planet. Wilderness, he announced, is entirely a cultural invention.[68] This was not just to say that the hand of man has set foot everywhere, whether through exploration or pollution or management, but that the very idea of nature is a human creation and that there is no way of relating to nature without culture. If Diamond represents environmental determinism, then perhaps Cronon represents cultural determinism. Each, however, insists that he is analysing an interaction. Diamond argues for human choice and Cronon argues that nature really exists and that there is a highly meaningful human cultural interaction with it. Most environmental historians find themselves in the broad middle ground between these two, although it is always more difficult for a scholar to define a balance than to stake out a radical position.

Another criticism of environmental history sometimes raised by other historians is that of presentism. These critics note that awareness of environmental problems is entirely a contemporary phenomenon. The very word 'environmentalism' did not emerge in general use until the 1960s, and environmental history became a recognizable subdiscipline only in the 1970s. The motive that led to the inquiry was a reaction to uniquely modern problems. Is environmental history, therefore, an untenable attempt to read late-twentieth-century developments and concerns back into past historical periods in which they were not operative, and certainly not conscious to human participants during the times? The problem with this criticism is that it is fundamentally an argument against history itself as an intellectual endeavour with application to the understanding of the present. Modern problems exist in their present forms because they are the results of historical processes. The relationship with nature was the earliest challenge facing humankind. It would take a particularly egregious form of denial not to see a precedent for the market economy in the exchange of a tribal nomad's meat and skins for a village agriculturalist's grain and textiles. The Greek philosopher Plato described soil erosion, and the Roman poet Horace complained about urban air pollution.[69] The Columbian transfer of Europeans along with their crops, weeds, animals and diseases to the New World in large part explains the history and present state of the Americas.[70] The study of past effects of environmental forces on human societies, and the impact of human activities on the environment, gives needed perspective to the dilemmas of the contemporary world.[71]

A third criticism, and one often heard at historical conferences, is that works written by environmental historians tend to be 'declensionist' narratives, that is, they describe a process by which a reasonably beneficial environmental situation became progressively worse due to human actions. For example, the Valley of Mezquital in Mexico, a highly productive agricultural region when farmed by the pre-Columbian Otomí people, was transformed through overgrazing by Spanish sheep into 'an almost mythologically poor place renowned for its aridity, for the poverty of its indigenous inhabitants, and for exploitation by large landowners', according to a compelling account written by Elinor Melville.[72] The biologically rich tropical forests of Brazil's Atlantic coastal region were hacked away from the time of discovery by Europeans down to the present, as another exemplary environmental history by Warren Dean puts it, *With Broadax and Firebrand*.[73] Today these forests are represented by scattered fragments, ostensibly protected by Brazilian law but still under attack in various forms. When expanded to the world scale, such regional examples become a story of global degradation, and it is hard to avoid the prediction of worldwide catastrophe, still more so where phenomena such as global warming are concerned. Since the process of destruction is still going on, and increasing exponentially in scale, it seems logical to extrapolate the trend toward future disaster. The declensionist narrative may even appear to have cautionary value. In the Middle Ages the Church taught an eschatology including the abolition of the earthly order and the Last Judgement of souls, and this was thought to frighten believers into good behaviour. Is environmental catastrophism simply the secular replacement for religious eschatology in world history? Of course historians generally avoid the future like the plague, since earlier historians who ventured to describe coming events often turned out to be spectacularly wrong – look at H. G. Wells, who predicted world order and lasting peace after World War I[74] – and environmental historians are no exception. Generally they resolve only to describe what has happened already and leave speculation to the reader, even when they secretly expect the worst to happen. Sometimes they break this resolution, however.[75] If history is generally held by its practitioners to exclude many forms of prediction, the validity of science is held to be tested by the accuracy of its predictions, and environmental history is, among historical subfields, perhaps uniquely open to the insights of science. To complicate the matter, however, the science most relevant to environmental history is ecology, and ecology is a historical science in which predictions are notoriously difficult to make, if not also undependable. Environmental historians are aware of this conundrum, however, and the charge of unsupportable catastrophism is on the whole unwarranted. The criticism of declensionist narration may be met in large part by the observation that deterioration of the global environment as a result of human activities is a fact revealed by careful research in many cases. To describe them otherwise would be to ignore the evidence.

The global environmental problems that first aroused the attention and interest of historians in environmental history have increased both in intensity and in number, and the interpretive value of environmental history has received wide acceptance. Nature and culture are, after all, interpenetrating notions that cannot be understood apart from one another. It is also notable that the number of scholars, particularly young scholars, engaged in the research and writing of environmental history has grown exponentially over the decades since 1980, and the list of nations where communities of such scholars exist has also grown. Environmental history seems certain to continue to influence the writing of world history in the twenty-first century. As Ellen Stroud puts it piquantly in a recent article which claims that environmental history is not merely a subfield of history, but an interpretive tool that stands ready for use by all historians,

If other historians would join us in our attention to the physical, biological, and ecological nature of dirt, water, air, trees, and animals (including humans), they would find themselves led to new questions and new answers about the past.[76]

notes

1. W. A. Green, 'Environmental History', in *History, Historians, and the Dynamics of Change* (Westport, CT: Praeger, 1993), pp. 167–90.
2. J. R. McNeill, 'Observations on the Nature and Culture of Environmental History', *History and Theory*, 42 (2003) 5–43.
3. R. Grove and J. Chappell (eds), *El Niño, History and Crisis: Studies from the Asia-Pacific Region* (Cambridge: White Horse Press, 2000).
4. Herodotus, *The Histories*, trans A. D. Godley (London: W. Heinemann, 1926) 2.5.
5. Thucydides, *The History of the Peloponnesian War*, trans. C. F. Smith (London: W. Heinemann, 1969) 1.2.
6. R. H. Grove, *Green Imperialism: Colonial Expansion, Tropical Island Edens and the Origins of Environmentalism, 1600–1860* (Cambridge: Cambridge University Press, 1995).
7. G. P. Marsh, *Man and Nature* (Cambridge, MA: Harvard University Press, 1965 [1864]).
8. Ibid., p. 11.
9. L. Febvre, *A Geographical Introduction to History* (New York: Alfred A. Knopf, 1925 [1924]).
10. W. M. S. Russell, *Man, Nature, and History: Controlling the Environment* (New York: Natural History Press for the American Museum of Natural History, 1969).
11. A. W. Crosby, *The Columbian Exchange: Biological and Cultural Consequences of 1492* (Westport, CT: Greenwood Press, 1972).
12. A. W. Crosby, *Ecological Imperialism: The Biological Expansion of Europe, 900–1900* (Cambridge: Cambridge University Press, 1986). See also Crosby, *Germs, Seeds, and Animals: Studies in Ecological History* (Armonk: M. E. Sharpe, 1994).
13. J. Diamond, *Guns, Germs, and Steel: The Fates of Human Societies* (New York: W. W. Norton, 1997).
14. McNeill, 'Observations on the Nature and Culture of Environmental History', p. 11.
15. M. Williams, 'The Relations of Environmental History and Historical Geography', *Journal of Historical Geography*, 20 (1994) 3–21.
16. I. G. Simmons, *Changing the Face of the Earth: Culture, Environment, History* (Oxford: Blackwell, 1989). Simmons also wrote a theoretical approach to environmental history, *Environmental History: A Concise Introduction* (Oxford: Blackwell, 1993).
17. A. Goudie, *The Human Impact on the Natural Environment*, 5th edn (Cambridge, MA: MIT Press, 2000).
18. A. Mannion, *Global Environmental Change: A Natural and Cultural History* (Harlow: Longman, 1991).

19. A. J. Toynbee, *Mankind and Mother Earth: A Narrative History of the World* (New York: Oxford University Press, 1976).

20. A. J. Toynbee, *A Study of History*, 12 vols (London: Oxford University Press, 1934–61).

21. C. Ponting, *A Green History of the World* (New York: Bedford/St. Martin's, 1991).

22. S. Boyden, *Biohistory: The Interplay between Human Society and the Biosphere* (Paris: UNESCO, 1992).

23. J. Radkau, *Natur und Macht: Eine Weltgeschchte der Umwelt* (Munich: Verlag C. H. Beck, 2000).

24. J. D. Hughes, *An Environmental History of the World: Humankind's Changing Role in the Community of Life* (London: Routledge, 2001).

25. H. Ibsen, *Mennesketts fotavtrykk: En oekologisk verdenshistorie* (Oslo: Tano Aschehoug, 1997).

26. S. Sörlin and A. Öckerman, *Jorden en ö: En global miljöhistoria* (Stockholm: Natur och Kultur, 1998).

27. S. C. Chew, *World Ecological Degradation: Accumulation, Urbanization, and Deforestation, 3000 BC–AD 2000* (Walnut Creek, CA: Altamira, 2001).

28. L. J. Bilsky (ed.), *Historical Ecology: Essays on Environment and Social Change* (Port Washington, NY: Kennikat Press, 1980).

29. D. Worster (ed.), *The Ends of the Earth: Perspectives on Modern Environmental History* (Cambridge: Cambridge University Press, 1988).

30. J. D. Hughes (ed.), *The Face of the Earth: Environment and World History* (Armonk, NY: M. E. Sharpe, 2000).

31. J. R. McNeill, *Something New Under the Sun: An Environmental History of the Twentieth-Century World* (New York: W. W. Norton, 2000).

32. R. B. Marks, *The Origins of the Modern World: A Global and Ecological Narrative* (Lanham, MD: Rowman & Littlefield, 2002).

33. M. Williams, *Deforesting the Earth: From Prehistory to Global Crisis* (Chicago, IL: University of Chicago Press, 2003).

34. R. P. Tucker and J. F. Richards (eds), *Global Deforestation and the Nineteenth-Century World Economy* (Durham, NC: Duke University Press, 1983).

35. L. E. Sponsel, T. N. Headland and R. C. Bailey (eds), *Tropical Deforestation: The Human Dimension* (New York: Columbia University Press, 1996).

36. S. J. Pyne, *World Fire: The Culture of Fire on Earth* (New York: Holt, 1995). Pyne also has a number of regional studies on the subject of fire.

37. E. Le Roy Ladurie, *Times of Feast, Times of Famine: A History of Climate Since the Year 1000* (Garden City, NY: Doubleday, 1967). Christian Pfister has published provocative and useful studies of climatic change as it relates to environmental history, but these are mainly limited to European regions. See C. Pfister, *500 Jahre Klimavariationen und Naturkatastrophen 1496–1996* (Bern: Paul Haput, 1999).

38. T. Griffiths and L. Robin (eds), *Ecology and Empire: Environmental History of Settler Societies* (Edinburgh: Keele University Press, 1997).

39. J. Young, *Sustaining the Earth: The Story of the Environmental Movement* (Cambridge, MA: Harvard University Press, 1990).

40. C. Merchant, *Radical Ecology: The Search for a Livable World* (New York: Routledge, 1992).

41. J. McCormick, *Reclaiming Paradise: The Global Environmental Movement* (Bloomington, IN: Indiana University Press, 1989).
42. R. Guha, *Environmentalism: A Global History* (New York: Longman, 2000).
43. For the first two authors and colleagues, see R. Costanza, J. Cumberland, H. Daly, R. Goodland and R. Norgaard, *An Introduction to Ecological Economics* (Boca Raton, FL: St. Lucie Press, 1997); and T. Prugh, R. Costanza, J. H. Cumberland, H. E. Daly, R. Goodland and R. B. Norgaard, *Natural Capital and Human Economic Survival* (Boca Raton, FL: Lewis Publishers, 1999).
44. H. French, *Vanishing Borders: Protecting the Planet in the Age of Globalization* (New York: W. W. Norton, 2000).
45. J. O'Connor, 'Is Sustainable Capitalism Possible?', in *Is Capitalism Sustainable?: Political Economy and the Politics of Ecology*, ed. M. O'Connor (New York: Guilford Press, 1994), pp. 152–75; and J. O'Connor, 'The Second Contradiction of Capitalism,' in *Natural Causes: Essays in Ecological Marxism* (New York: Guilford Press, 1998).
46. J. D. Hughes, 'Environmental History – World', in *A Global Encyclopedia of Historical Writing*, ed. D. R. Woolf, 2 vols (New York: Garland Publishing, 1998), vol. 1, pp. 288–91. See also J. D. Hughes, 'Global Dimensions of Environmental History', *Pacific Historical Review* 70(1) (2001) 91–102.
47. T. C. Smout, *Nature Contested: Environmental History in Scotland and Northern England Since 1600* (Edinburgh: University of Edinburgh Press, 2000).
48. M. Gadgil and R. Guha, *This Fissured Land: An Ecological History of India* (Berkeley, CA: University of California Press, 1992).
49. For articles and inclusive bibliography, see the *Indonesian Environmental History Newsletter*, No. 12, June 1999, published by EDEN (Ecology, Demography and Economy in Nusantara), KITLV (Koningklijk Instituut voor Taal-, Land-en Volkenkunde, Royal Institute of Linguistics and Anthropology), PO Box 9515, 2300 RA Leiden, Netherlands.
50. R. C. Hoffmann, *Fishers' Craft and Lettered Art: Tracts on Fishing from the End of the Middle Ages* (Toronto: University of Toronto Press, 1997); *Land, Liberties and Lordship in a Late Medieval Countryside: Agrarian Structures and Change in the Duchy of Wroclaw* (Philadelphia, PA: University of Pennsylvania Press, 1989).
51. W. TeBrake, *Medieval Frontier: Culture and Ecology in Rijnland* (College Station, TX: Texas A&M University Press, 1985).
52. P. J. E. M. van Dam, 'De tanden van de waterwolf. Turfwinning en het onstaan van het Haarlemmermeer 1350–1550' [The teeth of the waterwolf. Peat cutting and the increase of the peat lakes in Rhineland, 1350–1550], *Tijdschrift voor Waterstaatsgeschiedenis*, 2 (1996) 81–92. Includes a summary in English.
53. C. R. Bowlus, 'Ecological Crises in Fourteenth Century Europe,' in L. J. Bilsky (ed.), *Historical Ecology: Essays on Environment and Social Change*, pp. 86–99.
54. R. E. Zupko and R. A. Laures, *Straws in the Wind: Medieval Urban Environmental Law – The Case of Northern Italy* (Boulder, CO: Westview Press, 1996).
55. R. Meiggs, *Trees and Timber in the Ancient Mediterranean World* (Oxford: Clarendon Press, 1982).
56. R. Sallares, *The Ecology of the Ancient Greek World* (Ithaca, NJ: Cornell University Press, 1991).
57. T. W. Gallant, *Risk and Survival in Ancient Greece: Reconstructing the Rural Domestic Economy* (Stanford, CA: Stanford University Press, 1991).

58. G. E. Thüry, *Die Wurzeln unserer Umweltkrise und die griechisch-römische Antike* (Salzburg: Otto Müller Verlag, 1995).
59. H. Bender, 'Historical Environmental Research from the Viewpoint of Provincial Roman Archaeology', in *Evaluation of Land Surfaces Cleared from Forests in the Mediterranean Region during the Time of the Roman Empire*, ed. B. Frenzel (Stuttgart: Gustav Fischer Verlag, 1994), pp. 145–56.
60. K.-W. Weeber, *Smog über Attika: Umweltverhalten im Altertum* (Zurich: Artemis Verlag, 1990).
61. J. V. Thirgood, *Man and the Mediterranean Forest* (London: Academic Press, 1981).
62. J. D. Hughes, *Pan's Travail: Environmental Problems of the Ancient Greeks and Romans* (Baltimore, MD: Johns Hopkins University Press, 1994).
63. McNeill, *Something New Under the Sun*, p. 3.
64. R. W. Bulliet, P. K. Crossley, D. R. Headrick, S. W. Hirsch, L. L. Johnson and D. Northrup, *The Earth and Its Peoples: A Global History* (Boston, MA: Houghton Mifflin, 2004) is one text that adopts environment, along with technology, as a consistent theme.
65. J. Opie, 'Environmental History: Pitfalls and Opportunities', *Environmental Review*, 7(1) (1983) 8–16.
66. Diamond, *Guns, Germs, and Steel.*
67. W. Cronon (ed.), *Uncommon Ground: Toward Reinventing Nature* (New York: W. W. Norton, 1995).
68. Ibid., p. 70.
69. Hughes, *Pan's Travail*, pp. 73, 149.
70. Crosby, *The Columbian Exchange.*
71. See D. Worster, 'The Vulnerable Earth: Toward a Planetary History' in Worster, *The Ends of the Earth*, pp. 3–22, and 'Doing Environmental History', in ibid., pp. 289–308.
72. E. Melville, *A Plague of Sheep: Environmental Consequences of the Conquest of Mexico* (Cambridge: Cambridge University Press, 1997), quotation on p. 17.
73. W. Dean, *With Broadax and Firebrand: The Destruction of The Brazilian Atlantic Forest* (Berkeley, CA: University of California Press, 1995).
74. H. G. Wells, *The Outline of History*, 2 vols (New York: Macmillan, 1920).
75. C. H. Lewis, 'Telling Stories About the Future: Environmental History and Apocalyptic Science', *Environmental History Review* 17 (1993) 43–60.
76. E. Stroud, 'Does Nature Always Matter? Following Dirt Through History', *History and Theory* 42 (2003) 75–81.

recommended resources

Chew, S. C., *World Ecological Degradation: Accumulation, Urbanization, and Deforestation, 3000 BC–AD 2000* (Walnut Creek, CA: Altamira, 2001).
Cronon, W., 'A Place for Stories: Nature, History and Narrative', *Journal of American History,* 78 (1992) 1347–76.
Crosby, A. W., *Ecological Imperialism: The Biological Expansion of Europe, 900–1900* (Cambridge: Cambridge University Press, 1986).
Crosby, A. W., *Germs, Seeds, and Animals: Studies in Ecological History* (Armonk, NY: M. E. Sharpe, 1994).

Crosby, A. W. 'The Past and Present of Environmental History', *American Historical Review*, 100 (1995) 1177–90.

Diamond, J., *Guns, Germs, and Steel: The Fates of Human Societies* (New York: W. W. Norton, 1997).

Green, W. A., 'Environmental History', in *History, Historians, and the Dynamics of Change* (Westport, CT: Praeger, 1993), pp. 167–90.

Grove, R. H., *Green Imperialism: Colonial Expansion, Tropical Island Edens and the Origins of Environmentalism, 1600–1860* (Cambridge: Cambridge University Press, 1995).

Guha, R., *Environmentalism: A Global History* (New York: Longman, 2000).

Hughes, J. D., 'Ecology and Development as Narrative Themes of World History', *Environmental History Review*, 19 (1995) 1–16.

Hughes, J. D., 'Global Dimensions of Environmental History', *Pacific Historical Review*, 70(1) (2001) 91–102.

Hughes, J. D., *An Environmental History of the World: Humankind's Changing Role in the Community of Life* (London: Routledge, 2001).

Marks, R. B., *The Origins of the Modern World: A Global and Ecological Narrative* (Lanham, MD: Rowman & Littlefield, 2002).

McNeill, J. R., *Something New Under the Sun: An Environmental History of the Twentieth-Century World* (New York: W.W. Norton, 2000).

McNeill, J. R., 'Observations on the Nature and Culture of Environmental History', *History and Theory*, 42 (2003) 5–43.

O'Connor, J., 'What is Environmental History? Why Environmental History?', *Capitalism, Nature, Socialism*, 8(2) (1997) 1–27.

Pyne, S. J., *World Fire: The Culture of Fire on Earth* (New York: Holt, 1995).

Radkau, J., *Natur und Macht: Eine Weltgeschchte der Umwelt* (Munich: Verlag C. H. Beck, 2000).

Richards, J. F., *The Unending Frontier: An Environmental History of the Early Modern World* (Berkeley, CA: University of California Press, 2003).

Simmons, I. G., *Changing the Face of the Earth: Culture, Environment, History* (Oxford: Blackwell, 1989).

Sörlin, S., and Öckerman, O., *Jorden en ö: En global miljöhistoria* (Stockholm: Natur och Kultur, 1998).

Stine, J. K., and Tarr, J. A., 'At the Intersection of Histories: Technology and the Environment', *Technology and Culture*, 39 (1998) 601–40.

Thomas, W. L. Jr (ed.), *Man's Role in Changing the Face of the Earth* (Chicago, IL: University of Chicago Press, 1956).

Turner, B. L., Clark, W. C., Kates, R. W., Richards, J. F., Mathews, J. T., and Meyer, W. B., *The Earth as Transformed by Human Action: Global and Regional Changes in the Biosphere over the Past 300 Years* (Cambridge: Cambridge University Press, 1990).

White, R., 'American Environmental History: The Development of a New Historical Field', *Pacific Historical Review*, 54 (1985) 297–335.

Williams, M., 'The Relations of Environmental History and Historical Geography', *Journal of Historical Geography*, 20 (1994) 3–21.

Worster, D., (ed.), *The Ends of the Earth* (New York: Cambridge University Press, 1988).

12
world history education

deborah smith johnston

The recent growth in secondary- and university-level world history education reflects that of the field as a whole. Secondary schools in the United States are now mandating the study of world history, and elsewhere in the world, historians and teachers are beginning to question curricula that celebrate the nation state. Lest there be any doubt, these are not revamped Western civilization or British imperial history courses: this is a new world history, truly global in its orientation. As one teacher puts it, 'Rather than studying region by region, or Europe and the others, world history provides an opportunity to move the lens back aways and show how people interact with each other.'[1] The appeal of world history is not hard to see. None of us live in truly isolated places, and current events – global terrorism, bank failures in Argentina, environmental degradation in the Aral Sea, MTV in Paris or Delhi, or the women's movement in China, for instance – drive home the connections between peoples in often distant parts of the world.[2] World history has the potential to be the most exciting course in the curriculum. Students become excited when they recognize that world history involves a great number of diverse peoples, that it does not have to focus on memorization of names and dates, and that it connects to the world they live in today. Others legitimate world history based on its ability to help students develop a worldview. As Ron Edgerton has argued, world history 'gives students a sense of their humanity and how they have been influenced by activists across time and place, thereby creating a broader sense of common identity among all of us'.[3]

emergence

World history instruction first began in the United States in 1821 at the English Classical High School in Boston, and by World War I a number of schools offered a one-year 'general history' course which was nested in with other social science options. 'General History' was designed to better meet the diverse needs of an expanding student population. Aims, however, often fell short of reality. Historians were not satisfied with the content and rigour of the course, teachers were not happy with the pedagogy and students questioned its relevance. As Gambrill noted in a 1927 report, for example:

> These courses are increasing in number and textbooks are multiplying impressively... Yet is cannot be said that the high schools have really caught the idea of the new world history. Both the courses and the textbooks remain in nearly all cases overwhelmingly European in content and point of view, while the reasons for introducing them are in many cases utterly reactionary... the new course is introduced simply to cover as much ground as possible in the one year of history other than American which is offered, and the exigencies of a commercial or technical curriculum or the conflicting demands of other social studies are the real explanation, rather than any recognition of a World Community or of the need for a new world history.[4]

Despite critiques like this, however, enrolments rose across the country, and until the 1960s, 'Western Civilization' courses reigned supreme. Generally, 'Western Civ' courses delivered an account of European-led progress and the rise of the US as an international political and economic force. It provided postwar (World Wars I and II) North America with a sense of national unity and global positioning. Much of the rationale for teaching Western Civ courses changed, however, with international political events in the 1950s and 1960s. As Bullard commented:

> The Soviet launching of Sputnik had set the USA on her ear... When most of us try to recall what we were taught about human cultures from kindergarten through Grade 12, we remember only United States history, the history of our own home state, and what was lumped in a bag known as 'world' history, namely European, emphatically Western culture, commencing in Mesopotamia and the Nile Valley. Suddenly out of the 1960s, sprang Africa, Asia, Latin America, and Canada.[5]

With the 1958 National Defense Education Act, the United States Congress officially recognized the need to understand the world beyond its traditional periphery. Area-studies research and language support expanded, drawing graduate students to places all over the world. Educators like Leften Stavrianos, though, complained that these initiatives did not go far enough, and called for the teaching of world history as 'seen from the moon', or courses that would put stress on the interaction of the world's peoples.[6]

A common trend that emerged in the 1960s was the development of a two-semester, or two-year sequence in world history that started with a Western Civ survey and then moved on to a more or less historical tour of the 'non-West'. Courses designed to such a template did little to question the assumption that Europe had achieved a state of development that other countries would (and should) emulate.[7] As Jean Johnson, a teacher and consultant for the Asia Society commented on this approach:

> Students study the history of the West in detail and spend about six weeks each on various non-Western cultures where time constraints permit only a cursory look at geography and traditional ways of life before the class examines the impact of Europe. Ironically, this approach reinforces the importance of the West, because students study European imperialism again and again, each time Westerners conquer yet another non-Western culture. Students are often asked to make judgments without any real historical context for analysis, deciding, for example, whether 'caste is good or bad for India' or whether Mao's revolution helped or hurt China. With no examination of such things as the development of underdevelopment, students are encouraged to conclude that 'Hinduism is holding back progress,' but that India could enter the twentieth century by westernizing. In addition, hoping to make Area Studies interesting and relevant, and because they often have no background in the various non-Western societies, teachers emphasize cultural traits and have students dress in saris, perform tea ceremonies or make flower arrangements.[8]

Other public critiques identified pedagogical weakness, such as the inadequate use of audio-visual materials, irrelevant and repetitive content and the lack of recognition of student diversity.[9]

In the 1980s, commentators still argued that 'world history [education] retained the solid trunk and branches of Western civilization that it had possessed since the 1930s, but teachers continued to festoon it, indeed load it down, with the results of new research in social, economic and cultural history'.[10] In 1982, the American Historical Association (AHA) held a joint meeting with the US Air Force Academy to discuss ways to improve the teaching of world history. This led to the formation of the Rocky Mountain World History Association and later, the World History

Association (WHA). The first WHA Bulletin was published that year and the *Journal of World History* followed in 1990. From its foundation, therefore, the WHA showed a keen interest in promoting world history education.

The early years of the WHA coincided with efforts by educators and governments to improve education in the United States. Increasing communication between secondary schools and universities has generated both criticism of textbooks and approaches and new scholarship. A closer look at what was being taught in secondary world history classrooms revealed a lack of preparation – and a lack of enthusiasm – among teachers. Many had only a Western Civ background, and some did not even have that. What they taught was a 'collage of topics on ancient Rome, modern Europe, China and the like, all of which were presented without much of a connective structure'.[11] The National Standards project of 1994 attests to increasing attempts to foster dialogue between world history teachers at all levels of education and government bodies. The skills and outcomes recommended by the project elicited public complaints that world history education was 'un-American', but there is no doubt that the project fostered the embrace of secondary school world history education in many states. There are several significant factors that can be pulled from this account of the emergence of world history education in the US. First of all, it is clear that since the 1960s, there has been increased university and secondary school collaboration.[12] Second, it is apparent that syllabuses are more often products of political programmes than educational research and input. Third, there has been a relatively consistent commitment to world history survey courses.

Extensive research has yet to be done on world history education in other parts of the world. Anecdotal evidence reveals that in many places, though, world history is not taught or that it is viewed through the prism of national history.[13] In Britain, for instance, the National Curriculum has evolved into specialized units and not a broad survey course. In response, some critics have complained of 'the Hitler-isation of A-Level history' where a few individuals, narrow time periods or events are studied as isolated thematic units with an aim towards teaching historical skills.[14] World historians in Europe are quick to point out that the traditional 'Plato to NATO' curriculum is still prevalent in Western and now Eastern Europe, where few classes are devoted to Asian, Latin American or African history. Furthermore, most European textbooks are limited to modern history.[15] In China, despite over 40 per cent of PRC historians working in some field of world history or regional research, the world history curriculum remains infused with a Marxist (and Eurocentric) interpretation of the history of the global community, left over from Soviet educational influence prior to the Cultural Revolution.[16]

In Latin America, Commonwealth nations, India and Africa, much of the history curriculum continues to be dominated by colonial histories. In Latin America, new approaches seem to be heading in the direction of regional histories as opposed to global histories. History textbooks from Kenya, Zimbabwe and Tanzania, despite local presses, are organized using European (imperial) periodization and topics.[17] The choice of primary sources and imagery introduces global perspectives but the sequence of global processes covered conveys a European perspective. In Canada, the world history courses available focus on that nation's place in modern history.[18] And in Australia, some states present global education as part of 'social studies', but this is perceived to be disjointed from the practice of 'rigorous' history. In the one state where history is taught as a separate curriculum subject, New South Wales, world history does not appear.[19] Looking at approaches outside of the US, it is interesting to note how political influence has steered schools away from world history and towards national history.

teaching world history

World history is unique in that its scope, breadth and purpose necessitate different approaches to teaching historical thinking and understanding. To see the big picture, teachers and students need to use three conceptual frameworks – the building blocks by which students can learn, organize, retain and apply information – simultaneously. The *temporal framework* addresses how the course is organized in units of time: periodization and timelines. The *spatial framework* addresses units of social space: for example, should we think about empires, nation states, communities, commodities, regions or humanity itself? The *thematic framework* provides the overarching organizing tool for all the content in the course. What themes will be utilized in narrowing down the content in a world history survey? Students and teachers navigate amongst these frameworks using different lenses, scales and disciplines.

temporal framework

Students need to be given a temporal framework within which to place their prior knowledge – for example, their own lives as well as history learned in earlier coursework and through popular culture and current events – and their newly acquired knowledge. The issue is not memorization of endless dates but rather a general ability to put events into a meaningful sequence. Given the geographic breadth and the scope of time involved, a world history course can be overwhelming to students at any level. To complicate matters further, textbooks often use a 'switchback approach' where students are taken back and forward in time as they complete regional surveys. Temporal surveys of the non-West stretch across great temporal leaps, whereas European events are handled in shorter periods. Susan Douglass has also argued that events are often treated so as to suggest the inevitability of collapse or other outcomes.[20] Given these criticisms, there must be active discourse on time in world history courses. To raise awareness, teachers can use timelines, unpacking assumptions within periodization, and talking about what impact time has in society. New themes and evidence can also generate open discussion on periodization. For example, the traditionally conceived 'Age of Exploration' as a time when Europeans undertook voyages to Asia via Africa and the Americas may hold less significance as students study earlier voyages of the Vikings, Polynesians and Chinese.[21] The most important thing is for students to become comfortable with periodization as a dynamic, analytical activity, not as a fixed, unquestioned part of the course.

spatial framework

The teaching of world history is not only temporal but also spatial, demanding a basic understanding of geographic concepts and locale as well as the ability to move in scale from the local to the global, across time and place. World history is about movement, interaction, exchange and connection: all concepts that can be best understood spatially on a map or a graphic organizer. Geography is not about the memorizing of the world's capitals but it is about being able to talk about historical developments in a spatial context. A spatial understanding of world history also necessitates the ability to choose case studies that might be civilizational, imperial, regional, national, local, urban or maritime. The questions students pose when looking at these different scales of world history influence their ability to make connections between places and processes.

thematic framework

World historians use a variety of units of analysis to look at global processes. They do so partly because they cannot study or write about everything. Peter Stearns asserts that selection decisions in classrooms should be based on the best available scholarship about which episodes have had the greatest impact in shaping a society, culture or period, and they should be made explicitly... We need to examine the basic motors of society and culture, to make sure that they are conveyed to students, and, at the same time, that they will shape the unavoidable decisions about eliminating or reducing sheer quantities of data. One-damned-thing-after-another, the pattern followed in so many history courses, was never really effective, for it mixed big changes and small in a common mash. It has now become inexcusable because it prevents an analytical focus and distracts our attention from some of the additional topics necessary to grasp the big patterns.[22]

As teachers select themes, they select content. The thematic framework 'holds' content in patterns of relation. The framework needs to be evident to students throughout the course and the text so that they can use it to help filter case studies, see the developing narrative(s), and benefit from its organizational power. Designing a thematic course or textbook requires that we think carefully about the selection, not only in terms of periodization and units of analysis but also in terms of overall content relevance. In order to do that, criteria are needed to choose appropriate themes. Alfred Crosby, for example, defines a thematic approach in world history as 'that which affects the entire species, biological, especially disease, history – those which apply to humanity maximally. That usually means less politics than more.'[23]

Pedagogically, themes make sense. Themes provide students and their teachers with a means of selecting and organizing information. A thematic framework ensures a syllabus focused on an active, but limited, exploration of world history. When a theme contains an active verb, it encourages students to discuss it freely. For example, 'Finding Identity' empowers students to see the agency in history more freely than 'Identity' alone. World history is so broadly defined that by placing thematic limits on the scope it becomes less overwhelming and retains a clear focus. Themes provide an umbrella – an organizing tool around which students can group information. This has been called the 'Velcro effect' as students retain more information if they are able mentally to sort new data and attach it to some mental framework.[24] They like it because it helps them see linkages, remember things and connect to the content. Themes also allow for a focus on student interest. For example, issues of identity resonate for high school students. In times of conflict, world history teachers can connect their lessons to questions and discussions on human nature, human rights and international law.

educating for historical thinking

History has long been included in schools and universities as a means of fostering national pride and global awareness. History, we are told, teaches us what it means to be human. Debates over the past 100 years over exactly what to teach have revolved around content, with occasional shifts in the pendulum calling for more attention to skills. The tension between social studies and history has also increased as more teachers, trained in social studies, are called upon to teach history. Many history teachers are criticized, on the other hand, for not inspiring critical thinking in the classroom as they focus on an endless dissemination of information. These recent debates over what content to teach have left the impression that history is about facts and not process. In response, history educators argue that this has set up a 'false dichotomy between content and process – history teaching and history are similar in that they are both working with data and building argument'.[25] History provides the opportunity to teach the skills that social studies educators have infused in their classes, with more of a disciplinary coherence.

David Lowenthal asserts that the main reason all of us need history 'is not to give specific nuggets of data; it is to know how to think historically – to acquire, screen, and weigh evidence about anything past'. Fostering this historical thinking is at the heart of what history educators aim to do in the classroom. But what will give young people the ability to understand and act upon future historical events? Good history classes will and 'world history is the ideal arena in which to challenge stereotypical notions of how to study history'.[26] Due to the breadth and scope of world history, making content subsidiary to the historical thinking process is essential. In an address at the 1998 World History Association Meeting, Peter Stearns asserted that priority in world history education must be given to the development of historical analysis and thinking, with emphasis placed on reasoning, historical argumentation, and the skills needed to handle issues of change, continuity, comparison and causation.[27] The emphasis on historical thinking does not preclude knowing the facts. On the contrary, historical thinking cannot be employed without commanding historical evidence. But what is significant is the recognition that it is only through historical thinking that history can be appreciated and used.

In a recent Australian review of research into history education, studies are cited that provide evidence that historical thinking develops initially between the ages of 7 and 10, increases between the ages of 10 and 14 and becomes more advanced between 14 and 16. It is noted however, that with longer units of study and instructional strategies very young children can also attain complex levels of understanding.[28] The Bradley Commission, the National Council for the Teaching of History and others, have asserted that history education should be an integral part of the school curriculum and beyond. This remains the domain of cognitive psychologists to test, but without the existence of quality historical teaching materials for young ages, this seems a long-term goal.

There is no shortage of thinking on how history, and even world history can help to encourage historical thinking. A schema of particular interest is the US Advanced Placement World History Course. In designing the course, the College Board Committee believed that the main objective was good historical thinking amongst students. They devised a list of seven key historical skills, the last three of which they considered unique to world history:

- Constructing and evaluating arguments: using evidence to make plausible arguments;
- Using documents and other primary data: developing the skills necessary to analyze point of view, context, and bias, and to understand and interpret information;
- Developing the ability to assess issues of change and continuity over time;
- Enhancing the capacity to handle diversity of interpretations through analysis of context, bias, and frame of reference;
- Seeing global patterns over time and space while also acquiring the ability to connect local developments to global ones and to move through levels of generalizations from the global to the particular;
- Developing the ability to compare within and among societies, including comparing societies' reactions to global processes; and
- Developing the ability to assess claims of universal standards yet remaining aware of human commonalities and differences; putting culturally diverse ideas and values in historical context, not suspending judgment but developing understanding.[29]

And in dialogues after the introduction of the course, educators of all levels have shown a keen interest in identifying the developmental pathways of students in world history classrooms.

For students to understand that history is a dynamic process, they need to be exposed to how history is created, written and interpreted. Having them read book reviews and engage in historiographical debates demonstrates not only the historical thinking involved in such discussions but also the fact that there are often no black-and-white answers in history. Historiographical debates are important, especially in world history. For example, in preparation for a recent classroom roundtable on the 'Rise of the West', students read over a topical summary of how numerous historians interpreted the evidence. They then debated within small groups which factors were most convincing to them. In presenting their group's summative opinion, they had to identify which historian(s) they most agreed with. This accomplished several things: first it forced them to look at the body of evidence and interpret it; second, they had to assess what evidence was most convincing; and third, it helped them to gain an idea of what historical research and writing involves. World history is such a new field with the potential for such interesting debates that students need to understand that a textbook explanation is never the final answer.

Stearns argues that the humanities need to be taught as 'sources of new knowledge', as an 'on-going set of inquiries', not as a 'closed catechism, a set of questions already answered'.[30] It frustrates students to learn that there is no one right set of interpretations, devoid often of human agency. As Elizabeth Badger notes:

> We have been sanitizing the process of doing science (or history, or the analysis of literature or art), of all the human turmoil – personal, political, social, cultural – in order to present the final product as if it were the entirety of the subject. In doing so, we have deprived students of the excitement of scholarship, presenting a pre-cooked package of accepted theory – 'objective', impersonal, boring, static, and, essentially, untrue.[31]

In a one-year-long professional development experience in a public school district, an emphasis on historiography inspired teachers to do similar things in their classrooms. In Shelly Weintraub's view, as a result of this approach, teachers 'began to teach like historians'.[32] History is not black and white, and world history is even less so. As teachers and students alike discover the dynamism in the field, the joys of discovering new intellectual boundaries will make for better teaching and learning experiences.

History is not a subject that confines itself easily to disciplinary boundaries, since it draws upon fields as diverse as social and gender history, economics, politics, geography, anthropology and literature. Students will need to think about how other disciplines connect to history in order to think historically. By considering multiple perspectives, they will have a better sense of what historians draw upon as they do their own research. Another objective in world history education is to discourage students from thinking that peoples of 'other cultures' or of earlier times are necessarily 'exotic' or 'backward'. Furthermore, we can encourage students to think of *human* activities: for example, rather than looking at African and European perspectives of the slave trade, ask why did human beings behave the way they did in creating the Atlantic economy? Even a change of questions and a change in perspective can open up a new view on the past: the answer does not always lie with new teaching resources or new cultures.[33]

Historical thinking is fostered through the consistent interpretation of primary and secondary source documents, the use of multiple teaching strategies so as to encourage visual literacy, discussion, role plays, good question-asking, media analysis, debates, sequencing and assessment strategies which encourage multiple correct responses. These strategies are used regularly by history teachers at all levels, but in world history too often the content becomes the message rather than the medium, and in the grand pursuit of coverage, thinking skills are left behind.

World historians use a variety of historical methodologies in their research and their teaching. David Smith has suggested five ways of 'doing world history'. First, he talks of the 'Big Picture' as a means of ensuring that students have a broad, chronological overview of history, including an ability to judge significance and fair representation. Second, the idea of diffusion too is used to communicate to students the spread of natural entities, people and cultural items from one region to another. Third, syncretism refers to the process whereby enough items spread, resulting in the mixing of cultures to produce a new civilization. Fourth, comparison is used explicitly to look for differences and similarities between more than one place, process or event, but does not juxtapose them, thus avoiding parallelism. And fifth, Smith looks at common phenomena to assess the role natural or historical events may have if they affect more than one single civilization. This allows for an ecological element to enter into analysis.[34] Using all of these approaches in a world history classroom helps students to understand two things: first, that they are entering a growing and dynamic field; and second, that there is no single take on past events in classrooms and in research.

Bob Bain reminds us that world historians undergo significant mental shifts across methods and analytical frames as they work. Students need a lot of help to navigate their way through such mental gymnastics, but it is worth it, because in the process they acquire skills that are valued in a wide range of study and work contexts.

The problem of assuring and assessing learning in world history is not a new one. In commenting about the typical high school student, educators almost 70 years ago asserted that 'no historical knowledge will be of much use to him except in so far as he can make it a permanent part of the social memory pattern which enables him to function effectively in whatever activities he may engage'.[35] In 1934, several observations were made about the direction of change the world history survey needed to take. These included recommending a move away from the dissemination of rote facts that had little logical relationship with one another, the fostering of connections across the whole school experience of the student, and more discussion on the problems involved in teaching world history. Ironically, these are some of the same reasons given for a lack of retention and or learning in world history today. Debates on world history tend to be dominated by issues of *what* content should be *presented* rather than *how* selected content should be *processed* in a classroom. We want students to *retain* the ability to think historically; for them to develop conceptual frameworks allowing for the integration of new knowledge with old, but know that real learning cannot be assessed by their regurgitation of a familiar canon.

challenges

World history is big: the temporal and spatial scope is broad, the texts mammoth, and the tools of analysis numerous. This can make the course exhausting to teach and overwhelming to take. This is especially true when mass coverage is combined with rote memorization. A superficial coverage of many places over a long span of time results in a lack of depth with no sense of how these places, or times, connect. Such a compartmentalized vision of the world leads to places left out in the race against time. Selection decisions are made based upon a teacher's prior knowledge and often that means Europe remains central in a story about the 'West' and the 'Rest'. Teachers bogged down in details may also fail to get very far, leaving students wondering how issues connect with later times and even the present.

teacher preparation

Recent studies in the US show that 49 per cent of secondary teachers assigned to teach at least one section of 'World Civilization' do not have a history degree.[36] And of 75 world history professionals recently interviewed for my PhD dissertation, two people stated that they had degrees in world history, and only a few others were pursuing one.[37]

Most degrees were in area studies: African, Asian, European and American studies. World history preparation is almost non-existent in teacher training programmes and, although it is on the rise, few institutions of higher learning have programmes (or even courses) in world history. And yet the fastest-growing humanities secondary school course in the United States is world history. Almost inevitably this means that many teachers who are teaching the survey have little history background and even less world history experience.

Professional development in-service experiences need to be tailored to suit their audiences. This throws up a difficulty for those organizing sessions on world history, for there are large numbers of teachers who are required to teach world history and who have no vested interest in doing anything beyond the textbook. Even in classrooms where there is an attempt to really teach the world, the limitations of teaching training and textbooks result in compartmentalization. Successful pre-service programmes that provide student teachers with training and experience in world history are needed in order to provide all new teachers with a world history foundation. As one teacher has argued, 'The first year teaching world history is a conversion experience requiring a new language, but retraining needs to be happening at pre-service level in order to allow conversations to happen and background to be developed.'[38] Programmes need to address at a minimum the following three aspects in order to be effective at training new world history teachers: first, detailed content knowledge in world history, not just national histories or European history; second, interactive classroom strategies; and third, long-range planning and curriculum or syllabus design. This means that teachers need to feel comfortable with the larger historical context that comes from survey coursework as well as with case studies that they have encountered in regional specialties. As historians, they need to be able to see the changes that have occurred within the larger global patterns. The sheer volume of content, and the relative unfamiliarity of teachers with it, often results in a more top-heavy and textbook-driven approach. World history requires interactive teaching. Pre-service teachers need to be exposed to world history classrooms, modelling diverse teaching strategies. And they need to experiment with a variety of techniques. As part of this improved teacher training generally, it is argued that there needs to be 'more application of the art of teaching in World history'.[39]

Those who organize professional development programmes face a dilemma when it comes to how much content to include. Many people attending such programmes want a heavy dose of content because that is what they feel they are lacking. But an over-rich diet of information only will not allow for good *modelling* of content. World history should not be a mind-numbing factual Olympics. Finding that balance between content and pedagogy is then the penultimate challenge. As one teacher has put it, 'A successful professional development experience combines exposure to classic and recent scholarship with modelling of successful teaching techniques.'[40] And another:

> Teachers need more opportunities to see what others are doing. Teaching can be an isolating experience, and teaching world history can be overwhelming, so the more that world history teachers can discuss content and methodologies, the less isolated and overwhelmed they will feel. I recommend a variety of approaches to solving the problems of isolation and stress: listservs, conferences, workshops, some kind of newsletter or journal, videotaping myself, getting feedback from colleagues who watch me teach, teaming with other teachers offering the same course.[41]

It is not only secondary teacher contact that needs to nurtured, it is also necessary to encourage dialogues between high school and university teachers. Heidi Roupp is surely right when she notes that the 'split between teachers and professors continues as an endemic problem'.[42] Why is there such a split? There are a number of explanations that might be offered. Writing textbooks for secondary school consumption, for example, is not rewarded by academia in the same way that monographs and research articles are. There is no perceived institutional incentive to promote good teaching in the high schools. Additionally, as Ralph Crozier puts it, there is 'resistance in established history departments to world history specifically, especially since the younger generation is not necessarily more globally minded due to narrow specializations and the reward system in academia'.[43] Young historians often do not feel they can take the risk of dabbling in world history since it still has a questionable reputation historiographically. They feel the need to first cut their teeth to make their name and then think outside the box when they are older and tenured. Many of the big names in world history writing in the twentieth century have followed this path.

Knowing that the traditional reward system – exams and teacher promotions – does not look at how up to date the information teachers impart is, and that professional development continues, in many instances, to be about school structure and educational reform as opposed to content, how can new research hope to be integrated into daily instruction? The *Journal of World History* and *World History Connected* are the main means by which teachers can stay abreast of research and teaching developments. Pre-service coursework can also introduce future teachers to historiographical debates. Graduate coursework should promote the reading of new research and thinking about how that gets worked into the existing narrative(s). In-service experiences can include excerpts (passages, charts, maps, graphic organizers, visuals) from recent works that would be applicable to a wide range of audiences. During professional development experiences, participants should be engaging in dilemmas that also face those producing new scholarship. There also needs to be discussion at professional association meetings about pedagogy and how students learn. Dividing conference programmes into pedagogy panels and history panels, or holding professional development courses prior to annual meetings will not bring about needed dialogue.

So how can good world history come from a context in which most teachers are trained in national history and in which there is little incentive for universities to change that training? There is a common message in much of the scholarship on world history education, as well as from reports from panel presentations at the annual meetings of the AHA and WHA that can be summarized as 'be selective and look for places of intersection and comparison'. The biggest challenge to get over is the feeling that one needs to develop new materials on every place in the world. As Ross Dunn has suggested,

> World history teachers, for example, are likely to think they have neither the time nor the inclination in a busy semester to develop an individual unit plan on the Aboriginal peoples of Australia and Maori of New Zealand. Indeed, teachers would be ill-advised to represent these peoples as isolated and largely static 'cultures.' On the other hand, it is not hard to think of a number of interregional or comparative questions in world history whose investigation would be diminished if Aborigines or Maoris were not included among the significant actors: the problem of migration and settlement in the Pacific basin, the problem of early encounters between European settlers and indigenous populations, and the problem of social change amid rapid urbanization in the twentieth century.[44]

By thinking of these global processes, or themes, as the organizing framework, it seems more doable, though more intellectually challenging, to address multiple, large and small historical phenomena through time.

political and institutional resistance to change

World history educators struggle with issues of what to include and exclude, but this process is made easier through reflection on the analytical frames through which we want students to see the past. Often, though, teachers' aims collide with state requirements. Governments may dictate how a course is to be taught, and they can also mandate content and objectives. World history educators may therefore find themselves having to make compromises, or even having to deal with a curriculum that is so packed with content that they do not see that there is room for them to step outside of the bounds of lessons where textbook reading and regurgitation dominates.

commercial challenges

World history education also requires appropriate resources. Contacts with publishers might ensure that content and periodization is updated to reflect current research. Textbooks often lag long behind research, however, and teachers may feel that they are missing out on cutting-edge discussions. Textbooks are also produced for the most profitable locations, with little awareness of cultural differences: textbooks produced for US courses, for instance, may not be at all suitable for teachers in other parts of the world. Furthermore, textbooks often present information according to national history or regional studies structures: for example, discrete countries are presented, rather than interactions among peoples.

what next?

There are exciting changes that mark the start of the twenty-first century in the teaching of world history.[45] There is more dialogue about what world history *is* instead of *why* world history. At professional meetings, world historians have had a noticeable presence. There are more world history sessions at National Council for the Social Studies and AHA annual meetings. Textbooks are being written from scratch instead of merely being revised Western Civilization tomes. They are incorporating more and more new research in order to reflect the debates in the field. In classrooms, new approaches are being tried. Importantly too, there is increasing recognition of the need for secondary and collegiate scholars to collaborate and for pedagogy and scholarship to be intertwined. This is not just a US phenomenon. There has been a growth in receptiveness to world history in other parts of the world, perhaps as a result of contemporary problems that do not fit national boundaries.

University historians need to understand the distinct role world history has to play in their departments and in the larger secondary school market. Since the first real exposure to history for so many students is world history in secondary school, improved teaching in this field or agitation for its introduction can only help increase history enrolments at undergraduate and graduate levels. But that flow-through, of course, depends on training teachers at university level in ways of teaching world history. There needs to be a connection between the history department and the schools of education to ensure quality world history instruction. Exposure to this 'new world history' will help to start new teachers out on the right foot.

The improvement of world history teaching will be a long, ongoing process. Clearly, the solution is one that requires multiple steps: teacher training, policy directives which ask for teacher and student accountability in a way that does not require mind-numbing memorization of facts, curriculum reform, textbook revision and attention to good pedagogy in the world history classroom. As Ross Dunn sees it, 'Improving the teaching of world history is a "mammoth task." Work at both ends, school policy and pre-service training, is made more difficult when curriculum is continually changed by educational and cultural politics.'[46] State and national politicians are still unclear on the 'agenda' of world history. There remains the belief that students need to know how Western values shaped their nation's history and that the rest of the world's history does not connect to national identity.

Overcoming these barriers – financial, attitudinal and political – cannot be done without first addressing the bigger issues. Without adequate teacher training, educators cannot be advocates of world history. They need to believe in the course as an exciting means of teaching meaningful history. Across the United States, world history education is improving. The new AP World History programme is innovative. The course description communicates the overarching vision of a new world history that looks at global patterns over time in all places. The momentum that it has generated in the teaching of world history nationally and internationally has created a huge demand for teacher institutes. Over the past four years (1999–2004) the Educational Testing Service and the College Board have provided seed funding and organizational assistance to set up AP World History institutes and workshops. It is predicted that by 2004, over 45,000 students will take the AP World History exam. The course represents both opportunity and stimulus for real dialogue between university and secondary teachers. This interaction has resulted in an exchange of content and pedagogy. For example, at the 2000 National

Training Institute for AP World History held at Northeastern University, college faculty and high school teachers were among the participants. The conversations that went on over a very intensive week had the effect of deepening relationships and building respect. One university professor commented, 'I feel as though my circle of colleagues has considerably enlarged. And I've gained a new respect for high school teachers as partners in the world history enterprise.'[47] This same sentiment was echoed at the AP reading by scholars impressed by the student products and also by the standards to which the high school teachers held the essays. In addition, the AP course is providing a phenomenal boost for the discipline since it is showing historians that there is money to be made in world history.[48] New attention to the college world history survey is emerging as a direct result from the college faculty involvement in the AP programme. It is important that the AP programme be seen as only one of several alternatives to high school world history and that the course description itself be revisited over the next few years as teachers work through the curriculum.

World history is a new and dynamic field. This makes it both exciting and challenging to teach. It is imperative that teachers treat any world history curriculum as an evolving activity. If one is using a thematic approach, themes will change over the years with the times and interests of students. Similarly, new research is continually helping to discover, document, affirm or deny the existence of particular global patterns.

The challenges that the field faces include teacher preparation, the historical baggage of insular national curricula and political mandates, institutional resistance to change and commercial constraints. Perhaps even more challenging are the conceptual obstacles that educators must get beyond as they begin to teach world history. Teachers must make a shift from their own academic experiences where the historical units of analysis may have been nation states or regions. Changing to a process-driven course rather than civilizational or cultural area-studies is significant. Similarly, using themes in a chronological context to maintain historical integrity is important even as the underlying periodization is questioned. Lastly, moving from an emphasis on the accumulation of facts and details to a larger awareness of the overarching concepts is more difficult. Finding a balance between detail and the big picture is a constant tightrope walk.

The good news is that the world history teaching profession is already moving forward, full steam ahead. Driven in part by the teachers within the World History Association, by the momentum generated by the AP World History course, and by the efforts of thousands of classroom teachers, the train has left the station. But the possibility of derailments and incorrect switches looms ever present due to political, attitudinal, financial and professional obstacles. Getting past these is only half the journey, as we stop to pick up thousands of new passengers (teachers) unaccustomed to rail travel (world history). As we look for ways to make the trip easier, we need to sort out how to approach the journey – how do we select from the thousands of possible routes? And yet, as we bump along the tracks, we hear the roar of conversations among passengers of all walks of life who are collaborating on what to do next. The world history survey, whether it is a high school, college or AP course, needs to incorporate thematic, temporal and spatial conceptual frameworks in order to remain viable. In order for teachers to rethink the course, and for students to be able to develop the historical thinking skills necessary to navigate through these frameworks, professional development and teacher training programmes need to model these guidelines. The suggestions on implementation here help to provide a situation where new scholarship and collaboration is optimized so that the course can be infused with new life. Making it a course that survives political battles and trendy educational banter requires a revolution in how teachers experience world history themselves, in graduate programmes, pre-service training and with textbooks. Through a rethinking of world history, new temporal, spatial and thematic frameworks will help to shape a new experience for these teachers. These are heady times for world history as research is proliferating, more doctoral students are focusing on world-historical studies, the AP World History course has launched, and national requirements for world history have increased. World history educators must ensure that the vigour of the emerging research and the current momentum towards world history can be capitalized upon by improving the survey experience for all students.

The next big challenge for world history educators in the US is to connect with their colleagues in other parts of the world, to see the potential not just of information exchange but also of pedagogical exchange. World history courses are not available to all students around the world. And the courses offered outside the US vary in important ways. Our next step is therefore to seek the global connections that we encourage our students to see when we study the past together.

notes

1. M. Favretti, Scarsdale High School, New York. Phone interview, 18 February 2002. This is just one of 75 interviews that formed the basis of my recently completed PhD research project.

2. On this point, see C. Lockard, 'World History', in K. Boyd (ed.), *Encyclopedia of Historians and Historical Writing* (Chicago, IL: Fitzroy Dearborn, 1999), vol. 2, pp. 1330–1.

3. R. Edgerton, Professor of History, University of Northern Colorado. Phone interview, 20 February 2002.

4. J. M. Gambrill, 'The New World History', *Historical Outlook* 18 (1927) 267, as cited in Pulliam, 'Status of World History Instruction in American Secondary Schools', *ERIC Clearinghouse for Social Studies/ Social Science Education Interpretative Series Five* (1972) 9.

5. B. Bullard, 'Personal Statement to the President's Commission on Foreign Language and International Studies' (1979), as cited in B. F. Beers, 'World History in the Schools', in V. S. Wilson, J. A. Little and G. L. Wilson (eds), *Teaching Social Studies: Handbook of Trends, Issues and Implications for the Future* (Westport, CT: Greenwood Press, 1993), p. 102.

6. G. Allardyce, 'Toward World History: American Historians and the Coming of the World History Course', *Journal of World History* 1(1) (1990) 23–76.

7. S. Cohen, Walter Johnson High School, Maryland. Written interview, 8 February 2002.

8. Jean Johnson, 'Beyond Us and the Other: Standards for Mainstreaming Asia', *Education about Asia* 1(1) (1996) 14–15.

9. *Teaching American History: A Quest for Relevancy*, as cited by H. Hertzberg, *NCSS Yearbook* (Washington, DC: NCSS, 1974), p. 498.

10. G. Nash, C. Crabtree and R. E. Dunn, *History on Trial: Culture Wars and the Teaching of the Past* (New York: Alfred A. Knopf, 1998), pp. 89–90.

11. Beers, 'World History in the Schools', p. 109.

12. For example, curriculum writing projects and the web-based world history curriculum project at the National Center for Teaching History in the Schools, University of California Los Angeles; numerous NEH Institutes; the College Board AP World History programme; efforts by the AHA Teaching Division, the WHA *Bulletin* and the new *Connections* Editorial Board; collaborations between the OAH, WHC and History Day; the Standards project; National History Education Network; OPB Project; the World History Network; Teacher Institutes at WHA meetings, and many more.

13. As in the United States, the diversity of what is done in many countries makes generalizations difficult, though the underlying commonality does seem to be world history as an exception rather than the rule.

14. M. Baker, 'What is History For?', BBC News, 28 June 2002, online at <http://news.bbc.co.uk>.

15. Personal email correspondence with M. Middell, University of Leipzig, Germany, 29 February 2004, and Carol Adamson (Stockholm). Getting beyond universal and national histories remains the greatest challenge for European schools, as evidenced at a World History Conference in Leipzig in 1998.

16. Q. Edward Wang, 'Encountering the World: China and its Other(s) in Historical Narratives, 1949–1989', *Journal of World History*, 1(3) (1990) 332.

17. Books used in Kenyan and Zimbabwean schools in the 1990s included, for example, N. Parsons, *Focus on History Book 1* (Harari: College Press, 1985); D. Leeming, *World History I* (Nairobi: Longman, 1985), using as major topics Ancient civilizations, the Greek World, Christianity and Islam, the Renaissance, the Reformation and exploration; and D. Leeming, *World History Book 2*

(Nairobi: Longman, 1977), which includes revolutions, colonial systems, the United States, India, Russia, China, Africa (before and after colonial rule), and war and peace.

18. The contrast between provinces is clear as one looks at online sources from different regions. For example, consider the following: (Ontario) <www.edu.gov.on.ca/eng/document/curricul/secondary/grade1112/canadian/canadian.html>; (Atlantic Provinces) <http://apef-fepa.org/images/pdf/eng/social.pdf>, and (British Columbia) <www.bctf.bc.ca/psas/BCSSTA/comparativecivilizations.html>.

19. See for example <http://csf.vcaa.vic.edu.au/home.htm>.

20. S. Douglass, *Strategies and Structures for Presenting World History with Indian and Muslim History as a Case Study* (Beltsville, MD: Amana Publications with the Council on Islamic Education, 1994), pp. 140–1.

21. Students might be encouraged to debate the global accuracy of any of the following names and periods. There are certainly pros and cons for all: the point is more that students are having these discussions and raising evidence as historians do, to argue the relevance of a particular timespan or title. They are: Axial Age, 500 BCE–500 CE; Age of Exploration, 1450–1600; Exploding Technologies, 1914–present; Age of Social Change/Revolution, 1750–1900; Spread of Religions, 200 CE–1000 CE; Rise of the West, 1750–1914; Age of Imperialism, 1850–1950; Age of Southernization, 400–1300; Age of Forced Labour Systems, 1400–1800; Search for Identity, 1800–present; Age of gunpowder, 1450–1750; Age of the Atlantic, 1492–1940; and the Age of the Pacific, 1905–present.

22. P. Stearns, *Meaning over Memory: Recasting the Teaching of Culture and History* (Chapel Hill, NC: University of North Carolina Press, 1993), p. 189.

23. A. Crosby, University of Texas, Emeritus Professor. Written interview, 24 January 2002.

24. S. Cohen, Walter Johnson High School, Maryland. Written interview, 8 February 2002.

25. B. Bain, School of Education, University of Michigan. Phone interview, 5 February 2002.

26. P. Manning, 'Pedagogy and Historical Analysis in the *Migration* CD-ROM', *History Teacher* 32(3) (1999) 329–43.

27. P. Stearns, World History Association Keynote Address, Fort Collins, Colorado, 19 June 1998.

28. T. Taylor, *The Future of the Past Final Report of the National Inquiry into School History*, National Centre for the Study of History, Monash University, online at <www.dest.gov.au/schools/publications/2000/future/report.htm>. Additional information on teaching history to young learners may be found in J. D. Hoge, 'Achieving History Standards in Elementary Schools', ERIC Digest. Available at <www.ed.gov/databases/ERIC_Digests/ed373020.html>.

29. College Board, *AP World History Course Description* (Washington, DC: ACORN books 2002–3), p. 8.

30. T. Holt, *Thinking Historically: Narrative, Imagination and Understanding* (1990), as cited in Stearns, *Meaning over Memory*, p. 132.

31. E. Badger, 'Cultivating Historical Thinking', World History Institute, unpublished ms.

32. S. Weintraub 'What's this New Crap?', in P. N. Stearns, P. Seixas and S. Weinburg (eds), *Knowing, Teaching and Learning History: National and International Perspectives* (New York: New York University Press, 2000), p. 189.

33. R. Dunn, 'Constructing World History in the Classroom', in ibid., pp. 134–5.

34. David R. Smith, 'Teaching the "Doing World History" Method in the World History Survey', in H. Roupp, *Jumpstart Manual for World History Teachers*, July 1999.

35. C. Becker, as cited by E. Ellis, 'The Permanence of Learning in World History', *Social Studies*, 2 (1934) 133.

36. D. Ravitch, 'Educational Backgrounds of History Teachers', in Stearns et al., *Knowing, Teaching and Learning History*.

37. T. Mounkhall and D. Martin. Research in progress, as reported by Bill Ziegler and Linda Black, 2004.

38. M. Favretti, Scarsdale High School, New York. Phone interview, 18 February 2002.

39. H. Roupp, Former WHA President and retired Aspen Colorado teacher. Phone interview, 17 February 2002.

40. S. Cohen, Walter Johnson High School, Maryland. Written interview, 8 February 2002.

41. Ibid.

42. H. Roupp, Former WHA President and retired Aspen Colorado teacher, Phone interview, 17 February 2002.

43. R. Croizier, WHA Current President, University of Victoria BC, Emeritus Professor. Phone interview, 21 February 2002.

44. R. Dunn (ed.), *The New World History: A Teacher's Companion* (New York: Bedford/St. Martin's, 2000), p. 290.

45. L. Beaber, History Assessment Specialist, Educational Testing Service, AP Test Committee. Phone interview, 20 February 2002.

46. R. Dunn, Professor of History, San Diego State University. Phone interview, 20 February 2002.

47. See 'Sample Evaluation', AP Institute 2000, unpublished ms., Appendix 3.3.

48. B. Ziegler, Valhalla High School, California. Phone interview, 21 February 2002.

recommended resources

Dunn, R. (ed.), *The New World History: A Teacher's Companion* (New York: Bedford/St. Martins, 2000).

AP Central, online at <http://apcentral.collegeboard.com>.

Embree, A. T., and Gluck, C. (eds), *Asia in Western and World History* (New York: M. E. Sharpe, 1997).

H-World, online at <www.h-net.org/~world/>.

Manning, P., *Navigating World History: Historians Create a Global Past* (New York: Palgrave Macmillan/St. Martin's Press, 2003).

Nash, G., Crabtree, C., and Dunn, R., *History on Trial, Culture Wars and the Teaching of the Past* (New York: Alfred A. Knopf, 1998).

National Center for History in the Schools, *National Standards for World History* (Los Angeles, CA: National Center for History in the Schools, 1994).

National Center for History in the Schools, *Bring History Alive: A Sourcebook for Teaching World History* (Los Angeles, CA: National Center for History in the Schools, 1996).

National Council for the Social Studies, *Curriculum Standards for Social Studies*, (Washington, DC: National Council for the Social Studies, 1994).

Roupp, H., *Teaching World History: A Resource Book* (New York: M. E. Sharpe, 1996).

Smith Johnston, D., *'Rethinking World History: Conceptual Frameworks for the World History Survey'*. Unpublished PhD dissertation, (Northeastern University, May 2003).

Stearns, P. N., Seixas, P., and Weinburg, S. (eds), *Knowing, Teaching and Learning History: National and International Perspectives* (New York: New York University Press, 2000).

Stearns, Peter, *Meaning over Memory: Recasting the Teaching of Culture and History* (Chapel Hill, NC: University of North Carolina Press, 1993).

West, E. (ed.), *Improving the Teaching of World History* (Washington, DC: National Council for the Social Studies, 1949).

Williams, M., Ratte, L., and Andrian, R., *Exploring World History Ideas: for Teachers* (Portsmouth, NH: Heinemann, 2001).

Wineburg, S., *Historical Thinking and Other Unnatural Acts Charting the Future of Teaching the Past* (Philadelphia, PA: Temple University Press, 2001).

World History Center, online at <www.whc.neu.edu>.

World History Connected: the ejournal of Teaching and Learning, available at <www.worldhistoryconnected.press.uiuc.edu>.

World History For Us All, online at <http://worldhistoryforusall.sdsu.edu/>.

World History Network, online at <www.worldhistorynetwork.org>.

index

Printed in the United States
103467LV00002B/81/A

9 781403 912787